New American
Poets of the '90s ❖

New American Poets of the '90s ❖

EDITED BY
JACK MYERS
AND
ROGER WEINGARTEN

DAVID R. GODINE   *Publisher*   BOSTON

First published in 1991 by
David R. Godine, Publisher, Inc.
Horticultural Hall
300 Massachusetts Avenue
Boston, Massachusetts 02115

Library of Congress Cataloging-in-Publication Data
New American poets of the '90s / edited by Jack Myers and Roger
Weingarten.—1st ed.
p.   cm.
Includes bibliographical references and index.
ISBN 0-87923-892-5 (HC)—ISBN 0-87923-907-7 (SC)
1. American poetry—20th century.   I. Myers, Jack Elliott, 1941–
II. Weingarten, Roger.
PS615.N38 1991   91-7339   CIP
811'.54'08—dc20

Third printing, 1993

Printed in the United States of America

Contents

Foreword

New American Poets of the '90s is not attempting to confirm or usurp an existing canon of poetry, nor is it trying to establish a new one. Its aim is to publish a representative array of some of the best and most exciting poetry being written today by young to mid-career poets whose work, the editors feel, is provocative, timely, important, and accessible. If there is any implied bias operating in our selections, it admittedly might be toward choosing work that more closely aligns itself with the spoken word, and toward work that expresses both the unique and diverse character of the contemporary American experience, whether that character is rural or urban, aesthetic or political, outward-directed or self-reflexive, and whether it was written on an Indian reservation, Main Street USA, the university, or an urban ghetto.

It is of more than passing interest to note, as the poet Barry Goldensohn has observed of the English lyric tradition, that English-based poetry seems to be the only poetry in the world which periodically revolutionizes and refreshes itself by going back to the revitalizing roots of its spoken idiom. At the same time it displays a hunger for inclusiveness that borrows technique, theory, and vision from virtually every culture in the world. This must be what accounts for the diversity of its character and the attendant sense of an ongoing "progress" in the art.

Another aspect of the contemporary American poetry scene, which has undoubtedly helped to create the character of this anthology, is that over the last twenty years or so poetry anthologies have, thankfully, lost some of their previously exclusive, elitist aura. This move toward pluralism and decentralization of aesthetic-political power, which has most likely been brought about by the new technologies in production and communication and by the proliferation of workshops throughout the country, has had the end result of bringing more new poetry to the attention of more people than ever before, and has made it easier to find and gauge the pulse of the art. This recent turn of events seems to us a historic breakthrough both for the vitality of the art and for the practical effect of bringing poet and audience more closely together than has been the case thus far in this century. As editors we are happy to be a small part of this, and we feel confident in claiming that the work presented here is both vibrant and of lasting quality.

—Jack Myers
Roger Weingarten

New American
Poets of the '90s ❖

BARBARA ANDERSON ❖

Deuce: 12:23 a.m.

DR. BERMAN, my old lady listens to you
       ALL THE TIME.
You wouldn't BELIEVE IT, but YOU'RE FAMOUS
in all our conversations and arguments,
in EVERY room & bar and restaurant. I SWEAR,
       if you were a REAL LIVE GUY,
someone on the NEXT BAR STOOL I'd challenge your guts.
       SO HEY,
I'm a rehabbed convict, recovering addict,
someone YOU would walk THE OTHER WAY
from on the street, but I'm also
       into broadcasting LIKE YOU.
When I was in the joint, I was the HEAD HONCH,
       TOP-NOTCH DEEJAY, the main voice
over the caged waves, but once you've had
a tracheotomy, it's NEVER REALLY the same.
Well, now I GO TO SCHOOL where I study
       broadcasting and a little acting.
I've somehow BECOME DEPENDENT on school,
ANOTHER INSTITUTION like prison where you act
and where I SPENT HALF my life. I see it
as a function of my insanity OR SOMETHING.
I FOUND OUT from the prison shrink that I'M INSANE.
SAME with all my buddies—IN OR OUT of the joint.
       CRAZY!!!
All of them EXCEPTIONS TO THE RULES
of normalcy and convention AND THEREFORE
a bit juiced and whacked. But all smart as hell,
most smarter than me, and some of their women
       RICH AND BEAUTIFUL.
But back to THE MAIN POINT. I've BEEN OUT
for about 8 months now & I've FALLEN HARD
for this chick. Sometimes she's so honest with me,
like A MIRROR, and other times she's like a HUNK OF MARBLE
and I don't have no chisel, Y'KNOW?
Do you believe in MYSTICAL REALITY, DR. BERMAN?

Most Recent Book: JUNK CITY (Persea, 1987)

I spent the whole month of APRIL—
        THE CRUELEST month, right?—
in an isolation cell in the San Quentin prison
and IT WAS BEAUTIFUL. I swear, it's so easy
to GET INTO THOSE PLACES once you learn how.
But anyhow, I met this chick who's very candid
and to-the-point about HALF the time.
And now CONSEQUENTLY, I'm having trouble with
MY THOUGHT-LIFE. I think I would like to CAPTURE HER
for a couple days, JUST WATCH HER and MAYBE ASK
some questions, kind of LIKE AN INTERROGATION.
Do you know what I'M TALKING ABOUT?
INSTEAD of a relationship, we have A SERIES
of one-night-stands. But see, I want SOMETHING MORE.
        Is that TOO MUCH???
It's hard to know WHAT TO EXPECT FROM PEOPLE.
WHAT can I expect from her, OR YOU for that matter.
Dr. Berman, I believe that YOU'LL go to heaven,
and THAT THERE IS a heaven. I HAVE strong feelings
about WHAT WILL HAPPEN. I think it's been
THREE DAYS NOW that I've been sitting here,
HOLED UP in this room, I MEAN, MAN,
I haven't seen ANYONE but the room service kid.
THE FIRST NIGHT AFTER SHE LEFT,
I woke up feeling like I did the second day
into kicking a habit. THAT EMPTINESS, THAT DESPERATION,
accompanied by a mental clarity
that is very intense—a kind of insanity, YEAH,
but if you're insane in the first place
it's what sanity feels like, Y'KNOW?
It's WHAT HAPPENS when all my illusions get stripped away,
WHEN I SEE myself the way I am WITHOUT ALL THE BULL
I make up—A BIG DARKNESS COMES and then the spirit
is lifted right out of my body. I mean WHEN SHE BAILED OUT,
my impulse WAS TO TRACK DOWN another hot Betty,
but IT WASN'T ME. I mean, I have REAL VALUES, man.
Yeah, I done time, but I don't want TO PORTRAY MYSELF
as some kind of MONSTER/CRIMINAL. I was JUST DESTINED
to do these wild, exotic, and crazy things
and I COULDN'T BE a phony to that, man.
I COULDN'T BE one of those NO-ACCOUNT,
nonreal zeros you see WALKING AROUND
IN PURPLE POLYESTER, CHEATING on their wives,
those guys who aren't anything.

THAT'S ONE THING you learn in the joint—
there's no such thing as WHITE PROTECTION
because darkness is going to get you sooner or later—
	NOCHE. THE NOCHE OF THE SOUL
as the Mexican Dudes called it. YOU SEE,
it's not that I don't HAVE AN IDENTITY,
	THE PROBLEM IS I have too many.
MAYBE IF I'D BEEN LIVING IN THIS WORLD ALL MY LIFE
it wouldn't be too bad.
You see, she NEVER REALLY EXPLAINED them to me,
HER REAL FEELINGS. Man, I was just thinking this call
might sound MORE NEGATIVE THAN I actually am,
though I AM SOMETIMES SCARED ABOUT THIS NEW-LIFE I've got.
IT FEELS LIKE I'm wearing SOMEONE ELSE'S CLOTHES
and they don't fit. DO YOU THINK I'LL GROW
into them pretty soon? Do you GET MY DRIFT??
I'm 32 years old and THIS IS THE FIRST TIME
I've had a telephone in my own name.
	I'M DOING EVERYTHING I CAN
to stay clean and watch my company AND my cravings.
Y'KNOW, I once had this article by a famous doctor
that I wish I still had. It says something about a craving
LASTING, PHYSICALLY-in-the-body, only 90 seconds.
Doctor, I've been listening to you FOR THREE HOURS NOW
in this stupid room & I want to KEEP HONEST
	& STRAIGHT & KEEP THE FAITH.
Let's face it, man, either GOD EXISTS or else he doesn't.
	It's so strange BEING OUT HERE, man.
I can't understand the subtleties.
FOR INSTANCE, I know I'm in trouble
when I'm driving down the speedway
TRYING TO CONTROL THE TRAFFIC with my thoughts
and my foul mouth. I KNEW THAT STUFF in the joint,
where you could get the crap kicked out of you,
BUT OUT HERE, MAN, by the time I hit the red light,
the planet has already rotated a thousand miles.
Y'KNOW, in the prison library I read the works
of THE GREAT PHILOSOPHERS AND POETS AND SCIENTISTS,
	but THE GUY WHO SAID IT BEST
was this really spiritual black dude who lived
two cells down the block who believed
that you have to turn it all over to THE POWER.
The truth is—and I'm quoting this dude—is that a guy
can control his life about as well AS HE CAN CONTROL diarrhea.

CRUDE, I KNOW, but to the point.
I always manage to trip myself up, man.
It's like one night in prison I figured out THE PERFECT CRIME.
Except that I HAD TO TELL IT to somebody.
          YOU SEE?? I made it ANOTHER IMPERFECT CRIME.
You come up with the perfect crime,
but because IT'S SOOO PERFECT
you GOTTA TELL SOMEONE, making it imperfect.
Maybe I shouldn't have mentioned the Power.
          WHO KNOWS.
But to come back FULLCIRCLE TO THE MAIN POINT,
My old lady is an angel and she knows I'm saying this
to her favorite guy from another one of her favorite guys,
          & from my heart.
          I DEDICATE THIS TO HER.

RALPH ANGEL ❖

Man in a Window

I don't know man trust is a precious thing
a kind of humility   Offer it to a snake and get repaid with humiliation

Luckily friends rally to my spiritual defense
I think they're reminding me

I mean it's important to me it's
important to me so I leave my fate to fate and come back
I come back home   We need so much less always always
and what's important is always ours

I mean I want to dedicate my life to those who keep going just to see
     how it isn't ending

I don't know
Another average day
Got up putzed around 'til noon
took a shower and second-guessed myself and
all those people all those people passing through my
my days and nights and all those people and

Most Recent Book: ANXIOUS LATITUDES (Wesleyan University Press, 1986)

and you just can't stay with it you know what I mean
You can't can't stay with it   Things happen
Things happen   Doubt sets in   Doubt sets in and
I took a shower about noon you know and I shaved and
thought about not shaving but I
shaved   I took a shower and had a lot of work to do but I
I didn't want to do it I was second-guessing myself that's when doubt
     got involved

I struck up a
rapport with doubt   I didn't do any work and so
and so I said to myself I said well
maybe I should talk about something but I didn't learn anything
I couldn't talk about anything there was
lots of distraction today
A beautiful day   Lots of distraction   It had to do with
all these people all these too-many people
passing through my days and nights   But I
don't get to hear about ideas anymore know what I mean
Just for the hell of it   Talking about ideas
Takes the mind one step further
further than what it already knows   Doesn't
need to affirm itself   It's one step beyond affirming itself

Vulnerable in a way that doesn't threaten
even weak people   Those nice-guy routines
They come up to you
because they know how to be a nice guy

The River Has No Hair to Hold Onto

It's only common sense (not that they know the score,
they don't avoid it). And so one's life story
is begun on a paper napkin and folded into a coat pocket
to be retrieved later when it's darker
and cooler, and closer. And onward

to rockier ground, where conversation is impassable
and human beings matter more than
the light that glimmers beneath the horizon
before sinking into our own inaudible sigh (a long way
from these fur-covered hands). And somehow

the deal is struck. Money gets made.
And the small shocks one undergoes for no reason,
the bus driver handing you a transfer, a steamy
saxophone ascending the jungle. The city
lays down its blanket of rippling

lamplight as though exhaustion too
was achieved by consensus, and what one does
and how one feels have nothing to do with one's self.
No, this can't be the place, but it must be
the road that leads there, always beginning

when morning is slow and hazy, suffering to get somewhere
with all the memorable mistakes along the way,
piecing them together, arriving,
believing that one arrives at a point different from
the starting point, admitting things still aren't clear.

A rag doll on a dark lawn injures the heart
as deeply as the salt sea air filling one's lungs
with a sadness once felt in a classroom,
a sadness older than any of us.
And the dogs barking, challenging cars. And the willows

lining the sidewalk, lifting their veils
to the inscrutable surface of wood. (Someone
is trying to get a message through. Someone thinks
you'll understand it).

Shadow Play

She leaves the motor running.
I would too. I would like to marry her,
that face repeated a million times in this town.
In the exhaust next door a man twists
his wooden leg into an impossible position.
He doesn't even have to say, "I know,
I know, and nobody resents me."
He just grins.

On the vendor's tin scales, daylight
shifts and splinters. Blood on the black brick,
a shopkeeper sweeps glass from his eyelids.
A young man fidgets in a doorway,

cups his hands around a blue
flicker of panic, and leans back
into the shuffling papers and footsteps,
the noise that opens away from him
and is not noise.

Now a cleaning lady stops herself
and looks over her shoulder. And so does
the mailman, a traffic cop, a kid walking his bike.
And the perfect word lodges
deep in the throats of businessmen
talking gibberish, drawing lines around themselves
until obsessed and hailing taxis.
Only our loose clothes

between us, the linen tablecloths, white
as blindness. Only the putter of canal boats,
the vine-covered walls, some cursory
glance that empties our eyes, when they meet,
of options, and won't let go.
A person who might

grow older. People who will dash their dreams.
People who will come back and
live in the aroma of bread, in the sound of
a thousand doves unfolding the plaza.
I would like a glass of ice water.
It's the little thing, when I'm lucky
the world comes to me.

Breaking and Entering

Many setups. At least as many falls.
Winter is paralyzing the country, but not here.
Here, the boys are impersonating songs of indigenous
wildlife. Mockingbird on the roof of the Gun Shop,
scrub jay behind the Clear Lake Saloon.
And when she darts into a drugstore for a chocolate-covered
almond bar, sparrow hawks get the picture
and drive off in her car.

Easy as 8th & Spring Street,
a five-course meal the size of a dime.
Easy as vistas admired only from great distance,

explain away the mystery
and another thatched village is cluster-bombed.
Everyone gets what he wants nowadays.
Anything you can think of is probably true.

And so, nothing. Heaven on earth. The ruse
of answers. A couple-three-times around the block
and ignorance is no longer a good excuse.
There were none. Only moods
arranged like magazines and bones, a Coke bottle
full of roses, the dark, rickety tables about the room.
And whenever it happens, well, it's whatever it takes,
a personality that is not who you are
but a system of habitual reactions to another

light turning green, the free flow of
traffic at the center of the universe where shops
are always open and it's a complete
surprise each time you're told that minding your own business
has betrayed your best friend. But that's over,
that's history, the kind of story that tends to have an ending,
the code inside your haunted head.

Easy as guilt. As waking and sleeping, sitting down
to stand up, sitting down to go out walking,
closing our eyes to see in the nocturnal
light of day. "Treblinka
was a primitive but proficient
production line of death," says a former *SS Untersharfürer*
to the black sharecropper-grandchild of slavery
who may never get over
the banality of where we look.

Only two people
survived the Warsaw uprising, and the one
whose eyes are paths inward, down into the soft grass,
into his skeleton,
who chain-smokes and drinks, is camera shy,
wears short-sleeved shirts, manages to mumble,
"If you could lick my heart, it would poison you."

JIMMY SANTIAGO BACA ❖

I Am Here

for Jaime

I stopped my car on Gibson Avenue,
alongside the T-Bird Lounge, and asked
two policemen clubbing a drunk to stop.
       I was booked
          for obstruction of justice.
In the back seat with the drunk,
his grimy polyester coat
padded with wads of want-ads,
smelling of dog spittle and trash bins,
his eyelids cracked open
from their concrete numbness,
and his trembling hand reached
for an invisible Styrofoam cup
of black coffee on the floor mat.
He gummed thirsty lips
for a small postponement, just a sip,
he dreamed, as we passed liquor stores.

Behind bars, I stand
peering down into tiers.
Porters mill
leaning on mops and brooms.
Chicano in another cell
wears sunglasses
like ancestors wore their war paint.
Christ crucified across chest,
dragon on left arm
twirls through a trellis haze
of vines and roses.
Believer of blood duels,
faith that earth will crack someday
and Aztec warriors rise
to judge the heartless.
He whistles through branches of bars,
hand signing a friend

Most Recent Book: BLACK MESA POEMS (New Directions, 1989)

for brown powder to fertilize
vines of his veins
and make the rose bloom.

Tier guard
stands in front of my cell,
American flag
patched to shoulder above v-rank,
walkie-talkie dangling
from wide black leather belt,
brass buttons and silver badge
painstakingly
polished to impress authority.
"Charges been dropped! You're out! Come on!"
I follow the guard
to the end of the tier,
to a button-paneled cage
where a guard sprawls
like a fat wolf
reading a comic.

From a dark cell
as if from the hull of a slave ship,
I emerge into blinding noon deck-streets,
where sun hacksaws tin sheets of glistening air.

An unblinking anger
fills me. I stare
at strange pedestrians
returning from lunch to the office,
and a cut-checked anger burns my face,
anger that mumbles the world's end
                    over my bones.

I spent the rest of the afternoon
walking familiar streets.
        I withdraw and walk in a place
inside myself, trudging across fierce red sands
of my heart,
        and through the *arroyos*, sliding down,
turning over small rocks, patiently, searching
for something to describe me. . . .
            I am here—
        brown body, blood, bones,
living at Black Mesa outside of Burque.
                    To Them, I am found,

tagged with a number,
photographed cataloged
". . . fearless . . . violent prone. . . ."
"Mau-Mau warrior," one snickered
an aside.
Outlawed   in Their eyes,
to swing   Their picks,
to be jailed   in Their jails.

     I am here, scared, loving, helpful, brave,
     graying hair, meditative brown eyes, kind
     smile, angry eyes burning for equality.

        I am here.

Main Character

I went to see
How the West Was Won
at the Sunshine Theater.
Five years old,
deep in a plush seat,
light turned off,
bright screen lit up
with MGM roaring lion—
        in front of me
        a drunk Indian rose,
        cursed
        the western violins
        and hurled his uncapped bagged bottle
        of wine
        at the rocket roaring to the moon.
His dark angry body
convulsed with his obscene gestures
at the screen,
and then ushers escorted him
up the aisle,
and as he staggered past me,
I heard his grieving sobs.
        Red wine streaked
        blue sky and take-off smoke,
        sizzled cowboys' campfires,
        dripped down barbwire,

slogged the brave, daring scouts
who galloped off to mesa buttes
to speak peace with Apaches,
and made the prairie
lush with wine streams.
When the movie
was over,
I squinted at the bright
sunny street outside,
looking for the main character.

Green Chile

I prefer red chile over my eggs
and potatoes for breakfast.
Red chile *ristras* decorate my door,
dry on my roof, and hang from eaves.
They lend open-air vegetable stands
historical grandeur, and gently swing
with an air of festive welcome.
I can hear them talking in the wind,
haggard, yellowing, crisp, rasping
tongues of old men, licking the breeze.

But grandmother loves green chile.
When I visit her,
she holds the green chile pepper
in her wrinkled hands.
Ah, voluptuous, masculine,
an air of authority and youth simmers
from its swan-neck stem, tapering to a flowery
collar, fermenting resinous spice.
A well-dressed gentleman at the door
my grandmother takes sensuously in her hand,
rubbing its firm glossed sides,
caressing the oily rubbery serpent,
with mouth-watering fulfillment,
fondling its curves with gentle fingers.
Its bearing magnificent and taut
as flanks of a tiger in mid-leap,
she thrusts her blade into
and cuts it open, with lust

on her hot mouth, sweating over the stove,
bandanna round her forehead,
mysterious passion on her face
as she serves me green chile con carne
between soft warm leaves of corn tortillas,
with beans and rice—her sacrifice
to her little prince.
I slurp from my plate
with last bit of tortilla, my mouth burns
and I hiss and drink a tall glass of cold water.

All over New Mexico, sunburned men and women
drive rickety trucks stuffed with gunny-sacks
of green chile, from Belen, Veguita, Willard, Estancia,
San Antonio y Socorro, from fields
to roadside stands, you see them roasting green chile
in screen-sided homemade barrels, and for a dollar a bag,
we relive this old, beautiful ritual again and again.

STEPHEN BERG ❖

The Coat

for Jerry

Here's one of those warm simple letters in that big six-year-old scrawl of
yours, filling the whole page with your statement, clear, sweet, kind,
associating values with detail with Nietzsche with the glory of poetry with
some local flower or creature you bumped into yesterday and fell in love with,
with the rich tweed coat I gave you last time you were here. "Jews
understand coats, life-giving coats, protection against death," you say in the
letter, and "It's easy being crazy when the house is empty, thinking of birds
of prey wearing black hats." Jerry, the yellow Irish raglan-shoulder coat I
bought with money from my father is yours now, it's draped on your beefy
Hebrew shoulders in the sticks near Easton, Pa., where nobody has good taste,
nobody will admire its nubby random unassuming weave, its hand-loomed itchy
grain brimming with dots of pink. Where you live it's as if cities don't exist
yet, all's primitive, all's survival. Your neighbors pace the canal near your
house, naming weeds, studying the water level, diagnosing soil richness, filling

Most Recent Book: IN IT (University of Illinois Press, 1986)

plastic sandwich bags with specimens: butterflies, quavering nameless insects, leaves, semiprecious stones. But none of them know shit about coats, their cloudy bone buttons and waxed thread sewn crisscross over and over until there's a sharp lump the owner can rub his thumb across for comfort. It's a Burberry, you schmuck, and even you probably couldn't care less. It didn't fit from the day I picked it out, its long tent-like form comes from the past of animal pelts and capes and blankets with a slit cut in the middle, for living in nature not the city where people love clothes that "enhance" the body. Russians know coats, don't they? and Jews, those death-fearing, Godless, touchy, maniacs of the world who need their vulnerable, paranoid bodies ecstatic wrapped in a heavy expensive coat—so gas fumes can't penetrate, so torture can't swell their ankles and wrists, so the ideas of clean rigid Gentiles who believe in social justice, in eliminating obstructions to justice, can't get in, so the hands of strangers on a bus or in a street crowd can't reach their delicate skin, so even the hands of tender love can't change their mood. Eliot, Pound and Joyce bought themselves coats, showed off gorgeous Isle of Skyes, Meltons, Sheared Camel Hairs, hoping it would drop below zero just to test how absolute their coats were, whether they were true mortal coats that could give life, define life, save life. What a Jewish idea! But I believe it. A coat so well-made, so thick and fine it could actually prevent death: an immortality coat! Right now I want my coat back, Jerry, even though it's late May, it's the only coat I know that might help me live forever, but I give myself a stupid effeminate kiss in the long bathroom mirror instead, down to my crotch, I begin to lather and shave, a kiss instead of a coat, and feel the just sadness of how much I'll miss that sack of stitched woven hair come December. Naked, I shave, an hour before leaving to teach, zipping the blue plastic Good News across cheek over chin up to the lip under a nostril and it strikes me that I should lecture on coats today not poetry, inspired by the coat I gave you, which has probably fallen off its cheap wire hanger by now, a blurred heap among gashed rubber boots, the vacuum cleaner, outgrown ice skates, dark twisted hats and whatever else you've chucked down there to be sold at a yard sale. My lecture should explain the coat's power to stop death and somehow should, I think, represent divine coats in an act that uses a real coat somehow. I'll wear one of my coats to class. I walk in. Take out my note cards, still wearing my coat. I keep it on. Suddenly they're quiet. I'm talking about the coat, your coat, the coats. Brilliant. Euphoric. Letting my mind speak, wandering in all its honest blindness. And I add "Lusting for a hundred things this morning, I'd rather have a coat than anything, deep, unassailable wool to shield a back and chest on a cold night so securely that the man who wears it feels he can stand anything, do anything, survive even his own death, grateful for the feel of it, for the weight, the reassuring dense goodness against his bare hands, for the shiny trace of oil it leaves in a film on his palms and fingers." Then I call one student up and draw her inside my coat by opening it like Dracula, still lecturing, and button us in and feel her jump when my crazy stiff dick springs and pulses against her belly, still lecturing about coats, whispering, declaiming, gesturing, making scholarly digressions, invoking history, origins, fashion, cloth, hissing out of the side of my mouth to her—"Stay calm, don't let anybody know" as her hand slips it in a little and I sway a little, finishing, asking questions, answering questions, blithely in touch with their faces as she comes, three or four muffled tremors. All this time both our faces turned toward the class, and she's tittering as if the whole thing is merely a lecture on coats. "What a beautiful coat you have," she says, "so roomy, warm," and I thank her for the compliment, say "But you should see the one I gave Jerry," unable to recall one thing I've said to the class during the last few minutes. Ah, this life, which even the best coat can't protect us from; this death, too strong for the warmest coat there is. Nevertheless, there are coats that will never let us die—I know it. Every time I step into the hall closet and sniff its musty dark and rove my hands over the coats—first shoulders, then the long drape of the body— awed by their dark softness, and caress mine, I pray it's one of those coats, the holy ones, I close the door and stay in there as long as I can blindly nuzzling and singing.

Self-Portrait at Six

My wife hung it there, on the wall on the way to our bedroom. When you take the five steps up to the landing in front of our door, it's on your left, usually in shadow in a gold-rimmed, oval mat, Victorian oval walnut molding frame, the eyes already hurt, defensive in the way we think "open" means but is, actually, only a form of wariness. No steadiness, no self-assurance, no clarity of mind influence the face yet. The thick brown hair is mine, but the mouth is all wonder in a kind of sullen trance and pleads not to be wounded more. He fears the world can kill him, and will, the world is always mysterious, like disease. Being alone attacks him from the outside, saddening his look, he can't ignore it by simply playing. Instead it seems he can't defend himself, there's no courage of acceptance in his gaze. At my age now, I've come to imagine my mother, at the beginning of my life, as a young lovely woman, baffled by her pain, who found my helplessness too much like her own to let her simply reflect my emerging self. So, to extend the thought, my face on the stairwall, then, was already caught in the battles of identity and self-denial, of believing that freedom is impossible because another's self is who one is. Isn't that what our first taste of death is, invasion of another's pain? Isn't that how we first split ourselves into good and bad? Think of an awareness that lets you act without even a shade of sensing others are watching you, judging you, caring about you, so that desire and action diffuse, and there's no gap, no hint of pain that slows you. But this is memory, interpretation, the two great dangers of the mind. What it is I'm getting at, what it is that brings that picture back and stirs my ideas is the gnawing aloneness of people, of all things, of consciousness itself, and the opposite—that each of us lives in others' minds, as they live in ours, sometimes flaring in images, sometimes feeling each others' flesh. Each night before I go to bed I pass myself on the stairs, eternally helpless, caught with an early madness crossing my face, and it seems, as I tuck myself in, trying not to wake her, trying not to be seen or heard, that the entire universe is the dark fetal mound breathing on one side of our bed, that everything flows from it, everything returns.

And the Scream

The thirtyish, Irish, red-nosed carpenter
who works for Coonan—he rehabs houses up here—
is already half stoned on beer
before eight and chases his son past my front window,
screaming at him, the kid's glasses,
thick as my little finger,
bobbling on his nose.
Thin steady pewter drizzle,
long smudges yellowing the sky,
clouds darkening the street abruptly,
Pat and Jack Laurent's house gloomy
across from mine (they're away), even the embroidery
of lace curtains, the high-
arched Victorian double doors
incapable of lightening the mood.
That boy disappearing between houses
reminds me of when I
punched my whole arm through the glass door
between our dining room and kitchen
(the maid wouldn't leave it open)
and gashed my elbow so it bled on the floor
big splashes and wouldn't stop
and my mother's or the maid's or my
scream seemed to echo everywhere. That boy—
from my living room one night, in the dark,
I watched his father screaming, waving a beer bottle
above the mother stretched out in a slip in bed under
a hatless four-bulb ceiling fixture's neutral blue-white glare.
Nobody would call this poetry.

When I leaf through serious books, though, I see
blindings, suicides, revelations,
some lust that breeds disaster.
Families and blood are what we want—
because we need love or can't love?
For example, my mother tells me (we're face-to-face in her living room,
she will not look at me when she speaks)
her mother had to pick lice from her scalp when she was ten,
her piano-prodigy Christian Scientist brother
refused help from a doctor so he died at twenty-six,
coughing blood into a bucket while she watched. Poor. Crazy.
And so on, and so on, and therefore—
incomplete sentences, true,
sketches merely,
like watching a scream through glass, as I have twice lately,
filling in the detail of hearing
plus all the other crap: motives, stupidities,
money, sex, "the real reason," someone always dying.
But what I need to say is—
Yes, merely a sketch, that's it,
that's us, half-known, unredeemable animals,
and the scream, the scream.

LINDA BIERDS ❖

Off the Aleutian Chain

There is the sound of hail washed over a porthole, but
originating deeper, past the bunks
and galley, out
from the ship's icy center.
A door is opened. There—
it is the resonant swashing of claws:
king crabs in the hold stroking over one another,
their thousand bodies black and luminous.

This stroking, this echo of the weather,
is echoed again, just above, in a shuffle of limp cards.

Most Recent Book: THE STILLNESS, THE DANCING (Henry Holt & Co., 1988)

Flushed and exhausted, the fishermen
slump from their chairs. Their hands

and the wide bracelets of skin above their wrists,
have weathered to the color of salmon gills.
At their elbows are bottles of rye,
white cheese; here and there, the dried carcasses
of tea bags, like huge, toppled moths.

One man is smiling. Slowly,

he snaps down a trio of flat queens.
Judith, he laughs. *Rachel. The steamy Argine.*
And it is then, summoned by name, by chance,
that these women brush through:
powdered, good-natured,
their ruffs and twills slightly acrid,
their faces a patchwork of circumstance, history,
unique in the mind of each fisherman.

They are gone in an instant, like the memory of
hail. Outside, the night sky is clearing.
Frigid winds and the winter sea-spray

have coated the ship with ice. Everything—
the spars and rigging, the mosaic
of dredges, trawl lines—is turning to ice.

No one is threatened. It is winter.

The ship simply cups its vertical cargo—
these swimmers and queens—their
parenthesis of water—
rides with it into the morning.

For the Sake of Retrieval

As Whistler heard colors like a stretch of music—
long harmonies, violet to amber, double hummings of
silver, opal—so, in reverse, these three in their capsule,

free falling two hours through the black Atlantic, ears
popped then filled with the music of Bach or Haydn,
might fashion a landscape. Low note bring
a prairie perhaps, the sharps a smatter of flowers,

as the pip-notes of sonar spring back to the screen
in little blossoms. They have come for the lost Titanic

and find instead, in the splayed beam of a headlamp,
silt fields, pale and singular, like the snow fields
of Newfoundland. On its one runner blade the capsule slides,
slips out through drift hummocks, through
stones the ice-age glaciers dropped, its trail
the foot-thin trail of a dancer, who
plants, glides, at this head the flurry

of a ship's chandelier, at his back a cinch-hook of icebergs,
cast down through the winds of Newfoundland.
The music these three absorb
stops with the wreckage, with words
lipped up through a microphone:
flange, windlass, capstan, hull plating, then oddly, syllables,
at a slant, as light might slant through window slats,

stairsteps, doorknob, serving bowl, teacup, Bordeaux.
Mechanical fingers, controlled by the strokes
of a joy stick, brush over debris, lifting, replacing.
In jittery strobe lights, camera lights, all colors
ground down to a quiet palette,
angles return, corners and spirals
pull back to the human eye—as if from some

iced and black-washed atmosphere, boiler coal,
a footboard and platter, each common shape
brightened, briefly held for the sake of retrieval.
The current spins silt like a sudden storm.
With the intricacy of a body the capsule adjusts,
temperature, pressure. Some one coughs, then the three

sit waiting, as in Whistler's *Sad Sea*
three are waiting. All around them are dollops
of winter wind, everywhere beach and sea. No horizon
at all in this painting, just a grey/brown thrum
beach to sea. How steady his breath must have been
on the canvas, his hand on the brushstokes
of lap robes, of bonnets and beach chairs, the pull
of a red umbrella: each simple shape
loved and awash in the landscape.

The Stillness, The Dancing

I am indefinitely capable of wonder
—Federico Fellini

Long ago, in the forests of southern Europe,
just south of Macon, a woman died in childbirth.
She was taken, by custom, to the small slate
lip of a mountain. Legs bound at the knees
she was left facing west, thick with her still child.

Century by century, nothing disturbed them

so that now
the bones of the woman cup the small bones
of the child: the globe of its head angled
there, in the paddle and stem of her hips.

It is winter, just after midday. Slowly,
shudder by civilized shudder, a train slips over
the mountain, reveals to its weary riders

something white, then again, something
white at the side of the eye. They straighten,
place their lips to the glass, and there, far
below, this delicate, bleached pattern,
like the spokes of a bamboo cage.

What, someone whispers, and What, What,
word after word bouncing back from its blossom
of vapor, the woman and child appearing,
disappearing, as the train slips down through the alders—

until they are brands on the eyelid, until they are
stories, until, thick-soled and silent,
each rider squats with a blessing of ochre.

*   *   *

And so there are stories. Mortar. A little stratum
under the toenails. A train descends from a mountain,
levels out, circles a field where a team of actors
mimics a picnic. The billowing children.
On the table, fruit, a great calabash of chilled fish.
And over it all, a beloved uncle, long mad,
sits in the crotch of an oak tree.

He hears to his right, the compressed blare
of a whistle—each sound wave approaching shorter, shorter,
like words on a window, then just as the engine passes,
the long playing out.
He smiles as the blare seeps over
the actors, the pasture, the village

where now, in the haze of a sudden snowfall,
a film crew, dressed for a picnic, coaxes a peacock
to the chilled street. Six men on their knees
chirruping, laughing, snow lifting in puffs
from the spotlights. And the peacock,
shanks and yellow spurs high-stepping, high-stepping
slowly unfolds its breathless fan, displays
to a clamor of boxcars, clubcars—

where riders, excited,
traveling for miles with an eyeful of bones
see now their reversal.

In a ecstacy of color the peacock dips,
revolves to the slow train:
each rider pressed to a window,
each round face courted in turn.

LORNA DEE CERVANTES ❖

Raisins

Raisins are my currency
to date—slightly seedy,
prickled as my nipples,
black as pubis, colored
as my opened eyelids.
I tongue you
frictives into vowels.
I suck you
to the scabs

Most Recent Book: CABLES OF GENOCIDE: POEMS OF LOVE AND HUNGER (Arte Publico
Press, 1990)

you were, forbidden
fruit. Reminders.
Never mind
the way I found you
deserted in the depot
stall. No matter
how this small red box
was once a child's.
Lost wonder, you're
the gift of grace
swept up off
the bathroom floor.
You're my only food
today, the day I left
you, paper husband,
widowed name.
Our final meal
was sweet, you
hovered over me,
an open package,
beating blades
to froth, teething
me the way I like it,
both lips bit and shriveled
as our last *fuck you*.
You are black with rust
and will restore my blood.
You're my prize of faith,
stave against starve.
I eat it. Grateful
for the brief exchange.
Twenty-eight tips
of fate. Three good sweats
they soaked in sun
as you now soak
my spit, sweet
as acid, damp as rot.
This hunger, as your
memory, feeds
by chance.

Colorado Blvd.

I wanted to die so I walked
the streets. Dead night,
black as iris, cold as the toes
on a barefoot drunk. Not a sound
but my shoes asking themselves over,
What season is this? Why is the wind
stuttering in its stall of nightmares?
Why courage or the bravery
of dripping steel? Given branches
rooted to their cunning, a kind
of snow lay fallow upon the hearth
of dried up trunks, wan and musing
like an absent guitarist strumming
wildly what she's forgotten most.
Bats fell about me like fire
or dead bark from my brow beaten
autumn. A kind of passing through
and when it called, the startled bird
of my birth, I left it, singing,
or fallen from its nest, it was silent
as the caves of my footfalls left
ridden in their absent burials.
What good was this? My cold
hearing, nothing, more desire
than protection. When would it come?
In that clove of cottonwood, perhaps
that shape in the mist, secret
as teeming lions. Is it my own
will that stalks me? Is it in
the slowed heart of my beatings
or the face that mists when
I least expect it? Frost covered
the windshields of the left
behind autos. In his parking
lot, my savior rests, lighting
his crack pipe, semi-automatic
poised at my nipple or the ear
I expose to witches and thieves:
Here it is. Will you kill for it?

From the Bus to E.L.
at Atascadero State Hospital

for Juan Cuellar

Fall. Peppercorns
rouge into salmon roe.
The finished hills, blond
in Califas, get crew cuts
as cattle butch the hip grass
into flattops. Five o'clock
shadows singe and vanquish
without felling the scrub oaks
and manzanita snarls. Dusted
summer squash laze on the gone
lawns with ready pumpkins in the fields,
bright as plastic and faceless, their time
up, evident as flaring matches in the hole.
There's a town coming on. It shows
in the Greyhound windows, the mooned
mounds instantly green: fence
and civilize.
                    They sat you
here, where you stuck
like a poisoned dart
between the Idler Bar
and the Mud Hole Mini Mart.
Small wonder, vato, you
envisioned your Jupiterscapes
here in these martianed landings. What
messages they blew to this world, the seeds
of something generative.
Someday, you said, they would
blow us both away.
                    There was a code
to be read in the nothing of an empty page.
There was a plan to the shambles
of sage on the rocks or the bumbling
kooks on the blocked streets,
the nothing of a stranger
who refuses to give, the nothing
of a television mouthing
nothing to a nothing house full
of nothing, like on the morning they locked

you up for good.
You were here, Ed,
and there is nothing here. Moonscapes,
desert wastes. As it is, in this light,
the eyes read but register nothing: cables
and telephone trees, white fences, the immovable
air vanishing on the hips of comatose women.
Is this what you saw? Nothing
in the hedges, in the chopped ends, the panicking
roads where nothing is distanced
between ourselves and an abundance
of nowhere. The institutions of our lives
embed themselves in the shallows like the clumped
row houses of Camp Roberts, the wooden graves
of the suicidal dead or the wars where
they laid you to rest, resisting.
You could have gone on
to King City or the Temple
of Angels.   Instead,
You were here where the wounded
blackbirds warble jazz to a crazed wind,
where the dusk is as pure and uninimical
as law, devious as treaties; a substance
fills the night, the absence of light,
with whatever we imagine.   .
Think of it, spacetrips, vato
loco of the stars, this is what you get
in this life, the lockdown
of nothing.

DAVID CLEWELL ❖

We Never Close

Our Special Services manager is Helen Waite.
If you want special service, go to Helen Waite.

—taped on the wall in Tony's Chophouse

Some nights you need to get into the car and drive
until you find it, that familiar hash-house glow
that means Open All Night in Spokane or Hackensack
or anywhere between. But it's the brazen nature
of the promise spelled out in the window
that keeps you coming back: WE NEVER CLOSE.
Times like this nothing softer, nothing less
will do. You're a veteran of the edge of town,
an old hand at the middle of nowhere. Sometimes
you wake up and you're living your life
in the static between stations, between the prayer
and the answer: one lover and another. Between
jobs or novels or whole religions. You're looking
for something to hold onto between right now and
sunrise, two bad dreams, and some nights it takes
more than a feather pillow to sustain you.
There's something in the way the waitress
yells her orders to some guy five feet away,
the same short-order man you always see, same beefy
tattoo of a heart and words the years have finally blurred
into the vaguely Universal. Maybe *Born To* something. Maybe
something *Love*. Or the name of a ship that went down.
Or a woman. What matters is he's here unflinchingly
for you. He'll do Pig In A Blanket or Pie In The Sky
and even his mistakes with eggs are redeemed somewhere
in his imagination: Adam & Eve In A Padded Room,
Adam & Eve In Hell. With his spatula and maniacal grin
he always puts the fear of someone's God into you good.

Tonight the waitress recites a list of everything
she's out of. It's not much, compared to yours,
that litany of the gone and the going you sang softly
back to the radio. When she asks what you're having,

Most Recent Book: BLESSINGS IN DISGUISE (E. P. Dutton, 1990)

you know the obvious answer: *another one of*
those nights. But instead you take a guess out loud:
whatever's good, something you haven't had in a while.
And you're amazed that she can make it sound so special
for a minute, her own apotheosis of one more order
of the Usual. Your soup turns into Yesterday, Today, And
Always. Pin A Rose On It, and your hamburger's blessed
with a gigantic slice of raw. Coffee—Make It Sweet,
Sweetness And Light. And you're so lightheaded
with wonder you could almost ask her what she's doing
when she gets off. From where you sit it's hard
to tell the color of her eyes, but you'd have to guess
some shade of blue, the local color here:
Blue Plate Special, smoke on the rise from a dozen ashtrays,
the cop sweet-talking another Danish he won't pay for,
an entire row of songs in the jukebox, the blue-streak
chatter of the woman on the pay phone fingering the dark
blue bruise on the back of her neck, and suddenly
any blue you brought here with you pales in comparison.

It hurts just looking at it and thinking how
you'd hold up under that kind of wear, a pain
you could actually point to and insist *here's where . . .*
It All Began, or Went Bad, or Came To An End—
depending on who'll listen. Say you can tell
from the swelling it's no accident: runs too deep.
One night on the way in or out of the kitchen
the love she thought she had coming turned into
A Sudden Blur Of Hurt. After who knows how long
driving alone, this call is finally her way to
send it back. It's hard to make out very many
of her words, but you're jealous of whoever's
anywhere down the line to hear them.
Even if she rehearsed every mile of the ride out here,
she still doesn't sound sure, doesn't know how to say
no more, don't wait up, she won't be back, ever.
You want to see her slam that receiver into its cradle,
want it to sound like the irreversible thunk
of a car meeting something alive in the road.

The waitress drops a steaming plate
at the empty stool next to you. *Here's the lady's*
she says to no one in particular, and you realize
she could be talking to you again. Maybe
she's lumped you and the woman on the phone together

in the legion of the bruised, the day-old,
the bottom of the pot. You're stuck in the middle
between denying everything and confessing, when she winks
and out of nowhere assures you *it's working*.
No matter what she has in mind, you'd like to believe her.
She seems so sure that nothing else has broken down
or gone wrong since you got here. You'd like to take her home
where she could talk you through those days
of more dull ache than you can say.
And whatever hunger drove you here in the first place,
whatever you wanted so badly you could taste it,
you haven't seen anything yet.
Ask the woman now trying to convince the operator
this whole thing's been a mistake, one very long
wrong number. Ask the waitress who's already
running a hot bath in her mind.

Miles from here you'll be alone in the shower singing
whatever's left of your heart out, trying to remember
how it goes, this exalting of the ordinary.
If the night's not good enough the first time,
send it back: *Pin A Rose On It*. Yell out of love
at the top of your lungs if you have to: *Make It
Sweetness. Make It Light*.
And in the steamed-up bathroom mirror,
a little fainter maybe, but right where you wrote it
the last time: WE NEVER CLOSE. You'll see your own face
somewhere in that promise, and you'll be just barely
back in business again. Sometimes you stay open
so long it hurts. Ask the waitress who'll be no good
for anything tomorrow. Ask the woman down to her last
dime of crying. Or the short-order man. Put yourself
in his place, bent over the grill. The long haul
he's in it for, elbow-deep in another desperate creation.
Doomed to a life without sleep when some idiot
years ago unlocked the door and threw away the key.
He's logged so much time waiting for relief
that if someone punched in now and put on an apron,
he'd have to believe he was seeing things.

You'll be shivering in your towel,
afraid to admit you still can't help feeling
that no matter how long you've been living like this,
someone's going even longer out of her way tonight,
that any minute she'll walk back in from out of the blue.

She's spent all night working up the nerve.
It's what she wants, if you can find it in your heart.
Her hair will be the sheen of brown you remember
and her neck, perfect eggshell smooth.
Not a single wince in her body. Suddenly it hurts
just imagining it. Knocks the wind clean out of you
and drops you cold where you live.

You open your eyes and she's really here. Your waitress,
laying down everything you once hoped for on the counter,
and by now you're wishing it was something else completely.
She doesn't need to tell you: it's not working anymore.
She looks at the plate of eggs next to you,
the one the grill man's made up like a face
growing colder every minute: *I guess your friend's not
very hungry*. And you can't remember
what you ever saw in her. You don't remember asking
for any of this, but here it comes anyway.
With your name on it. Yesterday. Today. Always.
And for the first time in your lifetime of places
just like this, you can see the cockeyed wisdom
in the Hav-a-Hank handkerchiefs for sale
behind the counter, in the measured doses of Bromo
hanging over the cartoon outline of a man
with the fizz already gone out of him.
They're on hand for the sadness and the burning.
Tonight you understand
what you couldn't as a kid in the daylight
when all you could take seriously after lunch
was finally buying one of those unbreakable combs.
Hard to believe, but there it was, bent over nearly double
on its cardboard display: *Sweetheart—The Only One
You'll Ever Need*. One dime and it was yours
and it would last, that preposterous strength more than
you'd ever need. That good breeze blowing you perfectly home.

This Book Belongs to Susan Someone

on finding a copy of a friend's book, heavily marked
and underlined, in a second-hand bookshop

for Bill Kloefkorn

It's only her version of what you were trying to do
yourself: getting it down on paper, the right words
that will say it so it stays said that way forever,
whatever you once imagined *it* might be.
Reading her inky notations from this distance,
it's hard to tell. So often it seems to be her word
flush against yours, and who's to say, false modesty aside,
which one of you deserves believing more?
Surely once she must have had the profound feeling
she could think of better things to stay awake this late for.
The way I see it, she's up all night in bed
listening to the sound of your words in her mouth,
that figurative kiss she really wants no part of.
But she's so desperate to make out anything, no matter how
self-explanatory, that she writes *sad* here, *disappointing*
there. Turn the page and now it's *frustration*
all over the place, and it's absolutely palpable,
her side of it. Another page and it's raining
metaphor and *symbol* from a cloud of wishful thinking,
out of the blue felt-tip of habit pressing down
until finally she's writing *I don't get it*: the poem
like a joke, the love, the sleep she truly needs.

Because she knows what you've suspected for some time:
there will be a test on this, though hers will come
more tangibly and sooner. And while she shakes her head,
angry that she has to provide for this distraction
she never asked into her life, worried
she'll run out of coffee before enough of it sinks in,
she's writing her own anxious heart out
until it casts a shadow, takes on a life of its own, here
at the end of your book. I'm reading between the lines
when I suppose her motives were as pure as yours
because that's where she's put that small part of herself
trying to wish some connection into existence,
some sudden interstate that might finally replace
the slower backroads, those precarious hairpin turns
between the brain and the heart. It's obvious she's stuck
in the dark again. You've got to admire her for whistling.

By now her roommate's probably asleep, murmuring
in some dreamy *ur*-language that existed before the need
to speak it, before the urge to write its imperfections down.
Awake, it's trickier business, this saying
so deliberately what we can only hope means anything.
Especially when we're at it this late, weighing words
until they somehow seem to matter, until
we look at them again in the next day's excruciating light
and realize mostly we stayed up all night for not nearly enough.

And although she might have come to hate the very sound
of your name, the thought of everything you put her through,
I bet in other ways she's far too reasonable, too good
to be still carrying a grudge. More likely that night's
the farthest thing from her mind. Even if you can picture her
in the room full of people where she is tonight,
and even if she pauses between the drinks and dinner
to whisper a few words in her lover's ear, don't think
for a minute it has anything to do with you.
She's come a long way to get to this place in her life
where finally she's happy almost beyond words,
and these days if she knows any disappointment,
it's nothing she can say. If she'd had to rely on
the fragile wings of song, she'd still be back in her dormitory
sweating out those hours again before she passed her test,
but just barely. And you wherever you are,
with your own frantic pages of notes to get back to,
another night drunk down to the cold bottom of the cup,
imagining an even better poem somewhere in the margins
of the best you can do right now,
you know how that one goes.

PETER COOLEY ❖

The Soul

In their ascent from the pavement
the ten white fingers of my soul
should be drumming out their thanksgiving

Most Recent Book: THE VAN GOGH NOTEBOOK (Carnegie Mellon University Press, 1987)

I'm still alive. But they're too scraped, shaking.
I stand up. Now my feet, too, prove it:
I'm here, the alley of the downtown Y.
On the rooftops of the tenements around me
it is the same night coming down
I've always known though this time
the arm which reaches for my gym bag
could be a phantom limb, not mine,
while the full figure of myself against a wall
dances skeletal, dances a wildman in the cave.
As if for the first time I a man standing up . . .
I notice the stars I count on have begun to pulse
since I lay down, belly-flat, crying
at his command while he stood over me
while he cried back, you Mother, Mother,
repeating it as he tore my wallet for ten bucks,
all I had, and left the credit cards
while the pistol in his fist shook like his voice
and then decided I will sit down to dinner
this evening at the table whose edges I can grip
that the wine, the bread, my wife and children
be seen above water when I rise to them,
my vision rinsed in a white light
I never asked for from a man, weeping,
putting his finger on nothing he could name
until he turned and ran and chose to spare me.

Holy Family
Audubon Zoo, New Orleans

A mother, a father, a boy child, two maybe.
The lovers at the end of adolescence, when the glands
call to each other, demanding such oblivion
as only another can promise for a time.
Today, free day, they have left the shelter downtown
for a parkbench before the lions, the boy standing above parents
so they repeat that trinity the quattrocento did to death
though their poverty has probably something to do with oil
and there any connection to the Holy Land begins and ends.
I will see them later, younger, older
beneath the expressway when I drive downtown to teach,

bartering something I've never tried with an old man
who lives there any weather. Or child and mother alone
may beg the steps where the legless woman squats
at the abandoned church until police chase them away.
And the father, face expressionless as the Freshmen I face later,
can disappear in the Quarter and sell himself. So may his wife.
But one of them must keep the child, their savior,
alive and well so he will have a chance.
Listen to me! Preaching! Prophesying!
Probably the boy will be traded downriver or abandoned
in a shopping center I frequent after dinner
with my wife and son. We won't turn him in,
neither of us wanting any part of this. But someone will
and he'll appear if he's charmed in a special
at the end of the news which I turn off, exhausted,
bored or both, if grace descends to him.

The Zouave

Screw you. I don't give a rat's ass
if you think these flared vermillion pants,

puffed like a skirt, make me look the woman.
Where I sit, positioned over Death,

I roll on, cock of the walk, I roll off,
each time one of you fools comes to my picture.

Look, I've hit the public eye
a hundred years, you, longer than you'll live,

longer than your century may last.
Go on. Tell me I'm a brown monkey,

shaggy paws stuck over my crotch.
My answer? Death is just a bitch,

we pay enough, we get one who's a habit,
loving us more than we could ever itch,

crying, begging for us to come again—
and we promise if we've been granted paint,

song, paper, stone or precious metal,
promises we'll come back our sweet way.

Idiots, did I know what Van Gogh was,
foreigners the two of us in Arles—

me with nothing but soldiering and screwing scrawny ones
till he arrived, a paintbrush between his legs

to get me up for immortality.
Want to know, you, how we met, well, here it is:

one night, my favorite madam sent us both
upstairs to the same door: two piss-poor fuckers,

to see this Léontine, a new tart for us both,
and we shared her, first Vincent, then me, longer,

each of us alone, you, we're no perverts!—
Arles' dumbest, cheapest, fattest eighty-year-old!

Self-Portrait as Van Gogh

Before a mirror at midnight I compose myself,
donning the gold straw I tilt at just his angle
to assure the vision will stay caged.
I squint, ruffle my beard, henna the tips.

Or I bare my head, comb back the whorling locks
halfway to morning, tear all shades from the lamps
and rouge my cheeks, my pate, ruddy as the sun
turning the wheatfields in Arles to my vision.

Oh, the poses print can never flesh out!
The skullcap I snap on to play the bandaged ear,
hacking on a pipe, my throat inflamed . . .
The stupor assumed to lift an empty glass,
toasting the whores beaten off between my legs . . .
And then, at dawn, in my best suit, vest, gray bowler,
I stiffen to the pose of the finished gentleman,
the old disguise Vincent muffed until the end.
I sit down to breakfast sick. This is what they wrapped him in.

The History of Poetry

Once the world was waiting for a song
when along came this. Some said it was a joke
funny ha-ha but at the end too lachrymose
to last. Others that it was writ
holier than thou and should be catechized,
then set to turgid dirges, wept over
with gnashed fang, wrung palm.
The ancient declaimed it fad,
the young, old fogies' play.
Almost everyone agreed, except the children,
who didn't listen, it was kid stuff.

Centuries yawned and fell back, stuporous,
eons stretched out, soaking up beauty sleep.
Then one day a peasant, knowing he hurt too much,
remembered hurting too much, told his wife
he might have written it
if, in another life, he'd been born better,
at least literate.
And when the gods heard this
they hungered suddenly to become mortal
and join themselves with us in lecherous praise.
Thus hereafter follows the stories of their sins,
their cries made flesh by euphony and trope
they whispered to us that we take them down,
their great debauches, all made up
that we should emulate with our blood, pay in blood,
while they in the cheap seats, stomp the floor and clap—
all loss, all the fallible, all poetry.

MARK COX ❖

Archaic Torso of My Uncle Phil

Our broadcast day is over, I've unplugged
but there's still that perfect white dot
in the middle of the sky, still the smeary glow

Most Recent Book: SMOULDER (David R. Godine, Publisher, 1989)

of some distant transmission. What it reminds me of
is that bluish, phosphorescent dye they inject into you
before they stick the telescope up your astronomy. It's
the historyectomy of it, the rise and fall of the Roman
pulse rate, the existential yet plotted course
of our little dippers, that makes it so objectionable.
Some days I feel change coming on, but can't
tell if it's an airplane or my neighbor's chainsaw;
other days I just feel doomed. And tonight,
I feel certain I have both feet in the same sock,
that the moon is a head mirror on an Egyptian priest,
and a woman in Philadelphia
is carving the longboat with my name on it.
My whole body is a womb.
I'll miss everybody.
It hurts all over.

Geese

We were in love and his uncle had a farm
where he took me hunting
to try to be in love even more.

He wanted me to have what he had:
Black coffee,
toast buttered with bad light
in a truck stop splotched with smoke,

then moonlight on the hills and snow
like a woman stepping out of her dress.

And it was good even as we killed it.
The stalks lightening,
the sun rising like a worn, yellow slicker
over us, bent over panting
because it wasn't hit cleanly
and had run us both dizzy
before settling down.

There was a particular knife he used
to make the asshole bigger.
After that, one could just reach in
and remove anything that wasn't necessary,

and thinking about it now, I see
the old school desk behind his uncle's house
put there for that reason,
see my husband sadly hosing it down,
as if regretting how and what men are taught . . .

I'm lying . . .
Though the diner I see belongs
in a small town where I went to school,
the desk had no drawers, was in fact a table,
and he was whistling as he washed it.

The sun didn't rise
like something to keep the rain off us;
it hung, like a cold chandelier
in which I could see each filament
in each flame-shaped bulb
beating itself senseless against the light—
brilliant and hollow,

beautiful and inhumane . . .
But I wanted so badly
to forgive his hands, forgive his lovers,
and to forget how, driving home, I was fooled
by half an acre of decoys
and some camouflage netting,

how I wanted to honk but didn't,
and how the whole scene made me realize
that mannequins mate for life too,
in department stores, wearing back-to-school clothes,

made me remember that if you press hard enough
on a bird's dead breast, it will betray its own kind,
that when he took its neck and broke it
I said his first name.

Poem for the Name Mary

Like smoke in a bottle, like
hunger, sometimes light fits,
wraps itself around a person
or thing and doesn't let go.
The light becomes a name,

and that name becomes a voice
through which light speaks to us.
Maybe this is what a friend means
when she says there is a pair of lips
in the air, maybe this is desire
and need too. Or maybe
this is just how to love a potato,
how to see what the potato sees:
the childish, white arms that reach out
through its eyes into the dark of our cabinets
to bless them.

In This His Suit

Not his clothes, but their chimerical creases.
Not his body, but the gestures of his body
worn last and put unpressed
into its plastic. Not the hand,
but how he held it, palm buttressing head.
Not the meat, not words, but grace; not the mouth,
but the smoke, scratches on a plate, the
table's dulled edge.
Not absence, not presence. Not indentation,
but impression. Not not, but not is; not either
or neither. The hose's curve, the garden's
mounds, the slab walk's slope, the smell of the smell,
the sound of the sound, the book's missing page
found in another book.
Not the death, but his dying.
Not male, not female, not young, old, compassionate,
bitter, peaceful or sorrowed.
Not the life, but the living.

The Word

I get in between the covers as quietly as I can.
Her hand is on my pillow and I put my face as close
as I can without waking her up. We made salad yesterday
and her fingertips still smell of green pepper and onions.
I feel homey, almost safe, breathing this, remembering

the way we washed the vegetables under cold water, peeled,
then sliced them with the harmless little knife her sister
gave us for Christmas. I feel childish and gently pull
the blanket over my head, barely touching my lips
to the short, ragged fingernails she chews while talking
to her mother on the phone. These days there's so much bad news
from home. Old people who keep living and living awfully,
babies who stop breathing for no reason at all.
I am so close to her that if I were to speak one word
silently, she would feel it and toss the covers to one side,
and for this reason I'll say nothing as long as I can.
Let the sheet stiffen above us, I have nothing to say.
Not about their lives or my own life.
Not about the branches so weighted with snow
that they don't brush our window anymore.
Not about the fact that (anymore) the only way I can touch
at all, the only way I can speak, is by trying not to.
"What's left, what's left, what's left," my dog breathes
in his sleep. Lately I snore badly in a language
only he understands. I've been trying so hard to teach,
I've been trying so hard to switch bodies
with the young people in my classes, that last week, when the dog
woke me and wanted to go out, I took his face in my hands
and told him not to be afraid. "You know so much already," I said.
"You are talented and young, you have something to give people,
I wouldn't lie to you."
Rita told this story as we sat around the salad with friends,
repeating again and again how the dog closed his eyes and basked.
Sleep is also the only place I can type with more than three
fingers, I said. But I thought, it's true, all this,
I speak best and most fully in my sleep. When my heart
is not wrapped in layer after layer of daylight, not prepared
like some fighter's taped fist.
She sleeps, her hand next to my mouth, the number
for the 24-hour bank machine fading on its palm.
The word starts briefly from between my lips, then turns back.
The word sifts deeper into what my life is.

Christmas Party

It is my first Scotch tinkling
in the crystal glass as I talk to Léonel
in front of the fireplace. Fragrant and fresh,
greens bloom along the mantel, hidden lights
blinking among the dark, sleek needles of pine and fir.
Around us, women twirl in long dresses and gloves,
men in tuxedos, someone in a green, glisteny
turban, someone else in high gold heels
that click in lovely, drunken pirouettes
to the flute and cello playing
Vivaldi in the dining room.

Léonel is the only one not drinking. He is explaining
the war, and watching his fiancée, tiny and dark,
the most beautiful woman at the party. Beside her,
the rest of us look like fading moths, a dying breed.
Embarrassed at the tennis shoes she wears
among the delicate pumps and hand-embroidered evening slippers,
she sits on the sofa hiding her feet,
fingering an uneaten Christmas cookie,
and explaining she does not speak English well
though she understands.

It is all so far away, what Léonel says to me:
the shortage of bread, the way the wounded
bleed lonely in the jungle after the army passes through.
Perhaps Léonel does not want to speak of it
but I ask him anyway what is happening in his country,
ask him why he had to leave, ask him
if his family's in danger, exactly where they live,
persist in knowing precisely what happened when the farm blew up.

Here, as Léonel speaks in his calm, sore voice,
I feel my hand holding my glass of Scotch,
the tiny scratch of ice against the sides,
hear wood burning and falling through the grate,
smell the sweetish smell of applewood, the ghost of fruit.
Next to me, a hand with rings reaches

Most Recent Book: THE NIOBE POEMS (University of Pittsburgh Press, 1988)

into a silver bowl of tangerines and walnuts
and comes out full. The luxurious wool
of my trousers bothers me. I feel part
of a long chain of something rich and useless.
I lean forward to catch another word from Léonel. I touch
his arm. I force myself.

Bathing

He always bathed afterwards,
slipping his fine and sticky
genitals over the cool rim
of the porcelain sink.
She lay in the other room
smoking and staring tiredly
out the window. The tiny sounds
of the suds came to her
worrisomely. The *suck-suck*
sound of his hand lathering
soap into his tight, dark curls.
Then the farewell groan of the drain.
The energetic flap of the towel.
When he was before her again,
his teeth covered by a smile,
the sweat and stench removed,
she studied him from the crushed
bed, admiring his cruel
beauty, her body still marked
and odorous. His, clean
and unstained, amnesiac
already.

For Miklos Radnóti: 1909–1944

I.
When Radnóti wrote his last poem for his wife
he was weeks away from death.
He must have known it.
The landscape shook green and terrible
through the long retreat. The guards

pushed Radnóti and the other prisoners
harder, fed them less, whipped them more
often, killed more frequently, with less thought,
the fear of their own death and defeat
making it easier to pull the trigger.

In the midst of the six-month death march,
pissing blood, hair and teeth falling out,
Radnóti kept writing his way out of the nightmare,
tiny poems on postcards and matchbooks.
On the road to Budapest, the guards tortured
a retarded Hungarian boy before they shot him in the mouth.
It was the same in the poems: the prisoners died there, too,
blood running from the ear of Radnóti's friend, the violinist,
the body abandoned in a drainage ditch.

At the end, in the common grave
scrambled up with the human bodies he loved so well,
his poems went down with him,
fierce scraps of life in his coat pockets
that refused to be beaten.
Two years later, the poet gone back
to the earth, the poems remained,
exhumed and reborn,
when the widow plucked them from the fresh, young skeleton.

2.
In Harlem, housing projects shove their way up
out of the earth, all concrete and bricks,
iron bars at the windows, children locked inside
by themselves all day
while the mothers work and the fathers never come back.

I don't know how many people here
read poetry, or love it,
or know the name of Miklos Radnóti,
Hungarian poet dead almost forty years,
his one book out of print.
I know people love words and music,
listen to radios in the street,
jazz bands in the park,
memorize long passages of soul rap like poetry.
I know Radnóti would have loved my neighbors
who sit all night in Riverside Park
during the long weeks of the heatwave
singing and dancing in the breathless air.

From my window, I see a man on Broadway
propped against a concrete wall.
A brown joint dangles from his mouth
as the traffic rushes by obscuring him.
I remember the only photograph I've seen of Radnóti,
a homemade cigarette poked between his Jewish lips,
his wide sexual mouth breathing
the putrid air of World War Two.

When I close the book
the poems still sob around me.
When I turn off the light
the pages remain lit
like the blanched white slats
of a skeleton abandoned
in the war-torn night.
And across the street in Harlem:
the lights flickering on and
off, a chorus of frightened breathing,
a million human hearts
beating steadily in the endless darkness.

A NOTE ON THE POEM

Miklso Radnóti's death occurred as a result of Hungary's WWII
alignment with the Axis powers. During his short life, he was
interned several times in forced labor camps by the Hungarian
government. It was during the last internment, from May to
November 1944, that he was executed, either shot or clubbed to
death, and buried in a mass grave near Abda. The body was ex-
humed and the last poems retrieved in 1946.

TOI DERRICOTTE ❖

Blackbottom

When relatives came from out of town,
we would drive down to Blackbottom,
drive slowly down the congested main streets—Beubian and Hastings—
trapped in the mesh of Saturday night.

Most Recent Book: CAPTIVITY (University of Pittsburgh Press, 1989)

Freshly escaped, black middle class,
we snickered, and were proud;
the louder the streets, the prouder.
We laughed at the bright clothes of a prostitute,
a man sitting on a curb with a bottle in his hand.
We smelled barbecue cooking in dented washtubs and our mouths watered.
As much as we wanted it we couldn't take the chance.

Rhythm and blues came from the windows, the throaty voice of a woman
    lost in the bass, in the drums, in the dirty down and out, the grind.
"I love to see a funeral, then I know it ain't mine."
We rolled our windows down so that the waves rolled over us like blood.
We hoped to pass invisibly, knowing on Monday we would return safely
    to our jobs, the post office and classroom.
We wanted our sufferings to be offered up as tender meat,
and our triumphs to be belted out in raucous song.
We had lost our voice in the suburbs, in Conant Gardens, where each
    brick house delineated a fence of silence;
we had lost the right to sing in the street and damn creation.

We returned to wash our hands of them,
to smell them
whose very existence
tore us down to the human.

Christmas Eve: My Mother Dressing

My mother was not impressed with her beauty;
once a year she put it on like a costume,
plaited her black hair, slick as cornsilk, down past her hips,
in one rope-thick braid, turned it, carefully, hand over hand,
and fixed it at the nape of her neck, stiff and elegant as a crown,
with tortoise pins, like huge insects,
some belonging to her dead mother,
some to my living grandmother.
Sitting on the stool at the mirror,
she applied a peachy foundation that seemed to hold her down,
    to trap her,
as if we never would have noticed what flew among us unless it was
    weighted and bound in its mask.
Vaseline shined her eyebrows,
mascara blackened her lashes until they swept down like feathers;
her eyes deepened until they shone from far away.

Now I remember her hands, her poor hands, which, even then
    were old from scrubbing,
whiter on the inside than they should have been,
and hard, the first joints of her fingers, little fattened pads,
the nails filed to sharp points like old-fashioned ink pens,
    painted a jolly color.
Her hands stood next to her face and wanted to be put away, prayed
for the scrub bucket and brush to make them useful.
And, as I write, I forget the years I watched her
pull hairs like a witch from her chin, magnify
every blotch—as if acid were thrown from the inside.

But once a year my mother
rose in her white silk slip,
not the slave of the house, the woman,
took the ironed dress from the hanger—
allowing me to stand on the bed, so that
my face looked directly into her face,
and hold the garment away from her
as she pulled it down.

The Minks

In the backyard of our house on Norwood,
there were five hundred steel cages lined up,
each with a wooden box
roofed with tar paper;
inside, two stories, with straw
for a bed. Sometimes the minks would pace
back and forth wildly, looking for a way out;
or else they'd hide in their wooden houses,
even when we'd put the offering of raw horse meat
on their trays, as if
they knew they were beautiful
and wanted to deprive us.
In spring the placid kits
drank with glazed eyes.
Sometimes the mothers would go mad
and snap their necks.
My uncle would lift the roof like a god
who might lift our roof, look down on us
and take us out to safety.

Sometimes one would escape.
He would go down on his hands and knees,
aiming a flashlight like a
bullet of light, hoping to catch
the orange gold of its eyes.
He wore huge boots, gloves
so thick their little teeth couldn't bite through.
"They're wild," he'd say. "Never trust them."
Each afternoon when I put the scoop of raw meat
rich with eggs and vitamins on their trays,
I'd call to each a greeting.
Their small thin faces would follow as if slightly curious.
In fall they went out in a van, returning
sorted, matched, their skins hanging down
on huge metal hangers, pinned by their mouths.
My uncle would take them out when company came
and drape them over his arm—the sweetest cargo.
He'd blow down the pelts softly
and the hairs would part for his breath
and show the shining underlife which, like
the shining of the soul, gives us each
·character and beauty.

On the Turning Up of Unidentified Black Female Corpses

Mowing his three acres with a tractor,
a man notices something ahead—a mannequin—
he thinks someone threw it from a car. Closer
he sees it is the body of a black woman.

The medics come and turn her with pitchforks.
Her gaze shoots past him to nothing. Nothing
is explained. How many black women
have been turned up to stare at us blankly,

in weedy fields, off highways,
pushed out in plastic bags,
shot, knifed, unclothed partially, raped,
their wounds sealed with a powdery crust.

Last week on TV, a gruesome face, eyes bloated shut.
No one will say, "She looks like she's sleeping," ropes

of blue-black slashes at the mouth. Does anybody
know this woman? Will anyone come forth? Silence

like a backwave rushes into that field
where, just the week before, four other black girls
had been found. The gritty image hangs in the air
just a few seconds, but it strikes me,

a black woman, there is a question being asked
about my life. How can I
protect myself? Even if I lock my doors,
walk only in the light, someone wants me dead.

Is it any wonder I walk over these bodies
pretending they are not mine, that I do not know
the killer, that I am just like any woman—
if not wanted, at least tolerated.

Part of me wants to disappear, to pull
the earth on top of me. Then there is this part
that digs me up with this pen
and turns my sad black face to the light.

DEBORAH DIGGES ❖

Rock, Scissors, Paper

I

It ended when he popped one of the three of the order
coleoptera in his mouth. Two hands weren't enough even for Darwin—
He stares at a yellow flower for minutes at a time. His family
don't know what to do with him—.
                            The beetle stung his tongue, and like
      the dragon-
angel, who spit out the name of the fallen world's new genus
as he waded in an orchard through paradisaical weeds,

Darwin spat by a tree and laughed, son of the theological classes.

Now think of the mind, said Freud, as the Eternal City
(as if *angel* could mean *messenger* or *coin*, and *phylum*

Most Recent Book: LATE IN THE MILLENNIUM (Alfred A. Knopf, 1989)

tribe), think of the palaces of the Caesars on the Palentine
next to the temples of the gods. So many kingdoms

piling up—not one destroyed—residing whole, and every
sort of traffic there, the Tiber clogged. Our species

dreams across those rooftops. Why aren't we happy?—

2

like Marx's universal arming of the people, a species
crowded out imagining itself reborn among a rubble.

And yet the places, wrote Darwin, which most order
my thoughts are those, boundless, stratified as the nine legions
of angels, places without habitation, without trees, a kingdom

of food-gatherers, the fire-bearers upright before the herds.
See how they're moving toward the sea. Each lamp represents a family
along the lava beach. The nets they throw into the shallows
cannot contain their origins. They're happy here, *a class*

which has radical chains, which is the dissolution of all classes . . .

Freud: And do you remember how when we were young, we used, day
after day to walk Vienna's streets reciting psalms, as though the genus
of our race weren't something to be spat upon? And on Sundays
we'd go to the museums, peruse the fossils, name their phylums

3
in the long list of extinctions, Brother. Now here we are in Athens.
We have come a long way, as far as Babel from the new "linguistic
    phylums."

Europe's alive with talk. Outside the Prater
they're burning books, *The Talmud, The Origin of Species*,
and mine on jokes! What company! The fires
illuminate the ring of faces white with fear, fear's geniuses . . .

Rock smashes scissors, scissors cut paper,

paper covers rock, and the rest shall I set in order
when I come . . .

            No one knows the name of the ferryman
whom the good luck child advised, a precursor to the working classes.
I'm tired, he cried, of rowing. How do I get off this river?

When you reach the far shore, said the heir to the kingdom,
leap off! Hand the pole to your passenger.

Marx: In its earliest phases society took the form of the family,

4
the clan, the tribe. On what foundations are the present families
of the bourgois based? On capital. On private gain.

When the gods changed two Athenian sisters into birds, Philo-
mela became a nightingale. But could she sing without her tongue?
And did she know her sister, the swallow, whose kingdom
is the evening? Who does not sing? *Cruelty arises*

from the instinct for mastery, a trait not peculiar to our species.

And even birds (Darwin) have vivid dreams, a left and a right
cerebral hemisphere. Their songs are learned and can be classified
by dialect. A northern and a southern sparrow trill
a slightly different series.
                          We have our orders,
sang the young officers who took Anna Freud away.

I knew then, dying or not, that we must leave—. The genes

hold the journey. At the base of the cranial vault, hunger, thirst,

5
wanting, what is called *fight or flight* ignite the pulse, the genie
in the lamp. *When we stood up, we lost our way.*

Near eighty, Anna Freud (deceased) narrates home movies of the family
in which she is a girl bringing her father flowers she's picked,
she says, from her cousins' country gardens. *The orders*

came that spring. The women there—they are my father's sisters—died
in the camps, the ones waving, see? And the children beside them.
Phylloid,

their names on the tree diagrammed in the museum, set under glass,
protected from a million fingerprints, each thumb's swirl classified
at birth, black at the center, at the crow-eye of the funnel.

As children we made faces on our fists, some cross-species,
two blind eyes below the knuckle along the metacarpel index,

the thumb an awful mouth, an old man's, a tortoise's, saying: Then shall
    the kingdom
be likened unto a vineyard. Or heaven's a wedding.

6
It's exactly like a tree. Heaven's a door. The kingdom
is like a man traveling in a far country, *as if to make a marketable*
value out of virtue, love, etc. Heaven's congenital . . .

In fact, the hand-man sang, I want to marry a lighthouse keeper
and live by the side of the sea . . . , as though he were a specialist
of dreams, god of the big and the little shipwrecks,

his mouth torn open, half-dead, half-grinning, whispering the family

names, generation by generation, like the keepers of the flame,
those listed on brass plaques greening on any lighthouse, an extinct class.

And the robot beam clicks on clicks off above you
or the fog horn blasts the chlorophylled
air, blasts through you, merely matter, scissors-cut-paper,

who cannot fall out of this world. And if I cannot order
for myself (Freud) this 'oceanic feeling,' there's not a little

7
that is ancient still buried in the soil of the ordained
city. *Here is the church, here is the steeple*, here,

the cave whose rock swellings form the animal's haunches. The kingdom's
indivisible where the artist lay his hand under the herds
and through a blow-pipe spit his signature, even the phyllode
moons in his fingernails erased by his pigments

made from pollen, dirt, flower petals, blood, the colors fired and classified

on a wheel like a cornea, blind to itself.

                                        On the other side
we'll know the shaman by his blackened hand, as here, his genius
cannot fill the five-fingered emptiness. By my life, listen,

(Marx) I would create your own, and your families',
who will inherit nothing but these fields. I would be mediator,

lightning rod, dream and/or destiny machine between you. And the species
and you would know me as a part of your own nature . . .

Envoy: those first cold mornings our father blew into our hands to warm
them   and in the afternoons after our classes we were mad to be outside
       we'd bury one another in the leaves   we did not think *those who have
gone before us   the kingdom's progenitors*   not *the only species*   we
just lay down and closed our eyes as beech by oak by sycamore the leaf-
light disappeared and we stayed still awhile   *families at the gravesites*
       or leapt up shouting look and look at me   *but who will take my hand
first in the long receiving line*   watch me I'd call   *we have our orders*
       and sometimes they answered look at you   watch me I'd call from a
       branch
above the biggest pile of leaves   watch me and then I dove and I could
barely hear them calling *good-luck-to-yous   good luck   good luck   good luck*

STEPHEN DOBYNS ❖

Desire

A woman in my class wrote that she is sick
of men wanting her body and when she reads
her poem out loud the other women all nod
and even some of the men lower their eyes

and look abashed as if ready to unscrew
their cocks and pound down their own dumb heads
with these innocent sausages of flesh, and none
would think of confessing his hunger

or admit how desire can ring like a constant
low note in the brain or grant how the sight
of a beautiful woman can make him groan
on those first spring days when the parkas

have been packed away and the bodies are staring
at the bodies and the eyes stare at the ground;
and there was a man I knew who even at ninety
swore that his desire had never diminished.

Most Recent Book: BODY TRAFFIC (Viking Peguin, 1990)

Is this simply the wish to procreate, the world
telling the cock to eat faster, while the cock
yearns for that moment when it forgets its loneliness
and the world flares up in an explosion of light?

Why have men been taught to feel ashamed
of their desire, as if each were a criminal
out on parole, a desperado with a long record
of muggings, rapes, such conduct as excludes

each one from all but the worst company,
and never to be trusted, no never to be trusted?
Why must men pretend to be indifferent as if each
were a happy eunuch engaged in spiritual thoughts?

But it's the glances that I like, the quick ones,
the unguarded ones, like a hand snatching a pie
from a window ledge and the feet pounding away;
eyes fastening on a leg, a breast, the curve

of a buttock, as the pulse takes an extra thunk
and the cock, that toothless worm, stirs in its sleep,
and fat possibility swaggers into the world
like a big spender entering a bar. And sometimes

the woman glances back. Oh, to disappear
in a tangle of fabric and flesh as the cock
sniffs out its little cave, and the body hungers
for closure, for the completion of the circle,

as if each of us were born only half a body
and we spend our lives searching for the rest.
What good does it do to deny desire, to chain
the cock to the leg and scrawl a black X

across its bald head, to hold out a hand
for each passing woman to slap? Better
to be bad and unrepentant, better to celebrate
each difference, not to be cruel or gluttonous

or overbearing, but full of hope and self-forgiving.
The flesh yearns to converse with other flesh.
Each pore loves to linger over its particular story.
Let these seconds not be full of self-recrimination

and apology. What is desire but the wish for some
relief from the self, the prisoner let out

into a small square of sunlight with a single
red flower and a bird crossing the sky, to lean back

against the bricks with the legs outstretched,
to feel the sun warming the brow, before returning
to one's mortal cage, steel doors slamming
in the cell block, steel bolts sliding shut?

Shaving

It is really the most miniscule thing,
but you see sometimes when I shave,
my daughter follows me into the bathroom
to watch—she's sixteen months—and each
time she insists that I take the brush,
smear it around the lather in the cup,
then dab a small lump onto her hand,
which she studies, intently. Some mornings
I must do this five or six times before
I'm done scraping the remnants of yesterday
from my face. The brush is from a past life,
the present of an ex-girlfriend, and it's
at least ten times my daughter's age.
As for the badger, whose bristles
we are sharing, it must have been Swiss,
like the brush, and long turned to dust.
But I watch my daughter in the glass
and her pleasure seems so simple that I
don't mind the bother as she pokes
the lather, sniffs it, tastes it and
smears it over her hands and face up there
on the third floor of the house where I
shave in a small bathroom without windows.
I am forty-five. I had never thought,
actually, that to have a child at my age
would be different than any other age.
Probably, I'm even more patient. But
I think how in twenty years when she
is getting started, I'll be checking out,
that is, if all goes right between times.
Let them keep it, I've always thought.
Let them fend off the impending collapse.

But you know those parties where late at night
the whole place starts busting apart—
too many arguments, too many fights,
and you're just as glad to get moving,
that's how I always thought I would feel,
stepping into the big zero, but now
I see I'll be abandoning my daughter
there in the midst of the recklessness:
the bully with grabby hands, the lout
eager to punch somebody out, and my daughter,
who, in these musings while I shave,
is still under three feet tall and poking
at the lather smeared across her hand.
I joke, you know, I say we're raising her
to be the girlfriend of a Russian soldier,
or next week she'll begin karate lessons
and learn to smash carrots with a single blow.
But it all comes back as I watch her
in the mirror. Who is going to protect her?
Even now anything could happen. Last summer,
for instance, I rented a cottage from a fellow
who had a place up the hill, and one day I heard
these bees whipping past me, and you know what?
It was him, my landlord fooling with his .22,
shooting beer cans off a wall with me strolling around
down below. But that's how it is all the time,
the load of bricks crashing behind us
as the flowerpot smashes at our feet.
And cancer and car accidents, everyone's
got stories. How can I not think of this
when I watch my daughter messing
with the shaving lather? The whole
world gets vague and insubstantial, like
putting your finger through a wet tissue,
the muggers, rapists, terrorists, the Bomb.
It's just luck whether you escape or get hit,
making you feel about as safe as a light bulb
in a hailstorm which, of course, is exactly
how it is, except worse. But to have a child
means to expand the dimensions of the dark place,
until I wind up imagining this small
blindfolded creature toddling out on a rope
over the abyss and it's my daughter, my daughter,
this sweet morsel left over at the violent party,

this Russian girlfriend of the future. Well,
some mornings such thoughts crowd in on me
when I go upstairs to shave, and she
comes toddling after. That lather is so soft,
such a fragile conglomeration of white bubbles,
such a miniscule smidgin of possibility,
maybe that's why she likes it, dabbing it
with one finger, lifting it up, right there
by the pink ceramic toilet and torn green
shower curtain with silhouettes of fish,
sniffing this small heap of white bubbles,
touching it to her nose, then puff, just
blowing gently, so the bubbles hang, floating,
floating, and then they're gone of course.

Tomatoes

A woman travels to Brazil for plastic
surgery and a face-lift. She is sixty
and has the usual desire to stay pretty.
Once she is healed, she takes her new face
out on the streets of Rio. A young man
with a gun wants her money. Bang, she's dead.
The body is shipped back to New York,
but in the morgue there is a mix-up. The son
is sent for. He is told that his mother
is one of these ten different women.
Each has been shot. Such is modern life.
He studies them all but can't find her.
With her new face, she has become a stranger.
Maybe it's this one, maybe it's that one.
He looks at their breasts. Which ones nursed him?
He presses their hands to his cheek.
Which ones consoled him? He even tries
climbing into their laps to see which
feels most familiar but the coroner stops him.
Well, says the coroner, which is your mother?
They all are, says the young man, let me
take them as a package. The coroner hesitates,
then agrees. Actually, it solved a lot of problems.
The young man has the ten women shipped home,
then cremates them all together. You've seen

how some people have a little urn on the mantel?
This man has a huge silver garbage can.
In the spring, he drags the garbage can
out to the garden and begins working the teeth,
the ash, the bits of bone into the soil.
Then he plants tomatoes. His mother loved tomatoes.
They grow straight from seed, so fast and big
that the young man is amazed. He takes the first
ten into the kitchen. In their roundness,
he sees his mother's breasts. In their smoothness,
he finds the consoling touch of her hands.
Mother, mother, he cries, and he flings himself
on the tomatoes. Forget about the knife, the fork,
the pinch of salt. Try to imagine the filial
starvation, think of his ravenous kisses.

MARK DOTY ❖

Adonis Theater

It must have seemed the apex of dreams,
the movie palace on Eighth Avenue
with its tiered chrome ticket-booth,
Tibetan, the phantom blonde head

of the cashier floating
in its moon window. They'd outdone each other
all over the neighborhood, raising
these blunt pastiches of anywhere

we couldn't go: a pagoda, a future,
a Nepal. The avenue fed into the entry
with its glass cases of radiant stars,
their eyes dreamy and blown

just beyond human proportions to prepare us
for how enormous they would become inside,
after the fantastic ballroom of the lobby,
when the uniformed usher would show the way

Most Recent Book: BETHLEHEM IN BROAD DAYLIGHT (David R. Godine, Publisher, 1991)

to seats reserved for us in heaven.
I don't know when it closed,
or if it ever shut down entirely,
but sometime—the forties?—

they stopped repainting the frescoes,
and when the plaster fell they merely
swept it away, and allowed
the gaps in the garlands of fruit

that decked the ceiling above the second balcony.
The screen shrunk to a soiled blank
where these smaller films began to unreel,
glorifying not the face but the body.

Or rather, bodies, ecstatic
and undifferentiated as one film ends
and the next begins its brief and awkward exposition
before it reaches the essential

matter of flesh. No one pays much attention
to the screen. The viewers wander
in the steady, generous light washing back
up the long aisles toward the booth.

Perhaps we're hurt by becoming
beautiful in the dark, whether we watch
Douglas Fairbanks escaping from a dreamed,
suavely oriental city—think of those leaps

from the parapet, how he almost flies
from the grasp of whatever would limit him—
or the banal athletics of two or more men who were
and probably remain strangers. Perhaps

there's something cruel in the design
of the exquisite plaster box
built to frame the exotic
and call it desirable. When the show's over,

it is, whether it's the last frame
of Baghdad or the impossibly extended
come shot. And the solitary viewers,
the voyeurs and married men go home,

released from the swinging chrome doors
with their splendid reliefs

of the implements of artistry,
released into the streets as though washed

in something, marked with some temporary tatoo
that will wear away on the train ride home,
before anyone has time to punish them for it.
Something passing, even though the blood,

momentarily, has broken into flower
in the palace of limitless desire—
how could one ever be *done* with a god?
All its illusion conspires,

as it always has, to show us one another
in this light, whether we look to
or away from the screen.

Heaven

Tonight there's a mirror on the sidewalk,
   leaning against the steps of the cathedral.
      I want to think it's a work of art,
         or at least an intentional gesture:

anyone passing can see, reversed here,
   the rooftop Virgin's golden face
      ringed by light bulbs, looking up toward *us*.
         A few blocks down the searchlights revolve

atop some office tower's steely sheen.
   Where would they lead us, these beacons
      that sweep the dark and cut the steam
         billowing from the stacks, so the sudden sections

of clouds tumble in stunning and troubled currents?
   I have a friend who sometimes sells
      everything, scrapes together enough money
         to get to the city and lives on the streets here,

in the parks. She says she likes waking
   knowing she can be anyone she wants, keep any name
      as long as it wears well. She stayed with one man
         a few days; calling themselves whatever they liked

or nothing, they slept in the park
    beneath a silver cloth, a "space blanket"
        that mirrored the city lights, and the heat
            of his dog coiled between them would warm them.

I knew, she says, *I was in heaven.*
    Isn't that where those beams washing
        and disguising the stars have always called us:
            the anonymous paradise, where there isn't any telling

how many of these possible futures
    will be ours? It was enough to be warmed
        by steam blurring the cafe windows, to study
            how the grocers stacked the wet jewels

of produce and seem fed. Though the wine-flush
    would brighten everything, and dull the morning
        of working a thankless block. She held out her hand
            enough times to catch a torrent,

though little was offered but the sharpening chill
    of the street lacquered by rain, perfected
        and unyielding. *It's a little easier*
            for a woman to panhandle; that's why

my friend needed the dog. Sometime,
    when the weather turned, she'd go back home,
        at least till spring. Longer,
            maybe. But not before arriving at afternoons

when she wanted nothing, whole nights
    without desire, since everything passing
        was hers. Though she could not participate
            in the mortal pretense of keeping anything;

that lie belonged to the privileged,
    who hurried along the sidewalks
        just outside the stone boundaries of the park.
            And though they tried to warm themselves with it,

they still required those luxurious,
    frost-tipped pelts, the skins ripped and tailored
        out of their contexts. She knew she could lie there,
            with her stranger, with the living animal between them.

Night Ferry

We're launched into the darkness,
half a load of late passengers
    gliding out onto the indefinite
        black surface, a few lights vague

and shimmering on the island shore.
Behind us, between the landing's twin flanks
    (wooden pylons strapped with old tires),
        the docklights shatter in our twin,

folding wakes, their colors
on the roughened surface combed
    like the patterns of Italian book paper,
        lustrous and promising. The narrative

of the ferry begins and ends brilliantly,
and its text is this moving out
    into what is soon before us
        and behind: the night going forward,

sentence by sentence, as if on faith,
into whatever takes place.
    It's strange how we say things *take place*,
        as if occurrence were a location—

the dark between two shores,
for instance, where for a little while
    we're on no solid ground. Twelve minutes,
        precisely, the night ferry hurries

across the lake. And what happens
is always the body of water,
    its skin like the wrong side of satin.
        I love to stand like this,

where the prow pushes blunt into the future,
knowing, more than seeing, how
    the surface rushes and doesn't even break
        but simply slides under us.

Lake melds into shoreline,
one continuous black moire;
    the boatmen follow the one course they know
        toward a dock nearly the mirror

of the first, mercury lamps vaporing
over the few late birds
   attending the pier. Even the bored men
      at the landing, who wave

   their flashlights for the last travelers,
steering us toward the road, will seem
   the engineers of our welcome,
      their red-sheathed lights marking

   the completion of our, or anyone's, crossing.
Twelve dark minutes. Love,
   we are between worlds, between
      unfathomed water and I don't know how much

   light-flecked black sky, the fogged circles
of island lamps. I am almost not afraid
   on this good boat, breathing its good smell
      of grease and kerosene,

   warm wind rising up the stairwell
from the engine's serious study.
   There's no beautiful binding
      for this story, only the temporary,

   liquid endpapers of the hurried water,
shot with random color. But in the gliding forward's
   a scent so quick and startling
      it might as well be blowing

   off the stars. Now, just before we arrive,
the wind carried a signal and a comfort,
   lovely, though not really meant for us:
      woodsmoke risen from the chilly shore.

RITA DOVE ❖

Elevator Man, 1949

Not a cage but an organ:
if he thought about it, he'd go insane.
Yes, if he thought about it

Most Recent Book: GRACE NOTES (W. W. Norton & Co., 1989)

philosophically,
he was a bubble of bad air
in a closed system.

He sleeps on his feet
until the bosses enter from the paths
of Research and Administration—
the same white classmates
he had helped through Organic Chemistry.
A year ago they got him a transfer
from assembly line to Corporate Headquarters,
a "kindness" he repaid

by letting out all the stops,
jostling them up and down
the scale of his bitterness
until they emerge queasy, rubbing
the backs of their necks,
feeling absolved and somehow
in need of a drink. *The secret*

he thinks to himself, *is not
in the pipe but
the slender breath of the piper*.

Used

The conspiracy's to make us thin. Size three's
all the rage, and skirts ballooning above twinkling knees
are every man-child's preadolescent dream.
Tabula rasa. No slate's *that* clean—

we've earned the navels sunk in grief
when the last child emptied us of their brief
interior light. Our muscles say *We have been used*.

Have you ever tried silk sheets? I did,
persuaded by postnatal dread
and a Macy's clerk to bargain for more zip.
We couldn't hang on, slipped
to the floor and by morning the quilts
had slid off, too. Enough of guilt—
It's hard work staying cool.

Sonnet in Primary Colors

This is for the woman with one black wing
swept over her eyes: lovely Frida, erect
among parrots, in the stern petticoats of the peasant,
who painted herself a present—
wildflowers entwining the plaster corset
her spine resides in, that flaming pillar—
this priestess in the romance of mirrors.

Each night she lay down in pain and rose
to the celluloid butterflies of her Beloved Dead,
Lenin and Marx and Stalin arrayed at the footstead.
And rose to her easel, the hundred dogs panting
like children along the graveled walks of the garden,
until Diego appeared as a skull in the circular window
of the thumbprint searing her immutable brow.

Persephone, Falling

One narcissus among the ordinary beautiful
flowers, one unlike all the others! She pulled,
stooped to pull harder—
when, sprung out of the earth
on his glittering terrible
carriage, he claimed his due.
It is finished. No one heard her.
No one! She had strayed from the herd.

(Remember: go straight to school.
This is important, stop fooling around!
Don't answer to strangers. Stick
with your playmates. Keep your eyes down.)
This is how easily the pit
is waiting. This is how one foot sinks into the ground.

Persephone Underground

If I could just touch your ankle, he whispers, *there
on the inside, above the bone*—leans closer,

breath of lime and peppers—*I know I could*
make love to you. She considers
this, secretly thrilled, though she wasn't quite
sure what he meant. He was good
with words, words that went straight to the liver.
Was she falling for him out of sheer boredom—
cooped up in this anything-but-humble dive, stone
gargoyles leering and brocade drapes licked with fire?
Her ankle burns where he described it. She sighs
just as her mother aboveground stumbles, is caught
by the fetlock—bereft in an instant—
while the Great Man drives home his desire.

Cameos

Lucille among the flamingos
is pregnant; is pained
because she cannot stoop to pluck
the plumpest green tomato
deep on the crusted vine.
Lucille considers
the flamingos, guarding in plastic cheer
the bird bath, parched
and therefore
deserted. In her womb
a dull and husky ache.

If she picks it, Joe will come home
for breakfast tomorrow.
She will slice and dip it
in egg and cornmeal and fry
the tart and poison out.
Sobered by the aroma, he'll show
for sure, and sit down
without a mumbling word.
Inconsiderate, then,

the vine that languishes
so!, and the bath sighing for water
while the diffident flamingos arrange
their torchsong tutus.
She alone
is the blues. Pain drives her blank.

Lucille thinks: *I can't*
even see my own feet.

Lucille lays down
between tomatoes
and the pole beans: heavenly shade.
From here everything looks
reptilian. The tomato plops
in her outstretched palm. *Now*
he'll come, she thinks,
and it will be a son.
The birdbath hushed
behind a cloud
of canebreak and blossoming flame.

NORMAN DUBIE ❖

Radio Sky

The blue house at Mills Cross
Where the night's last firefly
Strikes its light out in a burst pod.

Under the cool stairs
You raised the chrome visor
On my aunt's old G.E.:
A faint band, green numerals
And a backlighting of amber tubes—
Each is glass, prophylactic,
With cosmic noise straight from the Swan.

Your sister,
Phyllis, had been unkind. It was hot.
Our towels floating in the tub upstairs,
We lit candles
And you poured the iced tea.

Later in bed you turned on the television
To where some station had signed-off;
Making adjustments in the contrast
We watched snow, what Phyllis said

Most Recent Book: GROOM FALCONER (W. W. Norton & Co., 1989)

Was literally the original light of creation.
Genesis popping like corn in a black room. Still,
Something out of nothing. Knowing

We can't have children
You watched the flecked light
Like a rash on your stomach and breasts.
Phyllis

Is a bitch was my reply.
We made love, shared strings of rhubarb
Leached with cream. We slept
In the blue snow of the television
Drifting under the familiar worn sheet.

Trakl

for Paul & Doug

In reality the barn wasn't clean, ninety men
Charged to you:
The burns, missing teeth, and dark jawbone
Of gnawed corn, gangrene from ear to elbow—
Even the dying
Returned to consciousness by the ammonia of cows.

You ran out looking beyond your hands
To the ground, above you a wind
In the leaves: looking up you found
Hanged partisans convulsing in all the trees.

Down the road in the garrison hospital,
In a cell for the insane, you were given
Green tea and cocaine . . .
With the blue snow of four o'clock
Came peace and that evening of memory
With Grete, her touch—in yellow spatterdock
She tied a black ribbon
Around the cock of a sleeping horse.
It was her *vivacious littles* as an admirer
Once put it. *Sister, trough*. . . .

How men talk. I read you first
In an overly heated room
Sitting in an open window. I left

For a walk in woods. Coming out
Into a familiar sinkhole, meadow
Now snow, deer ran over the crust—
Hundreds of them. I thought of my two uncles,

Their war, the youngest dead at Luzon,
The other, in shock,
At his barracks in California: Christmas evening
He looked up from the parade grounds and saw
An old Japanese prisoner
With arms raised, from the hands came
A pigeon. The bird climbed, climbed
Slowly and then dissolved

Like smoke from some lonely howitzer
Blossoming out over the bubbling bone pits of lye, over
The large sunken eyes of horticulture.

The Diatribe of the Kite

They come from the white barrier of noon
Where two forces of magnetism, one weak
And one strong, combine
To create a cruel sea of iron filings
Over which, as unlikely pilgrims, they journey.

As our sun rises, and they sleep,
Only then do they become
The ancestors of whom we are ashamed.

These two behemoths, one red and one green,
Sulk over willow sticks, rice paper
And a wooden pot of glue. There is gold leaf
Like raked fire between them.

They swallow blood with milk. They feast
On the roasted tongue of prisoner angels.

When they nap, in the late afternoon,
The earth moves. . . . They wake
Like simple accordians. And they are doomed.
Much of what they know, they learned
While grazing in the field with animals.

Their kite will be flown in a storm. It is
The crossed sticks of punishment
Above the city
Of their making. In time, they have taken

Two names: *Yang Baibing, Deng Xiaoping*.
In rhyme, they are joyously insane.
They are the immortality of the nursery
Where they reign—
Those ancestors for whom we are ashamed.

The Elegy for Integral Domains

You watched the slender narcissus wilt
In the vase below the pulpit.
You could never explain how the brain
Was packed with light, or that memory of a circus:
White undigested bone in tiger filth. The fear
Suddenly let go of you while you watched
The rich jeweler in the pew
Across the aisle. His hair fell down
That side of his face where the eyepiece stayed—
You wondered about skin wrinkled
From looking at jewels,
And then the fear left you with the wind
Over the pond, with the swelling
Of the church organ. There was the sweet smell
Of boiled corn in a cold night kitchen. The risible
Life of a spider living in a dry cracked flute,
And fog, you wrote, in the straw of the universe.

We can never be the undoubted stone.
Dice and mathematics. Music and the storm.
You loved the reticence of something
Heard first from the oboe. Some secret
Not heard from the solo instrument. And
Then runs of it in the orchestra. You heard of Schumann
In the asylum at Endenich near Bonn,
The white Schumann sprawled on the bed,
The attendant flicking at the tube to the enema bag.

You loved your wife, but the undoubted stone
Has no life in it. The diamondback pattern

On the cloth of the hose to the vacuum cleaner
Ran in and out of time, ran
From your mouth to the exhaust of the Plymouth.
Your brother gave me your journal, asking me
To write this. It made a hag of me in a night.
You loved life.
There is no way someone can make himself ready

To say this: a man dragging
A Christmas tree out of the woods found a body.

The Apocrypha of Jacques Derrida

The ruptured underbelly of a black horse flew overhead.
Bonaparte, is what the matron said to me,
Always condescending; vulgar, slowly separating
The three syllables. And it was the last thing she said.
The engine block struck the tree. Our faces
Making brook ice of the windshield. The vaulting black horse
Now on its side in the dust. I was left
With the road, with the memory of cities burning.
Matron seemed to sleep. My nose bleeding.
I went over to inspect the huge sunflowers
That were beyond the stonewall. The sunflowers
Marched with me in Italy. They were cut down.
There was gasoline everywhere. The attendants
Will come for me. It's back to the island.
I'll study English out in the cool stucco of the shed.
I don't really believe I am the Corsican. But then
Neither did he.
The car was now burning with the tree. The black
Brook ice bursting. The horse got up and left.
A back hoof snared by intestine . . .

I was once all game leg in a fast sleigh
Passing a half-frozen cook who asked a frozen orderly,
"Is he the snow?"
If only that cook had been my general.
It was that straggling long line that cost us.
If they had moved in a dark swarm, huddled together,
Cloud shadow over the Russian countryside, then
There would have been little trouble, a few men
Out on the fringes dropping to the snow for rest,

But still how
Like a forest they would have been
Moving over the land
Like that gang who came for Macbeth.
I know what you're thinking, that the land pell-mell
Is itself mostly obstacle
And this makes a road. But we were cloud shadow

Moving over snow.

STEPHEN DUNN ❖

The Routine Things Around the House

When mother died
I thought: now I'll have a death poem.
That was unforgivable

yet I've since forgiven myself
as sons are able to do
who've been loved by their mothers.

I stared into the coffin
knowing how long she'd live,
how many lifetimes there are

in the sweet revisions of memory.
It's hard to know exactly
how we ease ourselves back from sadness,

but I remembered when I was twelve,
1951, before the world
unbuttoned its blouse.

I had asked my mother (I was trembling)
if I could see her breasts
and she took me into her room

without embarrassment or coyness
and I stared at them,
afraid to ask for more.

Most Recent Book: BETWEEN ANGELS (W. W. Norton & Co., 1989)

Now, years later, someone tells me
Cancers who've never had mother love
are doomed and I, a Cancer,

feel blessed again. What luck
to have had a mother
who showed me her breasts

when girls my age were developing
their separate countries,
what luck

she didn't doom me
with too much or too little.
Had I asked to touch,

perhaps to suck them,
what would she have done?
Mother, dead woman

who I think permits me
to love women easily,
this poem

is dedicated to where
we stopped, to the incompleteness
that was sufficient

and to how you buttoned up,
began doing the routine things
around the house.

At the Smithville Methodist Church

It was supposed to be Arts & Crafts for a week,
but when she came home
with the "Jesus Saves" button, we knew what art
was up, what ancient craft.

She liked her little friends. She liked the songs
they sang when they weren't
twisting and folding paper into dolls.
What could be so bad?

Jesus had been a good man, and putting faith
in good men was what

we had to do to stay this side of cynicism,
that other sadness.

OK, we said. One week. But when she came home
singing "Jesus loves me,
the Bible tells me so," it was time to talk.
Could we say Jesus

doesn't love you? Could I tell her the Bible
is a great book certain people use
to make you feel bad? We sent her back
without a word.

It had been so long since we believed, so long
since we needed Jesus
as our nemesis and friend, that we thought he was
sufficiently dead,

that our children would think of him like Lincoln
or Thomas Jefferson.
Soon it became clear to us: you can't teach disbelief
to a child,

only wonderful stories, and we hadn't a story
nearly as good.
On parents' night there were the Arts & Crafts
all spread out

like appetizers. Then we took our seats
in the church
and the children sang a song about the Ark,
and Hallelujah

and one in which they had to jump up and down
for Jesus.
I can't remember ever feeling so uncertain
about what's comic, what's serious.

Evolution is magical but devoid of heroes.
You can't say to your child
"Evolution loves you." The story stinks
of extinction and nothing

exciting happens for centuries. I didn't have
a wonderful story for my child
and she was beaming. All the way home in the car
she sang the songs,

occasionally standing up for Jesus.
There was nothing to do
but drive, ride it out, sing along
in silence.

He/She

Brought up never getting punched
   in the mouth for saying more
      than the situation can bear,

she argues beyond winning,
   screams indictments
      after the final indictment

has skewered him into silence,
   if not agreement.
      The words she uses

mean she is feeling something large
   which needs words, perhaps
      the way Pollack needed paint.

Next day the words are unimportant
   to her, while all
      he's thinking about

are the words she used—
   if recovering from them
      is possible.

Years ago, the schoolyard taught him
   one word too many meant
      broken fingers, missing teeth;

you chose carefully, or you chose war.
   You were the last word
      you let live.

She was in the elsewhere girls were,
   learning other lessons,
      the ones men learn

too late or not at all; you took in,
   cared for, without keeping score
      you shaped a living space

into a kind of seriousness.
    Retract those words, he says.
      But she is only

sensing his reserve, his inability
    to perceive that her wrong words
      meant so much hurt and love.

LYNN EMANUEL ❖

Frying Trout while Drunk

Mother is drinking to forget a man
Who could fill the woods with invitations:
Come with me he whispered and she went
In his Nash Rambler, its dash
Where her knees turned green
In the radium dials of the '50s.
When I drink it is always 1953,
Bacon wilting in the pan on Cook Street
And mother, wrist deep in red water,
Laying a trail from the sink
To a glass of gin and back.
She is a beautiful, unlucky woman
In love with a man of lechery so solid
You could build a table on it
And when you did the blues would come to visit.
I remember all of us awkwardly at dinner,
The dark slung across the porch,
And then mother's dress falling to the floor,
Buttons ticking like seeds spit on a plate.
When I drink I am too much like her—
The knife in one hand and in the other
The trout with a belly white as my wrist.
I have loved you all my life
She told him and it was true
In the same way that all her life
She drank, dedicated to the act itself,
She stood at this stove

Most Recent Book: THE TECHNOLOGY OF LOVE (Abattoir Editions, 1988)

And with the care of the very drunk
Handed him the plate.

When Father Decided
He Did Not Love Her Anymore

Tonight I will remember the model
With the wide, sad mouth
Who used to pose for Father
Because I love the dangers of memory,
The boarded window and door,
Rooms where one bare bulb
Makes shadows swell up the wall.
And yet I recall only vaguely
The way her hem rustled on the floor
Like sand against tin
Laisse-moi tranquille, epicier,
It said because I want it to
Say something memorable.
I want her back
That brilliant, farfetched woman
Who drank coffee in our garden
And the days Father fed me
Absinthe through a sugar cube
So I would be asleep by noon
And wake to find Ramona posing
Naked with a tambourine.
Tonight the whole world is a garden
In which the immortal whispers
Something about art
And its opportunities:
Memory like a bolt of silk
In a tailor's arms
Can be made into anything
Especially misfortune,
Especially the year Ramona spent
In a wrath almost biblical
And so far from the world
Not even the moon could find
Her study in Paris
Where the doors opened to the river.

On Waking after Dreaming of Raoul

If Freud was right and dreams of falling are
dreams of having fallen then you must have been
the beautiful declivity of that hill, Raoul,
the speed was so seductive and the brakes so
unreliable, and so intricate and so abstract
that when I touched them they squeaked like a jar lid
coming loose and I was embarrassed, but not sad,
at being the one flat wheel that bumped down the hill
in an unsteady gulp of denial—oh no oh no oh no—
until I woke up chilly, damp, my breath unsteady.

In order to recover I sit at the desk studying the Order
of the Holy Ghost Retreat and Old Age Home
until dusk comes down the street elm by elm, here
where they've managed to cure them with a tincture
so poisonous, the leaves, though living, are frail
and blanched. I think of you, Ruby Flores'
half-brother and a thief and a cook.
Because what good is it, anymore, pretending
I didn't love you; after all these years you must
be jailed or dead, and it is a relief to give up
reticence which as you once said is merely
impetuosity held tightly in check.

Over the gold swells of sunset lawns the old
men come rolling in their iron chairs, pushed
around by nuns, their open mouths are Os
of permanent dismay. Far away the stars are
a fine talcum dusting my mother's one good black
dress, those nights she gunned the DeSoto
around Aunt Ada's bed of asters while you shortened
the laces of my breath. Despite the nuns, despite
my mother and my own notions of how bad girls
end up educated and alone the door opens and you
walk in; naked, you were narrow and white
as the fishing knife's pearl handle and you kiss me
until my resolve grows as empty as the dress
from which I stepped, both brave and willful.
I loved you, although I didn't know it yet,
anymore than these old men on the dole
of some nun's affectionate disdain
knew that they would end up poor,
mortgaged to a ghost, and living in a place like this.

Of Your Father's Indiscretions and the Train to California

One summer he stole the jade buttons
Sewn like peas down Aunt Ora's dress
And you, who loved that trail of noise and darkness
Hauling itself across the horizon,
Moths spiraling in the big lamps,
Loved the oily couplings and the women's round hats
Haunting all the windows
And the way he held you on his knee like a ventriloquist
Discussing the lush push of grass against the tree's roots
Or a certain crookedness in the trunk.
Now everything is clearer.
Now when the train pulls away from the station
And the landscape begins to come around, distant and yet familiar,
That odd crease of yellow light
Or the woods' vague sweep framed in the window forever
Remind you of the year you were locked up at the Hotel Fiesta
While father went out with fast black minks.
And how wonderful it was
When he was narrow as a hat pin in this tux
And to have come all that way on his good looks.
How wonderful to have discovered lust
And know that one day you would be on its agenda
Like the woman who drank and walked naked through the house
In her black hat, the one you used to watch
Through a stammer in the drapes.
In that small town of cold hotels, you were the girl in the dress,
Red as a house burning down.

Inspiration

I am tired of the tundra of the mind,
where a few shabby thoughts hunker
around a shabby fire. All day from my window
I watch girls and boys hanging out
in the dark arcades of adolescent desire.

Tonight, everything is strict with cold,
the houses closed, the ice botched by skaters.

I am tired of saying things about the world,
and yet, sometimes, these streets are so
slick and bold they remind me of the wet

zinc bar at the Cafe Marseilles, and suddenly the sea
is green and lust is everywhere in a red cravate,
leaning on his walking stick and whispering,
I am a city, you are my pilgrim,
meet me this evening, Love, Pierre.

And so I have to get up get up and walk downstairs
just to make sure the city's still secure
in its leafless and wintery slime
and it still is and yet somewhere on that
limitless, starlit seacoast of my past,

Pierre's red tie burns like a small fire.
And all at once my heart stumbles like a
drunken sailor, and I, an ordinary woman,
am adrift in the bel aujourd'hui of Pittsburgh.

Blond Bombshell

Love is boring and passe, all the old baggage,
the bloody bric-a-brac, the bad, the gothic,
retrograde, obscurantist hum and drum of it
needs to be swept away. So, night after night,
we sit in the dark of the Roxy beside grandmothers
with their shanks tied up in the tourniquets
of rolled stockings and open ourselves like earth
to rain to the blue fire of the movie screen
where love surrenders suddenly to gangsters
and their cuties. There in the narrow,
mote-filled finger of light, she loosens
her dazzling, disciplined torrent of platinum,
like the shaft of a waterfall. She is a blonde
so blond, so blinding, she is a blizzard, a huge
spook, and lights up like the sun the audience
in its galoshes. She bulges like a deuce coupe.
When we see her we say good-bye to Kansas.
She is everything spare and cool and clean,

like a gas station on a dark night or the cold
dependable light of rage coming in on schedule like a bus.

JOHN ENGMAN ❖

Mushroom Clouds

During the final minutes of the raid
Miss Nurvak made us kneel with our heads buried
between our knees—the blast that ruined our lives
was her yardstick breaking in half and confetti
she shredded over us was fallout. One boy threw up
Cheerios beneath his desk and then ran from class
with wet pants. The rest of us survived the drill
for milk and cookies during Miss Nurvak's nightmare
sermon on the Red Menace.

Miss Nurvak,
who said we had nothing to fear but fear itself,
was scared half-to-death. The shelter beneath her garden
was stocked with canned goods and sterilized water,
rations against the coming days of radioactive ash.
In gas mask and green fatigues, Miss Nurvak
would needlepoint and listen to the gramophone
until the fatal firestorms passed and she raised
her periscope, searching for pupils
from the lost second-grade.

So life was more serious than I thought.
And it was Miss Nurvak who made me want to be a man
as hard and strong as the stone man on the stallion
in the park, the general with epaulets of pigeon shit.
I imagined myself in crash helmet and bulletproof vest,
Miss Nurvak's periscope rising from the blackened grass:
how happy she would be to see a successful graduate
of Central Elementary who had not been reduced to ash,
whose ideals had not been shaken by the atomic blast,
who pushed the culprit forward with his bayonet,
a boy with wet pants.

Most Recent Book: KEEPING STILL (Galileo Press, 1983)

Atlantis

Everything that has been said for several centuries
is swept away by many hands and hurled through high windows
into a big hole my father calls *heaven* but I call *the sky.*
He looks angrily at me because I swore the human soul
was smaller and forlorn as any unmarked 8 oz. tin you pay
half-price for at the Railroad Salvage Grocery Store.

That was the night I thought he'd never learn
and I made foolish jokes about the boulevard in Minneapolis
where we both sat in darkness, watching yards where shadows
crawled between the bungalows like creatures from another world
and all the mothers who would never learn had hung loads
of white shirts and nighties like ghosts who are waiting

for Christ to return. I was 21 years old.
Already I had said too much: an immigrant from Norway, Michigan,
my father often spoke about another Norway where the sun
rose once but never set. *This world couldn't be your first,*
he said, and by calling my ideas "wise" he shut me up. Age
21, my father thought what *his* father thought

was ridiculous, and railroaded here
to find another Michigan where he was sure silence had
the last word. Where he and his son could sit in darkness
swapping silences until between us we produced a third and final
silence big enough to house the wild inhabitants and keep alive
the kingdom of a sunken island we could swim to, should it rise.

Another Word for Blue

On better days, I bathe with Wallace Stevens: dreaming his good
   dreams before I fall asleep, waves lapping, none of the poorly
   choreographed crashing they do around here, but waves
   that can read music.
And one afternoon, when I felt a new dream studying me closely,
   I kept my eyes shut and lay flat, but the dream flew off,
   leaving me alone again, asleep with reruns.
People who don't understand what it means to be an artist
   should be punished, and I know how: make them be one.
Make them write about their own mortal souls in the third person,
   make them enroll at college, where they will be forced to write

creative things about a piece of driftwood, forced to write
poems about their moods using colors like "cerulean,"
another word for blue.
People don't understand real artists: bottles with messages
wash up on the beach, always a heartbeat ahead of the sea.
It isn't always a matter of being in the right place at the right
time, wearing clothing that makes them notice you: black
satin jackets and green string ties, crocodile shoes.
Sometimes it's a matter of being in the wrong place at the wrong
time, unsinkable as Ivory Soap, an aesthetic theory
that isn't much more than a plain bad attitude.
All I ever wanted was an ice-cold beer and a booth with a view
of the local scene, that, and the adulation of multitudes.
There's a little place about a block from here where they never
heard of free verse.
When they say they took a bath, they don't mean they spent
an hour soaking with Esthétique du Mal, they mean
they lost big bucks at the track.
For all they care, Esthétique du Mal could be bath salts.
They know two things: on planet earth "being yourself" doesn't
mean much. And, there's no paycheck in pretending to be
somebody else.
So when I tell the waitress, oh yeah, I could have been another
Wallace Stevens—she tells me, oh yeah, so who needs two?
That's the kind of stuff that goes on in the poetry business.
And I am so pleased when I can refrain from expressing myself,
refrain from saying anything new: I like saying the same
old thing, words that stay put.
Words that don't go far, letting life remain a mystery for you.
Words I might say to a small group of friends someday, friends
who will sponge me down whenever I begin raving about free
verse back in the twentieth century, quoting at length
from my own modest book of poems, a visionary work
which sold poorly.

Staff

I got down on my knees with the little
weeds and whispered to them.
I counseled flowers, hey you stand up straight.
I hypnotized a crepe snake.
That's what I did for so many dollars an hour,

building a common garden of construction paper,
fingerpaint and Scotch tape in the rec room
of the Adolescent Long-Term Treatment Program.

That garden was a cost-effective therapy,
and the dance we held that evening
was a learning lab, therapy disguised as fun.
The kids made funny costumes from bedsheets
and danced beneath stars of aluminum foil.
They played crazy music on the radio
and danced like crazy. Rock, funk, soul.
Anything can be therapy. And with lights low,
if that is allowed, any shadowy dance
can be a beautiful scene from a Hollywood movie.

I poured sugarless punch into Styrofoam cups,
kept count of the dangerous plastic forks
and monitored touch. I stood back far enough
to translate body language, close enough to refeel
pain that might be used to document a diagnosis.
They were dancing like kids. Dancing like rabbits
behind wire mesh in the seclusion of a city garden.
Psychotic, arsonist, suicide—later, they'd suffer
the names life gave them. We tried everything.
And sometimes it was painful to watch them dance

with the skill they had to make dancing painful.
And when the dancing was done I uprooted the whole
garden, fashioned bouquets for the trash barrel
with fervor, like someone who needs psychiatric help.
Then dimmed the lights and sat in rec room darkness,
letting darkness fill me as an owl fills with wisdom,
a china owl in a city garden, waiting for something
human to happen and make sense, the patient approach.

One Minute of Night Sky

I worked for a year in the cellar
of an airtight clinic, trudged through a valley of cabinets
in a gray smock. My job was filing bulging folders of the dead:
I carried a wire basket through the alphabet, dumping envelopes
of aneurism, cancer and cerebral lesion into yawning racks.
I could travel decades in a few steps,

stop and page through a chart until
I was in the blue hills west of brain damage, dwindling hills
and rivers of red that met in flatlands on a black horizon,
ticker tape from the electroencephalograph. Stapled on last
reports of death there was a small snapshot from the morgue,
a face no larger than my thumbprint.

The work made me sick.
Reading histories of tumors and fatal transplants
until the lines on graphs convulsed and snarled like wiring
come loose in a circuit for the mind of God. Once, I saw
close-ups of the malignancy which killed a man my age,
nothing much on the X-ray,

a blemish vague as memory,
a burr which swam through nervous systems into his brain.
I could have sworn he was staring back at me from his worn
snapshot but, of course, he wasn't. He couldn't. His eyes
were shut. I put him away with unusual force and heard
his chart jar the rack, as if something

small had gone off, a mousetrap.
The next day I quit. For the first night in weeks, I slept.
But in my deepest sleep, even now, if the chemicals balance
and tissues are ripe, a synapse forms the memory: iron
spring slips, the trap shuts, my eyes fly open and all
the darkness around me wakes.

Supposedly, each human being
has a built-in mechanism for one minute of knowing
he or she will someday die. One minute of night sky: life
going on across the street where someone greets darkness
with tins of food and drink, where someone listens, pauses
by the door and throws the bolt and lets the animal in.

ALICE FULTON ❖

Cherry Bombs

At five I knew at twelve
the body's logic

Most Recent Book: POWERS OF CONGRESS (David R. Godine, Publisher, 1990)

would lead to blood, rah-rah
girly pom-poms, breasts, the secondary sex

signs shaved to lady-
likeness, arrayed in labial
pleats for the world's ease, a skirt
on an escalating gender:

the flatness developed in steps,
a corequake certain
to insinuate me up
despite my fast dissent.

I hated the world's complicitous give
in, give in.
Though the shot
silk slips, Lilt perms and Ambush

scent seemed lusciously adult
a suspicion lingered they were lures
to an unfixable forever
I deeply didn't want.

What did training bras train
breasts to do?
Hadn't I been told
when strangers offered dirty candy

to say no? I said no
to unselective service:
First comes love, then comes marriage,
then comes wifey with a baby carriage!

Prams pulled girls to ga-ga conversations
while boys made G.I. Joe advances
loving the loud sounds of their mouths.
At the beach I saw

the fate they called "expecting."
Labor was a squeeze and scream
we couldn't play at
making glamorous, like war.

I wanted no part of that combat, no
thank you, no
compulsory unsung heroics, please.
Please immunity. Please a dispensation.

Mother, are there monuments for women
dead of children?
Child, women are the designated weepers
at monuments for men.

But no one engraved spirits
behind the tiny engraved names.
We grew toward an undoing
punctual as mutual.

Boys put on ugliness young:
Filigreed cap pistols
swiveled them to targets,
chewed red spools and banged

on dots of dust
until the air smelled warm
as baking day but different.
Boys trailed their guns like magnets

drawn to polar charms.
Guns swirled like weathervanes
with boys instead of cocks above.
They dropped each other

into herohood, expecting
the chance of bullets
in their flesh, the mold
under their nails, the mold

of uniforms. They saved face
daily, scraping themselves free
of down and drowning
in Vitalis. They turned their hearts

to cherry bombs.
Of age and corseted
in shells, off they went
into the Aqua Velva yonder.

It wasn't that I wanted to be not
female. I wanted to be female
as I was. When another frilly being asked
Do you have the pretty kind?

I understood her
meaning: We loved our no-count

cunts and vulvas, though we lacked the words
till high school's titters,

its biology nuns all nuts
and bolts.
It's what up front that counts
sloganed the voice—

over selling filtered smokes.
At five I thought the secret
of eternal life was simple
as *keep breathing*: Out/in.

Girl/boy. Truth/lies.
No one could make me
null and void.
Would you rather be liquidated

or boiled in oil?
my sister's witch voice
drifted from the basement.
I thought about it

the rest of childhood, all day.

Powers Of Congress

How the lightstruck trees change sun
to flamepaths: veins, sap, stem, all
on brief loan, set to give all
their spooled, coded heat to stoves called
Resolute: wet steel diecast
by heat themselves. Tree, beast, bug—
the worldclass bit parts in this
world—flit and skid through it; the
powers of congress tax, spend, law
what lives to pure crisp form
then break forms' lock, stock, and hold
on flesh. All night couples pledge
to stay flux, the hit-run stuff
of cracked homes. Men trim their quick
lawns each weekend, trailing power
mowers. Heartslaves, you've seen them: wives
with flexed hair, hitched to bored kids,

twiddling in good living rooms,
their twin beds slept in, changed, made.

Self-Storage

"Doesn't that feel great?"
asks Aerobia, Goddess of the Body.
Those muscular curls, ribbons of fire
beneath her skin, give good definition
to the wilderness stashed within.
She's smoothing out the kinks and nicks:
perfection is necessary in a gift.

That's why we dress our presents
in foils and tissues.
Lions lie down with lambs
across each Christmas.
There's a nice democracy to it:
each thing entices equally,
and the trim prolongs the tension
before possession
when lessening begins.
So you want a pet and get
an air conditioner.
From this, you learn to want
what you are given.

When my mother was ill and I was little
I made her a mint jelly sandwich, which she ate
or hid because it was a gift.
The misprisions!
If only we got what we deserved.
In our family, plenty lay naked
beneath the tree on Christmas.
My parents didn't see the sense in wrapping
what we'd only rush to open.
"Let's get down to brass tacks."
That was one of their expressions.

So I was surprised last summer
to receive boxes done in holly wreaths and manger
scenes from home. Thick layers of "invisible"
tape held notes—"2 kitchen towels," "1 nightgown,"

as if to forestall false hopes.
The only mystery was my mother's candor.
And I was mystified at Christmas
to find she'd wrapped presents
for herself, even tagging them "For Mary."

But all the gifts dropped like hints
of what the giver wants
can't change the fact
of who is giving.
Whether roses come from boss or lover's
a distinction like that
between epidermis and skin.
"Though dadgummit," pants the Goddess,
"there's a point—lift . . . three . . . two . . .
one . . . —where it gets compulsive."

And where's that? Where
buyers spend big bucks on little nothings
at the cut-rate malls?
"We cash checks," each chain implores.
Last Christmas while shopping
I stood still, watching snow
machines forge the hills
to calendar art. "Michigan Collision"
stood beside "Self-Storage":
cubes holding the dislocated
against fire or theft. Near the freeway
where cars whisked by
like sweepings, the goods
and I stood to just one side.
A child swathed in floral layers
touched my hand
at last like something up for sale.
"That's not a fake lady," her mother
said, pulling her away.

Personally, I prefer gifts too big to wrap:
the inflammatory abstracts, say—
love, forgiveness, faith—
that sear through any paper
so packaging them's like tucking
flames into tuxedos.

Perhaps all presents are presumptions.
Giving, we test our affinity

with hidden wishes. Yet asking
changes both desire and deliverance,
as when lovers must say touch me
there. No matter.
Some things we'd gladly have
from any hand. Give us this day
in the pliable rain,
a solitude unlike a lidded wilderness,
a soft death—now doesn't that feel great?

I wouldn't say so. No.
What we want is another and another
day rising behind firm skylines,
a pink ridge shining into brick.
But when wasn't *always* not
less with dawn? Oh bright box
ripping in its own good time—

Tess Gallagher ❖

Each Bird Walking

Not while, but long after he had told me,
I thought of him, washing his mother, his
bending over the bed and taking back
the covers. There was a basin of water
and he dipped a washrag in and
out of the basin, the rag
dripping a little onto the sheet as he
turned from the bedside to the nightstand
and back, there being no place

on her body he shouldn't touch because
he had to and she helped him, moving
the little she could, lifting so he could
wipe under her arms, a dipping motion
in the hollow. Then working up from
the feet, around the ankles, over the
knees. And this last, opening
her thighs and running the rag firmly

Most Recent Book: Moon Bridge Crossing (Graywolf Press, forthcoming)

and with the cleaning thought
up through her crotch, between the lips,
over the V of thin hairs—

as though he were a mother
who had the excuse of cleaning to touch
with love and indifference
the secret parts of her child, to graze
the sleepy sexlessness in its waiting
to find out what to do for the sake
of the body, for the sake of what only
the body can do for itself.

So his hand, softly at the place
of his birth-light. And she, eyes deepened
and closed in the dim room.
And because he told me her death was
important to his being with her,
I could love him another way. Not
of the body alone, or of its making,
but carried in the white spires of trembling
until what spirit, what breath we were
was shaken from us. Small then,
the word *holy*.

He turned her on her stomach
and washed the blades of her shoulders, the
small of her back. "That's good," she said,
"that's enough."

On our lips that morning, the tart juice
of the mothers, so strong in remembrance, no
asking, no giving, and what you said, this
being the end of our loving, so as not to hurt
the closer one to you, made me look
to see what was left of us
with our sex taken away. "Tell me," I said,
"something I can't forget." Then the story of
your mother, and when you finished
I said, "That's good, that's enough."

Strange Thanksgiving

I don't know anyone at the table except
the friend who's brought me, who knows only
the host and hostess. I perch on my chair
like an egret, snowy and attentive. The man
to my left is the youngest son of an onion farmer.
The crop this year was ruined by rain.
His wrist is speckled blue from painting his
girlfriend's Chevy last night. We talk
about his hobby, building underwater cars. He
drove one off a dock into a lake. Nice
to putt around among the ducks, then wheel
on shore and go for burgers. Our host

draws up a chair, offers three kinds of pie.
He plays vicious squash to stay ahead of his bad
back. His wife will be near-dead
on the bathroom floor from swallowing pills
a few short nights away. But things
are holding now. Even that crumb at the edge of
my friend's mouth. I reach up
as if we're man and wife and brush it
away, that unconscious tenderness letting my hand
graze for a moment my own love's face
and so, submerged, fall heavily to sea in the homely
clatter of plates lifted suddenly

away. We're stalled out and anxious
in the chitchat before the hearth. Soon
into our coats and thank-yous. Getting to the car
down a fresh bank of snow, I steady myself
on my friend's sure grip. The ride home is better
than sleep, initialed over with afterthoughts we speak
out loud in that half-heard, half-said way—yet easy
to feel rescued by his debonair steering through
the unacknowledged coma of side streets. His intimacy
to know I'm beyond accompaniment and already
home, dividing myself with approach
like two moon-bright windows, seen after dark, across a field.

Red Poppy

That linkage of warnings sent a tremor through June
as if to prepare October in the hardest apples.
One week in late July we held hands like holding hearts
through the bars of his hospital bed. Our sleep
made a canopy over us and it seemed I heard
its durable roaring in the companion sleep
of what must have been our Bedouin god, and now
when the poppy lets go I know it is to lay bare
his thickly seeded black coach
at the pinacle of dying.

My shaggy ponies heard the shallow snapping of silk
but grazed on down the hillside, their little prayer flags
tearing at the void—what we
stared into, its cool flux
of blue and white. How just shaking at flies
they sprinkled the air with the soft unconscious praise
of bells braided into their manes. My life

simplified to "for him" and his thinned like an injection
wearing off so the real gave way to
the more-than-real, each moment's carmine
abundance, furl of reddest petals
lifted from the stalk and no hint of the black
hussar's hat at the center. By then his breathing stopped
so gradually I had to brush lips to know
an ending. Tasting then that plush of scarlet
which is the last of warmth, kissless kiss
he would have given. Mine to extend a lover's right past its radius,
to give and also most needfully, my gallant hussar,
to bend and take.

Now That I Am Never Alone

In the bath I look up and see the brown moth
pressed like a pair of unpredictable lips
against the white wall. I heat up
the water, running as much hot in as I can stand.
These handfuls of water over my shoulder—how once
he pulled my head against his thigh and dipped

a rivulet down my neck of coldest water from the spring
we were drinking from. Beautiful mischief
that stills a moment so I can never look
back. Only now, brightest now, and the water
never hot enough to drive that shiver out.

But I do remember solitude—no other
presence and each thing what it was. Not this raw
fluttering I make of you as you have made of me
your watch-fire, your killing light.

After the Chinese

By daybreak a north wind has shaken
the snow from the fir boughs. No disguise
lasts long. Did you think there were no winds
under the earth? My Tartar horse prefers
a north wind. Did you think
a little time and death would stop me?
Didn't you choose me for the stubborn
set of my head, for green eyes that dared
the cheat and the haggler from our door?
I've worn a little path, an egg-shaped circle
around your grave keeping warm
while I talk to you. I'm the only one
in the graveyard. You chose well. No one
is as stubborn as me, and my Tartar horse
prefers a north wind.

LOUISE GLÜCK ❖

Brown Circle

My mother wants to know
why, if I hate
family so much,
I went ahead and

Most Recent Book: ARARAT (The Ecco Press, 1990)

had one. I don't
answer my mother.
What I hated
was being a child,
having no choice about
what people I loved.

I don't love my son
the way I meant to love him.
I thought I'd be
the lover of orchids who finds
red trillium growing
in the pine shade, and doesn't
touch it, doesn't need
to possess it. What I am
is the scientist,
who comes to that flower
with a magnifying glass
and doesn't leave, though
the sun burns a brown
circle of grass around
the flower. Which is
more or less the way
my mother loved me.

I must learn
to forgive my mother,
now that I'm helpless
to spare my son.

Paradise

I grew up in a village: now
it's almost a city.
People came from the city, wanting
something simple, something
better for the children.
Clean air; nearby
a little stable.
All the streets
named after sweethearts or girl children.

Our house was gray, the sort of place
you buy to raise a family.
My mother's still there, all alone.
When she's lonely, she watches television.

The houses get closer together,
the old trees die or get taken down.

In some ways, my father's
close, too; we call
a stone by his name.
Now, above his head, the grass blinks,
in spring, when the snow has melted.
Then the lilac blooms, heavy, like clusters of grapes.

They always said
I was like my father, the way he showed
contempt for emotion.
They're the emotional ones,
my sister and my mother.

More and more
my sister comes from the city,
weeds, tidies the garden. My mother
lets her take over: she's the one
who cares, the one who does the work.
To her, it looks like country—
the clipped lawns, strips of colored flowers.
She doesn't know what it once was.

But I know. Like Adam,
I was the firstborn.
Believe me, you never heal,
you never forget the ache in your side,
the place where something was taken away
to make another person.

Widows

My mother's playing cards with my aunt,
Spite and Malice, the family pastime, the game
my grandmother taught all her daughters.

Midsummer: too hot to go out.
Today, my aunt's ahead; she's getting the good cards.
My mother's dragging, having trouble with her concentration.
She can't get used to her own bed this summer.
She had no trouble last summer,
getting used to the floor. She learned to sleep there
to be near my father.
He was dying; he got a special bed.

My aunt doesn't give an inch, doesn't make
allowance for my mother's weariness.
It's how they were raised: you show respect by fighting.
To let up insults the opponent.

Each player has one pile to the left, five cards in the hand.
It's good to stay inside on days like this,
to stay where it's cool.
And this is better than other games, better than solitaire.

My grandmother thought ahead; she prepared her daughters.
They have cards; they have each other.
They don't need any more companionship.

All afternoon the game goes on but the sun doesn't move.
It just keeps beating down, turning the grass yellow.
That's how it must seem to my mother.
And then, suddenly, something is over.

My aunt's been at it longer; maybe that's why she's playing better.
Her cards evaporate: that's what you want, that's the object: in the end,
the one who has nothing wins.

Lullaby

My mother's an expert in one thing:
sending people she loves into the other world.
The little ones, the babies—these
she rocks, whispering or singing quietly. I can't say
what she did for my father;
whatever it was, I'm sure it was right.

It's the same thing, really, preparing a person
for sleep, for death. The lullabies—they all say
don't be afraid, that's how they paraphrase

the heartbeat of the mother.
So the living slowly grow calm; it's only
the dying who can't, who refuse.

The dying are like tops, like gyroscopes—
they spin so rapidly they seem to be still.
Then they fly apart: in my mother's arms,
my sister was a cloud of atoms, of particles—that's the difference.
When a child's asleep, it's still whole.

My mother's seen death; she doesn't talk about the soul's integrity.
She's held an infant, an old man, as by comparison the dark grew
solid around them, finally changing to earth.
The soul's like all matter:
why would it stay intact, stay faithful to its one form,
when it could be free?

Amazons

End of summer: the spruces put out a few green shoots.
Everything else is gold—that's how you know the end of the growing
    season.
A kind of symmetry between what's dying, what's just coming to bloom.

It's always been a sensitive time in this family.
We're dying out, too, the whole tribe.
My sister and I, we're the end of something.

Now the windows darken.
And the rain comes, steady and heavy.

In the dining room, the children draw.
That's what we did: when we couldn't see,
we made pictures.

I can see the end: it's the name that's going.
When we're done with it, it's finished, it's a dead language.
That's how language dies, because it doesn't need to be spoken.

My sister and I, we're like amazons,
a tribe without a future.
I watch the children draw: my son, her daughter.
We used soft chalk, the disappearing medium.

Albert Goldbarth ❖

How the World Works: an essay

That's my topic. How complex, Alhambran arabesques of weather
(seen computer-screened by satellites); and the weathering eddies on tiles
in the courtyards and intimate tryst-rooms and policy chambers
of The Alhambra itself: construe a grander pattern.
How the west wind whipples the osiers. How the slivery, eyeless
cave fish in Mexico slip through their fissures unerring.
In Nepal, a poacher reams a spoonful of musk
from that orifice near the urethra, holding—with his other
gloved hand—the deer's small death-kicks steady; and in
mid-Manhattan at 3 a.m., at Chico's place, the Pimp Prince
enters swimming in coke, with one new frou-frou dewy-cunted
acolyte on each eelskin sleeve, and he reeks of a vial
of musk. I'm singing the rings-in-rings song of the planet,
its milks, its furnaces, its chlorophyll links. One

suddenly clear blue afternoon (when I was 8) of the kind
Lake Michigan unhoards at winter's thinner end,
the sky: a child soprano's pure high-C struck after
months of ugly gutturals . . . a copper (as my father still
referred to them), a copper of the old school, beefy, easy, from
the one-foot-on-the-runningboard days of Chicago ticketdom,
stopped us *slam* in the midst of our shoreline spree, the flasher
calling all of Heaven's attention, I thought, to this misfortunate
second-hand dent-bodied Chevy. "Officer, have you had
breakfast?" "Why, no sir." And he wetted his finger and thumb
(he always did this with money) and from (as my father
still called a wallet) his billfold, a 5 (you could do it for 5
in those days) sleeked on over. Later, educative and high on this
his mastery, he winked and told me that was how the world

worked. This was part of an interlocked system for him as
sure as the ecoconnectedness in the italic stance of a cattle egret,
the living shoulders it tweezes, lice that graze this egret's
feather-flesh, and dungbugs shitting the bull's more generous
shit back incremental and rich to the grasses . . . all
neat, clean, a perfect processional circle of textbook arrows.
So: you invited "the Boss" to dinner and used

Most Recent Book: HEAVEN AND EARTH: A COSMOLOGY (University of Georgia Press, 1991)

the holiday silver and chortled at jokes which
were "a riot," and thus you "advanced"; you shmoozed
the waitress, and her service upgraded. This was a very clear
flow chart, and I sing the song of its unctious functioning-well.
I was 8: I believed him. He believed himself. For
thousands of years, for that matter, the planet revolved
Ptolemaically, managing beautifully, thank you. Once

a woman I knew in my days of believing repeated sex
meant knowing a person, said, from out of some vaporous cranial
nowhere, "Do you think we come from monkeys, or little
enemas in the water?" and after the ripplings of pity and comedy
through me, I began the task of explaining the planet: I still
have the cocktail napkin that cartoonily shows Earth
axis-spit and pivoting, and that crudely rules a B.C./A.D. timeline.
This was long ago; I'd like to apologize, now, for that
initial pity: once I saw the tiny beads of bravery she needed
to restring each morning just to face the next
dyslexic day, I understood—too late to do love any good—
the shadows she walked through the rest of us didn't. And
by then of course I'd also come to understand my father
wasn't sharp or slick but small in a way

that makes me tender toward him: one more anyone
with his salesman's satchel, and son, and wife, like counters
in some global game, "Advantage," tycoons and brigadiers play. Well
now he's *in* the globe, beyond maneuvering. I saw him
lowered; now he's part of the parfait striations I'm singing of,
part of the nitrogen/flywheel/hovel-and-palace totalityworks
called Terra—where the butterfly fish
at mating time, the vivid-hued and specifically-patterned
butterfly fish, fights rivals with its colors for weapons,
its cinnabars and its veridians, deepening, quivering, them . . .
while out back of Chico's, the Pimp Prince stands
his gaudy ground in front of a would-be usurper,
plumed hats, ostrich boots, gold neckchains,
one a ruby ring, one jade . . . Oh the world

not only works but networks, rarefiedly, in
topnotch geewhillikers form. The ever-ravenous protozoa
in the rumen-goop of that bull I earlier mentioned, burbling
away at their cellulose walls . . . by one hashbrowns-surrounded
breakfast steak, they *are* connected to some soul-weary
salesman in 1929 pulling in to a roadside diner architected to be a
giant coffeepot on Pacific Highway outside South Tacoma.

Let the sign of that connection be the thready, heady
olfactory-waft of ant saliva the anteater rides like radar
unto its repast. And so there *is* a mode, an almost diagrammable
order, albeit on levels sub and supra while we sit around
in the dark with our luminous human desires confusing the
everything that they're a part of. Still we need
to remember, against our own small breakdown days. Once

after my father had died but before the family car was sold,
I joyrode with a lady, one-handed wheeling us up
the curves past Lighthouse Point. A cop clocked our speed:
an hour later I was in custody—a shabby, crapped-up,
roach-infested custody—for attempting to bribe. It was
bad, but I was good, and it was brief. What's longer and
sticks with me more is being dropped off back at the car,
too tired even to feel defeated, somewhere on damp sand
miles from anywhere 3 or 4 in the morning. When
the engine wouldn't turn, that last indignity, all I could do
was sit stupidly humming—not singing just humming—
on the hood, and stare at the first gray rhythmic swashing
in-and-out of the water, sure that nothing ever does, or
ever had really, or ever would, work.

The Nile

Elijah this.
The Children of Israel that.
And Moses. Moses in the bulrushes, Moses
blahblahblah. The doors closed
and the dark, fake-woodgrain paneling casketed us
away from the world for an hour and 45 minutes every afternoon
in Rabbi Lehrfield's neighborhood Hebrew School. Here, as one,
the pious and the derelict chafed equally. The vehicle
of Rabbi Lehrfield's narrative drive was Obedience,
all the wonder in those stories was run down methodically
and left behind like so many roadkills. Methuselah
something. Somethingsomething Ezekiel. And Pharaoh
set the infant Moses in front of a crown and a plate of embers,
testing if this was the child it was prophesied
would steal his reign. And Moses
did reach for the crown. But the Lord set an angel to guard him,
who now did guide that hand to lift an ember, and so did Moses

thereby burn his tongue and lo would stammer all his life long.
Did I care? *His speech limped, but he lived.*
Did I listen? Every night I'd read another chapter
in those actionful schlock-epic books by Edgar Rice Burroughs,
the ones where Mars (Barsoom, the natives call it) is
adventured across by stalwart Terran John Carter, *Jeddak*
(Warrior-King) and husband of the gauzey-saronged and
dusk-eyed Dejah Thoris, Princess of all those red-duned climes.
It made more sense to me
than God is a great bush of fire. All the while
Moses stuttered in front of the Living Flame, I
silently practiced Martian. It was Rabbi Lehrfield's
Martian School for me the whole lackluster time.

Out of what we've learned to call
"deep structures," Lindsay Nichol, my niece, is pursing
the first of her organized sounds. They're . . . oh,
no words; but they take sure place in a pattern
as repeated as the crib bars, with a little
occasional lingual fillip
as decorative as the headboard's gnomish carving.
Slurp and gurgle, out of whatever
increasingly subatomic deliveryline of chevals
flashes the message of neural language-wiring on up
from meiotic gel unbroken to this 9-month-old
soliloquizer, Lindsay Nichol
is wailing, gooing, composing juicy musics, here
on the quantifiable, witnessed edge of a process that
starts somewhere magic.—Someone
pointing to a tree, and saying: "tree," a heart, and: "heart,"
the first time; being with a word so new it's glass
not fully hardened yet, it's going to be a tree soon, or a heart,
but now it's rainwater, and the morning sun is living
yolk in its skin . . .
          In Moccasin County,
once, the night a full moon orb'ed the giant crosshairs
of a steeple, and any spirit-commingling was possible, and the line
between the Trinity and 3 tossed shots of cornmash likker
wavered in tremulous hoochiecoo veils of feeling . . . I could see
such language settle out of the air. They spoke in tongues. A woman
frenzied like a telegraph key on the sawdust-clumped church floor.
Galvanic bluebolts straight from Heaven twitched her limbs.
A man was shaking like sheeted foil. What they said was
clearly speech, although I didn't know the words

/M'lash k'HAB chebawby HEI-HEI-HEI ZH'BO/ was clearly
not a sloshy gibberish, but something
from the templates in the brain that give us English, only
singular and more shimmering with its source: a kind of
manna spangled over their tongues. If anything
I've also seen comes close, it's in films of some early
jazz guys jamming through the thirties, with the drapes
of cigarette smoke in those backroom clubs befuddling the stage,
and joy and concentration being the same thing, and
between their rumpled and utterly brotherly selves
a field I can only call "vocabulary" occurs and unites
and they play, in great asyncopated waves,
where the cells of the blood are notation,
where the nerves of the body are staves . . .

                                                  I have this
daydream: squares and circles and triangles
floating out of the sky. My friends
are lifting them. Licking them. Taking intimate
oral pleasure off of these perfect lines. And after that,
nothing is ever the same. We're marked.
We've nursed on the "high structures" Plato says
precede the smutched units of Earth.

In my family, stories are normally softened
over the years.—As if a tragedy,
or even marrow-wiffling celebration, any
abandoning of the blandest mean, was shameful.
By the time my life is second-hand
or third-explained to Lindsay, I'll be
anyone, and flatter than the nondescript stone marker.
Once I met my cousins Izzy and Rebecca,
only once—they'd come in for a wedding.
They were in their middle-'70s then, 2 crease-faced German Jews
from when a Jew in Germany meant you wore a number
dyed into your arm. And so I heard some stories directly.
"They were after me," he says. "I wasn't afraid
from their fists. But some had broken bottles. See."
He lifts his shirt. "I hid in a barrel. A barrel
of pigshit. Yes, really. It covered my head. In this, even
they didn't search. The worst part was the burning
against the cut, this pigfire, filthfire, eating my skin.
But then they gave up and I crawled out. It's a blur then,
really, until Becka and America." She says, "My mother
begged my sisters not to get into the truck. One was 15.

Meeseleh, she was only 12. The driver told her 'You
think you'll miss them so much, you get in too.' She
did, without a second's hesitation. In part, I think, to get them
all on their way before I was discovered in the haypile.
Well of course—they went up the chimneys, in the Camps.
Who knows what went on in those places? 20 years later,
we were in New Jersey then and settled, a neighbor
gave me a little set of scented soaps, and I saw on the box
they were made in Germany, and—Izzy will tell you
it's true—I threw up. For a week after that, I threw up."
To reach America, they "did things" too—"not so nice,
if you want to know. These were not pretty times."
There are anecdotes of innocent German countryside couples
clubbed for their clothes. The irony is, they
reached their haven, Liberty lifting her torch high,
just when anti-German sentiment reached its peak.
"And so our accents—you know? For years
Americans beat us up in the streets." He shakes his head
as if the past could be shooed like a fly.
"So, anyway. Everyone's here for the wedding, a happy time,
now let's be happy." He hooks his arm around Rebecca's arm.
His speech limped, but he lived.

God doesn't speak in the language of people
or need to. God speaks out of what first hurt us.
So of course, on the mountain, Moses understood
what was said by the fire.

I'm 40. I know, by now, my life, my friends' lives . . .
we will never wake to face some all-consuming
deific announcement. But I also know: hurt is inevitable.
Then: so is some Godtalk, sized to that hurt.

Now Lindsay's asleep, and quiet, quiet . . .
Finally the long dark river of night
will deliver her crib to its tanglement
in the first pale reeds of the morning.

"The more you're meat, the less they treat you human," Kendall says
amid the general beer-tone party brouhaha. She's
just been hired as a hospital's Emergency Unit desk clerk.
"If you come in with a broken leg they'll talk to you
while setting it, explain things, chat. But
someone comes in mangled from a tractor toppling over and he's
just bloodied-up parts to assemble." This is all

new to her. She ledges out her lower lip in concentration.
"I suppose there are reasons." Later,
                                              an hour maybe, I
see her hazily through a window. She's left the gaudy talk and
rock-&-roll, and walks by herself in the midnight yard,
around the substantial base of its guardian tree.
She's talking softly—to herself—or to some self-of-her
that's taken form invisibly out of the molecules of the night, and
walks beside her. Kendall's
musing. She's "working things out." Whatever
infinite hallways of pain and laboring tissue she's seen opened
in the bodies wheeled past her for the last week, these
are first inventing words to hold
small conversation with her. Moonlight's
whittled by the bough to a handspan conical shape; and
Kendall halts as if to press her ear against this
hearing-trumpet floating in the blackness, and be privy
for a moment to the murmurstuffs the electrons of Earth
exchange with the protons of Luna.
                                              Soon
she's back: she's wagging ass to some sperm-powered shout
in an early Rolling Stones hit. What I come
to understand, though, is that everyone—these
friends o' mine, my tender lads and lassies—needs some time
outside, alone, by the tree, in its Whispering Zone.
Now Casey leaves the very public hubbub for this quiet
domain, now Rita . . . Some of them touching the bark
that's textured like the rope sole of an espadrille,
and some of them simply moving their lips in silence,
under stars that must be Cosmic Esperanto's
punctuation. "Albert, YO!"—I'm
                                              back in Stonesville,
avocado chip dip, argument, flirtation. When I look
next time, a 14-year-old boy is in the yard. He's . . .
a translucent 14-year-old boy. So shy.
So pained by anything in this world. No wonder
he's practicing Martian. "Thark," I hear him say
in a familiar cracking voice. "Tars Tarkas. Jasoom."
No wonder I love these friends I have now. When
I start to say a word of encouragement to him, he
distorts into a mist, he's air now, and my single gasp
inhales him . . .
                          No wonder I love my people. We're
all woozey-eyed with partying by now, we're tired

empathetic heaps lounged out on the pillows . . .
My sweeties, my grownups who have come so far, what are we
here in midlife, but
the scars of healing from where we once burned

our tongues on the Other Language.

BECKIAN FRITZ GOLDBERG ❖

The Possibilities

After a wife's death a man may talk
to his horse with a great tenderness
as if, just this morning, he had tried on
her pink slipper. And if he has no horse
he may crack his window a little
wider when it lightly rains to confirm
the roofs and trees are made
of paper. If there is no rain
he may make himself a meal at midnight,
sweet artichokes and Danish cheese,
a glass of red wine. If there is
no red, then white. He may suck the knife
clean with his tongue. Later

lying awake he may hear the wild lung
of a motorcycle far off on a far road.
If there is no motorcycle, a dog
trying for any syllable in any known
language. Something falling suddenly in
the closet, according to some law.

Nearness in the dark is a kind of beauty
though it is only a lampshade, a shoulder
of the walnut chair. If there is no chair,
then a shelf. A shelf of books with the devil's
violet fedora tossed on top. Or something
exotic from the sea, manta ray

like the pulse in the ball of his foot.
A man may walk ten steps behind

Most Recent Book: BODY BETRAYER (Cleveland State University Press, 1990)

his life. It may be sorrow or fear.
He may see her back like two doves rushing
up where a boy has flung a handful
of pebbles. If no pebbles, leaves
where a masked prowler hunches, his belt of
lockpicks, his bag of velvet like the one
from which memory snatches. These are

the possibilities, the immaculate
like miracles which are nothing
in themselves, but in this world a sign
of angels, ghosts, supernatural beings
who watch us. Who listen. Who sometimes
helplessly let us stumble on
their pyramids, their crude observatories
or let us, generation after
generation, speak to the broken horse
of the human heart.

Monsoon

The heaviness of twilight at noon. Stillness
like a thug in the wings. The sky thinks
over glass. A man stares at the telephone.
There is the moment that waiting becomes
luminous, the roundness of the air visible
as he had always guessed. He hangs in the dome
with a few green leaves. Then darkness

cinches the house up in its sack.
And you know how people think of things once
inside. Sometimes he thinks of dialing the number
that used to bring his mother's voice. Would it
ring, would it reach a woman with flour
like moon seas on her apron, string
around her finger. A reminder.
Perhaps it is connected

to the voice that says I'm sorry.
To the man who is passing the booth.
Perhaps he would interrupt a robbery or love.

The cloud smashes open like fruit.
The ozone of junipers rinsed in gin.

He thinks when the dead die, children go in
and lift the lids of the music boxes
in their rooms. They discover how jewels are places
lonelier than darkness. The rain better

than a thousand mothers.

In the Middle of Things, Begin

Bees rode the scalloped air of the garden.
The table, glazed bowls set for the afternoon meal,
trembled. A woman flashed in the archway
clutching her jewel box and an infant,
shoving them into a cart. The sleep was over.

I am near the mountain when you wake me,
the darkness ancient as the tongue
in a stone. You had slept a few hard hours
and then did not know where you were.
Small room on the Italian coast, it is strange
to us. I hear you touch things. I put up

my hand. I say *here, here*. We still
love each other. But this was years ago.
In the morning, we wander the ruins
of Pompeii, rooms cracked by golden
broom flowers, dry mosaic of a pool where
blind boy Cupid stands, the limed

jet in his loins. We step inside
the tepidarium, pale corruptions of pipe
and wall, and circle slowly the people
of ash, molded to their moment behind
museum glass. Cocooned so perfectly
in the postures of death, their bodies

tire us, even the dog's legs curled
to the tickle of stillness, torso
torqued almost playfully. We forget
it was the cloud they died from, not
the burning, not the fire. But the gray world.
Woman lying with her knees drawn up, cheek
resting on her hands. Man with his head

turned, hands flat, arms bent like a mantis
as if to push away the kiss of earth.
I am remembering them now in the middle
of things, like the married in their
separate fitful sleep. Suffocation
and climax: Same slow drag of the mouth. Same
gouged bread of the face.

To a Girl Writing Her Father's Death

Sometimes the lake water writes and writes and gets
no answer. You tell me, It was just October.
That is good. His voice was full of love and laughter. Not
so good. Full of copper, jacks-of-diamonds, cubes
of honey, I could believe. But I did not know
your father. The moment when the cable snapped from
the boat has, however, its drama. Yet is not
enough. Try to understand the need out here for
gestures, wind, raw sound. Was it a spasm
of sex in the motor, light shingling
his black hair as the boat spun
on its wide iris down? Were you standing?
I know this must be painful, standing
at the edge of your white page with someone
gone under. You were sixteen and he called you
Princess, though it is a cliché to be
called Princess. And to be sixteen. Yet
I have looked at you and you are not now
much older. You could wear tiaras,
your blonde waves pure as the back
of the knee. Though you wear your carrot rouge
in clumsy circles, which makes me
love you. I have not lost a father
except in dreams. But each one has left
my mouth open. Speak. Make holy
detail. Let the water bead over you like cold
eyeballs. Let in the scream and the lining of the scream
and the prismic figure eights of oil
mad on the wake—and forgive me
for asking. You have to think of the world
which gave and took your father.
The world which asks for him now.

There's no sense writing poems unless
you see the mob: We who gather for the red
pulse of every ambulance, we who crowd
lifeguards kissing the still blue lips of
children on the beach, and murmur who
and how, hungry for every morsel
of this life that is not ours, not really. Not
for long. But for the asking.

In the Badlands of Desire

If there is the statue of a saint
whose toes are worn smooth from old women
kissing, if there is an animal whose name
is sleep, if there is a hill
whose bones are broken, I
will remember me in the next life.

If there is an onion with the hundred
smaller and smaller faces
of wet light, if there is a mirror
whose shoulders drift
the museum of shoulders, if

there is a spider like a dud star
which catches the empire
from table leg to corner, if there are communists,
and useless lingerie, and rubies
snatched at night from jewelers' windows,
I will be the butcher's white

paper, the hook raving in frost.
If there is a tongue still moving
toward its mother silence, mint still breaking
its unimaginable green fist
through old aqueducts where the drunk

meet to be lonely and violet
as nets sieving the shine of nothing,
if there is a plaza in a town
where the stones break out
like hives from the plaster, and pigeons
blow their cool oboes of love,

I will be the look given to a door
when it closes by itself. After
it closes, wondering
was it some hand, some wind. And if it is painted
blue, like the faded crepe of old hours, if
a wolf bares its teeth to its tail
on the doorstep, there will be a hard winter,
a demon spring.

BARRY GOLDENSOHN ❖

The Marrano*

*Art is the remedy for the worst diseases
of the mind, the corruption of consciousness.*
            —Collingwood

God wants the souls of the faithful,
not their corpses. He has carrion enough.
In *The Golem* it explains
from moments of the highest danger
he saves us, always in the form of wonders,
like making a new man. For this truth
we struggle in disguise.
I moved to Hamburg or Seville, bought
a bakery or clothing store, a new name,
and lived openly, spoke like a native. I was
a kind of native, the most internal exile.
I could not change my name
because I was committed to disguise,
from Weiss to Scheiss, Hermano to Marrano.
I am His pig. To hide Him I renounce Him.
My teacher cared for me, a prize student.
To spare my feelings he asked me to leave the class
during his diatribes against the Jews.
I listened from the hallway, grateful

* The *Marranos* (the swine) was the name given to the converted Jews
in Spain, the "new Christians," more specifically those who converted
from mid-fourteenth century onward, usually under great duress.

Most Recent Book: THE MARRANO (National Poetry Foundation, 1988)

for this lesson in accommodation.
Modesty and secrecy are virtues of the chosen.
Study the pig for modesty. The cat
buries the emblem of the world. We learn
in secret, through closed doors, all love.
I welcome the need to convert, create
an adequate corruption of the mind
fit for understanding, for the sacred,
the one text, the one ungainly text,
saying *Alles in Ordnung ist*,
meaning another, unimaginable order.
The Gnostics were right, the world is made of shit.
I made my life a work of art expressing this.

American Innocents, Oberlin, Ohio, 1954

I
You were the ball I was trained to keep
my eyes on, with your alien blonde hair
and eyes of the alien blue, staring at me
hanging over the plate, myopic, dazed

by the light tent of hair you loved to spread
over us, your gift for music and math,
long legs, a careful way with words:
you said I had "a semi-recumbent walk."

I barely knew the difference between
Gentile and Jew, and wanted to marry you.
But you knew. Your lawyer-father knew.
Silver Springs had one or two. He threatened

to cut you off. The night you got his call
you stepped out of the dorm for air, to clear
your head, and when I followed you were gone,
running down the street, your yard-long hair

streaming straight back, your silhouette
flashing to gold at each distant streetlight.
I chased you four blocks and when I caught you
you didn't know who you were, or me.

I steered you to a small cafe, you stared
an hour at rings of light in the black coffee.

I was afraid to breathe and make them waver,
and when you raised your face I didn't know

if you were back. "This is forbidden," you said
in a child's voice, and you sang for another hour
with absolute pitch to the tune of *Là ci darem*,
legato, your submission and consent:

"No, no, no-no, no, no, no."

2

The *Anschluss* could not prepare me for this
midnight invasion by the red-eyed,
white-faced American children, nor could Vienna—
there they posture grandly for a week,
shrug and console themselves with the less messy
and preserve the order of acts in the family romance,
not hurrying so, content with the pace of *la ronde*,
diseases and love-wounds in tolerable doses.

My first exile, in Jerusalem,
with my neighbors Martin Buber and Max Brod,
the starker ones, prepared me better for them,
and for my wife, her pure Quaker service,
for all the unaccommodating spirits
who scream as they bend, as they must bend.

Now the tall yellow one, after her hours tonight
of little hysteria is afraid she will lose her mind.
She feels in the muscles of her face
and throat a new and terrifying looseness.
Nothing is broken in her American soul—
I have watched them from my windows as they raced
with one another on their bicycles
to their tutorial on Kafka with me.

I have heard them chatter about the Book of Job,
these young who have never been herded against a wall
or awakened and arrested. So I said to this child:
"In this situation a gentleman should withdraw."
And he will, and tonight, educated out
of the world he's constructed from innocence into exile,
and learn to love with his eyes over his shoulder
searching for the handle on the door.
And she will regress to a greater loyalty.

Honeymoon

On a piece of our honeymoon
my aunt and uncle lay
(he was a crude-mouthed clown)
one thickness of sheetrock away.
I never learned to bear
his bullying idiot humor.
It was no win. If we
roared to our bodies' content
and let the booming slats
play ground bass
or eased into love in silence
his jokes would be equally foul.
But we were good—a slow
grind and discreet gasps
and the next day on the dock
his rancid patter made
my shy wife writhe
and I iced to contempt for life.
His life, and my own.
My mother was there. For years
she let me know how shamed
she was by the dirt ingrained
deep in the hollows of my ankle
on show on the dock before
her idiot brother-in-law.
Again the lawless child
trying hard to be good
and betrayed by his filthy body
in their spanking boisterous world
that I fled for the precincts of art
in sneakers without socks
and a carefully preserved
shredded turtleneck
with my unacceptable wife.
Now nearly everyone's dead—
but the wish to be forgiven,
to forgive, to give, to get,
burns in this need to complete
the broken cycle of debt.

Post Mortem as Angels

When we meet then after death we will merge
easily, without the forced reserve
of our betraying bodies, the great routine
or the restraint with which we kept ourselves, alive.
There will be no husband then, or wife.
We will be all truth. Nothing to defend,
not one boundary. We will be one great friend.
No drama of discovery, nothing left to find.

We'll be so bored. Dissolved, the high theatre,
costumes, spooky music, uncovered letters,
devoted love jealous of him or her,
the reassuring masks we tried to wear
flung together in the backstage mirror.
We're buried with open eyes in dreamless order.

JORIE GRAHAM ❖

Salmon

I watched them once, at dusk, on television, run,
in our motel room halfway through
Nebraska, quick, glittering, past beauty, past
the importance of beauty,
archaic,
not even hungry, not even endangered, driving deeper and deeper
into less. They leapt up falls, ladders,
and rock, tearing and leaping, a gold river
and a blue river traveling
in opposite directions.
They would not stop, resolution of will
and helplessness, as the eye
is helpless
when the image forms itself, upside-down, backward,
driving up into
the mind, and the world
unfastens itself

Most Recent Book: THE END OF BEAUTY (The Ecco Press, 1987)

from the deep ocean of the given. . . . Justice, aspen
leaves, mother attempting
suicide, the white night-flying moth
the ants dismantled bit by bit and carried in
right through the crack
in my wall. . . . How helpless
the still pool is,
upstream,
awaiting the gold blade
of their hurry. Once, indoors, a child,
I watched, at noon, through slatted wooden blinds,
a man and woman, naked, eyes closed,
climb onto each other,
on the terrace floor,
and ride—two gold currents
wrapping round and round each other, fastening,
unfastening. I hardly knew
what I saw. Whatever shadow there was in that world
it was the one each cast
onto the other,
the thin black seam
they seemed to be trying to work away
between them. I held my breath.
As far as I could tell, the work they did
with sweat and light
was good. I'd say
they traveled far in opposite
directions. What is the light
at the end of the day, deep, reddish-gold, bathing the walls,
the corridors, light that is no longer light, no longer clarifies,
illuminates, antique, freed from the body of
the air that carries it. What is it
for the space of time
where it is useless, merely
beautiful? When they were done, they made a distance
one from the other
and slept, outstretched,
on the warm tile
of the terrace floor,
smiling, faces pressed against the stone.

What the End Is For
(Grand Forks, North Dakota)

A boy just like you took me out to see them,
    the five hundred B-52s on alert on the runway,
fully loaded fully manned pointed in all the directions,
    running every minute
of every day.
    They sound like a sickness of the inner ear,

where the heard foams up into the noise of listening,
    where the listening arrives without being extinguished.
The huge hum soaks up into the dusk.
    The minutes spring open. Six is too many.
From where we watch,
    from where even watching is an anachronism,

from the 23rd of March from an open meadow,
    the concertina wire in its double helix
designed to tighten round a body if it turns
    is the last path the sun can find to take out,
each barb flaring gold like a braille being read,
    then off with its knowledge and the sun
is gone. . . .

That's when the lights on all the extremities, like an outline like a dress,
    become loud in the story,
and a dark I have not seen before
    sinks in to hold them one
by one.
    Strange plot made to hold so many inexhaustible
screams.
    Have you ever heard in a crowd mutterings of
blame

that will not modulate that will not rise?
    He tells me, your stand-in, they *stair-step* up.
He touches me to have me look more deeply
    in
to where for just a moment longer
    color still lives:
the belly white so that it looks like sky, the top
    some kind of brown, some soil—How does it look

from up there now
    this meadow we lie on our bellies in, this field Iconography

tells me stands for sadness
     because the wind can move through it uninterrupted?
What is it the wind
     would have wanted to find and didn't

leafing down through this endless admiration unbroken
     because we're too low for it
to find us?
     Are you still there for me now in that dark
we stood in for hours
     letting it sweep as far as it could down over us
unwilling to move, irreconcilable? What *he*
     wants to tell me,

his whisper more like a scream
     over this eternity of engines never not running,
is everything: how the crews assigned to each plane
     for a week at a time, the seven boys, must live
inseparable,
     how they stay together for life,
how the wings are given a life of
     seven feet of play,

how they drop practice bombs called *shapes* over Nevada,
     how the measures for counterattack in air
have changed and we
     now forego firepower for jamming, for the throwing
of false signals. The meadow, the meadow hums, love, with the planes,
     as if every last blade of grass were wholly possessed

by this practice, wholly prepared. The last time I saw you,
     we stood facing each other as dusk came on.
I leaned against the refrigerator, you leaned against the door.
     The picture window behind you was slowly extinguished,
the tree went out, the two birdfeeders, the metal braces on them.
     The light itself took a long time,

bits in puddles stuck like the useless
     splinters of memory, the chips
of history, hopes, laws handed down. *Here, hold these* he says, these
     grasses these
torn pods, he says, smiling over the noise another noise, *take these*
     he says, my hands wrong for

the purpose, here,
     not-visible-from-the-sky, prepare yourself with these, boy and
bouquet of

thistleweed and wort and william and
timothy. We stood there. Your face went out a long time
    before the rest of it. Can't see you anymore I said. *Nor I,*
you, whatever you still were
    replied.
When I asked you to hold me you refused.
    When I asked you to cross the six feet of room to hold me

you refused. Until I
    couldn't rise out of the patience either any longer
to make us
    take possession.
Until we were what we must have wanted to be:
    shapes the shapelessness was taking back.
Why should I lean out?
    Why should I move?
When the Maenads tear Orpheus limb from limb,
    they throw his head

out into the river.
    Unbodied it sings
all the way downstream, all the way to the single ocean,
    head floating in current downriver singing,
until the sound of the cataracts grows,
    until the sound of the open ocean grows and the voice.

MARK HALLIDAY ❖

Reality U.S.A.

I feel I should go to Norfolk Virginia and drink
gin with sailors on leave from the *Alabama*, talking
baseball and Polaris missiles and Steve Martin movies,
another gin with lime juice, then Balto, Balto,
hitchhike in and out of Baltimore for days
back and forth for days in a row discussing the jobs
of whoever gives me rides, salesmen, shippers,
small-time dispatchers of the much that can be
dispatched. For the ACTUALITY of it!

Most Recent Book: LITTLE STAR (William Morrow, 1987)

Books dominate my head. I read in them, I read at them,
I'm well into my thirties. What about real life?
The woman in the light-blue skirt
on the cigarette billboard has such big thighs!
What is it about thighs? Smooth and weighty,
weighty and smooth: you can tell there's really
something *there*. And to think that
the woman must really exist, it's a photo after all
not a painting, she is somewhere in America—
and to think that some guy gets to lie down
on her and her thighs . . . She's a model,
she probably lives in New York, New York baffles me
I know I could never find her there—but
listen, her sister lives in Baltimore,
hanging out sheets to dry from the balcony
of a light-blue house, lifting her arms—
reality. Along with

her dimly dangerous ex-husband, her speed pills,
his clumsy minor embezzlement of funds from
Pabst Auto Supply, and what else?
The boxing matches he goes to, and the stock-car races
and—maybe I should go to Indianapolis?
But I feel sure I'd be bored in Indianapolis
despite the smoky reality of Indianapolis.
But it's this idea of American experience how I don't
have it, how I ought to know the way things are really
and not just from Hemingway or Dreiser, John O'Hara or
James T. Farrell
or, say, Raymond Carver or Bruce Springsteen
but directly: firsthand: hands-on learning.
What if I were to take a Greyhound to Memphis,
quit shaving, learn to drink whiskey straight,
lift some weights (maybe I should do the weights before I go)
and get a tattoo on one bicep saying KISS OFF
and meet a guy named Eddie who chain-smokes
and rob a record store with Eddie! Yes,
we smash the glass at 3 a.m. on Davis Avenue in Memphis
and grab 300 albums and 200 8-track tapes
pile them into Eddie's red pickup and bingo, we're gone
in five minutes. Next day we paint the pickup yellow
and change the plates, no sweat. Eddie knows,
he knows stuff, he knows how to fence the loot
and he says next we hit a certain TV store,

he slugs my shoulder laughing, I get my piece of cash
but really it's not the cash I care about,
it's the being *involved*.
                    Eddie thinks that's weird,
he says "You're weird, man"
and starts to act mistrustful so I leave town.
Kansas City here I come.

No, skip Kansas City, I want to save Kansas City.
Just in case.
—In case what? What am I talking about?
How many lives does a person get,
one, right? And me,
                    I love my life with books!—
Of course it's not *just* books, I've got bills
and friends and milkshakes, the supermarket, laundromat
oh shit but still I keep feeling this thing about
reality—
the world is so loaded: a green beer bottle is chucked
half-full from a speeding Ford Mercury and that beer sloshes
exactly like this loaded world—what?
Forget the world, just take America,
sure there's the same hamburgers everywhere
and gasoline fumes but among the fumes and burgers
there's *de*tail, tons of it, you can smell it.
There are variations . . . All the stuff
Whitman claimed he saw, there's the really *seeing* that stuff!
There's—
I don't know—there's a waitress in an Arby's Roast Beef
and her name is either Donna or Nadine,
you buy the Special on the right day and you get
a free Batman 10-ounce glass, she makes a joke about it,
you say "What time do you get off work" (only this time
it's really happening) and that night Donna
or Nadine does for you what you thought they only did
in fiction . . . That's right. Next morning
her bottom in the light from the window looks so pearly
it's like home, just glad to be home.
It's April, all cool and sunny,
and across the street from Arby's there is
a ten-year-old black boy wearing red hightops
and we talk about the Braves (this is in Georgia, now,
and the asphalt glistens) and the kid says
something beautiful that I'll never forget.

Good. So then, the kid's uncle sells me some cocaine
or teaches me how to aim a pistol
or takes me for a ride in his helicopter—
there must be a few black men who own helicopters?
Up we go roaring over Georgia!
The roofs and poles and roofs
the components,
the components!
Ohhhh . . . Already they've worn me out.

Population

Isn't it nice that everyone has a grocery list
except the very poor you hear about occasionally
we all have a grocery list on the refrigerator door;
at any given time there are thirty million lists in America
that say BREAD. Isn't it nice
not to be alone in this. Sometimes
you visit someone's house for the first time
and you spot the list taped up on a kitchen cabinet
and you think Yes, we're all in this together.
TOILET PAPER. No getting around it.
Nice to think of us all
unwrapping the new rolls at once,
forty thousand of us at any given moment.

Orgasm, of course, being the most vivid example: imagine
an electrified map wired to every American bed:
those little lights popping
on both sides of the Great Divide,
popping to beat the band. But
we never beat the band: within an hour or day
we're horny again, or hungry, or burdened with waste.
But isn't it nice not to be alone in
any of it; nice to be not noticeably responsible,
acquitted eternally in the rituals of the tribe:
it's only human! It's only human and that's not much.

So, aren't you glad we have such advanced farm machinery,
futuristic fertilizers, half a billion chickens
almost ready to die. Here come the loaves of bread for us
thup thup thup thup for all of us thup thup thup
except maybe the very poor

thup thup
and man all the cattle we can fatten up man,
there's no stopping our steaks. And that's why
we can make babies galore, baby:
let's get on with it. Climb aboard.
Let's be affirmative here, let's be pro-life for God's sake
how can life be wrong?
People *need* people and the happiest people are
surrounded with friendly flesh.
If you have ten kids they'll be so sweet—
ten really sweet kids! Have twelve!
What if there were 48 pro baseball teams,
you could see a damn lot more games!
And in this fashion we get away
from tragedy. Because tragedy comes when someone
gets too special. Whereas,

if forty thousand kitchen counters
on any given Sunday night
have notes on them that say
I CAN'T TAKE IT ANYMORE
I'M GONE, DON'T TRY TO FIND ME
you can feel how *your* note is
no big thing in America,
so, no *horrible* heartbreak,
it's more like a TV episode,
you've seen this whole plot lots of times
and everybody gets by—
you feel better already—
everybody gets by
and it's nice. It's a people thing.
You've got to admit it's nice.

Seventh Avenue

Late Tuesday afternoon the romantic self weaves
up Seventh Avenue amid too many lookers, too many
feelers: romance hates democracy;

how can *you* be so great and golden inside
if your trunk is shouldered among other trunks
block after block, block after block—

you can't help glimpsing an otherness in others
that is not just surface: they ache,
their aches ache away north and south all Tuesday

in murmurous torsos like yours . . .
What apprehension blossoms even now in Manuel
shifting steaks at the ten-foot grill of Charley O's

beneath the towering chef's hat they make him wear?
When I was twenty I'd have written
that he was only thinking of Cadillacs and sex;

now I'm afraid he's just as worried as I am
about love vs. lesser things and the point of it all.
Manuel, stay there at the sizzling grill till midnight

and then just drink or sleep, man,
don't write poems—
do me that favor. It's loud enough already

out here on Seventh Avenue with that cat's boombox
and these three giggle girls being Madonna together
and that guy hawking wind-up titans wielding laser lances.

Who's Wordsworth for any extended period on Seventh Ave?
In this predusk traffic you catch the hint
that Manuel and thou if seers at all are seers only

for seconds—now the steak, taxi, buttocks, headline
and wallet resume their charismatic claim to be what counts.
Soul on Seventh is a sometime on-off quick-flip thing . . .

What I want is a poem long as Seventh Avenue
to sprinkle gold on every oppressed minority,
every young woman's subtly female hips,
every sad and suspicious American face
and the quiddity of every mud-tracked pizza shop;
proving, block after block, stanza by stanza
that I'm not just one skinny nervous pedestrian
but the one who matters because he sees and says.
I want that. The Avenue grins and says
"You want that? How does it feel to want?"

JOY HARJO ❖

Santa Fe

The wind blows lilacs out of the east. And it isn't lilac season. And I am
walking the street in front of St. Francis Cathedral in Santa Fe. Oh, and
it's a few years earlier and more. That's how you tell real time. It is here, it
is there. The lilacs have taken over everything: the sky, the narrow streets,
my shoulders, my lips. I talk lilac. And there is nothing else until a woman
the size of a fox breaks through the bushes, breaks the purple web. She is
tall and black and gorgeous. She is the size of a fox on the arm of a white
man who looks and tastes like cocaine. She lies for cocaine, dangles on the
arm of cocaine. And lies to me now from a room in the DeVargas Hotel,
where she has eaten her lover, white powder on her lips. That is true now;
it is not true anymore. Eventually space curves, walks over and taps me on
the shoulder. On the sidewalk I stand near St. Francis; he has been
bronzed, a perpetual tan, with birds on his hand, his shoulder, deer at his
feet. I am Indian and in this town I will never be a saint. I am seventeen
and shy and wild. I have been up until three at a party, but there is no
woman in the DeVargas Hotel for that story hasn't yet been invented. A
man whose face I will never remember, and never did, drives up on a
Harley Davidson. There are lilacs on his arm, they spill out from the
spokes of his wheels. He wants me on his arm, on the back of his lilac
bike touring the flower kingdom of San Francisco. And for a piece of time
the size of a nickle, I think, maybe. But maybe is vapor, has no anchor
here in the sun beneath St. Francis Cathedral. And space is as solid as the
bronze statue of St. Francis, the fox breaking through the lilacs, my
invention of this story, the wind blowing.

Blue Elliptic

All the lights in the house are burning.
In the other room Zinger still wheezes,
then puts her raggy head between her paws
and sleeps. She leaps but it is not
real. Already she anticipates your return,
hears the van pulling up, cracking the
iced asphalt, the rattle of equipment, and

Most Recent Book: IN MAD LOVE AND WAR (Wesleyan University Press, 1990)

your lullabye voice smoothing her ear. All
her nerves run on that sound. And in the
other room the fish swim musically in their
watery cage. Their sense of concave horizon
points to a foreign sky. The heater shakes
and blows from the basement, and outside
someone loses their voice, calling to an angel
they have never seen before. And all I can
remember to tell you is the talk of a meteor
shower. To drive to it is impossible in
this weather, but close by are velvet deer
stalking the moon on the shaggy ice. And
closer still you are in Vail playing the
gorgeous blues with Maxine and the crazy
quartet. The Geminids are falling falling
from one sky to another, onto the antlers
of the luminescent deer, onto the roof
of this house and did you see

as your fingers climbed your tenor for
the smell of a flower that would never
prosper in this world, did you see

as you made that frightening leap
through the diminished world
into the lapis asylum

did you see

Petroglyph

for Jaune Quick-to-See Smith

Everyone had turned off their televisions to watch the meteor shower
flood midnight. Who named them Delta Aquarids? And what names were
sealed on the lips of the grandparents who'd slipped from their
disassembling bones, back onto resurrected horses, roaming the cities
where there were no longer cities but cleansing wind threading the leaves?
In Corrales the horse named Sally knew what love was about when she
lifted up her head to acknowledge the flying stars who were nodding to
her, and to our humanness worn about us like rags in this war to survive
with dignity. Even the chickens who had become too civilized clucked in
assent in their dreams, the one place they remembered how to fly over the
walls of the chickenwire, their skirts forgotten, the pull of worms

underground the rudder for perfect flight. And dogs, the chosen companions for humans had long since made the choice to stay, not out of pity but love. Rudy in particular danced around the feet of the painter who poured herself another cup of coffee before going outside to catch the blessing of stars that would suddenly light up the world. Even though it was something the painter didn't think about (with words) she recalled the metallic flavor of minerals (how the stars must taste) scratching at the root of her tongue, which led to nerveways of the bones where the imprint of all symbols surfaces to the fingers, where spirits ride horses through the colors needed to form any coherent universe. And never far away is the lightning of the heart that quickens the need to understand the night sky as a word with which you can create in the same manner that you were created, as were the stars talked into painting our vision with promise of eternity. Petroglyphs on a ridge of stones overlook Corrales. Everything is going on if you look close enough, a similar version of the pageant of whirling stars, arrows finding their way to the sun, a child who has lost her way but will find it, and the painter who stands out in the rain of horses where the night is always a puzzle of origins. And how did she know that someone hadn't conceived of her, as they ran out of their house to watch the falling stars, light years away (in the language of the enemy) but as close as the pulse in her wrist counting the surge of love? As she stands outside the kitchen door, drawn in by the whirling patterns of the electric stars, she can see herself painting the dawn as it elopes over the Sangre de Cristos, the crisp nostrils of Sally the horse snorting cool breaths into clouds, Rudy the collie dog brushing the ground with her tail as she anticipates the presence of the human she has chosen to take care of, forgetful chickens scratching for seed, and the grandparents on horses with grandchildren in front of them, forming the border of the composition.

Grace

for Wind and Jim Welch

I think of Wind and her wild ways the year we had nothing to lose and lost it anyway in the cursed country of the fox. We still talk about that winter, how the cold froze imaginary buffalo on the stuffed horizon of snowbanks. The haunting voices of the starved and mutilated broke fences, crashed our thermostat dreams, and we couldn't stand it one more time. So once again we lost a winter in stubborn memory, walked through cheap apartment walls, skated through fields of ghosts into a town that never wanted us, in the epic search for grace.

Like Coyote, like Rabbit we could not contain our terror and clowned our way through a season of false midnights. We had to swallow that town with laughter, so it would go down easy as honey. And one morning as the sun struggled to break ice, and our dreams had found us with coffee and pancakes in a truckstop along Highway 80; we found grace.

I could say grace was a woman with time on her hands, or a white buffalo escaped from memory. But in that dingy light it was a promise of balance. We once again understood the talk of animals, and spring was lean and hungry with the hope of children and corn.

I would like to say, with grace, we picked ourselves up and walked into the spring thaw. We didn't; the next season was worse. You went home to Leech Lake to work with the tribe and I went south. And Wind, I am still crazy. I know there is something larger than the memory of a dispossessed people. We have seen it.

ROBERT HASS ❖

Human Wishes

This morning the sun rose over the garden wall and a rare blue sky leaped from east to west. Man is altogether desire, say the Upanishads. Worth anything, a blue sky, says Mr. Acker, the Shelford gardener. Not altogether. In the end. Last night on television the ethnologist and the cameraman watched with hushed wonder while the chimpanzee carefully stripped a willow branch and inserted it into the anthill. He desired red ants. When they crawled slowly up the branch, he ate them, pinched between long fingers as the zoom lens enlarged his face. Sometimes he stopped to examine one, as if he were a judge at an ant beauty contest or God puzzled suddenly by the idea of suffering. There was an empty place in the universe where that branch wasn't and the chimp filled it, as Earlene, finding no back on an old Welsh cupboard she had bought in Saffron Walden, imagined one there and imagined both the cupboard and the imagined back against a kitchen wall in Berkeley, and went into town looking for a few boards of eighteenth-century tongue-in-groove pine to fill that empty space. I stayed home to write, or rather stayed home and stared at a blank piece of paper, waiting for her to come back, thinking tongue-in-groove, tongue-in-groove, as if language were a kind of moral cloud chamber through

Most Recent Book: HUMAN WISHES (The Ecco Press, 1989)

which the world passed and from which it emerged charged with
desire. The man in the shop in Cambridge said he didn't have any old
pine, but when Earlene went back after thinking about it to say she was
sure she had seen some, the man found it. Right under his feet, which
was puzzling. Mr. Acker, hearing the story, explained. You know, he
said, a lot of fiddling goes on in those places. The first time you went
in, the governor was there, the second time he wasn't, so the chap sold
you some scrap and he's four quid in pocket. No doubt he's having a
good time now with his mates in the pub. Or he might have put it on
the horses at Newmarket. He might parley it into a fortune.

Vintage

They had agreed, walking into the delicatessen on Sixth Avenue, that
their friends' affairs were focused and saddened by massive projection;

movie screens in their childhood were immense, and someone had
proposed that need was unlovable.

The delicatessen had a chicken salad with chunks of cooked chicken in
a creamy basil mayonnaise a shade lighter than the Coast Range in
August; it was gray outside, February.

Eating with plastic forks, walking and talking in the sleety afternoon,
they passed a house where Djuna Barnes was still, reportedly, making
sentences.

Bashō said: avoid adjectives of scale, you will love the world more and
desire it less.

And there were other propositions to consider: childhood, Vista Vision,
a pair of wet, mobile lips on the screen at least eight feet long.

On the corner a blind man with one leg was selling pencils. He must
have received a disability check,

but it didn't feed his hunger for public agony, and he sat on the sidewalk
slack-jawed, with a tin cup, his face and opaque eyes turned upward in a
look of blind, questing pathos—

half Job, half mole.

Would the good Christ of Manhattan have restored his sight and two-
thirds of his left leg? Or would he have healed his heart and left him
there in a mutilated body? And what would that peace feel like?

It makes you want, at this point, a quick cut, or a reaction shot. "The taxis rivered up Sixth Avenue." "A little sunlight touched the steeple of the First Magyar Reform Church."

In fact, the clerk in the liquor store was appalled. "No, no," he said, "that cabernet can't be drunk for another five years."

A Story about the Body

The young composer, working that summer at an artist's colony, had watched her for a week. She was Japanese, a painter, almost sixty, and he thought he was in love with her. He loved her work, and her work was like the way she moved her body, used her hands, looked at him directly when she made amused and considered answers to his questions. One night, walking back from a concert, they came to her door and she turned to him and said, "I think you would like to have me. I would like that too, but I must tell you that I have had a double mastectomy," and when he didn't understand, "I've lost both my breasts." The radiance that he had carried around in his belly and chest cavity—like music—withered very quickly, and he made himself look at her when he said, "I'm sorry. I don't think I could." He walked back to his own cabin through the pines, and in the morning he found a small blue bowl on the porch outside his door. It looked to be full of rose petals, but he found when he picked it up that the rose petals were on top; the rest of the bowl—she must have swept them from the corners of her studio—was full of dead bees.

Privilege of Being

Many are making love. Up above, the angels
in the unshaken ether and crystal of human longing
are braiding one another's hair, which is strawberry blond
and the texture of cold rivers. They glance
down from time to time at the awkward ecstasy—
it must look to them like featherless birds
splashing in the spring puddle of a bed—
and then one woman, she is about to come,
peels back the man's shut eyelids and says,
look at me, and he does. Or is it the man
tugging the curtain rope in that dark theater?

Anyway, they do, they look at each other;
two beings with evolved eyes, rapacious,
startled, connected at the belly in an unbelievably sweet
lubricious glue, stare at each other,
and the angels are desolate. They hate it. They shudder pathetically
like lithographs of Victorian beggars
with perfect features and alabaster skin hawking rags
in the lewd alleys of the novel.
All of creation is offended by this distress.
It is like the keening sound the moon makes sometimes,
rising. The lovers especially cannot bear it,
it fills them with unspeakable sadness, so that
they close their eyes again and hold each other, each
feeling the mortal singularity of the body
they have enchanted out of death for an hour or so,
and one day, running at sunset, the woman says to the man,
I woke up feeling so sad this morning because I realized
that you could not, as much as I love you,
dear heart, cure my loneliness,
wherewith she touched his cheek to reassure him
that she did not mean to hurt him with this truth.
And the man is not hurt exactly,
he understands that life has limits, that people
die young, fail at love,
fail of their ambitions. He runs beside her, he thinks
of the sadness they have gasped and crooned their way out of
coming, clutching each other with old, invented
forms of grace and clumsy gratitude, ready
to be alone again, or dissatisfied, or merely
companionable like the couples on the summer beach
reading magazine articles about intimacy between the sexes
to themselves, and to each other,
and to the immense, illiterate, consoling angels.

William Hathaway ❖

A Poem in Response to Doom

All summer long the smartypants
at the egghead writers' conference
lectured on the end of the world.
Mainly, alchemy and acronym: dioxins,
polycarbons, PCB, SDI, and AIDS—
AIDS loomed large. Seals had caught
it and in each voice a big finger
poked holes in air. My friend and I
had come mainly to meet brainy women
and secular sermons discouraged us.
I slumped sullen and pouty, but
whenever the public address system
crackled that word "Apocalypse,"
I blinked awake and leaned forward
to hear what revelation was at hand.

Of course the new death is old death.
We couldn't play outside, my sister
told me, because a "rabbit fox"
was loose. She was the one who found
this fox at last sprawled by
the railroad tracks on our way
to school. We clustered two feet
all around it to watch it be dead.
A boy named Shep cut its bushy
tail off but his father burned it
and the lunchbox he'd put it in.
He was the first prick I ever met.
We didn't know Switzerland even
had an army then. Our jackknives
were all named after cowboys.
Horrible flies in splendid colors
strutted up and down its toothy grin.

It seemed savage with smug cunning
and malice but, in retrospect,
I see wry regret. It's fun to imagine

Most Recent Book: Looking Into the Heart of Light
(University of Central Florida Press, 1988)

this fox snarling blood-flecked foam
and springing with insane barking
into the teeth of the locomotive.
But anyone who's grown to know
the bewilderment of delirium knows
better. If such poetry isn't silly,
it's cruel. There isn't even a whimper,
finally. Just death's dull gray
glazing the eyes that speak of what?
Mercy! And if I don't take the pain
of pity full to me then, it will wait
to swarm through me like disease.

Apocalypse: I love to say its sound
even better than Armageddon, holocaust,
or soft consonants and sibilances
in venereal names. All the new diseases
were always in us waiting to be loosed.
It's so clear I can say it in the real
poetry of prose: Nature is without pity.
More cruel than kind, no virus even cares
about not caring. Harmony without love.
We are chaos of purpose; the proper study.

But anarchy to poets who chant names
of nuts and berries the way acolytes
sing-song the mass. Quavery solemnity
to summon back a naive awe in response
to awfulness. Puffed like emphysema:
a beautiful word. Which is how someone
got all Spain to lisp. By the time
the mail delivered our cards pasted in
Art and signed to the girl with polio
named Donna, she'd died. My first time
when the awful gloat of death got too
chill to thrill. Helpless and stupid-
hearted with fear I carried home
the gift she never got. Returned
to sender, crushed in my lunchbox
with all the silly pictures and papers
all stinking together like tuna fish.
I barely knew her. Like vampires,
any Spot or Fluffy carried germs
of sudden slathering hate. Toilets
and swimming pools seethed with death.

And behind the blandest faces on our
block communism was plotting in Russian.
Sealed tight in the sour bomb shelter
under the girl-next-door's backyard,
we crouched beneath stacked cans
dripping with mildew and examined
each other's genitals with flashlights.
I thought my heart would explode
from both joy and terror. My yard
was just a yard. If the world blew up,
we'd stand out in the hot wind
of the last Apocalypse. I imagined
angels decked out in flowers and fruit
shimmying and bumping toward us
in a magnificent splutter of golden
fire. But that's why poetry is so silly
and sad: saying all the sounds so
you're left alone with whatever's left.

Wan Hope

for Robert Pinsky

After we got suckered and lost the war
there weren't jobs or any place to roost,
so we just humped along close to the coast
scrabbling one day at a time. Now, on this
one evening, see? We've tied up the boat
and we're clanking down a vaulted hall
looking for dinner, a bath, maybe a girl
when Aeneas stops dead like he's been
coldcocked and starts juicing the inside
of his elbow with this noble flood of tears
and snot over nothing but pictures
on the wall. Then I see it too and I can't
believe my eyes! There's Anchises, Hector,
Priam—all of us, both living and dead
stiff as hell configured in the doing
of deeds. And the war just a few years old!
The rest of us just have to wait it out
while Aeneas blubbers over how beautiful
sadness is for about fifteen minutes,

dabbing at our eyes like a gnat's got in
there and all tensed up to an acute
knowledge that there's nowhere natural
to put your hands in this world. I'll tell
you the truth, doomed and gloomed as anyone
there, it was me who unfroze this poignant
tableau back on reel. Real casual I put
my arm on my pal, "How's that new helmet
liner, still chafing?" And in the echo
of our own hollow clanging, we walked on
then. "Tough-guy swagger," a critic might
say. "A wise-ass trivialization of human
grandeur and tenure revealing naught
but the poet's own spiritual paucity."
Whew! And wanly, my pale fish-hand in
a dazed drift up to the bait, I could
only say, "Well, at least I was there."

But that's crap; I wasn't there. This
part's been just a poem, a parable
meant so cold souls can't understand
and be forgiven. But now I'll tell
the story behind the story. A school pal
and I bartended fraternity parties
and at one in the pre-dawn wreckage
when only the team's star tackle
was left with his toxic fear and rage,
and his vicious sycophants, and two
high-school girls, deaddrunk, who
shouldn't have been there, those cruel
thugs told them to undress and beat
them when they wouldn't. My friend said,
"Hey, you bastards, leave them alone!"
and they beat us too. They cracked
his ribs and his jaw and made his gut
bleed. I fought hard until they re-broke
my nose and then—what the hell—
begged for mercy. They took the cutest girl
upstairs, clamped her neck in a windowsash
and ganged her from behind. We sat
out on the curb away from the light
under a sickle moon with the other girl
who just whimpered when we spoke
and wouldn't let us touch her. My pal

began to cry, a terrible weeping without
hope or dignity, and he beat his knuckles
on the asphalt. Then I said this, "Listen,
those girls should have known; we did
all we could." Which is crap, of course,

and I suppose on the blackboard of an ethics
course before a warm crescent of faces
some yellow chalk could screech this
so a rubber-tipped pointer could jab it:
accidie. Cowardice in greek, as doctors
always scribble names of sickness. The point,
again, is that I was there—again
and again and again in places so stupid
they're hidden not merely from cunning
but from wisdom itself. And I never saved
anyone for Love and Freedom and Art—
in fact, all those I drank and fought
with got turned to pigs and run off
cliffs. Even now, most of these I put
my arm around still smoke cigarettes
though every cough rumbles with warning
like an inscrutable parable, righteous
and merciless. My soul? It is like this:
a gray barmop, all sweetness soured
by shame, but no matter how sodden
with bitter spillage or the biles
that ferment with grief inside of men
you can wring this thing of tears again
and again. And whatever words I've said,
no matter how churlish and wrong, I meant
them for pity's sake and if I could I'd
soak all the world's anguish up inside
me and save the living and the dead.

EDWARD HIRSCH ❖

After the Last Practice

Grinnell, Iowa, November 1971

Someone said, I remember the first hard crack
Of shoulderpads on the sidelines before a game,
And the bruises that blossom on your arms afterward.
Someone else remembered the faint, medicinal smell
Seeping through the locker room on Saturday mornings,
Getting your ankles taped while a halfback

Frets in the whirlpool about his hamstrings:
Steam on three mirrors, the nervous hiss
        Of the first hot shower of the morning.
We talked about the tension mounting all day
Until it became the sound of spikes clattering
Across the locker-room floor, the low banter

Of the last players pulling on their jerseys,
Our middle-linebacker humming to himself
And hammering a forearm against the lockers
While an assistant coach diagrammed a punt
Return for the umpteenth time on his clipboard
For two cornerbacks looking on in boredom . . .

Eventually, it always came down to a few words
From the head coach—quiet, focused, intense—
While a huge pit opened up in your stomach
And the steady buzz of a crowd in the distance
Turned into a minor roaring in your skull
As the team exploded onto the field.

The jitters never disappeared until the opening
Kickoff, the first contact, until a body
Hurtled down the field in a fury
And threw itself against your body
While everything else in the world faded
Before the crunching action of a play, unfolding . . .

I remember how, as we talked, the flat Midwestern
Fields stretched away into nowhere and nothing,

Most Recent Book: THE NIGHT PARADE (Alfred A. Knopf, 1989)

How the dark sky clouded over like a dome
Covering a chilly afternoon in late November
On the prairie, the scent of pine cones
And crisp leaves burning in the air,

The smoky glow of faces around a small fire.
Someone spoke of road trips and bridge games
In the back of a bus rolling across the plains,
The wooden fenceposts ticking off miles
And miles of empty cornfields and shortgrasses,
Windmills treading their arms, as if underwater,

The first orange lights rising on the horizon—
Jesus, someone said, I never thought it would end
Like this, without pads, without hitting anybody.
But then someone mentioned stepping out of bounds
And getting blindsided by a bone-wrenching tackle;
Someone else remembered writhing in a pile

Of players coming down on his twisted body.
Torn ligaments. Sprained wrist. A black coin
Blooming under your left eye on Sunday morning.
After all those years of drills and double practices,
Seasons of calisthenics, weightrooms, coaches
Barking orders—missed blocks, squirming fumbles—;

After all those summers of trying to perfect
A sideline pass and a buttonhook, a fly, a flag,
A deep post, a quick pass over the middle;
After the broken patterns and failed double teams,
The July nights sprinting up the stadium stairs
And the August days banging against each other's bodies,

The slow walks home alone in the dusky light—;
After all those injury-prone autumns, not
One of us could explain why he had done it.
What use now is the language of traps
And draws, of power sweeps and desperate on-side
Kicks, of screen passes, double reverses?

But still there was the memory of a sharp cut
Into the open and the pigskin spiraling
Into your hands from twenty yards away,
The ecstasy of breaking loose from a tackle
And romping for daylight, for the green
Promised land of the empty endzone.

Someone said, I remember running into the field
And seeing my girlfriend in the stands at midfield—
Everyone around her was chanting and shouting
And the adrenaline was coursing through my body;
I felt as if I would explode with happiness,
As if I would never falter, or waver, or die . . .

Someone else recollected the endless, losing,
Thirteen-hour drive home after he had bruised
A collarbone on the last play of the game,
The whole bus encased in silence, like a glass
Jar, like the night itself, clarified. Afterward,
He recalled the wild joy of his first interception . . .

The fire sputtered and smoldered, faded out,
And our voices trembled in the ghostly woodsmoke
Until it seemed as if we were partly warriors
And partly Boy Scouts ringed around the flame,
Holding our helmets in our arms and trying
To understand an old appetite for glory,

Our raging, innocent, violent, American
Boyhoods, gone now, vanished forever
Like the victories and the hard losses.
It was late. A deep silence descended
As twilight disintegrated in the night air
And the fire glowered down to embers and ashes,

To red bits of nothing. But no one moved. Oh,
We were burning, burning, burning, burning . . .
And then someone began singing in the darkness.

Art Pepper

It's the broken phrases, the fury inside him.
Squiggling alto saxophone playing out rickets
And jaundice, a mother who tried to kill him
In her womb with a coat hanger, a faltering
God-like father. The past is a bruised cloud
Floating over the houses like a prophecy,
The terrible foghorns off the shore at San Pedro.

Lightning without thunder. Years without playing.
Years of blowing out smoke and inhaling fire,
Junk and cold turkey, smacking up, the habit
Of cooking powder in spoons, the eyedroppers,
The spikes. Tracks on both arms. Tattoos.
The hospital cells at Fort Worth, the wire cages
In the L.A. County, the hole at San Quentin.

And always the blunt instrument of sex, the hurt
Bubbling up inside him like a wound, the small
Deaths. The wind piercing the sheer skin
Of a dark lake at dawn. The streets at 5 a.m.
After a cool rain. The smoky blue clubs.
The chords of Parker, of Young, of Coltrane.
Playing solo means going on alone, improvising,

Hitting the notes, ringing the changes.
It's clipped phrasing and dry-ice in summer,
Straining against the rhythm, speeding it up,
Loping forward and looping back, finding the curl
In the wave, the mood in the air. It's
Splintered tones and furious double timing.
It's leaving the other instruments on stage

And blowing freedom into the night, into the faces
Of emptiness that peer along the bar, ghosts,
Shallow hulls of nothingness. Hatred of God.
Hatred of white skin that never turns black.
Hatred of Patti, of Dianne, of Christine.
A daughter who grew up without him, a stranger.
Years of being strung out, years without speaking.

Pauses and intervals, silence. A fog rolling
Across the ocean, foghorns in the distance.
A lighthouse rising from the underworld.
A moon swelling in the clouds, an informer,
A twisted white mouth of light. Scars carved
And criss-crossed on his chest. The memory
Of nodding out, the dazed drop-off into sleep.

And then the curious joy of surviving, joy
Of waking up in a dusky room to a gush
Of fresh notes, a tremoring sheet of sound.
Jamming again. Careening through the scales
For the creatures who haunt the night.

Bopping through the streets in a half-light
With Laurie on his arm, a witness, a believer.

The night is going to burst inside him.
The wind is going to break loose forever
From his lungs. It's the fury of improvising,
Of going on alone. It's the fierce clarity
Of each note coming to an end, distinct,
Glistening. The alto's full-bodied laughter.
The white grief-stricken wail.

TONY HOAGLAND ❖

One Season

That was the summer my best friend
called me a faggot on the telephone,
hung up, and vanished from the earth,

a normal occurrence in this country
where we change our lives
with the swiftness and hysterical finality

of dividing cells. That month
the rain refused to fall,
and fire engines streaked back and forth crosstown

towards smoke-filled residential zones
where people stood around outside, drank beer
and watched their neighbors' houses burn.

It was a bad time to be affected
by nearly anything,
especially anything as dangerous

as loving a man, if you happened to be
a man yourself, ashamed and unable to explain
how your feelings could be torn apart

by something ritual and understated
as friendship between males.
Probably I talked too loud that year

Most Recent Book: HISTORY OF DESIRE (Moon Pony Press, 1990)

and thought an extra minute
before I crossed my legs; probably
I chose a girl I didn't care about

and took her everywhere,
knowing I would dump her in the fall
as part of evening the score,

part of practicing the scorn
it was clear I was going to need
to get across this planet

of violent emotional addition
and subtraction. Looking back, I can see
that I came through

in the spastic, fugitive, half-alive manner
of accident survivors. Fuck anyone
who says I could have done it

differently. Though now I find myself
returning to the scene
as if the pain I fled

were the only place that I had left to go;
as if my love, whatever kind it was, or is,
were still trapped beneath the wreckage

of that year,
and I was one of those angry firemen
having to go back into the burning house;
climbing a ladder

through the heavy smoke and acrid smell
of my own feelings,
as if they were the only
goddamn thing worth living for.

Sweet Ruin

Maybe that is what he was after,
my father, when he arranged, ten years ago,
to be discovered in a mobile home
with a woman named Roxanne, an attractive,
recently divorced masseuse.

He sat there, he said later, in the middle
of a red, imitation leather sofa,
with his shoes off and a whiskey in his hand,
filling up with a joyful kind of dread—
like a swamp, filling up with night,

—while my mother hammered on the trailer door
with a muddy, pried-up stone,
then smashed the headlights of his car,
then drove herself home
and locked herself inside.

He paid the piper, was how he put it,
because he wanted to live,
and at the time knew no other way
than to behave like some blind and willful beast,
—to make a huge mistake, like a big leap

into space, as if following
a music that required dissonance
and a plunge into the dark.
That is what he tried to tell me,
that afternoon we talked,

as he reclined in his black chair,
divorced from the people in his story
by ten years and a heavy cloud of smoke.
Trying to explain how a man could come
to a place where he has nothing else to gain

unless he loses everything. So he
louses up his work, his love, his own heart.
He hails disaster like a cab. And years later,
when the storm has descended
and rubbed his face in the mud of himself,

he stands again and looks around,
strangely thankful just to be alive,
oddly jubilant—as if he had been granted
the answer to his riddle,
or as if the question

had been taken back. Perhaps
a wind is freshening the grass,
and he can see now, as for the first time,
the softness of the air between the blades. The pleasure
built into a single bending leaf.

Maybe then he calls it, in a low voice
and only to himself, *Sweet Ruin.*
And maybe only because I am his son,
I can hear just what he means. How
even at this moment, even when the world

seems so perfectly arranged, I feel
a force prepared to take it back.
Like a smudge on the horizon. Like a black spot
on the heart. How one day soon,
I might take this nervous paradise,

bone and muscle of this extraordinary life,
and with one deliberate gesture,
like a man stepping on a stick,
break it into halves. But less gracefully

than that. I think there must be something wrong
with me, or wrong with strength, that I would
break my happiness apart
simply for the pleasure of the sound.
The sound the pieces make. What is wrong

with peace? I couldn't say.
But, sweet ruin, I can hear you.
There is always the desire.
Always the cloud, suddenly present
and willing to oblige.

Poem for Men Only

It wasn't easy, inventing the wheel,
dragging the first stones into place,
convincing them to be the first house.
Maybe that's why our fathers,
when they finished work,

had so little to say. Instead,
they drifted—feet crossed on the divan,
hands folded over stomachs like a prayer
to middle age. They watched the game,
or snored and dreamed of flying naked

through a storm of bills. When,
like a weighty oak, my father fell,

chopped down by a streak
of lightning through his chest,
when he went on living at the height

of an adjustable bed,
below a chart of pulse and respiration lines,
then I understood what it meant to be a man,
and land on your back in the shadow

of all your solitary strength,
listening to the masculine ticker tape of leaves
whisper judgmentally above you.
Weakness is so frightening. You speak
from the side of a sagging mouth,

hear a voice you never wanted to produce
ask for some small, despicable, important
thing—a flexible straw, a channel
change. I stared through the window,
across the institutional lawn,

seeking what to feel. Sparrows
darted to and from a single
emerald pine, a sort of bird motel.
Light purred into the grass. I tried
to see all men as brief

as birds—inhaling the powerful oxygen,
flying the lazy light, having their afternoon
as sort of millionaires,
then at evening, to reenter the collective shade
and shrink, remembering their size. When I looked

for my father, when my father finally
looked for me, it was impossible. We kept
our dignity. But when did I learn
to leave everyone behind? When did I get
as strong as my old man? Out of your strength,
you make a distance. Then you see,

and start to cross. You think
of what you want to say,
and you forget, deliberately.
Go back to the beginning. Think about it.
Take, if you like, all day.

Jonathan Holden ❖

The Wisdom Tooth

for Bill Strutz

In the days when it was still stupendous
to be a "millionaire," I thought money
was something you could fan
out all over the floor, like what we toted home
on Halloween, in shopping bags,
the salary that all us children got
for doing the only job we knew how to do—
going to school, addressing grownups in falsetto
solemnly, being cute. But when at last
alone, skipping the peanuts, the endless
jelly beans (useless as pennies),
skipping Mrs. Garrity's homemade cookies,
skipping even Ackerman's fresh apples,
we delved straight to the bottom of the bag,
scrounging for the jackpot, a candy bar.
Glittering in its star-spangled wrapper
like some early Christmas present from Las Vegas,
a Milky Way gave off a tiny halo, it seemed
to float above the floor, a minor
miracle. We craved only the most tawdry stuff,
junk so sweet its sugars
almost hurt your head to eat—
the very thing, my fourth-grade teacher, Mrs. Lee,
with a vinegar expression on her mouth,
promised us could rot the character
of Eagle Scouts, of even the whitest,
four-square Christian teeth.
The world beyond that window
(she made this clear) is booby-trapped.
There were little pills, she hissed,
that made a boy feel powerful, so good
that if you popped just one into your mouth
you wanted more and more, you couldn't stop.
And so, each week she trotted out

Most Recent Book: Against Paradise (University of Utah Press, 1990)

this trusty wisdom tooth she kept
in a glass of stale Pepsi, and we would peer
into the amber glass museum
where that lucky tooth basked in its corruption—
a tooth gone soft, its edges slurred with rust,
"Probably in pain," said Mrs. Lee.
And we would nod, solemnly,
and play along with her, dreaming
of someday being millionaires, of buying
all the Milky Ways and all the Mars Bars
and nougat-dripping, thick Forever Yours
we'd ever wanted, and dream
of the forbidden and delicious world,
about which Mrs. Lee would drop her voice
and speak in confidence to us,
of being corrupt.

Against Paradise

> *Is there no change of death in paradise?*
> —Wallace Stevens

The hounds that heralded the rich
would wake us up at six
on Sunday morning, hounds squandering
their cries, hounds begging
the very air for blood,
hounds poring over stones, zigzagging,
their avid noses thumbing
through the grasses, reading
our shabby field down by the swamp,
reading through our lawn,
an open library of appetites.
When, from cover in our rickety woods,
the fox hunters issued in a posse,
I'd pretend they were the British.
Outlaw in my pajamas, behind
the curtains, I'd draw my bead
on brokers, financiers, on girls
desexed in britches and strait coats,
on local names like Wheelwright, Miller,

Reeve, names with a quaint,
almost an ancient sound.

Miles from where they lived on higher ground,
like golfers or rare birds
errant in the rough,
they'd sit there, high
and in no hurry at all,
surveying our ramshackle little field
with its gnarled pear tree,
as if they were the owners
in their old costumes—redcoats
we could no longer recognize.
But later, when I'd mow the lawn,
not knowing any better,
I longed to give it the elegiac look
of their estates, thinned groves
arranged like furniture
within the neat ballroom of a field
where the grass, uniform and smooth
as indoor carpeting stretched wall-to-wall.

To show off your station (which is your name)
the grounds of your estate must be
conspicuously false and very trite—
the pond a polished tabletop "like glass,"
the trees "stately," the pastures
"rolling" and "idyllic," the bases
of the bushes drained of leaves,
the farthest line of trees a hazy backdrop
for some diorama where, in the foreground,
kittens "sport" by a picnic basket,
fawns "gambol." Your dog,
like those dignified, melancholy dogs
varnished on the backs of playing cards,
should have a pedigree. It should maintain
a solemn, philosophical expression
and be named "Rex" or "Rusty."

Sometimes, Sunday afternoons, a rich kid
named Bradley Wheelwright asked me
over to his home to play.
The house was stifling.
It was crepuscular all day.

Always, Bradley's parents would be out,
the curtains drawn on parlors
muffled as stuffed birds, where Bradley
or the maid, like museum guards, cautioned
nothing must be touched,
as we trespassed over carpets thick
enough to suffocate our steps, past walls
of massive, leather novels, past stilled
encyclopedias, under chandeliers
and up a back staircase
to the upper stories, to the only
messy room in the whole place,
where, dutifully, Brad dragged
his Electric Baseball out.

And suddenly I'd wish that I were home
practicing my curve
against the south side of the garage,
my threadbare tennis ball alive
in the dead air—the only terms I had
back then for something I half knew but
hadn't yet learned how to say,
something about how monuments go bad,
how all that wealth can do
is to magnify a banal appetite,
but how it hangs on anyway, inherently,
like a species—this pure desire
that the names of things stay fixed
while customary services go on,
that the same torpid statuary
remain sprawled around the pool
up at the country club (a pool bluer
than the sky, a pool like glass),
nymph, fawn, satyr wired
in their casual positions,
secured in paradise—that all those precious, old,
well-tended, not-especially-happy names
might be made fast
high on some wall as if alive,
perfectly composed in their huge frames.

Tumbleweed

> *Arms with hands grasping seek to clutch at the prows. Bodies thrown recklessly*
> *in the way are cut aside.*
>
> —William Carlos Williams

This morning the March wind is huge, and there are many of them
struggling across the fields, but they travel singly.
They do not know each other. Sometimes one, like a chicken
just beheaded, shudders in a spasm across the road,
gets caught on a bumper, and the car wears it for awhile
like a badge, though it stands for nothing, a poor man's jewelry,
a burr. A fat one, like the architecture
of a small cumulus cloud, hesitates in the right-hand lane,
makes its move. "Hit it!" my son urges. Wind buffets us.
We catch it flush, feel its shriveled limbs clutch
the bumper and, clinging, travel with us, its weightless anatomy
continuing in a new direction, perpendicular
to the rest of their southern migration
as we forge westward through it, casting guilty glances
north where more of them are bouncing in the distance, bouncing
in place, and we notice, closer, the barbed-wire hedge,
how they are plastered to it, stuck, clawing like insects
begging, determined to climb it and to cross
the highway. *Why did the chicken cross the road?* Tourists,
we stare out the window at fields, a roaring tundra
spread-eagled under the force of the sky, at the tumbleweed
endlessly bobbing toward us as if eager for something,
and feel a kind of pity for the dead, who are truly homeless,
at the way the body, when it's shed its soul
is physically driven on, regardless, a bristle of matter. Wind
leans on the car, and we wonder if we, ourselves, aren't
being buffetted across some frigid field as randomly
as these mops of tumbleweed snagged on the barbed-wire
perimeter, shivering there in a row, miles of prisoners
facing the moat they have to get across
as the gods sail by all day, at sixty miles an hour, free.

GARRETT HONGO ❖

The Legend

In Memory of Jay Kashiwamura

In Chicago, it is snowing softly
and a man has just done his wash for the week.
He steps into the twilight of early evening,
carrying a wrinkled shopping bag
full of neatly folded clothes,
and, for a moment, enjoys
the feel of warm laundry and crinkled paper,
flannellike against his gloveless hands.
There's a Rembrandt glow on his face,
a triangle of orange in the hollow of his cheek
as a last flash of sunset
blazes the storefronts and lit windows of the street.

He is Asian, Thai or Vietnamese,
and very skinny, dressed as one of the poor
in rumpled suit pants and a plaid mackinaw,
dingy and too large.
He negotiates the slick of ice
on the sidewalk by his car,
opens the Fairlane's back door,
leans to place the laundry in,
and turns, for an instant,
toward the flurry of footsteps
and cries of pedestrians
as a boy—that's all he was—
backs from the corner package store
shooting a pistol, firing it,
once, at the dumbfounded man
who falls forward,
grabbing at his chest.

A few sounds escape from his mouth,
a babbling no one understands
as people surround him
bewildered at his speech.
The noises he makes are nothing to them.

Most Recent Book: RIVER OF HEAVEN (Alfred A. Knopf, 1988)

The boy has gone, lost
in the light array of foot traffic
dappling the snow with fresh prints.
Tonight, I read about Descartes'
grand courage to doubt everything
except his own miraculous existence
and I feel so distinct
from the wounded man lying on the concrete
I am ashamed.

Let the night sky cover him as he dies.
Let the weaver girl cross the bridge of heaven
and take up his cold hands.

Four Chinatown Figures

In a back alley, on the cracked pavement slick with the strewn waste
of cooking oil and rotting cabbages, two lovers stroll arm in arm,
the woman in furs and a white lamé dress with matching pumps,
her escort in a tux casually worn—the black tie undone,
the double-breasted, brushed-velvet coat unbuttoned.
They're a Wilshire lawyer and city planner out on the town.
When they pass the familiar curio of the wishing well
with its Eight Immortals spouting aqueous wisdoms
through their copper mouths and baggy sleeves, they spend a minute
considering the impotent, green nozzle of its fountain.
The reflecting pool, speckled blue willow or streaked turquoise
as a robin's egg from the small litter of coins wintering on its bottom,
catches starlight and red neon in a tarn of winged ephemera
streaking across the black glaze of homely water. The lawyer
kisses his date and tosses some bus change, balls up
the foil wrapper from an after-dinner mint and throws that,
while she laughs, shaking her head back so the small,
mousse-stingered whips on the ringlets of her hair shudder
and dress sequins flash under the sore, yellow light of streetlamps.
Two dishwashers step from the back door of the Golden Eagle
arguing about pay, about hours, about trading green cards
with cousins for sex, setups with white women, for cigarettes
or a heated hotel room to sleep in on a dry, newspaper bed.
Bok-guai, they curse with their eyes, *Lo-fahn*, as the four nearly collide,
separate galaxies equal in surprise as they wheel to face each other.
The lawyer thinks little of these punks in T-shirts and Hong Kong jeans,

but the woman rhapsodizes, for no reason, in suspense/thriller prose—
slender and boylike, the bull's ring curl to their flimsy moustaches;
they must be cold in this dry, winter chill of late December in L.A.—
the sky a high velvet, indigo-to-black as it vaults, lazily,
from the city's fluorescent glow to the far azimuth
where the bear and huntsman drift casually into nothing.
Without jackets, the Chinese have bundled themselves in castoff,
cotton aprons stained with intricate patterns of lard and duck's blood
and wrapped like double-slings around their shoulders and folded arms.
Something grins on the face of the taller, fairer-complected one,
glints from his foxteeth, smolders in breathfog, camphor about to flare.
She tells herself, *Forget it, c'mon,* and, with a hooked finger,
snaps at the man's satin cummerbund. They turn away.
Without a gesture, in the greasy dark, the two Chonks turn away too,
back towards each other, and hear, quickening away behind them,
steps receding into the light din of street noise and sidewalk chatter.
The fair one says, audibly and in English, *Kiss me, white ghost,*
and, briefly staggered in the amniotic burst of light
from a passing tourist's flash, shrugs off his gruesome apron,
pulling out a pack of Gauloises, blue-wrapped, *especial,*
and strikes a match, holding it in the orange well of his hands
as, dragonlike, they both light up and puff, posed on a street vent,
hunching their thin shoulders and turning uptown against the wind.

The Underworld

Under the cone of flurried light
blued with cigarette smoke,
we sat in the false, morphined shade
of L.A.'s old Orpheum,
a once lavish Fox now gone to skinflicks,
horror fests and community matinees,
laughing at the silliness on-screen—
two comics, a black and a Jew,
both Afroed and dressed in chicken outfits,
trying to rob a suburban bank.
The black housewives around us
laughed too, nursing and cooing
at their infants who bawled
during the lulls and gunfight scenes,
shushing their older ones

who jounced in their seats, miming
the robot-dance or tossing popcorn, bored.
A few rows up from us was a stagpile
of the unemployed, bachelors in their twenties,
middle-aged fathers graying in cigar smoke,
all of them dressed in satins and polyesters
softly gleaming in the spill-light from the screen.
There was one in particular—a ghetto blade
in green velours—he wore a purple hat too,
and its feather, a peacock's unblinking eye,
bounced and darted, faintly luminous in the dark.
He cackled through the escape and arrest scenes,
calling out to his partners
phrases I couldn't quite make out,
then laughing and muttering deep *Yeahs*
in the rhythm of the talking around him.
I suppose they shared a thrill of recognition,
that old slap five and *I heard that*
from the street corner session,
but something passed among them,
a common pain or delight in, just once,
another's humiliation. It was Monday
or Thursday, and though no rain
was coming down in the streets
outside that I could see,
everybody seemed nonetheless well.
My friend talked about the opulence around us—
coal-black interior walls frescoed
with a chain of demons intertwined,
the stalled parade of aisle and exit lamps
(red grottoes, archipelagoes of colored light)
and plush chairs with their flower-carved fabric
and scalloped backs, the gabled balcony overhead—
everything so ornate and particularized,
designed on a theme of descent
into an irretrievable world—
summer afternoons of phosphates and cowboy serials,
or love made more than potential,
corporeal on-screen, a starlet's hair
undone and almost in your lap, *so real*
that the soul stirred in the body
like a river of cold light sliding
through a forest petrified in winter.

When we left, shuffling out behind
the small crowd lighting up their Kools,
almost embarrassed to be seen
in the harsh house lights, everyone went quiet
from the dissonance of our being there.

We stepped outside to the chill blast
of the low desert turning to fall,
city buses hissing and squeaking by,
slurs of Spanish and disco and rap,
a cop's traffic whistle, a street vendor's call,
the day's last, feeble light
streaked in the eyes, fuzzy Giotto halos
like the stiff, polyester hats
on the shimmering, mingled throngs of the poor.

MARIE HOWE ❖

The Split

I.

She'd start the fires under the bed.
I'd put them out.

She'd take the broom stick and rape all the little girls.
I'd pull them aside, stroke their cheeks, and comfort them.
—How they would cry.

Brit would fight the German soldiers.
She'd crouch by the banister waiting for them
when I was too scared.

And sometimes, she would push me farther into the back woods than I
        wanted to go.
But I was glad she did.

She was mean and she liked it.

She'd take off her clothes and dance in front of the mirror
and she'd say things and she'd swear.

Most Recent Book: THE GOOD THIEF (Persea, 1988)

She'd laugh at the crucifix, turn him upside down and watch him hang.
And she'd unhinge that piece of metal cloth between his legs
and run when she heard somebody coming
leaving me.

Mean as she was, I miss her.

Only twice have I heard her laugh since then.
Once, lying on my back in a yellow field,
I heard something like me in the back of my head
but it was Brit,

and just now, making love with you, it's hard to tell you
but I heard her laugh.

2.

It began as a fear.
There was something, not me, in the room.

And translated into a dumbfounding
forgetfulness

that stopped me on the street
puzzling

over what year it was, what month.

I began to watch my feet carefully.
Nevertheless, I suffered
accidents.

The bread knife sliced my thumb
repeatedly

the water glass shattered on the kitchen floor
and in its breaking there was a low laugh.

Looking up, I saw no one

but felt the old cat stretch inside me
feigning indifference.

Marie, I'd hear in a crowd, *Marie*
the air so thick with ghosts it was hard
breathing.

One afternoon, the trucks were humming like vacuum cleaners
in the rain.

It was impossibly lonely,
No one but me there.

I called out Brit, the city is burning,
Brit, the soldiers are coming

and she laughed so sudden and loud I turned
and saw her for one second

all insolent grace, pretending
she wasn't loving me.

Without Devotion

Cut loose, without devotion, a man becomes a comic.
His antics are passed

around the family table and mimicked so well, years
later the family still laughs.

Without devotion, any life becomes a stranger's story
told and told again to help another sleep

or live. And it is possible
in the murmuring din of that collective loyalty

for the body to forget what it once loved.
A mouth on the mouth becomes a story mouth.

It's what they think *they* knew—what the body knew
alone, better than it ever knew anything.

Without devotion, his every gesture—
how he slouched in the family pantry, his fingers

curled into a fist, the small thing he said
while waiting for water to boil—

becomes potentially hilarious. Lucky for him
the body, sometimes, refuses translation,

that often it will speak, secretly,
in its own voice, and insist, haplessly,

on its acquired tastes. Without devotion, it might
stand among them and listen, laughing,

but look, how the body clenches,
as the much discussed smoke intermittently clears.

It has remembered the man standing, wearing
his winter coat.

Watch how it tears from the table, yapping, ferocious
in its stupid inarticulate joy.

Part of Eve's Discussion

It was like the moment when a bird decides not to eat from your hand,
and flies, just before it flies, the moment the rivers seem to still
and stop because a storm is coming, but there is no storm, as when
a hundred starlings lift and bank together before they wheel and drop,
very much like the moment, driving on bad ice, when it occurs to you
your car could spin, just before it slowly begins to spin, like
the moment just before you forgot what it was you were about to say,
it was like that, and after that, it was still like that, only
all the time.

Death, the Last Visit

Hearing a low growl in your throat, you'll know that it's started.
It has nothing to ask you. It has only something to say, and
it will speak in your own tongue.

Locking its arm around you, it will hold you as long as you ever wanted.
Only this time it will be long enough. It will not let go.
Burying your face in its dark shoulder, you'll smell mud
        and hair and water.

You'll taste your mother's sour nipple, your favorite salty cock
and swallow a word you thought you'd spit out once and be done with.
Through half-closed eyes you'll see that its shadow looks like yours,

a perfect fit. You could weep with gratefulness. It will take you
as you like it best, hard and fast as a slap across your face,
or so sweet and slow you'll scream give it to me give it to me until it
        does.

Nothing will ever reach this deep. Nothing will ever clench this hard.
At last (the little girls are clapping, shouting) someone has pulled
the drawstring of your gym bag closed enough and tight. At last

someone has knotted the lace of your shoe so it won't ever come undone.
Even as you turn into it, even as you begin to feel yourself stop,
you'll whistle with amazement between your residual teeth oh jesus

oh sweetheart, oh holy mother, nothing nothing nothing ever felt this
    good.

LYNDA HULL ❖

Love Song During Riot with Many Voices

Newark, 1967

The bridge's iron mesh chases pockets of shadow
and pale through blinds shuttering the corner window

to mark this man, this woman, the young eclipse
their naked bodies make—black, white, white,
black, the dying fall of light rendering bare walls

incarnadine, color of flesh and blood occluded

in voices rippling from the radio: Saigon besieged,
Hanoi, snipers and the riot news helicoptered
from blocks away. All long muscle, soft

hollow, crook of elbow bent sequinned above the crowd,
nightclub dancers farandole their grind and slam
into streets among the looters. Let's forget the 58¢

lining his pockets, forget the sharks and junkyards
within us. Traffic stalls to bricks shattering,
the windows, inside her, bitch I love you, city breaking
down and pawnshops disgorge their contraband of saxophones

and wedding rings. Give me a wig, give me
a pistol. Hush baby, come to papa, let me hold you

through night's broken circuitry, chromatic
and strafed blue with current. Let's forget this bolt
of velvet fallen from a child's arm brocading

pavement where rioters careen in furs and feathered hats
burdened with fans, the Polish butcher's strings

Most Recent Book: STAR LEDGER (University of Iowa Press, 1991)

of sausages, fat hams. This isn't a lullaby a parent
might croon to children before sleep, but all of it
belongs: in the station torn advertisements whisper
easy credit, old men wait for any train out of town

and these lovers mingling, commingling their bodies,
this slippage, a haul and wail of freight trains

pulling away from the yards. With this girl
I'll recall black boys by the soda shop, other times
with conked pompadours and scalloped afterburns
stenciled across fenders. Through the radio

Hendrix butanes his guitar to varnish, crackle
and discord of "Wild Thing." Sizzling strings,
that Caravaggio face bent to ask the crowd

did they want to see him sacrifice something
he loved. Thigh, mouth, breast, small of back, dear
hollow of the throat, don't you understand this pressure

of hotbox apartments? There's no forgetting the riot
within, fingernails sparking to districts
rivering with flame. What else could we do

but cling and whisper together as children after
the lullaby is done, but no, never as children, never

do they so implore, oh god, god, bend your dark visage

over this acetelyne skyline, over Club Zanzibar
and The Best of Three, limed statues in the parks, over
the black schoolgirl whose face is smashed again

and again. No journalist for these aisles of light
the cathedral spots cast through teargas and the mingling,
commingling of sisters' voices in chapels, storefront
churches asking for mercy. Beyond the bridge's

iron mesh, the girl touches a birthmark
behind her knee and wishes the doused smell
of charred buildings was only hydrants flushing hot concrete.

Summertime. Pockets of shadow and pale. Too hot
to sleep. Hush baby, come to papa, board
the window before morning's fractured descant,

a stacatto crack of fire-escapes snapping pavement
and citizens descending, turning back with points of flame

within their eyes before they too must look away.
At dawn, the first busses leave, their great wipers arc
like women bending through smoke

to burdens, singing terror, singing pity.

Frugal Repasts

After the ribboning fever of interstate, after freight yards
& tinsel towns, through the cranked-up mojo of radio signals,
through the moteled drift of nonsleep, comes the arms crossed

over the chest, the mind's blind odometer clicking backwards,
comes sifting over years the musk of those opened crates spilling

into that room, the abandoned building. Just me & him. Comes
the torn Army jacket & Detroit voice, dusky, the sweat-grayed
T-shirt. A cup of snow-water melted on the ledge. No light—

simply candles pooled in wax across the floor, nothing more, but
those crates of rose crystal, hot out the backdoor of some swank shop.

While shadows flickered bare lathes, while he spasmed
the strung-out toss of too much hunger, too long, I set out
the beautiful *idea* of feast. Rose crystal plates & saucers

lined the mattress's thin margin of floor, guttering flames,
those teacup rims. Just me & him, that nameless jacket,

olive drab. I wanted to catch the cries, the ragged breath, how
we used to say come the revolution we'd survive anything, anything,
& condemned to that frugal repast we were, somehow, free.

Snow-water melted in the cup rinsed his forehead, that pure
juncture of clavicle & shoulder. Better this immersion

than to live untouched. I wanted to be the cup & flame,
I wanted to be the cure, the hand that held the river back
that would break us, as in time, we broke each other. Wait.

Not yet. While great news presses crashed over next day's
headlines, while alley cats stalled beyond the wrenched police-lock

in a frieze of ferocious longing, his arms clenched the flawless
ache of thigh, damp curls. No clinic till break of day to break
the stream of fever I rocked with him toward the story I told

as a girl: the perfect city, luminous in the back of the radio,
jazz turned down so low it ghosted improvisations that let me fly

immune above skyscrapers, the endless gleaming arguments
of streets. I set out the platter, a delicate tureen & then
we *were* spark & fever, all frequencies tuned until

that piss-poor stinking room seemed shouldered through torn skyline.
Through spark & fever, shouldered beyond the folly of others

set adrift: the room of the girl who bends to gas-flame deciding
coffee or suicide, beyond Roxbury's Emperor of Byzantium
alone on his Murphy-bed throne, tinfoil minarets & domes.

Condemned & oddly free, my hand following his ribs' dark curve,
the ridge of muscle there & there. James, what's the use?

After the broken arpeggios of all these years, comes this waking,
this stooping to the gas-flame, comes the learning & relearning
through the long open moan of highway going on towards

a stream of crimson lifting away from the horizon. I wanted to
be the hand that held back the river, destiny. Comes this new day

cruelly, unspeakably rich, as that drenched grisaille of morning
came pouring then over blackened wicks, over all that crystal
fired empty & clean. Better this immersion than to live untouched.

Shore Leave

She wears the sailor suit—a blouse with anchors,
skirt puffed in stiff tiers above her thin
knees, those spit-shined party shoes. Behind her
a Cadillac's fabulous fins gleam and reflected
in the showroom window, her father's a mirage.
The camera blocks his face as he frames
a shot that freezes her serious grin,
the splendid awkwardness of almost-adolescence.
He's all charm with the car dealer and fast-talks
them a test-drive in a convertible like the one
on display, a two-tone Coupe de Ville. But once
around the corner he lowers the top and soon
they're fishtailing down dump-truck paths,
the Jersey Meadows smoldering with trash fires.
He's shouting *Maybelline why can't you be true,*

and seagulls lift in a tattered curtain across
Manhattan's hazy skyline. Dust-yellow clouds
behind him, he's handsome as a matinee idol,
wavy hair blown straight by sheer velocity.
Tall marshweeds bend, radiant as her heart's
relentless tide. They rip past gaping Frigidaires,
rusted hulks of cranes abandoned to the weather.
Her father teases her she's getting so pretty
he'll have to jump ship sometime and take her
on a real whirl, maybe paint the whole town red.
For her *merchant marine* conjures names like
condiments—Malabar, Marseilles—places where
the laws of gravity don't hold. She can't believe
her father's breakneck luck will ever run out.
He accelerates and spins out as if the next thrill
will break through to some more durable joy.
So she stands, hands atop the windshield and shouts
the chorus with him, and later when they drop the car
he takes her to a cocktail bar and plays Chuck Berry
on the juke box. She perches on a bar stool and twirls
her Shirley Temple's paper umbrella, watches
the slick vinyl disks stack up, rhythms collecting,
breaking like surf as her father asks the barmaid
to dance with him through "Blue Moon," then foamy
glass after glass of beer. The barmaid's sinuous
in red taffeta, a rhinestone choker around
her throat. Her father's forgotten her and dances
a slow, slow tango in the empty bar and the dark
comes on like the tiny black rose on the barmaid's
shoulder rippling under her father's hand.
The girl thinks someday she'll cover her skin
with roses, then spins, dizzy on the bar stool.
She doesn't hear the woman call her foolish
mortal father a two-bit trick because she's whirling
until the room's a band of light continuous
with the light the city's glittering showrooms throw
all night long over the sleek, impossible cars.

TERRY HUMMER ❖

Austerity in Vermont

Astral blue of old mountains, ridge after rising ridge
Blurring the western horizon just after the sun goes down,
And there, up five degrees, the cold yellow evening star
My almanac says will be Saturn this month, the bastard god nobody
Wants for a father—not much light, but it's all Vermont conceives
Now that September's come and I feel like losing weight.
What is this voice I hear that tells me *Less flesh?*
Where does it go, the meat of the belly, when I stop
Drinking beer and run my groaning mile a day
Into the Yankee wind that articulates a whole
Future of frost in the darkening perpendiculars of maples?
All flesh has a fate, sure enough, though it's clear no body believes
This moment's horoscope, Saturn in the sixth house descending,
Pissed-off cannibal planet of constipation and infanticide—
But what can you do if you're being born right now
In a ward in Burlington? They're about to cut the cord
Just as that point of luminescence the color of urine on snow
Crowns at the lip of the sky's birth canal. Will you scream
At the doctor to wait just five minutes more with his surgical steel—
Hold on, get back until that terrible light tips over the edge
And dissolves into somebody else's birthday? But look,
It's too late, there's a snip and you're bleeding, your flesh
And your mother's are suddenly lives apart,
And there you lie, naked in that planet's damning radiation.
That's how destiny works—you'll never be a stockbroker,
You'll have five kids of your own, you'll live on a farm in Vermont
Rolling stones up a hill for years until one afternoon you come home
And open fire with your old shotgun on everybody in sight.
Right at the moment, gasping for air, I'm trying to remember
How it felt with the doctor shagged me loose from the rope of blood
That strained me down toward the good sleep of the placenta,
And I was myself apart, zapped from a dozen angles
By all the essences of my future—Mercury, Venus, Mars,
The whole merciless pantheon of necessary acts
That impressed themselves in my blue flesh turning red
With its own bloody weight. And look at me now,

Most Recent Book: THE 18,000-TON OLYMPIC DREAM (William Morrow, 1990)

Out on a road in Vermont at sunset, running, trying to choose
To make the bulge in my belly disappear the way my mother's did
After the lying-in, after the labor, after the voice
In the anesthetic stopped its mindless song, and some stranger
Lay there beside her with a body already growing
   Ascetic, unbelieving, refusing her, demanding nothing not its own.

Mississippi 1955 Confessional

It would have been, I think, summer—it would have been August, I think,
Somewhere near midway between solstice and equinox,
When the tractors move all daylight in mirages of their own thrown dust
And the farmhands come in the back gate at noon, empty,
   with jars in their hands.
Imagine yourself a child with a fever, half delirious all that month,
And your sisters lift you in your white wooden chair, carry you to the edge
Of a hayfield, set you down in hedgerow shade and leave you
While they go into woods to turn, you think, into swans—
They are so lovely, your sisters, in their white sundresses
That appear and disappear all afternoon among the dark trunks of trees.
None of this ever happened. But remember the body-heat of the wind
As it came from behind the tenant shack just there on the eastern border
Of your vision to touch you with its loving nigger hand? And there you are,
A white boy brought up believing the wind isn't even human,
   the wind is happy
To live in its one wooden room with only newspaper on the walls
To keep out what this metaphor won't let me call the wind—
But don't worry about that, your sisters in the woods are gathering
Beautiful fruit, you can hear it falling into their hands,
And the big pistons of the tractors drive thunderously home into cylinders
Steel-bright as the future. You are five years old. What do you know?
Your fever is a European delicacy, it burns in your flesh like fate,
A sign from God, cynosure, mortmain, the intricate working out
Of history in the life of the chosen. O listen, white boy, the wind
Has a mythic question only you can answer: *If all men were brothers,*
Would you want your sister to marry one? Let me tell you, white boy, the wind
Is in the woods with its cornmeal and its black iron skillet,
It's playing its blues harp in the poison oak where your youngest sister,
The one with hair so blonde you think it looks like a halo of rain,
Is about to take off her dress. You sit there dreaming your mild fever dream.
You tap your foot to the haybaler's squared rhythms.
   They've dressed you in linen.

From the woods where your sisters lie suddenly down, you burn, snow-white.
I've seen your face. I remember your name. I prophesy something
        you can't imagine
Is coming to kiss you. And you thought I was reaching back to you in words
To tell you something beautiful, like *wind*.

A Heart Attack in the Country

Something is shattering high in the frozen
Twilight pines. It makes a weightless rattling
Like layers of isinglass in the window
Of an antique woodstove, brittle with years
Of inward flaming, finally letting go.
The postcard vistas of Vermont collapse
With the icy weight of this moon's condensation,
This circumscribed sky's breaking down its old
Familiar persona with murderous transparency,
Arcing toward blackness and the poisonous
Chromates of starlight. In the valley
That disappeared half an hour ago
Under the shadow of a minor mountain,
The coroner's house radiates its porchlight.
Twenty miles northwest, in Burlington,
Post-rush-hour headlights constellate
The street in front of the shabby red-brick
County morgue where he left the body
Half dismantled at quitting time. Nights like this
There's a border in the air nobody can see
Where the inner and outer bleed into each other
Painlessly: What death by drowning ought to be
But probably isn't. Who knows? It's just
One more landscape when you go down,
Just one more expanse of one damned thing
Next to another. But this steady sound
High in the growing blindness of the air
Is a tinnitus like the detonation
Of nitroglycerine in the blood,
A scraping of ice against ice.
The woman turned herself inside out for him.
Caucasian female, he wrote on the chart, *sixty-five*.
Scalpels for the belly-flesh, a small bright saw
For the sternum: A layman can hardly imagine

The sounds in an insulated room
When the doors of the body open.
In that interior space, a textbook order appears:
Contour of stomach, liver, spleen, one lung
Laid next to another. All these things remain
Defined as long as the darkness holds
Everything up on the curve of its surface tension,
Keeps clear the veins and meridians
Of this night, still glazed with the afternoon's
Freezing rain. Pines arrange themselves in icy
Starlight outside the room where the woodstove glows,
Where the man stares down at his sterile hands
As they lay out the cutlery, the plates.
Cause of death, he wrote: *Congestive heart failure,
Massive*. Sleet rattled on the windows
Of the morgue all afternoon. He cut
The ruptured heart loose, raised it like a newborn
Into the artificial whiteness of surgical arclight.
Buy coal, he wrote at five o'clock, as February twilight
Made its professional incision in the tissue
Of clouds, and the mercury went down. Tomorrow,
He knows, the body will be the same, all cause
And consequence, a naked arrangement
Of temporary questions. Here, over his honed roofbeam,
Over the driveway where his car is parked,
Over the aureole of the mountain, the arbitrary track
Of a meteor slits the sky between the breasts from groin to throat.
What sound does it make, cutting through
That elevated breathlessness? Such silence is specialized
Knowledge a layman can hardly imagine, no matter
How the evening sky sharpens its clarities.

Spring Comes to Mid-Ohio in a Holy Shower of Stars

On the clearest night of the earliest spring of my life,
An Easter Sunday, come in March by the luck of the draw,
I saw a streak of light in the sky like the middle finger of God,
But it did not come down on me. It was the brightness
William James heard about
      from a housewife-turned-saintly-spiritualist
That she said she always saw when the dead were about to touch her

In that certain way the dead have. I saw it effloresce and vanish.
Standing there on the road next to the blacked-out body of an oak,
I wanted to trance myself into the past, to get in touch
With the ectoplasmic other side.
                                    I wanted some strangeness to speak
Out of the unpragmatic crystal ball of my larynx and name itself,
In the timbre I whisper to lovers in, my life. But then another
Finger gestured godlike halfway down from the zenith, another, another,
And the sky burned with the print of a whole left hand.
That's the way the past works:
                                    brilliance, and a slap in the face.
Years later, in winter, when the rusted iron wheels
Of snowplows gave their spiritual groans in the heat-dead midnight
      streets,
I would dream God's immaculate body could suddenly be struck
With a human palm the color of fever, and darken, and die.
But that night in mid-Ohio,
                            I knew what the housewife knew
When James sat in her dingy seance parlor with his notebook clumsy on
      his knee:
That nothing you ever dreamed of saying comes of its own free will.
It has to be beaten out of you, word by impossible word, until the dead
Spread themselves in your flesh like March dogwood spreads through the
      dark,
And you speak,
                  and a stranger writes everything down.

CYNTHIA HUNTINGTON ❖

Rhapsody

Beat it with a shoe
because it can't talk, because it won't shut up,
because it makes those noises about its loneliness
endlessly. Beat it with a shoe
over and over, beside the door, on the balcony;
beat it because it's yours,
because you've had enough. Beat that shoe
your foot's orphan, like a leather club

Most Recent Book: THE FISH WIFE (University of Hawaii, 1985)

against its side, around its head, with short sharp blows.
Beat it to make it stop crying.
Show you mean business.
Because it's dumb, because you told it once
or a thousand times; beat it because it ought to know
better by now. Beat it with a shoe
because it feels good—
beat it *until* it feels good.
Beat the crap out of it. Beat it senseless. Beat it
within an inch. Because it's worthless and dumb,
shitty, and loud, and dirty.
Beat it because there is pain in the world.
Beat it because it's yours.

The Hackeysack Players

Try to see them as Monet would,
alive in the shadows of open doors,
beside the spare architecture of bicycles
thrown down on the pavement:
the four tall youths by the open garages,
standing, or half-lifted from the ground,
balanced midway in motion. See the pink
just under their skins, loose waistbands
of cropped blue jeans, bare backs twisted
with vigor of the kick-up, the turn
to the side, happy and concentrated.
Include, off to the side, the girl in the bikini
face up to the sun on a blanket, her nose
skyward, balancing her interest and her
distance from the game. And the mother
on the upstairs porch, leaning over
to call to her boy, held there
in the game that repeats itself into
the afternoon. Compose,
in this version or view of things,
something to show the radios blasting the air,
maybe a preoccupation in the players' pose,
a cocked head, an air of listening and
not listening, of being under the music. See first
the flesh colors—bare chests and legs and arms—
then the clothes' fullness covering

the bodies' mass, their density,
but also their liveliness, knowing
it is their hour to be alive. This Monet saw
and kept his seeing, seeing it go by,
a movement they cannot feel now,
being entirely inside it.
See how the flesh is a permeable boundary,
blood flushing up through the skin,
lighting the muscles' sculpture, or how
the dark a boy moves into to retrieve
the sack kicked under the car set up on blocks
throws the heaviness of old use over him,
as they fade together against the grey stretch of asphalt.
See what the sunlight is doing, how it loves the actual,
blessing these loud boys caught
in our vision, distracted and unaware
of time, not realizing the day
is brief, or that it is endless,
with no terror in the light moving over
their bodies and down the side of the world. Try
to see without criticizing
the junk in the driveway, the dead brown
of garage rows no light can waken, the game
dragging on for hours
as they kick the leather pouch angrily
and gaze off down the alley and down the street
with unfocused eyes. See only perfection:
this only-once in which we breathe
and give off heat, and touch
the earth with shadows. The joy of substance,
as Monet would see it, alive,
able to see because he has stepped away
from them, as every observer must stand
beyond that boundary to notice,
or even think something like: "The sun is warm
on the bodies of the young men, on the first day
of summer, on a Sunday."
Try not to think of the viewer as standing
on the other side. Try not to see
the emptiness behind the shadows
the boys make when they move. How cold
it must be inside those shadows, how endless
it is inside their minds,
these boys who will not be men,

playing a loud and tired game on Sunday,
under a colored sun
in this century, on this street,
in the afternoon that touches
infinity. The utter length of it,
the distance they look into
without markers. A vacancy and scope
humans no longer fill, or even inhabit.

Breaking

The holy light of loneliness
shines within a single cell, lit up
across the alley tonight, in the block-long
grid of apartments and hallways
and garage doors. A boy, sixteen,
has hung a bedspread across the span
of the single garage, and placed
a red bulb in the ceiling fixture.
Music resounds against
concrete; the walls send back chords,
increasing force. The sound crashes
against limits, grows huge and
slams the air. In the hot night,
in a room without windows,
he rides a three-foot board
and throws himself forward on wood
and rubber wheels, to perfect
a mastery, a somersault
in air that will return him
to earth still flying. He breaks
his flight against the wall,
and falls and retreats, and returns.
In dimensions of twelve by eighteen,
in the cave of his faith, hot
and red, with strange music
for food, he tests
his soul and slams his body,
his bone-jutting fragile boy's shoulders,
down hard on the concrete, and rising does not
weep, or even hesitate, again.

Party

You and I, darling, here in the dark
rooms with the ghostly furniture
at one in the morning, after the baby's fever has broken,
his crying gone into a waveless pink sleep.
And the party downstairs has hired a stripper.
Thump through the walls of the bass
drive she thumps to and yelp of men's voices urging
Do it baby, baby, yes, and we sit in separate chairs,
too tired to turn on the lights.

In the windows' glow I see you drinking
from a water glass with absolute care,
slowly, opening your mouth wide as if the liquid were dense,
heavy, and you needed to make room for it.
Wet crib sheets are knotted in the hall;
in the kitchen a stack of ice trays and spoons,
a red clot of medicine hardening in each silver curve.
The floor rises and falls beneath us; we hear doors slam and cars
circling the block.

They turn the music louder and beat
their shoes on the floor and yell. Then the squeal
of tires in oil slick ecstasy rounding a corner
on two wheels and a blast: it's a party,
a party, and downstairs she's a hit,
a specialist, a hooter with tricks and everything shaking.
You have gone to the bedroom to lie still and curse the ceiling.
I'm here in my red robe,
a milk spill hardening on the sleeve.
I rub it absently and pick the nap,
then take it off and hold it against me
like a very thin lover. The floor moves;
the walls contract and expand to the weight
and pressure of desire. I hear the men scream
at each other how much they like it.
Whistling and pounding their feet. Just to *see* a girl do it.
Something about how she could pick up a dime.
The party is happy, except for the three young men
outside on the curb
who say they would rather, for the money,
have seen the donkey show in Tijuana.

We saw the donkey movie once, Ass Flicks, in Amsterdam
three years ago as tourists excited by dark freedoms,
sex for sale. The street excited us
with its promise of safe evil
but we laughed at the movie, it was so bad.
Later though I wondered what happened to the woman
to make her do that, and you thought you knew
and told me, and we walked out in another mood,
gentled, separate from expectation, seeing
the way everyone wanting something looks from one side
of a window or the other, and some can buy
and some need to sell; the world and all of us
colluding in this market of desire, souls
kissing rings, and buying horsepower and fire-power,
buying power, and guns and milk.
So the women lit up in the windows
seemed just like us, their poses
like purgatorial moments, their lives connected
to us right then, like us, making do in this time.

It seemed we were all suffering and getting better for it
together in separate windows, so our lovemaking that night
was tender and grave, and seemed to belong to everyone, to be
something done for the world, a feeling
I could not call back by morning, or even quite believe again.
Your gracile body was long and cool
on the clean sheets of the huge hotel bed;
in sunlight we turned to find each other.
There was only us then, just us there,
and I closed my eyes and fell back into it,
and there was only me.

RICHARD JACKSON ❖

Homeric

She just hauls out and smacks him
on the side of the head which sends him reeling
against the plate window of the Krystal

Most Recent Book: WORLDS APART (University of Alabama Press, 1987)

hamburger shop while the old couple inside,
she in the print dress, he in the light orange
polyester suit, just watch because they've seen this
a hundred times, maybe a thousand, and there's never
any reason to speak of, so that the boy just
straightens up, lowers his head, and walks
behind his mother. The old folks are there because
the Krystal hamburgers are steamed and soft
to their gums, and me because my new root canal
won't take too much pressure yet, and the mother
and son because there's not a hell of a lot to do in
Chattanooga, the Bible Belt, on a hot June morning, 1989.
There are a couple of choices:—you can walk away,
letting the scene continue for generations and make, if you
know words, obscene art from someone else's pain;
you can abduct the kid in a dramatic rescue, which will
add to your pain and his; you can lecture the mother
in which case she'll take it out on the boy; or maybe
slap her silly, which is what I would have done
thirty years earlier, the year I discovered Homer's
rosey fingered dawn, as preached by Sister Michael,
was really the bloody one Hector, Ajax and the others
made for themselves, and the one I knew then
on Lawrence and Haverhill streets,—the chains,
the black taped flashlights, the kick boxers,
the knuckles, the whisper of zip guns,—the year I had
enough of it from Charlie Pilch and his brother, and
so pushed them against the chain link fence, amazed
as they were at how fast my fists were hitting them
until they fell bloody beneath me, no Homeric dawn,
no heroic fight, and then ran home to get sick
for my own stupid cruelty. I don't know how
I escaped that world where you were either lucky
or nearly dead, where we drank Hollihan's ale
behind the brewery when the night shift sold us
illegal, and we argued how we should have joined
the Hungarians throwing bottles of gasoline at Russian
tanks, not for nobility of freedom, but because that was
the way, how we should have dropped the bomb,
beat it out of any one who said we couldn't. I don't
know if the world I've entered is much better
because I'm clenching my fists inside my jeans,
biting so hard it's only my foolish and rootless
tooth that warns me back from the woman,

and I have looked over the rough idea of the world
this has become, the endless cars making their way
down Brainerd Road with their own gritted angers
to face, the polyester man snapping at is wife,
the hot sun which is just another star angry with itself,
the street preacher who's taken up his cross
with its bloodied spots for wrists and ankles, not
even him, none of them even noticing that boy
who has already walked off the world of poems,
who may or may not be lucky enough to escape
this or that world, drive his car, some used junk,
out to the levee or dam, look back over the city
lights that are okay even if they are not the tent lights
of the noble Greeks on the plains of Troy,
where he will remember from that safe distance,
like some Achilles still brooding over a small loss,
how his life, too, almost came to an end
on several occasions, some worth it, some not.

A Violation

Whatever they said, those ten foot lips pouting across
the screen at the Den Rock Park Drive-In, and they were
glistening with the light rain falling on some Balkan city,
my father was prepared to be earnestly embarrassed that night
he took three of us friends to see John Wayne in *Horse Soldiers*
and had to wait for this romance to be over. I was afraid we could
walk up to the screen like little cameras zooming in to see
the pores, the pimples, the ugly mole hair I had read Swift's
Gulliver describe, and which so violated my sense of romance.
But we were supposed to hate it, we were supposed to head
to the concession stand for Cokes. Instead, we crouched
behind an old Rambler where we thought we wanted to be touched
by anyone, by the lovers silhouetted in those lips. It was
Arthur who snapped the picture with his pocket Brownie,
and it was Eddie who turned away for some pain we couldn't see,
not for the woman on the screen, though whatever love
or life she was pleading, she spent those last few frames
wandering the streets from one doorway to another
after refusing someone's love, until her life was lost among
the subliminal messages of the intermission ads. It would be

years before I thought of her again, in front of a perfect madonna
painted by Bellini, her small, sensual mouth bringing me back
to that same hopeless love, and once in front of a Balkan gypsy
I was photographing in a world I still thought was all romance.
It was romance I wanted us to be dreaming that night.
But it was two years before we learned the truth, how earlier
that summer Eddie had been found standing beneath a signal maple,
his jeans and underwear pulled down to his ankles, his tiny
sex bruised and red, his thighs raw from someone's switch—
he never said who—shivering probably as much as he did
that night at the drive-in we teased him to tears he couldn't stop.
I can't stop remembering him now. I remember this:
someone had taken pictures. Someone had left the yellow
film boxes scattered around his feet. He must have closed
his eyes. He must have stood there in his own dark, imagining
we would swarm over the ridge the way those horse soldiers might.
It was only today I remembered all this. I was standing
in a small church near Trieste where there still hangs a picture
of Mussolini peering from shadows the way Eddie's attacker must have,
peering at the shawled women who hobble up the aisle to the altar
to light a votive candle, to kiss the wounds, the feet of the crucifix,
trying to find forgiveness for the love they refused or denied,
il Duce violating their prayers, invading their dreams.
Everyone's, that is, except the photographer, blind since youth,
and his wife,—except those two beside me, taking pictures,
he said, of our sounds, the hush of our shame, *the Mussolinis
of each cruel act*, he whispered, seeing not things but the echoes
between things, what they had been or what they might become,
our secret fears, our dreams of romance—that was it—he was
taking pictures of our dreams, more than we could ever imagine
at the Den Rock Drive-In, what with all our blown up images
and that shattered life before us, Eddie Trainor, who in a few years
refused to see anything, trying to move his lips to speak,
motioning us away, the same motion that gypsy woman made,
a kind of madonna herself, trying to stop me from taking her
picture, her soul, and the souls of her two young children,
the girl hugging her thigh where they sat on the curbing, the boy,
Eddie's age, starting to work the evening tourist crowd,
for this too was a kind of rape, as so much has become—
what my father could not stop, holding Eddie in his arms,
for the love of life, he would cry, not knowing the story either,
the horse soldiers charging, the Mussolinis shouting, the madonna
weeping, her lips moving, her lips closing, the shutter not quitting.

The Angels of 1912 and 1972

It is a long time since I flapped my wings,
a long time since I stood on the roof of my house
in Lawrence, Mass., or Michael's in No. Andover,
a little whiskey in one hand, the past slipping
through the other, a little closer to the heaven
of dreams, letting the autumn wind, or the spring
wind, or maybe just the invisible breath of some
woman lift me up. It is a long time since I have flown
like a swallow, or even the clumsy pigeon, into another
time, practicing miracles, dodging the branches
of lost dreams that cut against the sky,
and the rocks thrown by small boys, finding
the right nest under the eaves of some pastoral age
even the poets have forgotten, or fluttering
to a slow landing on some ledge above the buses
and simple walkers of this world. It is a long time.
From where we stood I could see the steeple of the French
church. Further back, it was 1912, and I could almost
see the tenements of the French women who worked
the fabric mills, weaving the huge bolts of cloth,
weaving the deadly dust into their lungs.
They could hardly fly, these angels. I could
almost see them marching down Essex Street and
Canal Street to the Everett mills, the Essex mills,
pushing against the police horses for two bitter years,
thousands of them, asking for bread and roses, asking
something for the body, something for the soul.
If I did not fly so far I could see my mother's father,
years later, stumble to the same mills, nothing gained.
Or I could have looked ahead to this very year, and seen
Bob Houston and I standing on a roof in Bisbee, Arizona,
two desert sparrows flying blind against the night
once again, remembering the union workers herded
into boxcars and shipped from there into the desert
a few years after my French weavers flew down
Essex Street. But it was 1972 and we still believed
we could stop the war with a rose, as if there were
only one war and not the dozens of little ones
with their nameless corpses scattered like pine cones.
It was 1972 and we stood on the roof like two angels
lamenting the news that John Berryman had leaned out

over the Washington Avenue bridge in Minneapolis,
flapped his broken wings, dropped to the banks below him.
I am a nuisance, he wrote, unable to find a rose for his soul.
We thought we could stand on that roof in 1972, two
Mercuries waiting to deliver his message to another time.
I should have seen what would happen. I should have seen
my own friend on his bridge, or the woman who could have
descended from one of those French weavers leaning
on the railing of the north canal in Lawrence because
all hope had flown away, or my own father starting
to forget my name that same year. If there is anything
I remember now, it is the way he looked at me in his
last year, wondering who I was, leaning back against
his own crushed wings, just a few years after he told me
to fight the draft, to take flight, or maybe he leaned
as if there was a word no one would ever speak
but which he knew I would believe in, that single word
I have been trying to say ever since, that means
whatever dream we are headed towards, for these
were the angels of 1912 and 1972, the ones we still
live with today, and when you love them, these swallows,
these desert sparrows, when you remember the lost fathers,
the soldiers, when you remember the poets and weavers,
when you bring your own love, the bread, the roses—this is flying.

MARK JARMAN ❖

Ground Swell

Is nothing real but when I was fifteen
going on sixteen, like a corny song?
I see myself so clearly then, and painfully—
knees bleeding through my usher's uniform
behind the candy counter in the theater
after a morning's surfing; paddling frantically
to top the brisk outsiders coming to wreck me,
trundle me gawkily along the beach floor's
gravel and sand; my knees ached with salt.
Is that all that I have to write about?

Most Recent Book: THE BLACK RIVIERA (Wesleyan University Press, 1990)

You write about the life that's vividest,
and if that is your own, that is your subject,
and if the years before and after sixteen
are colorless as salt and taste like sand—
return to those remembered chilly mornings,
the light spreading like a great skin on the water,
and the blue water scalloped with wind-ridges
and—what was it exactly?—that slow waiting
when, to invigorate yourself you peed
inside your bathing suit and felt the warmth
crawl all around your hips and thighs,
and the first set rolled in and the water level
rose in expectancy, and the sun struck
the water surface like a brassy palm,
flat and gonglike, and the wave face formed.
Yes. But that was a summer so removed
in time, so specially peculiar to my life,
why would I want to write about it again?
There was a day or two when, paddling out,
an older boy who had just graduated
and grown a great blond moustache, like a walrus,
skimmed past me like a smooth machine on the water,
and said my name. I was so much younger,
to be identified by one like him—
the easy deference of a kind of god
who also went to church where I did—made me
reconsider my worth. I had been noticed.
He soon was a small figure crossing waves,
the shawling crest surrounding him with spray,
whiter than gull feathers. He had said my name
without scorn, but just a bit surprised
to notice me among those trying the big waves
of the morning break. His name is carved now
on the black wall in Washington, the frozen wave
that grievers cross to find a name or names.
I knew him as I say I knew him, then,
which wasn't very well. My father preached
his funeral. He came home in a bag
that may have mixed in pieces of his squad.
Yes, I can write about a lot of things
besides the summer that I turned sixteen.
But that's my ground swell. I must start
where things began to happen and I knew it.

The Black Riviera

for Garrett Hongo

There they are again. It's after dark.
The rain begins its sober comedy,
Slicking down their hair as they wait
Under a pepper tree or eucalyptus,
Larry Dietz, Luis Gonzalez, the Fitzgerald brothers,
And Jarman, hidden from the cop car
Sleeking innocently past. Stoned,
They giggle a little, with money ready
To pay for more, waiting in the rain.

They buy from the black Riviera
That silently appears, as if risen,
The apotheosis of wet asphalt
And smeary-silvery glare
And plus inner untouchability.
A hand takes money and withdraws,
Another extends a sack of plastic—
Short, too dramatic to be questioned.
What they buy is light rolled in a wave.

They send the money off in a long car
A god himself could steal a girl in,
Clothing its metal sheen in the spectrum
Of bars and discos and restaurants.
And they are left, dripping rain
Under their melancholy tree, and see time
Knocked akilter, sort of funny,
But slowing down strangely, too.
So, what do they dream?

They might dream that they are in love
And wake to find they are,
That outside their own pumping arteries,
Which they can cargo with happiness
As they sink in their little bathyspheres,
Somebody else's body pressures theirs
With kisses, like bursts of bloody oxygen,
Until, stunned, they're dragged up,
Drawn from drowning, saved.

In fact, some of us woke up that way.
It has to do with how desire takes shape.

Tapered, encapsulated, engineered
To navigate an illusion of deep water,
Its beauty has the dark roots
Of a girl skipping down a high school corridor
Selling Seconal from a bag,
Or a black car gliding close to the roadtop,
So insular, so quiet, it enters the earth.

The Shrine and the Burning Wheel

On the way to the evening reading,
Stopped at a Quick Stop for cigarettes,
I saw, as did everyone else parked there
Or passing, a gang of boys,
     Local boys probably,
Burning the front wheel of a ten-speed.
The bicycle, turned upside-down,
Stood on the dumpster-side of the store,
And one boy glanced from the corner
     Through the front window.
     Transcendence, that's what
It means to want to be gone
As, turning the eye's corner
To the sudden glare of fire,
The local terror stares in your face.
     I got the hell out of there,
And kept the spidery intaglio
Of the one, their lookout, peeping
Into the store window at—it must have been—
     The boy who owned the bicycle
     In his clerk-smock
     Making change from the safe.
At the evening reading, as the poet was
Introduced at length, she rested her head
     On the heel of her left hand,
     Full hair falling to the propped elbow,
And, as the prologue ran on,
Shook a little dandruff from her hair.
And what I saw was no longer her gesture
But the memory of Nora and Bo Dee Foster
     And the crowd at the Shrine Auditorium
     In Los Angeles, long ago, listening

To "Renascence" and "A Few Figs from Thistles"
And one that rhymed "stripèd pants" and "Paris, France."
        Bo Dee remembers how
        As Huxley went on
And on introducing her,
Edna Millay shook the dandruff from her hair.
        Transcendence is not
        Going back
To feel the texture of the past
Like the velvet nap of the loges
In the Shrine. It is wanting to be
        Anywhere else.
        Clearly, I don't understand.
The wheel spins. It is not hard to ignite
The hard lean tire with lighter fluid.
It flashes and a round of smiles
Breaks in the dismal circle
        Of the boy pack
        From the apartment complexes.
In their stripèd pants they open doors
Of sedans to men in maroon fezzes.
But they are men themselves, Nobles,
And wear ruby rings set with diamonds
        And symbols.
Searchlights mortar the clear night.
"Thank you, Noble," says one man
Helping his wife to the curb.
        She, white as a fez's tassel,
        And the grandchildren
Will see a Chinese girl-prodigy at the piano,
Jugglers on unicycles,
And, the reason they've come,
        Edgar Bergen and Charlie McCarthy,
        Aging and never to age.
Here at the Shrine, with its swag tent ceiling
And Arabic signs, hands of the crowd
        Grip in ways
        That cannot be revealed.
        But now the amps are on.
Big Brother and the Holding Company are on.
The rapid fire of strobes cuts, cuts.
But that's too much, too soon.
        Instead, it's the Boy Scout Expo.
        Let it be calm for awhile

As it would be at a state fair
Inside a great pavilion.
      Here are the Scouts displaying
      Their skill at fly casting.
      The arc ends in a splash.
Fly-blue or fly-green, it hits the pool
Among the crowd, under the roof
Of the Shrine Hall. There is quiet.
Then a cheer. Now the speakers start up.
      Janis Joplin, shapeless and small
In the loose Madras fabric of her dress,
Flares and thrashes in the wind
      Her body makes to the music,
      Cut and cut and cut
      By the strobe lights across her hair.
Transcendence is what she wants
Or not what she wants, to live
In the world or out of it,
      To be anywhere else
      Or here, as a studied voice
Says its poetry of heaven and earth,
And meshed with it, hidden,
A wheel of history turns,
And the boys burn the wheel.

RICHARD JONES ❖

The Bell

In the tower the bell
is alone, like a man
in his room,
thinking and thinking.

The bell is made of iron.
It takes the weight
of a man
to make the bell move.

Most Recent Book: COUNTRY OF AIR (Copper Canyon Press, 1986)

Far below, the bell feels
hands on a rope.
It considers this.
It turns its head.

Miles away,
a man in his room
hears the clear sound,
and lifts his head to listen.

The Mechanic

It's dark in the garage. The mechanic
goes down into the concrete grave
with his trouble light, while the day
rushes past outside on the highway.

Standing in the pit beneath an old engine,
he works patiently, with a kind of gentleness.
Looking up, he could be in a field at night
staring into the sky for answers.

In the afternoons, when the owners come back
for their cars, he stands around with the other men,
drinking beer, pushing one another around, cursing.
He works the kinks out of his neck, squints into the sun.

The Hearing Aid

My mother—half-deaf,
a small metal box
pinned to her blouse,

and beneath the gray locks
the hidden earphone,
the wire running across

her heart to its home
in her ear—can barely
hear me anymore. I'm

just someone's voice
lost years ago, trying now
to make myself clear,

deliberately now,
so she will see how
hard the words come.

Bent to her breast, I speak
to the heart, almost hopeless,
where hardly anyone

is ever heard.

Certain People

My father lives by the ocean
and drinks his morning coffee
in the full sun on his deck,
talking to anyone
who walks by on the beach.
And in the afternoons he works
part-time at the golf course—
sailing the fairways like sea captain
in a white golf cart.
My father must talk
to a hundred people a day,
yet we haven't spoken in weeks.
As I get older, we hardly speak at all.
It's as if he were a stranger
and we had never met.
I wonder, if I
were a tourist on the beach
or a golfer lost in woods
and met him now for the very first time,
what we'd say to each other,
how his hand would feel in mine
as we introduced ourselves,
and if, as is the case
with certain people, I'd feel,
when I looked him in the eye,
I'd known him all my life.

The Birds

When I try to say something about the birds
living around my house, or about the jay
tearing the cold insides from a mouse
I murdered and tossed in the yard,
I find myself writing instead
about Anne, the secretary I knew
in New York. She was afraid of people.
Even when the phone rang,
she'd sometimes start crying
and lock herself in the ladies' room.

I bet Anne could write a poem about the birds
for me. She'd know what to say
about the cream-colored bird I saw yesterday,
the way it made me think not about birds,
how they starve in winter,
but about the life of the soul.

I'd like to know what happened to crazy Anne.
The last time I saw her was in Times Square, after work.
Snow was falling and for once she wasn't crying.
She said, "My best friend's been murdered."
She was staring at neon reflecting
on the wet pavement, the snow
falling as in a dream, repeating
the dead girl's name over and over,
the same as hers,
Anne, Anne. . . .

Leaving Town after the Funeral

After the people and the flowers
have gone, and before the stone
has been removed from your mother's house
and carved into a cross, I come back
on my way out of town
to visit your grave. And nothing
is there—only the ground,
roughed up a little, waiting for rain.
I sit down beside you

in my dark glasses
and put my hand on the earth
above your dead heart.
Two workmen are mowing grass
around the graves beside us.
They pretend not to see
I am crying. Quietly,
they walk over to their truck
to give me time.
The day is hot. They hold paper cups
under the water cooler on the flatbed
and drink together.
They are used to this.
The heat. The grief.
After a few minutes the younger one
walks back to work.
He gets down on his knees
and blows cut grass off a stone.
I believe he wants me to know
he will take care of you.
But hard as it is,
I know the truth:
when you drowned, your body
sank into the river forever.
Ten minutes to eight.
Darkness came down quickly.
And now it will be night
for a long, long time.
The workman gets up and goes on
with his work. I get up
and walk back to the car.
Andrew, we know the truth:
the cold child in the casket
is not the one I loved.

Wan Chu's Wife in Bed

Wan Chu, my adoring husband,
has returned from another trip
selling trinkets in the provinces.
He pulls off his lavender shirt
as I lay naked in our bed,

waiting for him. He tells me
I am the only woman he'll ever love.
He may wander from one side of China
to the other, but his heart
will always stay with me.
His face glows in the lamplight
with the sincerity of a boy
when I lower the satin sheet
to let him see my breasts.
Outside, it begins to rain
on the cherry trees
he planted with our son,
and when he enters me with a sigh,
the storm begins in earnest,
shaking our little house.
Afterwards, I stroke his back
until he falls asleep.
I'd love to stay awake all night
listening to the rain,
but I should sleep, too.
Tomorrow Wan Chu will be
a hundred miles away
and I will be awake all night
in the arms of Wang Chen,
the tailor from Ming Pao,
the tiny village down river.

RODNEY JONES ❖

Mule

Here is this horse from a bad family, hating his burden and snaffle,
        not patient
So much as resigned to his towpath around the sorghum mill,
        but pawing the grist,
Laying back his missile ears to balk, so the single spoke of his wheel
        freezes, the gears lock.
Not sad, but stubborn, his temperament is tolerance,
        though his voice,

Most Recent Book: TRANSPARENT GESTURES (Houghton Mifflin Co., 1989)

Old door aching on a rusty hinge, blasts the martins from their gourds,
    and he would let
Nothing go behind him: the speckled hen, the green world
    his blinders magnify.
With the heel of one ecclesiastical hoof, he would stun goats or gods.

Half-ass, garrulous priest, his religion's a hybrid appetite that feasts
    on contradictions.
In him Jefferson dreamed the end of slavery and endless fields,
    but the labor goes on
In prefabricated barns, by stalled regiments of canopied tractors,
    in offices
Where the harvest is computed to the least decimal point,
    to the last brown bowl of wheat.
Not with him, the soil yields and futures swell into the radio.
His place, finally, is to be loved as a curiosity, as an art
    almost dead, like this sulfurous creek
Of molasses he brings oozing down from the bundles of cane.

Sometimes in the library I pause suddenly and think of the mule,
    desiring, perhaps, some lost sweetness,
Some fitful husk or buttercup that blooms wildly beyond the margins.
Such a peace comes over the even rows, the bound volumes
    where the unicorn
Bows his unearthly head, where the horned gods of fecundity rear
    in the pages of the sun.
All afternoon I will think of the mule's dignity, of his shrunken lot—
While the statistics slip the tattered net of my attention,
While the lullabies erect their precise nests in the footnotes.

I like to think of the silver one of my childhood, and the dark red one,
    Red.
Avuncular, puritanical, he stands on hooves as blue as quarries,
And I think his is the bray I have held back all of my life,
    in churches
Where the offering passed discreetly from one laborer to the next,
    in the factories of sleep,
Plunging a greased hand into the vat of mineral spirits.
And I think I have understood nothing better than the mule's cruelty
    and petty meanness:
How, subjugated, he will honk his incomparable impudence;
    stop for no reason;
Or, pastured with inferiors, stomp a newborn calf on a whim.

This is the mule's privilege: not to be governed badly by lashes,
    nor to be turned

Easily by praise; but, sovereign of his own spirit, to take his own time,
To meditate in the hardening compost under the rotting collars.
To sleep in wet straw. To stand for nothing but himself.
In August he will stand up to his withers in the reeking pond.
    In the paradise of mules,
He will stand with the old cows, contemplative, but brooding a little
    over the sores in his shoulders,
Remembering the dull shoes of the cultivator and the jet heads
    of the mowing machine.
Being impotent and beautiful, he will dream of his useless romances.

Caught

There is in the human voice
A quavery vowel sometimes,
More animal than meaning,
More mineral than gentle,

A slight nuance by which my
Mother would recognize lies,
Detect scorn or envy, sober
Things words would not admit,

Though it's true the best liars
Must never know they lie.
They move among good-byes
Worded like congratulations

We listen for and hear until
Some misery draws us back
To what it really was they
Obviously meant not to say.

And misery often draws us
Out to meadows or trees,
That speechless life where
Everything inhuman is true.

Mother spoke for tentative
People, illiterate, unsure.
Thinking of it her way is to
Reduce all words to tones

The wind might make anytime
With a few dead leaves. Our

Own names called in the dark
Or quail rising. Sounds that

Go straight from the ear to
The heart. There all the time,
They are a surface too clear
To see. Written down, no

Matter how right, they are too
Slow and vain as those soft
Vows we spoke in childhood to
Wild things, birds or rabbits

We meant to charm. When
My mother mentioned oaks,
They could be cut down, sawn
Into boards and nailed together

As rooms, and she was mostly
Quiet, standing in the kitchen,
Her pin rolling like law
Across plains of biscuit dough

While dark ripened, wind
Died on the tongue of each leaf.
The night broke in pieces
If she cleared her throat.

The Weepers

How could they do it, as though a smoky wind
had blasted their inflamed eyes or they sat
in a shut cupboard dicing a basket of leeks,
when they were not hurt and had hurt no one?
Their tragedies were average. It was not
the age of tears, yet often I saw them start,
kneeling at plain altars or leaning over bars,
their first glove-muffled sobs like the first
tremors of an earthquake that heaves up cities
or those first salty jars that prime the pump,
promulgating the troughs, creeks, and rivers
that fill the famous lakes and oceans of tears.
How they shook then. In hiccuppy assaults.
With the full mortal heart. They wept spasms.

They wept in great, undignified, blubbering fits,
and what could we do to console them?
How would we dry them out or pick them up
who went to pieces, broke down, or burst out,
invoking, in their sniffling, our own names,
our bleak deeds, our most embarrassing dreams?
Did they prefer things streaked and blurred,
the colors of houses merging with the colors
of trees, the lawns melting into the streets,
the dun sky running and smearing the station
where the vague buses were always going away?
Pity was too common for them, and sympathy.
Neither were they truly sad. They wept best
when there was no legitimate reason for tears,
no recent widow walking her mongoloid son,
no deaf student sodomized behind the gym,
no mendicant with his lyrics of a suicidal girl.
They did not believe in despots or atomic bombs.
They wept on celebration days, when picnics
were spread by pretty lakes or bronze plaques
were engraved with their names. They wept
sagas and epics. It was their talent to weep.
Their happiness was as fluent as their grief.
And yet I did not like them. Their seriousness
was exclusive and oppressive. I sat in the back
with the stoics while they moved to the front
in strict allegiance to the superiority of tears.
I could not resist the temptation to test one
with a practical joke, a dirge pitched off-key,
an orange water pistol trained on lamentations,
a Chaucerian fart let against momentousness.
I hated those sycophants who followed them,
porcupines of funeral homes, elderly senators
with patriotic speeches, nostalgic Irish priests—
those whores who knew all the tricks to arouse
the prolonged and mystical coming of tears.
But when I cried, all casket-rattling stopped,
jokes withered, my own life rose like bread,
and no one, not in the whole becalmed world
of measured feeling, was so ripely green, freed
in that compulsive, purblind, repetitious release.

RICHARD KATROVAS ❖

A Dog and a Boy

Joe Brickhouse saw his dog
get smashed by a garbage truck
in Elizabeth City, North Carolina.
He was twelve and smoked Luckies
and had a glass eye.
I won't tell you about the games of marbles
or how he fucked his sister,
nor shall I discuss in the abstract
his deep-seated contempt for authority
or why he kicked my ass
just because I was his friend and he loved me.
For this is about a dog and a boy
and has virtually nothing to do with Mark Twain
and the rest of American literature.
It's about a garbage truck
that backed up over a beautiful Lab
and a white kid who wrapped his arms
around the dead animal and gasped for air
and his face turned red then bluish,
whose tears streamed
onto the blood-caked fur of the dog,
and who howled and screamed so loud
at gray and porch-lit 5 a.m.
windows all down Merrimac scraped open,
and T-shirts, drawers, scrungy robes
hobbled onto porches
to stare in wonder
at a human being
who had learned so young
how to talk to the dead.

Most Recent Book: THE PUBLIC MIRROR (Wesleyan University Press, 1990)

The Beating

I will never forget my only beating
at the hands of a stranger, or that you
got down on hands and knees to pound the grass
and scream that I, ten years old, should be a man
and not just lie there pinned, weeping,
and breathless with defeat.

I saw an old man push a shopping cart
down Royal Street last night. From his cache
of crushed aluminum and chipped bottles
poked a little brown head with floppy ears
and a black nose. The man, so used to hunger
he'd attained a slow and mournful gracefulness,
paused in neon-blue bar light, then rasped
a chuckle as he gently shoved
the little head back under.

The kid who beat me up became my friend
out of pity, I think. Not because he
ever regretted having sat on my chest
and punched my face till I couldn't see
through the blood, but because after his knuckles
were so sore he had to slide, exhausted,
off my body, you grabbed me by the hair
and lifted me and tore your belt
from its loops and whipped my neck and back and legs.

I am just barely too smart
to blame my intermittent rages
on you and your insane code;
I'm referring to the many times
I've played the insulted ass with officialdom,
the ranting idiot whose "rights"
are violated by some poor jerk
whose soul is violated hourly
by his boss the computer.
I'll blame that on Brecht,
Nietzsche, Marx and television.

No, there is another rage
which is kin to a horse fly's bumping
on a pane of glass in late summer,

a wholly un-self-conscious rage of the body
which we may feel even when
something is gentle with us.

The Public Mirror

When I was a kid I froze
before a long Men's Room mirror
and the knowledge that I was nothing special,
that indeed I would never be,
tore God from the sky.

Seconds earlier I'd stood with other males,
young and not, some relieving themselves,
some wetting their hands and posing,
making private checks of their public faces.
They'd left at once through the swinging door.

Others would enter any second;
it was a very busy facility.
I just happened to be there in a lull;
not at all by design had I lingered.
I had decided to wash my hands:

As I'd wrung them under the cool water,
the swinging door thrumped again and again,
and boys and men reentered the halls leading to streets.
I'd thought nothing of their departures until I looked up
at the reflected white urinals and empty stalls,

the paper-towel dispenser, and the door
still creaking. I knew any moment a man
or boy would enter and take no notice of me,
would observe himself beside someone who was I.
But that moment I was alone before the public mirror,

ordinary and full of God, God
who never again would stand on the night
looking down at what I was doing,
I who suddenly was a hair more than nothing,
whom I could destroy simply by closing my eyes.

My Friends the Pigeons

The American Experiment has entered
yet another critical phase.
My friends the pigeons, who rent
a ledge in the nine hundredth block
of St. Louis, seem painfully aware of this.
I hope I am not merely projecting
my own dread onto them, but if I am
I do so with trepidation,
for pigeons are, by their very nature,
conduits of urban grief, though if
studied with an open, critical mind,
refract anemic sentiments. Oh sage
pigeons of the nine hundredth block
of St. Louis Street! What next?
The Christian Right is gaining force.
The Christians who march with placards
on Bourbon Street . . . Will the crowds
cease to laugh at them?
A blight on that day the happy crowds
no longer laugh at them!
A blight on the idiocy of the Christian Right!
I have watched them on television
and shivered with grief.
They are forcing me to embrace
what otherwise I might shun,
such as ugly, mite-infested pigeons,
surrogate angels for those
never told their bodies were evil.
I thank my sweet, dead mother
for never telling me my body was evil,
and for laying a big, dirty feather
on my pillow one Christmas Eve.

BRIGIT PEGEEN KELLY ❖

Young Wife's Lament

The mule that lived on the road
where I was married
would bray to wake the morning,
but could not wake me.
How many summers I slept
lost in my hair. How many
mules on how many hills singing.
Back of a deep ravine
he lived, above a small river
on a beaten patch of land.
I walked up in the day and walked down,
having been given nothing
else to do. The road grew no longer,
I grew no wiser, my husband
was away selling things to people who buy.
He went up the road, too, but
the road was full of doors for him,
the road was his belt and,
one notch at a time, he loosened it
on his way. I would sit
on the hill of stones and look down
on the trees, on the lake
far away with its boats and those
who ride in boats
and I could not pray. Some of us
have mule minds,
are foolish as sails whipping
in the wind, senseless
as sheets rolling through the fields,
some of us are not given
even a wheel of the tinker's cart
upon which to pray.
When I came back I pumped water
in the yard under the trees
by the fence where the cows came up,

Most Recent Book: TO THE PLACE OF TRUMPETS (Yale University Press, 1988)

but water is not wisdom
and change is not made by wishes.
Else I would have ridden something,
even a mule, over
those hills and away.

Those Who Wrestle with the Angel for Us

I

My brother flies
A plane,
            windhover, night-lover,
Flies too low
Over the belled
                and furrowed fields,
The coiled creeks,
The slow streams of cars
                        spilling
Like lust into the summer
Towns. And he flies
                when he
Should not, when
The hot, heavy air
                breaks
In storms, in high
Winds, when the clouds
                    like trees
Unload their stony fruit
And batter his slender
                    wings and tail.
But like the magician's
Dove, he appears home safely
                        every time,
Carrying in his worn white
Bag all the dark
                elements
That flight knows,
The dark that makes
                his own soul
Dark with sight.

Even when he was a child, his skin was the white
Of something buffed by winds at high altitudes

Or lit by arctic lights—it gleamed like fish scales
Or oiled tin, and even then he wished to be alone,

Disappearing into the long grasses of the Ipperwash dunes
Where the gulls nested and where one afternoon

He fell asleep and was almost carried off by the sun—
In his dream he was running, leaping well, leaping

High as the hunted deer, and almost leaping free,
But like the tide, my gentle-handed mother hauled him back

With cold compresses and tea, and after that he favored
The dark, the ghostly hours, a small boy whistling in our yard

As he dragged a stick along the fence rails, and listened
To the slatted rattle of railroad cars, and knew by

Instinct how railroad lines look from the air, like ladders
Running northward to the stars, to the great constellations.

And he began then tracking his way through the names
Of all our fears, Cassiopeia, Andromeda, the shining Ram,

Tracking the miles and years he logs now, the lonely stretches
Where he finds the souvenirs that light our narrow kitchens—

Buckles and pins, watches and rings—the booty
That makes our land-locked, land-bound souls feel the compass

In our feet, and see in those who never speak, who
Slouch in with the dust of the northern wind on their backs,

The face of the angel we ourselves must wrestle with.

Wild Turkeys: The Dignity of the Damned

Because they *are* shame, and cannot flee from it,
And cannot hide it, they go slow,
One great variegated male and his harem of four wild hens

Halting our truck as they labor
To cross the road into the low fields they are indentured to.
They go slow, their hearts hardened to this;

Those laughing-stock, shriveled, lipstick red hearts—
Swinging on throat and foreneck
Beneath the narrow heads that are the blue

Not of the sky but of convicts' shaved skulls—
Have been long indurated by rains and winds and filth
And the merciless exposures of the sun.

They do not look up, they do not fly—
Except at night when dark descends like shame,
When shame is lost to dark, and then,

Weak-winged, they heave themselves
Into the low tree roosts they drop from in the morning,
Crashing like swag-bellied bombers

Into the bare fields and stingy stands of trees
They peck their stones and seeds from.
Yesterday they were targets, but now they go slow,

As if this lacuna between winter and spring, still gray,
But full of the furred sumacs' pubescent probings,
And the faint oily scent of wild onion vials crushed open,

Gave hope to even them, or as if they knew
All seasons to be one, the going back,
The crossing over, the standing still, all the same,

When the state you defend is a lost state,
When lurching into an ungainly run
Only reminds you that there is nowhere to run to.

And this movement, this jerking
Of these heavy goffered carapaces forward,
This dumb parading that looks at first glance furtive,

Like skulking, the hunkered shoulders, the lowered heads,
Reveals, as we watch, the dignity that lines
Of pilgrim-sick possess as they halt toward some dark grotto—

A faith beyond the last desire to possess faith,
The soldiers' resolve to march hump-backed straight into Death
Until it breaks like oil over them

And over all that is lost.

Silver Lake

Fast-locked the land for weeks. Of ice we dream.
Of ice and the low fires the fishermen feed on Silver Lake.
All the lakes are called silver here, though none are that.
And this one now is white and shot through with fishing holes.
It looks like the blasted back of one of those huge turtles
That summer drags out of the weeds with the lure of sweeter bogs.
They lumber with the ponderous slowness of some interminable sermon
And they are easy game for the long-legged boys in pickups
Who hack their backs with axes to make thick soup. Years
In that soup. Unseen years and depths to mull the blond meat
That my great great Uncle Lusty in England made his fortune from.
But that is another story. Now the lake—with its toppled shrine
And the memory of its lone heron, seasonal and proud—is sealed;
And on these frigid fog-bound days the sun comes late,
If at all, comes like a slow yellow age stain on linen,
Or like the muted blare of the fluorescent lights you can see
Through the smeared windows of the Gulf Station garage.
Sometimes it has the iridescence of spilled oil, and always
In the fog you can look straight at it, as you can look
At the sun in Medjugorje, and it will not burn your eyes;
Though here we are not changed much by such sights.
Once you were alone on the ice. Too cold for the rest.
All day the wind was rank with the metallic smell of old snow,
Blowing over and over itself, tangling like lost laundry,
And even the hungry packs of snowmobiles—that sound
As they cross the cornfields with their shrill chain-saw whine
As if they are felling whole forests—were silent.
Dusk was coming on. And I watched you for a long time.
I was in the open, though you did not see me, did not turn
To where I stood in the high grasses the weather had stained black.
You sat on your three-legged stool by a numb fire, your boot
Cocked on the coughed-up collar of ice the awl leaves,
And waited for the fish to spring your trap, spring
The pink plastic flag that made me think of the lawn flamingos
In the yard of the Kinkel's Corner antique shop. Few stop there
Because the highway's hairpin curves are deadly and blind,
But one morning I stood among the flocks of those plastic birds
And the statues posturing in the yard. Virgins and trolls.
Saints and satyrs and naked women with no arms. "Things
That keep and do not change," as the proprietor told me.
And he pointed to the painted figure of a shirtless slave

Up the narrow walk to his house. "See that colored boy," he said.
"I've had him sixty years, and all he needs is a little varnish."
The lower rims of the man's eyes belled forward and were very red
And it was impossible not to look at that soreness . . .
You sat for so long on the ice my tongue went numb in my mouth
And I woke to see you paying your line out slow as a delicious thought
Into the circled dark. There was a pause before whatever contract
You made with the darkness was complete, the wind repeated
Its wolf whistle in the reeds, and then the prisoner was released—
The orange-winged, green-and-black striped perch flew up, flew fast,
Iced by the fire's light, scattering bright hot pellets as it flew,
The way the priest scatters holy water during the Asperges
At Easter Vigil. And when you put your hand on the fish
I felt how it burned your flesh, burned for the two worlds to meet . . .
I don't lie to myself. This is what men love the best.
The thoughts they deal from the dark. Better than any woman's flesh.

YUSEF KOMUNYAKAA ❖

Venus's-flytraps

I am five,
  Wading out into the deep
    Sunny grass,
Unmindful of snakes
  & yellow jackets, out
    To the yellow flowers
Quivering in sluggish heat.
  Don't mess with me
    'Cause I have my Lone Ranger
Six-shooter. I can hurt
  You with questions
    Like silver bullets.
The tall flowers in my dreams are
  Big as the First State Bank,
    & they eat all the people
Except the ones I love.
  They have women's names,
    With mouths like where

Most Recent Book: DIEN CAI DAU (Wesleyan University Press, 1988)

Babies come from. I am five.
  I'll dance for you
    If you close your eyes. No
Peeping through your fingers.
  I don't supposed to be
    This close to the tracks.
One afternoon I saw
  What a train did to a cow.
    Sometimes I stand so close
I can see the eyes
  Of men hiding in boxcars.
    Sometimes they wave
& holler for me to get back. I laugh
  When trains make the dogs
    Howl. Their ears hurt.
I also know bees
  Can't live without flowers.
    I wonder why Daddy
Calls Mama honey.
  All the bees in the world
    Live in little white houses
Except the ones in these flowers.
  All sticky & sweet inside.
    I wonder what death tastes like.
Sometimes I toss the butterflies
  Back into the air.
    I wish I knew why
The music in my head
  Makes me scared.
    But I know things
I don't supposed to know.
  I could start walking
    & never stop.
These yellow flowers
  Go on forever.
    Almost to Detroit.
Almost to the sea.
  My mama says I'm a mistake.
    That I made her a bad girl.
My playhouse is underneath
  Our house, & I hear people
    Telling each other secrets.

Sunday Afternoons

They'd latch the screen doors
& pull venetian blinds,
Telling us not to leave the yard.
But we always got lost
Among mayhaw & crab apple.

Juice spilled from our mouths,
& soon we were drunk & brave
As birds diving through saw vines.
Each nest held three or four
Speckled eggs, blue as rage.

Where did we learn to be unkind,
There in the power of holding each egg
While watching dogs in June
Dust & heat, or when we followed
The hawk's slow, deliberate arc?

In the yard, we heard cries
Fused with gospel on the radio,
Loud as shattered glass
In a Saturday-night argument
About trust & money.

We were born between Oh Yeah
& Goddammit. I knew life
Started from where I stood in the dark,
Looking out into the light,
& that sometimes I could see

Everything through nothing.
The backyard trees breathed
Like a man running from himself
As my brothers backed away
From the screen door. I knew

If I held my right hand above my eyes
Like a gambler's visor, I could see
How their bedroom door halved
The dresser mirror like a moon
Held prisoner in the house.

Blackberries

They left my hands like a printer's
Or thief's before a police blotter
& pulled me into early morning's
Terrestrial sweetness, so thick
The damp ground was consecrated
Where they fell among a garland of thorns.

Although I could smell old lime-covered
History, at ten I'd still hold out my hands
& berries fell into them. Eating from one
& filling a half gallon with the other,
I ate the mythology & dreamt
Of pies & cobbler, almost

Needful as forgiveness. My bird dog Spot
Eyed blue jays & thrashers. The mud frogs
In rich blackness, hid from daylight.
An hour later, beside City Limits Road
I balanced a gleaming can in each hand,
Limboed between worlds, repeating "One dollar."

The big blue car made me sweat.
Wintertime crawled out of the windows.
When I leaned closer I saw the boy
& girl my age, in the big backseat
Smirking, & it was then I remembered my fingers
Burning with thorns among berries too ripe to touch.

Temples of Smoke

Fire shimmied & reached up
From the iron furnace & grabbed
Sawdust from the pitchfork
Before I could make it across
The floor or take a half step
Back, as the boiler room sung
About what trees were before
Men & money. Those nights
Smelled of greenness & sweat
As steam moved through miles
Of winding pipes to turn wheels

That pushed blades & rotated
Man-high saws. It leaped
Like tigers out of a pit,
Singeing the hair on my head,
While Daddy made his rounds
Turning large brass keys
In his night-watchman's clock,
Out among columns of lumber & paths
Where a man & woman might meet.
I daydreamed some freighter
Across a midnight ocean,
Leaving Taipei & headed
For Tripoli. I saw myself fall
Through a tumbling inferno
As if hell was where a boy
Shoveled clouds of sawdust
Into the wide mouth of doubt.

My Father's Loveletters

On Fridays he'd open a can of Jax,
Close his eyes, & ask me to write
The same letter to my mother
Who sent postcards of desert flowers
Taller than a man. He'd beg her
Return & promised to never
Beat her again. I was almost happy
She was gone, & sometimes wanted
To slip in something bad.
His carpenter's apron always bulged
With old nails, a claw hammer
Holstered in a loop at his side
& extension cords coiled around his feet.
Words rolled from under
The pressure of my ballpoint:
Love, Baby, Honey, Please.
We lingered in the quiet brutality
Of voltage meters & pipe threaders,
Lost between sentences . . . the heartless
Gleam of a two-pound wedge
On the concrete floor,
A sunset in the doorway

Of the tool shed.
I wondered if she'd laugh
As she held them over a flame.
My father could only sign
His name, but he'd look at blueprints
& tell you how many bricks
Formed each wall. This man
Who stole roses & hyacinth
For his yard, stood there
With eyes closed & fists balled,
Laboring over a simple word,
Opened like a fresh wound, almost
Redeemed by what he tried to say.

SYDNEY LEA ❖

Museum

> recalling George MacArthur
> and Donald Chambers

Small thunder cuts my autumn doze on the porch.
Trotting by, two thoroughbreds—skittish, slender.
Dream is at once a heavy and delicate thing.

Donald's wrinkles could hold a week of rain.
Every fall, he told me, he'd bleed his horse.
A horse's waters thicken, summering over.

Or did he say he bled her after winter?
He spoke so much, so often, I ought to remember.
He said and said and said—I wasn't there.

A horse don't mind, she didn't mind, he said.
He'd make a jutting movement into air.
You put the knife-point, quick as you could, inside.

A Belgian would barely flinch, God was his witness.
He swore the roan mare didn't care.
Only a little prick in the palate's softness.

Most Recent Book: PRAYER FOR THE LITTLE CITY (Charles Scribner's Sons, 1990)

It's America, it's 1988.
Shy, the thoroughbred pair, and thin in the leg.
Soft and bright, the riders' clothes—like mine.

Queenie, he whispered, she lowered her trunk of a neck.
Her look was almost bored, she seemed to yawn.
There stood a barrel, and blood came pouring down.

You needed to stanch it with alum right on time.
A horse was a thing you wanted not to lose.
By God you wanted a rugged horse back then.

Back then the trees got bigger than they do.
My road was just a path in the swamp, of course.
I wasn't there, repeat, not there, repeat.
You can't remember somebody now by a horse.
Not by a horse that really works, at least.
All I recall is Donald telling me of it.

Queenie, he'd whisper, repeating himself. He loved it.
You can't recall a person by a canoe.
I'm thinking now of George as well, awake.

Not a canoe you use, you really use.
You had to portage then from here to the lake.
Riverman, trapper, river of words, Bard.

The only roads were tote roads, so George said.
Repeating himself, repeating—I wasn't there.
You could borrow the loan of a horse if you were tired.

A timber horse, well-bled and -fed, was strong.
A Belgian would hardly pay a canoe attention.
You lashed it onto a sledge and drove it on.

George and Donald were there, who now are gone.
And this may be the realm of imagination.
When the Black ducks flew from the lake they covered the sun.

When a he-bear coughed in the woods, the great flanks trembled.
You threw wet trout on the garden to feed your corn.
You bled a horse in autumn—or was it spring?

Good smell of flesh and blood, the hay, the hovel.
Even in January the flanks would steam.
Vaporous song for New England. Imagination.

Useless, swift and helpless, the thoroughbreds.
Dream's domain: song and talk, museum.
You have to make sure that too much blood don't spill.

They told me so, they laughed, they frowned, they said.
There were rocks, rapids, currents you couldn't feel.
Solid things and spectral, redundant winds.

There were widow-makers, limbs that fell without sound.
Sometimes, though, the horses seemed to hear.
Sometimes they'd bolt, and a ton of horse can maim.

That much horse is a delicate thing all the same.
So Donald always suggested—I wasn't there.
You could fix any boat you didn't completely lose.

Sometimes I lose it, even the shadow from slumber.
Canvas and cedar, ash ribs, gunwales of spruce.
Mist. Recalls: Donald and George, New England.

Horses, canoes, talk, men, museum.
Thunder: wood-scrap, green cloth going under.
The old men's regal faces could hold the rain.

One twitches the horse's lip, the knife jabs in.
Riders wave to me from the road all cheerful.
I think the Belgian mare's big legs will buckle.

I think we're late, and blood brims over the barrel.
Its stain is the shade of these Indian-summer maples.
It's 1988, the canoe is fragile.

The spindly trot comes liquid through autumn air.
Words I repeat and repeat for George and Donald.
I say and say. And say who wasn't there.

Prayer for the Little City

> January 6

Hushed plane, the pond. Ice-fishers' lights. Still little city.
Men hug their whiskey jugs inside as they loiter among
whiffs of bait, potbelly smoke, sock-wool and sweat.

Laconic chat: an idle joke; or God damn that
or God damn this, although such words aren't even angry,
but ordinary. Snowmobile roads thread our shacks

one to another; now and then, Big Lou throws open
his door (like an oven's, infernal within) and cries to a neighbor,
"Doin' some good?" Or dirty Duane, the one we call

"Blackfly," will call words much the same and the neighborhood
will rally from silence a moment or two, then sink back in.
It's half past ten. Blackfly and Lou and all the quietened

others stay through the darkness till dawn, whether or not
the small smelt bite. What *of* this town, this bobhouse crew?
What of Ben, who's outside skimming his ice-hole's O's?—

he sniffs and blows, thinks vaguely of women, and thinks to name
some part of their bodies out loud across the frozen surface:
a shout all worthless, directionless, a shout all shoddy

with platitude, devoid of embrace, containing nothing,
not even longing . . . at least for sex. Just part of a mood
and situation much at odds, it might be imagined,

with a hopeful season, season of gods, of resolution
to start anew. Outside, the flags on their planted poles
in the utter chill are utterly slack, betraying no

visionary prey down under to clasp our lures.
The dullness is pure. No signs, no wonders, no mystery . . .
except it be the care with which all night men linger,

as if in prayer for a novel fish, or a novel way
by which to address some thing they're feeling. Surely this is
part of what holds us under crude ceilings beaded with pitch,

amid this fetor with speechless friends. Surely, surely
a sense that early, before the dawn (or sooner, or later)
our flags will all at once, together, tremble and shimmy.

Epiphany—o bright palaver! o every hole
a yodel of steam! So runs our fancy in the absence of sound
in this merest of towns, although our shanties' very beams

of light seem bored. O little city, we think, it's cold;
city, how still, how still we see thee. Still, the stars
go by above, even here, and still may love

       embrace the year.

LI-YOUNG LEE ❖

The Cleaving

He gossips like my grandmother, this man
with my face, and I could stand
amused all afternoon
in the Hon Kee Grocery, amid hanging meats he
chops: roast pork cut from a hog hung
by nose and shoulders, his entire skin burnt
crisp, his
flesh I know
to be sweet,
his shining face grinning
up at ducks dangling single file,
each pierced by black
hooks through breast, bill, and steaming from a hole
stitched shut at the ass.
I step to the counter, recite, and he, without even slightly
varying the rhythm of his current confession or harangue,
scribbles my order on a greasy receipt,
and chops it up quick.

Such a sorrowful Chinese face,
nomad, Gobi, Northern in its boniness
clear from the high warlike forehead
to the sheer edge of the jaw.
He could be my brother, but slighter,
and, except for his left forearm, which is engorged,
sinewy from his daily grip and
wield of a two pound tool, he's delicate, narrow-
waisted, his frame so slight,
a lover, some rough other,
might break it down its smooth
oily length.
In his light-handed calligraphy
on receipts and in his moodiness, he is
a Southerner from a river-province;
suited for scholarship,
his face poised above an open book,

Most Recent Book: THE CITY IN WHICH I LOVE YOU (Boa Editions, 1990)

he'd mumble his favorite passages.
He could be my grandfather;
come to America to get a Western education
in 1917, but too homesick to study,
he sits in the park all day, reading poems
and writing letters to his mother.

He lops the head off, chops
the neck of the duck
into six, slits
the body
open, groin
to breast, and drains
the scalding juices,
then quarters the carcass
with two fast hacks of the cleaver,
whose blade has worn into the surface of the round
foot-thick chop-block
a scoop that cradles precisely the curved steel.

The head, flung from the body, opens
down the middle where the butcher cleanly halved it
between the eyes, and I
see, foetal-crouched
inside the skull, the homunculus,
gray brain grainy
to eat.
Did this animal, after all, at the moment
its neck broke,
image the way his executioner
shrinks from his own death?
Is this how
I, too, recoil from my day?
See how this shape hordes
itself, see how little it is.
See its grease on the blade.
Is this how I'll be found
when judgment is passed, when names
are called, when crimes are tallied? This
is also how I looked before I tore my mother open.
Is this how I presided over my century, is this how
I regarded the murders?
This is also how I prayed.
Was it me in the Other

I prayed to when I prayed?
This too was how I slept, clutching my wife.
Was it me in the other I loved when I loved another?

The butcher sees me eye this delicacy.
With a finger, he picks it
out of the skull-cradle
and offers it to me.
I take it gingerly between my fingers
and suck it down.
I eat my man.

The noise the body makes
when the body meets
the soul over the soul's ocean and penumbra
is the old sound of up-and-down, in-and-out,
a lump of muscle chug-chugging blood
into the ear; a lover's
heart-shaped tongue;
flesh rocking flesh until flesh comes;
the butcher working at his block and blade
to marry their shapes by violence and time;
an engine crossing, recrossing salt water, hauling
immigrants and the junk
of the poor. These
are the faces I love, the bodies
and scents of bodies
for which I long in various ways at various times,
thirteen gathered around the redwood,
happy, talkative, voracious at day's end,
eager to eat four kinds of meat
prepared four different ways,
numerous plates and bowls of rice and vegetables,
each made by distinct affections
and brought to table by many hands.
Brothers and sisters by blood and design,
who sit in separate bodies of varied shapes,
we constitute a many-membered
body of love.
In a world of shapes of my desires,
each one here is a shape of one of my desires,
and each is known to me and dear by virtue
of each one's unique corruption
of those texts, the face, the body:
that jut jaw

to gnash tendon;
that wide nose to meet the blows
a face like that invites;
those long eyes closing on the seen;
those thick lips to suck the meat of animals
or recite 300 poems of the T'ang;
these teeth to bite my monosyllables; these cheekbones
to make those syllables sing the soul.
Puffed or sunken
according to the life,
dark or light according to the birth,
straight or humped, whole, manque, quasi, ëach
pleases, verging
to utter grotesquery.
All are beautiful by variety.

The soul too
is a debasement
of a text, but, thus, it
acquires salience, although a
human salience, but
inimitable, and, hence, memorable.
God is the text.
The soul is a corruption and a mnemonic.

A bright moment, I hold up an old head
from the sea, and admire the haughty
down-curved mouth
that seems to disdain all the eyes are blind to,
including me, the eater.
Whole unto itself, complete
without me, yet its
shape complements my mind's shape.
I take it
as text and evidence
of the world's love for me,
and I feel urged to utterance, urged
to read the body of the world,
urged to say it in human terms,
my reading a kind of eating, my eating a kind of reading,
my saying a diminishment,
my noise a love-in-answer.
What is it in me
would devour the world to utter it?
What is it

in me will not let the world be,
would eat
not just this fish,
but the one who killed it, that butcher who cleaned it.
I would eat the way he
squats, the way he
reaches into the plastic tubs
and pulls out a fish, clubs it, takes it
to the sink, guts it, drops it on the weighing pan.
I would eat that thrash
and plunge of the watery body in the water,
that liquid violence between the man's hands,
I would eat
the gutless twitching on the scales,
three pounds of dumb nerve and pulse,
I would eat it all
to utter it.
The deaths at the sinks, those bodies prepared
for eating I would eat,
and the standing deaths
at the counters, in the aisles, the walking
deaths in the streets, the death-far-from-home, the death-
in-a-strange-land, these Chinatown
deaths, these American deaths.
I would devour this race to sing it,
this race that according to Emerson
managed to preserve to a hair
for three or four thousand years
the ugliest features in the world. I would
eat these features, eat
the last three or four thousand years, every hair
And I would eat Emerson, his transparent soul, his
soporific transcendence. I
would eat this head,
glazed in pepper-speckled sauce,
the cooked eyes opaque in their sockets.
I bring it to my mouth and—
the way I was taught, the way I've watched others before me do—
with a stiff tongue lick out the cheek-meat
and the meat over the armored jaw, my eating—
its sensual, salient nowness—punctuating
the void
from which such hunger springs and to which it proceeds.

And what is this I excavate with my mouth?
What is this ribbed, hinged,
plated architecture, this *carp head*,
but one more articulation
of a single nothing
severally manifested?
What is my eating,
rapt as it is,
but another shape of going,
my immaculate expiration?

O, nothing is so
steadfast it won't go
the way the body goes.
The body goes.
The body's grave,
so serious
in its dying,
arduous as martyrs
in that task and as
glorious. It goes
empty always
and announces its going
by spasms and groans, farts and sweats.

What I thought were the arms
aching *cleave*, were the knees trembling *leave*.
What I thought were the muscles
insisting *resist, persist, exist*,
were the pores
hissing *mist* and *waste*.
What I thought was the body humming *reside, reside*,
was the body sighing *revise, revise*.
O, the murderous deletions, the keening
down to nothing, the cleaving.
All of the body's revisions end
in death.
All of the body's revisions end.

Bodies eating bodies, heads eating heads,
we are nothing eating nothing,
and though we feast, are filled, overfilled,
we go famished.
We gang the doors of death.

That is, our deaths are fed
that we may continue our daily dying,
our bodies going
down, while the plates-soon-empty are passed
around, that true direction of our true prayers,
while the butcher spells his message, manifold,
in the mortal air.
He coaxes, cleaves, brings change
before our very eyes, and at every
moment of our being.
As we eat we're eaten.
Else what is
this violence, this salt, this
passion, this heaven?

I thought the soul an airy thing.
I did not know the soul
is cleaved so that the soul might be restored.
Live wood hewn, its sap springs from a sticky wound.
No seed, no egg has he
whose business calls for an axe.
In the trade of my soul's shaping,
he traffics in hews and hacks.

No easy thing, violence.
One of its names? Change. Change
resides in the embrace
of the effaced and the effacer,
in the covenant of the opened and the opener;
the axe accomplishes it on the soul's axis.
What then may I do
but cleave to what cleaves me.
I kiss the blade and eat my meat.
I thank the wielder and receive
while terror spirits
my change, sorrow also.
The terror the butcher scripts in the unhealed air,
the sorrow of his Shang dynasty face,
African face with slit eyes. He is
my sister, this
beautiful Bedouin, this Shulamite,
keeper of sabbaths, diviner
of holy texts, this dark
dancer, this Jew, this Asian, this one
with the Cambodian face, Vietnamese face, this Chinese

I daily face,
this immigrant,
this man with my own face.

DAVID LEHMAN ❖

Spontaneous Combustion

Under the mattress was a day-old newspaper rolled into a scroll,
And in the scroll was a small fortune in bank notes.
They all went up in smoke. First the sheets caught fire,
Then the mattress, the newspaper, the money. Finally,
The bed itself began to rise, ascending to the heights
Of a wandering cloud suspended between rival promontories
In the Alps. The bed disappeared into the cloud and then,
And only then, could the lovers be seen
For the first time, in the splendor of their absence,
As if a blaze of light bulbs had outlined their bodies
In the midnight sky, just to the north of the archer.

It was as if the boy had stayed in the big store
After it closed for the night, had hidden in the men's room
When the lights went out and the clerks went home,
And all at once became aware of music in the darkness,
And crept out to witness a masquerade ball of mannequins.
That dancer, there, in the slippers and pearls! He wanted her
And would have her if only . . . if only her body weren't just
A function of the mind that designed her dress and never
Entered the nave of her nudity. And yet . . . and yet the body
Shedding that dress was real, and equipped with the lips
And hair angels lack: the proof lay there beside him
In the bed. A lover of paradox, he turned away
From the big bright cancellations of night
That announced the new day, and let sleep overcome him,
Him and her, in the levitating bed, in the flames.

Most Recent Book: OPERATION MEMORY (Princeton University Press, 1990)

Operation Memory

We were smoking some of this knockout weed when
Operation Memory was announced. To his separate bed
Each soldier went, counting backwards from a hundred
With a needle in his arm. And there I was, in the middle
Of a recession, in the middle of a strange city, between jobs
And apartments and wives. Nobody told me the gun was loaded.

We'd been drinking since early afternoon. I was loaded.
The doctor made me recite my name, rank, and serial number when
I woke up, sweating, in my civvies. All my friends had jobs
As professional liars, and most had partners who were good in bed.
What did I have? Just this feeling of always being in the middle
Of things, and the luck of looking younger than fifty.

At dawn I returned to draft headquarters. I was eighteen
And counting backwards. The interviewer asked one loaded
Question after another, such as why I often read the middle
Of novels, ignoring their beginnings and their ends. When
Had I decided to volunteer for intelligence work? "In bed
With a broad," I answered, with locker-room bravado. The truth was, jobs

Were scarce, and working on Operation Memory was better than no job
At all. Unamused, the judge looked at his watch. It was 1970
By the time he spoke. Recommending clemency, he ordered me to go to
    bed
At noon and practice my disappearing act. Someone must have loaded
The harmless gun on the wall in Act I when
I was asleep. And there I was, without an alibi, in the middle

Of a journey down nameless, snow-covered streets, in the middle
Of a mystery—or a muddle. These were the jobs
That saved men's souls, or so I was told, but when
The orphans assembled for their annual reunion, ten
Years later, on the playing fields of Eton, each unloaded
A kit bag full of troubles, and smiled bravely, and went to bed.

Thanks to Operation Memory, each of us woke up in a different bed
Or coffin, with a different partner beside him, in the middle
Of a war that had never been declared. No one had time to load
His weapon or see to any of the dozen essential jobs
Preceding combat duty. And there I was, dodging bullets, merely one
In a million whose lucky number had come up. When

It happened, I was asleep in bed, and when I woke up,
It was over: I was 38, on the brink of middle age,
A succession of stupid jobs behind me, a loaded gun on my lap.

Perfidia

You don't know who these people are, or what
They'll do to you if you're caught, but you can't
Back out now: it seems you agreed to carry
A briefcase into Germany, and here you are,
Glass in hand, as instructed. You rise to dance
With the woman with the garnet earrings, who is,
Of course, the agent you're supposed to seduce
And betray within the hour. Who would have known
You'd fall in love with her? Elsewhere the day
Is as gray as a newsreel, full of stripes and dots
Of rain, a blurred windshield picture of Pittsburgh,
But on the screen where your real life is happening
It is always 1938, you are always dancing
With the same blonde woman with the bloodshot eyes
Who slips the forged passport into your pocket
And says she knows you've been sent to betray her,
Or else it is seventy degrees and holding
In California, where you see yourself emerge unscathed
From the car crash that wiped out your memory,
Your past, as you walk into a gambler's hangout
On Sunset Boulevard, in a suit one size too large,
And the piano player plays "Perfidia" in your honor
And the redhead at the bar lets you buy her a drink.

Fear

The boy hid under the house
With his dog, his red lunch box, and his fear
Thinking God is near
Thinking It's time to leave the things that mean
Just one thing, though you can't tell what that is,
Like God or death. The boy held his breath,
Closed his eyes, and disappeared,
Thinking No one will find me here—

But only when his parents were watching.
When they weren't, he slipped away
And hid under the house
And stayed there all night, and through the next day,
Until Father (who had died that December)
Agreed to come home, and Mother was twenty
Years younger again, and pregnant with her
Darling son. Hiding under the house,
He could see it all, past and future,
The deep blue past, the black-and-white future,
Until he closed his eyes and made it disappear,

And everyone was glad when he returned
To the dinner table, a grown man
With wire-rim glasses and neatly combed hair.
Fear was the name of his dog, a German shepherd.

Enigma Variations

1

Sir Winston Churchill advised against suicide
"Especially when you may live to regret it."
After an endless faculty meeting at Princeton,
Einstein revised his theory of eternity.
"Just a run in time's stocking," said Nabokov.
The child grows older while everyone around him
Stays the age they were when he was born.

The painter and his model change places.
The nude wears a mask. Otherwise she is nude.
Otherwise she is just like all the other passengers
On this hijacked jet suspended over Manhattan.
One terrorist says: Let the death be as illuminating
As the resurrection. Everyone else has frozen
Into the age they were when he was born.

2

Let the alcoholic transcend his religious upbringing.
Let the Leaning Tower of Pisa stabilize its tilt.
Let the spaces between Pollock's "Blue Poles"
Vibrate with the music of the spheres and
Let the death be as illuminating as the resurrection,

And as beautiful. A million degrees centigrade:
The sun's corona during a total eclipse.

If the world has terrors, said Rilke, then
We must learn to love them, for they belong to us.
Notice the "if." If among all these skeletons
One stood up to denounce his tormentors
Crying "We shall outlive them!" in triumph as if
His escape did not mean his destruction:
The sun's corona during a total eclipse.

3

The driver of the hearse seen from the hospital window
Says, "There's room for one more inside,"
And so does the bus conductor the next afternoon.
We know it will crash, but it's our destiny
And we can't escape from our destiny, though
We refuse to climb aboard. A used syringe was found
In the toilet in the back of the bus.
They would never have permitted it in the hospital.

The lovers dreamed in parallel lines that converged
When they woke up, midway between heaven and no place.
I was the blind painter who could see his model
Only by touching her. We met on the bus
Which didn't crash, except when we were asleep
And we could see the place exactly as it was
Except that we were missing from the picture.
They would never have permitted it in the hospital.

4

Terror links the father, the son, and the sacrificial ram.
Thanks to a choice typo in *Time*,
The Allies snatched victory from "the jews of defeat,"
The chosen people, who live across the street,
Having babies and working for a living.
The law requires a medical examination before execution:
The law of self-preservation, which doesn't exist,
If we can commit suicide and live to regret it.

The terror of transgressing angels, looking homeward,
Is ours, because there's no one else to blame.
We are the chosen people, choosing to laugh
At a practical joke that isn't all that funny.

The Appian Way is now Highway 7, and Icarus
In his plane need fear no more the heat of the sun
As he flies, fatherless, midway between heaven
And no place: a suicide who lived to regret it.

LARRY LEVIS ❖

The Widening Spell of the Leaves

The Carpathian Frontier, October, 1968

Once, in a foreign country, I was suddenly ill.
I was driving south toward a large city famous
For so little it had a replica, in concrete,
In two-thirds scale, of the Arc de Triomphe stuck
In the midst of traffic, & obstructing it.
But the city was hours away, beyond the hills
That were shaped like the bodies of sleeping women.
Often I had to slow down for herds of goats
Or cattle milling on those narrow roads, & for
The narrower, lost, stone streets of villages
I passed through. The pains in my stomach had grown
Gradually sharper & more frequent as the day
Wore on, & now a fever had set up house.
In the villages there wasn't much point in asking
Anyone for help. In those places, where tanks
Were bivouacked in shade on their way back
From some routine exercise along
The Danube, even food was scarce that year.
And the languages shifted for no clear reason
From two hard quarries of Slavic into German,
Then to a shred of Latin spliced with oohs
And hisses. Even when I tried the simplest phrases,
The peasants passing over those uneven stones
Paused just long enough to look up once,
Uncomprehendingly. Then they turned
Quickly away, vanishing quietly into that
Moment, like bark chips whirled downriver.

Most Recent Book: THE WIDENING SPELL OF THE LEAVES
(University of Pittsburgh Press, 1990)

It was autumn. Beyond each village the wind
Threw gusts of yellowing leaves across the road.
The goats I passed were thin, gray; their hind legs,
Caked with dried shit, seesawed along—
Not even mild contempt in their expressionless,
Pale eyes, & their brays like the scraping of metal.
Except for one village that had a kind
Of museum where I stopped to rest, & saw
A dead Scythian soldier under glass,
Turning to dust while holding a small sword
At attention forever, there wasn't much to look at.
Wind, leaves, goats, the higher passes
Locked in stone, the peasants with their fate
Embroidering a stillness into them,
And a spell over all things in that landscape,
Like . . .
                    That was the trouble; it couldn't be
Compared to anything else, not even the sleep
Of some asylum at a wood's edge with the sound
Of a pond's spillway beside it. But as each cramp
Grew worse & lasted longer than the one before,
It was hard to keep myself aloof from the threadbare
World walking on that road. After all,
Even as they moved, the peasants, the herds of goats
And cattle, the spiraling leaves, at least were part
Of that spell, that stillness.
                    After a while,
The villages grew even poorer, then thinned out,
Then vanished entirely. An hour later,
There were no longer even the goats, only wind,
Then more & more leaves blown over the road, sometimes
Covering it completely for a second.
And yet, except for a random oak or some brush
Writhing out of the ravine I drove beside,
The trees had thinned into rock, into large,
Tough blonde rosettes of fading pasture grass.
Then *that* gave out in a bare plateau. . . . And then,
Easing the Dacia down a winding grade
In second gear, rounding a long, funneled curve—
In a complete stillness of yellow leaves filling
A wide field—like something thoughtlessly,
Mistakenly erased, the road simply ended.
I stopped the car. There was no wind now.
I expected that, & though I was sick & lost,

I wasn't afraid. I should have been afraid.
To this day I don't know why I wasn't.
I could hear time cease, the field quietly widen.
I could feel the spreading stillness of the place
Moving like something I'd witnessed as a child,
Like the ancient, armored leisure of some reptile
Gliding, gray-yellow, into the slightly tepid,
Unidentical gray-brown stillness of the water—
Something blank & unresponsive in its tough,
Pimpled skin—seen only a moment, then unseen
As it submerged to rest on mud, or glided just
Beneath the lusterless, calm yellow leaves
That clustered along a log, or floated there
In broken ringlets, held by a gray froth
On the opaque, unbroken surface of the pond,
Which reflected nothing, no one.

                           And then I remembered.
When I was a child, our neighbors would disappear.
And there wasn't a pond of crocodiles at all.
And they hadn't moved. They couldn't move. They
Lived in the small, fenced-off backwater
Of a canal. I'd never seen them alive. They
Were in still photographs taken on the Ivory Coast.
I saw them only once in a studio when
I was a child in a city I once loved.
I was afraid until our neighbor, a photographer,
Explained it all to me, explained how far
Away they were, how harmless; how they were praised
In rituals as 'powers.' But they had no 'powers,'
He said. The next week he vanished. I thought
Someone had cast a spell & that the crocodiles
Swam out of the pictures on the wall & grew
Silently & multiplied & then turned into
Shadows resting on the banks of lakes & streams
Or took the shapes of fallen logs in campgrounds
In the mountains. They ate our neighbor, Mr. Hirata.
They ate his whole family. That is what I believed,
Then . . . that someone had cast a spell. I did not
Know childhood was a spell, or that then there
Was another spell, too quiet to hear,
Entering my city, entering the dust we ate. . . .
No one knew it then. No one could see it,
Though it spread through lawnless miles of housing tracts,
And the new, bare, treeless streets; it slipped

Into the vacant rows of warehouses & picked
The padlocked doors of working-class bars
And union halls & shuttered, empty diners.
And how it clung! (forever, if one had noticed)
To the brothel with the pastel tassels on the shade
Of an unlit table lamp. Farther in, it feasted
On the decaying light of failing shopping centers;
It spilled into the older, tree-lined neighborhoods,
Into warm houses, sealing itself into books
Of bedtime stories read each night by fathers—
The books lying open to the flat, neglected
Light of dawn; & it settled like dust on windowsills
Downtown, filling the smug cafés, schools,
Banks, offices, taverns, gymnasiums, hotels,
Newsstands, courtrooms, opium parlors, Basque
Restaurants, Armenian steam baths,
French bakeries, & two of the florists' shops—
Their plate-glass windows smashed forever.
Finally it tried to infiltrate the exact
Center of my city, a small square bordered
With palm trees, olives, cypresses, a square
Where no one gathered, not even thieves or lovers.
It was a place which no longer had any purpose,
But held itself aloof, I thought, the way
A deaf aunt might, from opinions, styles, gossip.
I liked it there. It was completely lifeless,
Sad & clear in what seemed always a perfect,
Windless noon. I saw it first as a child,
Looking down at it from that as yet
Unvandalized, makeshift studio.
I remember leaning my right cheek against
A striped beach ball so that Mr. Hirata—
Who was Japanese, who would be sent the next week
To a place called Manzanar, a detention camp
Hidden in stunted pines almost above
The Sierra timberline—could take my picture.
I remember the way he lovingly relished
Each camera angle, the unwobbling tripod,
The way he checked each aperture against
The light meter, in love with all things
That were not accidental, & I remember
The care he took when focusing; how
He tried two different lens filters before
He found the one appropriate for that

Sensual, late, slow blush of afternoon
Falling through the one, broad bay window.
I remember holding still & looking down
Into the square because he asked me to;
Because my mother & father had asked me please
To obey & be patient & allow the man—
Whose business was failing anyway by then—
To work as long as he wished to without any
Irritations or annoyances before
He would have to spend these years, my father said,
Far away, in snow, & without his cameras.
But Mr. Hirata did not work. He played.
His toys gleamed there. That much was clear to me. . . .
That was the day I decided I would never work.
It felt like a conversion. Play was sacred.
My father waited behind us on a sofa made
From car seats. One spring kept nosing through.
I remember the camera opening into the light. . . .
And I remember the dark after, the studio closed,
The cameras stolen, slivers of glass from the smashed
Bay window littering the unsanded floors,
And the square below it bathed in sunlight. . . . All this
Before Mr. Hirata died, months later,
From complications following pneumonia.
His death, a letter from a camp official said,
Was purely accidental. I didn't believe it.
Diseases were wise. Diseases, like the polio
My sister had endured, floating paralyzed
And strapped into her wheelchair all through
That war, seemed too precise. Like photographs . . .
Except disease left nothing. Disease was like
An equation that drank up light & never ended,
Not even in summer. Before my fever broke,
And the pains lessened, I could actually see
Myself, in the exact center of that square.
How still it had become in my absence, & how
Immaculate, windless, sunlit. I could see
The outline of every leaf on the nearest tree,
See it more clearly than ever, more clearly than
I had seen anything before in my whole life:
Against the modest, dark gray, solemn trunk,
The leaves were becoming only what they had to be—
Calm, yellow, things in themselves & nothing

More—& frankly they were nothing in themselves,
Nothing except their little reassurance
Of persisting for a few more days, or returning
The year after, & the year after that, & every
Year following—estranged from us by now—& clear,
So clear not one in a thousand trembled; hushed
And always coming back—steadfast, orderly,
Taciturn, oblivious—until the end of Time.

ROBERT LONG ❖

Have a Nice Day

> *We live in an age of hyenas.*
> —Reuben Nakian

The romance of police in their shiny cruisers washes
Across television screens as well as everyone's windows,
Here in New York, through the first-floor triple-locked
Kind as well as the big, barroom plate-glass type,
Street level, blurred with transient figures: going to work,

Going home, etc. Today I noticed, in the new
Sears catalogue, that those old-fashioned, gathered curtains
Which adorned kitchen windows of the fifties
Are called "Priscillas." Cottage Priscillas.
Double- or single-draw Priscillas. Double ruffle Priscillas.

I used to be a professional chef, but I never made anything
That remotely resembles the fried chicken you get
In this neighborhood: it comes in Styrofoam boxes,
With compartments of greasy macaroni salad, soggy yellow fries,
And a piece of white bread. On the lid, in relief,
"Have a Nice Day," next to an image of smiling balloons
And exclamation points scattering like bowling pins.

Life is full of surprise. Discovering the official name
Of familiar objects: one trims one's nails with pinch clippers.
The state of New York boasts good quantity

Most Recent Book: WHAT HAPPENS (Galileo Press, 1988)

Of the following varieties of blackberry: Lawton's,
Minnewaska, and Rathburn. My next-door neighbor's dog,
The one I'd been calling "Hunter" for the last two years,

Is actually named "Putter." But back to today's topic:
Cookery. One time this guy I worked with
Told me I made the worst meat loaf he'd ever tasted *in his life*.
Another time, a drunk woman sent word, via a waiter,
That her eleven-year-old made a better Bolognese sauce. Nonetheless,

I persevered in my craft, so that, someday, I could afford
This box of slimy chicken, the one describing a parabola
Across the room, and live to write about it, on my IBM Model C.
Mostly, these days, we just sit around and vacuum the cats,
Play gin rummy and watch the police cars go by.
This is why I love television. Any drug that subtle
Deserves the kind of acclaim normally reserved

For a '59 Haut Brion or (I've tasted these) a '45
Cheval Blanc. Just think of all those tuxedoed sommeliers
Stumbling from cellar to dining room, wearing
What a younger generation might see as an awesome coke spoon,
The terrific clank of it against onyx shirt studs.
This is why I love restaurants. This is one of the reasons
I like to write. It's a quiet occupation.
It's a nice day out; it's crow season here by the bay.
A man is starting up his powerboat for the first time this year.
Clouds Vuillard never painted twirl to the west.
The dog goes off barking, into the brush.

What Happens

> Let's say that grief has insisted that you
> carry its luggage. That you have no choice.
> —Mekeel McBride

Let's say that what I miss
Is the sound of your car door whining open,
Then slamming lightly, and the two minute delay
While you walked up the little hill,
Carrying folders and pens, or a soccer ball, or, once,
A tackle box with a snapping turtle shut inside.
You found him on the road. We called him Marcel.

He lay for weeks on the bottom of his tank,
And never got used to it, though he ate raw meat
Thoughtfully, one half-inch chunk at a time.
He was a meditative creature; he stared into the corners
Of his little home for whole days. He wasn't impressed
When we'd stare back, or talk to him, or play music.

But enough of strange pets. It's not enough,
Remembering events as though they held such significance—
Such nearly physical import—that they could matter.
What's the use. What's the right way to say good-bye?
Maybe it means throwing out words like these:
Old blue sweatshirt. One bottle rubbing alcohol.
A quart jar reading WATER. Letters.
It's impulse that rules us, the impulse that causes
Certain days to be memorable, this possibility:
Anything can happen, and will. It's the feeling
That anytime now, this hot July sun will fade
Behind stratocirrus, that sheets of rain will lacquer
These windows. Here today, and gone tomorrow,
All you've got coming is the moment.

When we let the snapping turtle go,
He plonked like a stone dropped casually into the pond.
As the rings on the water grew thoughtfully distant,
Highway noise drifted in. I remember touching you
Lightly, on the shoulder. A kid dropped his toy boat,
On the opposite shore. We headed back to the car,
Just after the little bubbles glugged to the surface.
I shut my door. The clouds were passing above
In confident gangs, and we drove the twist of roads home,
The place by the water, the home you'd leave in a matter of days,
Our lives as confused and clear as hieroglyphics. This moment:
Leaves turning silver. A backache that comes and goes.

Saying One Thing

Today, the angels are all writing postcards,
Or talking on the telephone.
Meanwhile, in Nowheresville,
A rabbit is running into a bush. This, I tell my friend,
Means good luck. The next day,
The sun is out, the fix is in,

And we're ready to throw in the towel.
Anytime now, our number might come up,
And the telephone will finally stop ringing:
Don't call before three,
Knock four times,
Show me the way to go home,

Back and forth and back again,
Like some idiot boomerang.
"Kerpow" and "schlock" are our favorite words,
Lately, and are about what things are amounting to.
Still, the stories of airplane disasters
And overnight flings in far-off cities have a kind of allure,

Like metallic paint, or something expensive
You want but can't have.
O toothpaste commercials, common house fly,
Fall is in the air again. On this spaceship
The code word is "blond," or "good dog."
Night begins to fall, the atmosphere is electric.

Found and Lost

Let's tell the story of the man
Who worked in a factory, making chocolate cigarettes,
Who ran over a squirrel on his way to work
One morning: it belched a cloud of CO_2,

Vanished in the mirror. The man
Mourned. He began collecting photographs
Of squirrels. The walls of his home
Bore them: soon, he became

A recognized authority on the squirrel,
Its anatomy, its habits, its relationship
To other rodents. People became tired
Of his singular devotion, began

Posting bills on walls all over town,
Posters reading "Down With Squirrels," and
"Turn on the TV so I can see if I'm alive."
The man moved to North Dakota,

Where he died. Let's call him Harry.
He wasn't much fun. Sometimes I can almost feel

How he must have felt, that burden
Of guilt, that siege of unpopularity.

Distance has its disadvantages. You're
In Paris, trying on shoes, and I'm wondering
If it's really snowing out or if it's just
Blowing off the trees. The distance

From me to you a slow motion stretch
Of ocean air, nearly palpable, heavy,
Heavier by the second. It's late fall,
And it's too late to start over.

Fumetti

When Madame Bovary sat up shrieking
Toward the end of the hilarious novel
Of the same name, poison eating away at her innards,
Flaubert described her posture as that of
"A galvanized corpse"; it seemed she thought
She was locked in a nightmare she couldn't escape. And so

She died, as indicated by all that "black liquid"
That poured from her mouth when Charles and Hommais, that pig,
Propped her up in bed. Next example:
When Tony thinks Maria's dead, at the end of *West Side Story*,
And runs gasping around Hollywood's version of 110th and Amsterdam
Jangling playground fences it seems so cruel: it turns out

She's alive. Tony gets shot. The Sharks are upset. Life
Imitates art, and it isn't fair, but it goes on, anyway, at least
For the rest of us. On the bay this morning
Rest several nun buoys, red from this distance, faded close-up,
To a nail polish color: *dusk blush*, or *Santa Fe embarrassment*.
Their shapes suggest new approaches to the figure, metaphors,

Or, as Adrienne Rich would have it, "metafirs," for the slinkiness
Of our lives, lately, sliding from one minor crisis
To the next, sidling up to yesterday's celebrities in the streets,
Languishing in a salon of ineptitude. And suddenly heaven's doorbell
Rings: it's a gas-pumping boy from New Jersey holding a clump
Of witch hazel, he is an accretion of yellow light,

Smells I recall, blur of traffic. And so we come to you today
In a haze of amyl nitrate, paint spattered T-shirts,

In a big silver car, confused in the brilliance of the day,
Wrapped in white aprons and dusting cans of tomato puree,
Dutifully collecting phone numbers and jotting down license plates,
Trimming the hedges and clearing the decks,

Throwing together the fall collection, catching quick naps between takes.
O otherwise lovely day, day of achingly blue skies,
Cacophony of birds in lush late May oaks, you seem a gift
In your modest, headlong passage.

ADRIAN C. LOUIS ❖

*Wakinyan**

Puppy Luppy, our super sleek black Lab
was missing for two days, running
with the pack after a Spaniel in heat
and because the day was warm, we walked
down to the pow-wow grounds by the creek
to look for that goofy boy.
We had a lot of money and love invested
in him and he'd never been out for two days.
We sat in the shade of the squaw cooler
underneath the boughs of rusted pines
for a minute to catch our breath
before we headed for the tick-infested creek.
It had snowed heavily a week earlier so
it must have been the heat that brought
the opening buds of the cottonwoods and willows
and the spiderlike ticks who, once attached,
would turn to big, green grapes on my dogs.

Wakinyan, the thunder beings, kicked us
in the crotch before we got to the creek.
The sky turned violet, lightning cracked
and crackled sideways, not up and down.
Rain slapped down so hard, for an instant
I heard strains of Junior Wells at a Chicago
nightspot twenty years past.

* *Wakinyan* is a Sioux word meaning "thunder beings."

Most Recent Book: FIRE WATER WORLD (West End Press, 1989)

That didn't last long. The rain hardened
into hail and we ran past the music in my mind
and huddled in a large clump of wild cherry.
Broken bottles, buried frogs, and reason rushed
all around us in swollen rivulets of rain and hail.
The thunder beings had driven us to humanity.
Inside the thicket across from us were two winos,
coats thickened by greasepuke and woodsmoke,
shivering with shivering eyes.

It was early spring and the day was sweating wet.
God had emerged for the first time since creation
and had decided to show his magnificent mirth.
Four Indians in a bush were being pelted
by golf ball-sized pellets of ice.
We laughed aloud and the two winos did too.
We stared at them in silence and they stared
back with yellow, empty eyes.
We quickly left the bush and entered the storm.
Pain is easier to deal with than spirits.

Rhetoric Leads to Cliché

The young white ranchers with chew drippings
down the door panel of their pickup
have never heard of *communitas*
because it is foreign to their twenty-watt concept
of America where all men are equally constituted
upon a quaint document which they praise
with conceit and deceit in their hearts.
That is the nature of the beast and breast
be damned. Violence condoned in the name of goodness
decries innocence; a word soon discarded
when discovered the savages already possessed it.

I am an Indian born upon Indian land
and I've been battered by myself and others
for nine rounds but I am raging and ready
for the tenth and final spurt of manhood.
When the rednecks passed me in their white pickup
and dropped a beer can in their wake
I tromped the gas pedal and passed them back
stupidly, since the roads were sheet ice.

I hovered in front of them for a minute
then fishtailed toward the horizon feeling good.
I hit the reservation line and then slowed down.
I remembered what my bumpersticker read:
Life is a bitch and then you die.

Life is a bitch and then you die?
Hours later at home waiting for the old lady
to get home and cook my beans
I stared at the icebox landscape of Pine Ridge
and through the faint
mirrored ghost of my own reflection
upon the winter pane
some wino's coat frozen in the yard
half under snow, a rigid arm extended
reaching for air in this ghost scene
the dogs dragged home
this replication of what we all have seen
in that famous picture of 1890
by the hysterical Nebraska Historical Society:
The Minniconjou chief Bigfoot, frozen solid,
one gnarled and bony arm extended
into the chilled air of his cousins' land
a simple why in his death grimace:
"*Tunkasila*,* these white men
hate all that is good
and we don't know why."

Indian College Blues

Friday's all-staff meeting dissolves
into structure because time is money
and the *wasicu*† neo-colonials in charge
have learned to ignore "Indian time."
The breed guest speaker is dressed
in black like a skinny witch Johnny Cash.
Self-proclaimed as an Indian expert

* *Tunkasila* is a Sioux word meaning "grandfather" or implying deceased
males of the tribe, or as an address to the Great Spirit.
† *Wasicu* is a Sioux word which literally is "taker of fat," but has commonly
come to mean "white man."

she launches into her talk about the ancient
Indian astronomy inherent
in a tribal history she herself has conjured
according to fullbloods sitting near me.
They ignore her and talk about the rodeo
or who got shot at and missed by his old lady
then wrecked his car like he was in a movie
after eluding the tribal cops
by speeding through a herd
of a thousand whiteface steers.
The cops threw him to the ground, cuffed him,
and then rubbed his face in fresh bullshit
only because the cops were his cousins.

The strange skinny woman lulls my mind away
from overhearing the story of the chase
because part of me pities her
and her bat-winged words whisk me away
with a brief, daft vision of Copernican Sioux.
Distracted momentarily, my ears
wander back to the renegade car crasher.

In the image of his cousins rubbing his face
into fresh cowshit I know he saw stars
and in his sight I see ancient campfires
twinkling in our ancestors'
earthly imitation of the night sky.

Somehow the witchy speaker does not know
the lessons of her own blood.
Her own people cannot see her
and her own people cannot hear her
but I am transported by the cowshit grace
of our Indian race
until the meeting so mercifully ends.

Couch Fantasy

In the mandolin air of pistons
sweat hammers down the pale face
of the movie U-boat captain
gliding his steel shark through
the canyons of the North Atlantic.

In a womb of silence
he cuts his engines and genuflects
at the keyhole periscope.
Upon the crucifix crosshairs I see
he sees a Teutonic dream with blue eyes
of Delft and tresses of cascading bronze.
My hand sneaks to my groin until I remember
the blonde cleavaged clerk in K-Mart yesterday
and a depth charge explodes in my brain.
She insulted my woman and me because our check
had a reservation address.
Her supervisor and her supervisor's supervisor
verified us. We were Indians with good credit!

When we left Pine Ridge in the morning we
saw a hobbling puppy on the street.
It was eighteen below outside.
Halfway to Rapid City we saw a woman hitching,
young, raggedy coat, black eye and smiling.
It was eighteen below outside
and any submarines had yet to sail.

The First of the Month

Undeodorized and radiant in rags
she squats sullenly
upon the crooked earth
and pokes her brown finger
at fat, red ants
dragging a dead fly home.
My reflection in her eyes
dazzles the air from my lungs.
I shrivel inside
the vacuum of formic arms.
Now's hourglass is frozen.
The bubbling brook is foetid
and the ancient, wondrous
songbirds are chancrous.
Against my dark void
of memories
of blood upon blood

White Clay, Nebraska, explodes
with a thousand faces
of my drunken race
cashing their welfare checks.

HEATHER McHUGH ❖

Earthmoving Malediction

Bulldoze the bed where we made love,
bulldoze the goddamn room.
Let rubble be our evidence
and wreck our home.

I can't give touching up
by inches, can't give beating
up by heart. So set the comforter
on fire, and turn the dirt

to some advantage—palaces of pigweed,
treasuries of turd. The fist
will vindicate the hand,
and tooth and nail

refuse to burn, and I
must not look back, as Mrs. Lot
was named for such a little—
something in a cemetery,

or a man. Bulldoze the coupled
ploys away, the cute exclusives
in the social mall. We dwell

on earth, where beds
are brown, where swoops
are fell. Bulldoze

the pearly gates:
if paradise comes down
there is no hell.

Most Recent Book: SHADES (Wesleyan University Press, 1988)

Inflation

Language wasn't any
funny money I was playing with,
no toy surprise, no watch or wooden
nickel, not
a nickel nickel either, twice
removed, sign of a sign.
I meant to make
so deep a song

it held no end of love.
But now I'm dumb
to frame the stream
of stills I feel,
stuck in the onrush without any
one that I was singing to,
without a you, and currents go on running up
a bill of silver senselessness—the seconds counted
in the hundreds, in the thousands, in the billions, till the till

is burst. Remember how enormous one
old swollen moment used to be?
Remember how we loved
position 99, the one where you
look forward? Man, as I look back, I wonder how

did numb get so comparative?
How did the verb to come
(our childhood's bright
infinitive) become
so narrow a necessity?

Place Where Things Got

I always thought if I could just
remember where I started I
could understand the end. The cat upon my lap
infolds itself, intends itself;
it makes itself a compact package, perfectly adapted to
the transient circumstance of my repose,
and chooses out of live adjacency

best balance, fewest gestures,
all intelligence, no thought.
It wraps the rest around itself and settles.

For a time its engine runs
continuous, it bumbles and it hums and drones
and then slows down, so little
interludes of stiller stuff occur, some
quietude in patches, here and there, and then
another strength of hum crops up to just
drop off, drop deep and deeper in
to dream, to stir,
to dream, till only
little nubs of noise arise, the
intermittent particles of purr . . .

 *

When moments hadn't melted
into ages yet, my sister Jan and I
would grind the sounds of sentences
down past the word to syllables,
the syllables to letters and
the letters into even less:
the grindstone was the voice's slow control;
you spoke so gradually symbol turned
to substance, curve to its
constituents; you shifted rpm until
the voice was gravel and the gravel grain and then
the particles themselves became distinct. If you
could utter utterances slow enough you found
the sand inside a saying, molecules like those
Superman is made of, held up close (as duplicated
supermen will be, by little people).
Grown-ups wouldn't tell us
what is IN a loaf of time or life of story, what's inside
a voice, in other words—away from what
the English teachers wanted and away
from what the elders took for granted,
what's *in* there, aside
from coins of meaning? That is why

we took the trail of crumbs, broke breadstuff down,
backtracked from mines of money toward the mill
where dough turned into grain and grain

to seed and seed to cell and there
beyond iotas of the minuscule we found
a place where things got huge again.

Third Person Neuter

Is God mad? Was Christ
crazy? Is the truth
the legal truth? (Three PhDs who swear

the human being who believes
a human being God
is what, in fairness, speaking

clinically, we call
a nut.) No jury,
given sacred laws

of science and democracy, would now
forgive so big a claim as Christ's—a claim
for good. (The wounded get

their settlements in millions, not
worlds-without-end.) We think of bliss
as ignorance, and heaven as naïveté: the doctor's

a philosopher, the priest a practicing
apologist. Not one of them
will let me see

with my own eyes my friend again.
When experts gave him time, it made
his luck and language die. What good

was love? It was the ultimate
authority to quit.
He had no use

for flesh at last
and, Christ,
I'm made of it.

LYNNE McMAHON ❖

Convalescence

And we, who are going to live after all,
get up from our day beds, chaise lounges, settees,
pull off the twisted linen, brush our hair back
into bright bands, and smoothe the color,
lipstick, back into our cheeks. How well
we look! How clearly we are the portrait
of well-being, gathering ourselves at the pond's
edge and spreading out our blankets; so
sun-enamored we hardly recognize this future,
so brownly we burn, so whitely our secret parts
shine, as if these two tones were our own
invention and not the Nature's that saves us
as a gift for Eros—you know him—the Hungry One.

Devolution of the Nude

In Whitman's day there were the secret bathers
spied on by his poem's spinster, yearning
behind the glass; in Emerson's day
and Thoreau's; in the Utopian societies eager
to transmute the dross of Puritanism into the gold
of burnished flesh; in every century or half-
century there have been faddists who know
the six openings of the body must go
unstoppered, that the distinction between man
and woman is holy, and the expulsion from
the garden was the garment district's
first advertisement ploy.
                    In our day
there are perhaps fewer of these: acid rain
and factory seepage combine to forecast another
ice-age (this time the glacier greens with alloys),
have made stoppering hygenic;
and we've discovered in place of the open,

Most Recent Book: FAITH (Wesleyan University Press, 1988)

the principle of the closed, the Victorian tenet
that covered is more alluring than bare,
that Shame's the secret passageway
to Eros. And though we may laugh at Marianne
Moore's remark—"I like the nude," she said,
handing back Kenneth Clark's book, "but
in moderation"—it is us
                              we find
swathed in bedclothes, as if we were asthmatic
invalids under covers, calming ourselves
with penlights and turn-of-the-century novels
whose characters' cumbersome cloaks
and flannel layers protect them, protect *us*,
from what is only whispered of: the difficult
birth in the back room, the laying out
of the dead in the parlor, the two occasions
for nakedness that are dreadful
and not for our eyes—
                              not yet.

Barbie's Ferrari

Nothing is quite alien or quite recognizable at this speed,
Though there is the suggestion of curve, a mutant
Curvature designed, I suppose, to soften or offset
The stiletto toes and karate arms that were too
Angular for her last car, a Corvette as knifed as Barbie
Herself, and not the bloodred of Italian Renaissance.
This is Attention. This is detail fitted to sheer
Velocity. For her knees, after all, are locked—
Once fitted into the driving pit, she can only accelerate
Into a future that becomes hauntingly like the past:
Nancy Drew in her yellow roadster, a convertible,
I always imagined, the means to an end
Almost criminal in its freedom, its motherlessness.
For Barbie, too, is innocent of parents, pressing
Her unloved breasts to the masculine wheel, gunning
The turn into the hallway and out over the maiming stairs,
Every jolt slamming her uterus into uselessness, sealed,
Sealed up and preserved, everything about her becoming
Pure Abstraction and the vehicle for Desire: to be Nancy,
To be Barbie, to feel the heaven of Imagination

Breathe its ether on your cheeks, rosying in the slipstream
As the speedster/roadster/Ferrari plummets over the rail
Into the ocean of waxed hardwood below. To crash and burn
And be retrieved. To unriddle the crime. To be
Barbie with a plot! That's the soulful beauty of it.
That's the dreaming child.
Not the dawn of Capital, or the factories of Hong Kong
Reversing the currency in Beijing. Not the ovarian
Moon in eclipse. Just the dreaming child, the orphan,
Turning in slow motion in the air above the bannister,
For whom ideas of gender and marketplace are nothings
Less than nothing. It's the car she was born for.
It's Barbie you mourn for.

Little Elegy for the Age

We've sworn off nostalgia
this time for good, no more recounting the sixties
and those astronaut hairdos giving way to a wilderness
of plaits and frizz and blonde Marianne Faithfull falls;
or the beautiful freak embroidery above the monochrome
of blue; or the music, or the aphorisms, on the front
porch, on the grass, on the courthouse steps.
The tatterdemalion aggregate's slangy shorthand
cutting through to God or beauty *was* a kind of beauty,
a transcendent sloganeering that got the mind out
of the way of the body. It was Byronic, at least part
of the time, for the aloof and tormented. It was
certainly Shelleyan: accumulating lovers, sending
poems and manifestos out to sea in Molotov
cocktail bottles whose tiny conflagrations Shelley
and Mary and Claire Clairmont watched from shore
in a miserable joy, exacting love's price only later.
Italy without glooms, poetry part politics, part
Mont Blanc—that was the portion we appropriated.
Sexual carouse and anarchy. But Mary Shelley later
wrote: "He died, and the world showed no outward
sign." That's the part we come to now. The scale
of grief, and losses, that for all their grandeur, were
only personal. It's the *only* that rends our hearts,
now that we too are only personal, private now
and retreating to houses we'd not foreseen, on streets

where demolition goes on in cordoned sections
struck off by carnival flags and cones, and where,
showcased at the front curb, we find ourselves,
our life really, frozen for a moment—foot lifted,
or hand, as if to signal the life on the street—
arrested by the beauty of measurable diminishment,
concrete crushed into smaller and smaller bits until
it is just dust, a gray-whiteness on our shoetops,
then not even that.

Ann Lee

> founder of the First Church
> of the Millennium (Shakers)

A serenity so arduously maintained, and at such
frightful cost (but one needn't consider
that anymore), the soul could at last unbend
and become the female Christ, sanctified
in the company of glossy fruit in a plain bowl
and the unadorned cherrywood sconce
holding a single candle, everything "in the neatest
conceivable style," reported the *Richmond Virginia
Inquirer* in 1825. And the superlative
of neat conceiving was precisely the point.
After four hemorrhaging births, the children
all lost in infancy, and a brute husband,
she left for America, leaving behind abhorrent
intercourse—"the flesh consumed upon my bones,
and bloody sweat pressed through the pores
of my skin"—and was revealed to be
the celibate divine.
                              Done with blood,
with semen, with the torn body of penetration
and delivery, she was at last the spiritual
mother of painless ghost-children
who would live forever in shining separate
houses. Where there had been coal dust
and stinking mill effluent, there was lemon
oil and lye-scrubbed boards.
Where there had been the rags of aspiring
gentility—lace trimmings, or High Church

embroideries the poor cleaned themselves
to look at but couldn't touch—there was
the planed surface, whitewashed walls, pegs
to hang the chairs on. No altar, or gold,
or carvings. And she, the Manchester slum
girl, could, for the first time
in her life, simply rest.
                              It was better
than death. It was death-in-life.
The body clean, the room clean, the mind
could be drawn out of grossness and float
over the beautifully, artfully rock-tumbled
fences into the acres of immaculate pasture.
The shakings and hallucinations, the leadership
quarrels and canvassing for converts, all
the business of religion, came full-force later,
when she was too far gone into her light-flooded
mind to assume corporeal form.
She had been substance. Now she was essence.
She had spent four crucifixions, had been
impaled on the sex of brutish inevitability,
her daily round had been the Gethsemane
of alleys and verminous warrens.
                              And now
was the peace that passeth understanding.
The congress of the elect, the Lost Tribe
of Israel, Joseph Smith and Chief
Nez Perce, American History stalking
through the dining hall like a poltergeist,
impregnating the prettiest girls, spiking
the scurvy-curing double lemon pies
with aphrodisiac and psychotropic dust—
all that was still to come. Civil War
was still to come. The Kentucky
settlement would be set upon by soldiers
from both sides, the best horses and men
conscripted, and only the elderly left,
who would die out, prisoners of the body
after all.
She could, perhaps, foresee it.
She could no longer care about it.
The message had been conceived and delivered
and she was finished. A legacy
of furniture, some boxy buildings, and

tiny separate beds: all she amounted to
was in the end all she wished to leave.
To see God in a plain room,
to fix serenity in a single bed . . .
The principle was sound,

and would come round again.

Gail Mazur ❖

Phonic

As if my answering machine were a rejection,
you'd leave your forlorn message:
Call your father. . . . Then, a dial tone.
Guilty of being out, or busy,
I never thought to save the tape,
to keep some resonance and pitch of you,
if only in those four syllables—
tremulous, demanding, but tangible

as the snapshot I found today,
a torn dwarf, her plump gray face
shadowing as she squatted on our front porch,
tight braids, strange frown, white Mary Janes.

I'd forgotten that silent child
until I held her flattened image;
My peopled past is curled and tattered,
tucked into envelopes and albums;
it reconstitutes itself in dreams,
a *richesse* of repeat performances—
a friend's touch become sweetly erotic,
my children, peachy and clinging again,

you, saying you're not afraid of dying. . . .
I wish I could listen to your voice
instead of the staticky measures
of a cassette's repetitive erasures.

Although sometimes in my edgy sleep,
I hear a *Gail!* that snaps me awake,

Most Recent Book: The Pose of Happiness (David R. Godine, Publisher, 1986)

an urgent extrasensory appeal
I take for mortal emergency.
I feel sure it's you, calling
for something I don't understand
and never did. Then, it disappears.
The voice is nowhere in my wakefulness,

not kept in memory's burr—
no tender disinterested utterance
you never quite pulled off in life,
good as you were.

Family Plot, October

I'm digging at my father's grave,
my mother holding the rusty mums
she's carried here to make a little garden

before the first frost. Three years today,
and the grass is a damp brown rectangle
over his cryptic body that's guarded

by earth from my more morbid speculations.
Perpetual care's contracted out here,
so no one's responsible for the dried-out

tap, the graveyard's shameless posture
of neglect, certainly not this pair
of purposeful mourners with trowels

and sturdy annuals we've chosen
for their profusions of unopened buds.
I'm not good at this, thudding my shovel

at stones, setting pots in the ground
off-center. Alone, I'd plant a little dogwood,
a Japanese drift of flowing branch

above his name, but my mother sees this
as her future home and wants, as usual,
something else, whatever's harder to nurture.

I'll never lie here. I don't want anyone
to stand, icy-handed, imagining
my ruined body. My father liked so much

to laugh—would he enjoy his clumsy girl,
hacking away at clumps of sod, or his wife's
sensible blue shoes sinking in mud?

It doesn't matter. I can't even say
if he or I believed in God,
or in any kind of hereafter. . . .

A drizzle mists the raw new hole,
mists the one white rose from my table,
and the pebble I place on his headstone

like a good Orthodox daughter
leaving a memorial relic
as if it were a talisman of devotion

that nothing—no eternities of neglect
by myself or others, no drought or blight
or storm or holocaust—could erode.

May, Home after a Year Away

Bridal wreath. White rhododendron. Dogwood.
My town. At dawn, six or seven people—
hard to know if one shape's just a bundle—
sleeping on the Common's tender new grass
and on the granite benches. Dandelion
puffs cluster in the green; didn't we once
take deep breaths and blow the gossamer off
and make a wish? With each return home,
I seem to love it more, yet with less terror.

What would I wish for now? What wasn't working,
still isn't. My friends' sorrows, mine again.
If only we could carry this sweet spring
in us anywhere . . . I hope I die in May, some
one to scatter my ashes—
                              Is that it, Gail,
the wish you make in your happiness?

Spring Planting

This is the season
when our friends may and will die daily.
—Robert Lowell, "Soft Wood"

Last year's sunflower stalks blacken
at dusk, their huge exploded suns
droop like the heads of mourners,
frozen in somber procession.

I carry my seedlings from the car—
snap peas, radishes, an experimental
pole bean . . .
          My little green homunculi,
my hostages to a future season, you've
hardened in April's tonic breeze.

We say you'll bear in so many weeks,
that we'll be here to share the fruit—
it's easy to imagine the future wrong.

The four-year mimosa tree stands pale
and spring-naked, a body's length taller
than last year, and seems to belong.

Years back, at Temple Israel Sunday School
on Saturdays, we donated flattened one-dollar bills
for planting trees in newborn Israel.
Survivors would "make the desert bloom"—
Reform American kids helped prevent erosion.
I imagined dark enormous pines,
my father's sweet name
a plaque on one I'd never find . . .

My friend, your last days among us,
you were such a frail leaf tossing
in pain's hurricane, until morphine
finally took you to sleep with my other
lost ones in a distant forest . . .
                    I place
the flats on the ground by a rusty trowel.
Soon, when the mimosa blossoms again,
its delicate pink blooms will sway
in the Cape's harsh wind, and drop—

oriental creature, its feathery flowers
are evanescent as the colorless smoke
your last cigarette blew across my room.

SUSAN MITCHELL ❖

Havana Birth

Off Havana the ocean is green this morning
of my birth. The conchers clean their knives on leather
straps and watch the sky while three couples
who have been dancing on the deck of a ship
in the harbor, the old harbor of the fifties, kiss
each other's cheeks and call it a night.

On a green velour sofa five dresses wait
to be fitted. The seamstress kneeling at Mother's feet
has no idea I am about to be born. Mother
pats her stomach which is flat
as the lace mats on the dressmaker's table. She thinks
I'm playing in my room. But as usual, she's wrong.

I'm about to be born in a park in Havana. Oh,
this is important, everything in the dressmaker's house
is furred like a cat. And Havana leans right up
against the windows. In the park, the air
is chocolate, the sweet breath of a man
smoking an expensive cigar. The grass

is drinkable, dazzling, white. In a moment
I'll get up from the bench, lured
by a flock of pigeons, lazily sipping the same syrupy
music through a straw.
Mother is so ignorant, she thinks
I'm rolled like a ball of yarn under the bed. What

does she know of how I got trapped in my life?
She thinks it's all behind her, the bloody
sheets, the mirror in the ceiling
where I opened such a sudden furious blue, her eyes

Most Recent Book: THE WATER INSIDE THE WATER (Wesleyan University Press, 1983)

bruised shut like mine. The pigeon's eyes
are orange, unblinking, a doll's. Mother always said

I wanted to touch everything because
I was a child. But I was younger than that.
I was so young I thought whatever I
wanted, the world wanted too. Workers
in the fields wanted the glint of sun on their machetes.
Sugarcane came naturally sweet, you

had only to lick the earth where it grew.
The music I heard each night outside
my window lived in the mouth of a bird. I was so young
I thought it was easy as walking
into the ocean which always had room
for my body. So when I held out my hands

I expected the pigeon to float toward me
like a blossom, dusting my fingers with the manna
of its wings. But the world is wily, and doesn't want
to be held for long, which is why
as my hands reached out, workers lay down
their machetes and left the fields, which is why

a prostitute in a little *calle* of Havana dreamed
the world was a peach and flicked
open a knife. And Mother, startled, shook
out a dress with big peonies splashed like dirt
across the front, as if she had fallen
chasing after me in the rain. But what could I do?

I was about to be born, I was about to have
my hair combed into the new music
everyone was singing. The dressmaker sang it, her mouth
filled with pins. The butcher sang it and wiped
blood on his apron. Mother sang it and thought her body
was leaving her body. And when I tried

I was so young the music beat right
through me, which is how the pigeon got away.
The song the world sings day after day
isn't made of feathers, and the song a bird pours
itself into grows tough as a branch
lifting with the singer and the singer's delight.

Feeding the Ducks at the Howard Johnson Motel

I wouldn't say I was dying for it.
But he was already undressed, trousers, socks, shirt
in a heap on the floor. Now it's four in the morning and he
wants to feed the ducks. I tell him the ducks are sleeping.
The ducks are awake, though, floating
around and around on the pond
like baby icebergs. It's a wonder they don't freeze,
it's a wonder there aren't videos
in every room with ducks clouding the screens.

When I was six, my parents took me
to the Jungle Queen, family dining, with portholes
over every table. Fish swam past my nose,
dull-whiskered carp, shadowy
as X-rays. I tried to squeeze crumbs
through the glass, but now I think those fish fed
on one another. He saved bread
from dinner, and throws a piece to the biggest
duck, paddling in circles. Even the taste

of our bodies comes from so far away,
from bodies and bodies where we have washed
ourselves clean and hard as stones.
If a duck shuddered into him, it would
shatter. If my tongue blew away, I might know
what to tell him. Instead, I say, Why does the orange
bedspread look hideous when duck feet, the same
color, are beautiful? He throws again
and again, the bread sinking right

in front of their beaks.
I have been hungry so long I could
lift an empty glass to my mouth and savor the air
for hours. Each time I throw bread,
I feel like a child, my arm reaching out across
the pond, pitching as hard
as it can the fat balls of dough. Only
now I am aware of their dumbness,
their duck stupidity, how

they do not even see the bread, which glows
as it falls, every crust and crumb
shining under lights of the motel. Suddenly I
think of his teeth, hard
behind his lips; how, if a duck
bit me now, my hand
would open its heart, the rich
smell of something baking rising
from my flesh.

The Face

is what I always imagined
I would look like
if there were any justice in the world, which
is not to say the face is handsome or a
face anyone would want
to sit across from, let alone possess.

Mother used to say, in the days when
mother and I went around
together, "That's how I feel" and point to a girl
of sixteen, her long hair streaming
as she ran to catch a cab. I
never felt sixteen.

I felt like this man's face, so
it's surprising to discover the face
has been in prison, and not for doing anything
bad, but for doing something good.
My friends don't want to look
at the face, they want an angel

to appear and roll the tight fists
of its wings between them and the lions
jaws, clamping shut the icy draft, the animal
roar, which is the sound a cave
gives off in its silence. There was one
occasion where I shied away

from my own face, I was in
a hospital where some fool had hung a mirror
across from the bed, so that anyone could
see the nose tubes streaming

from their nostrils and tied back into
a machine that decorated the wall. I would rise

from the bottom like a wave towering
above its own strength or like that Nova Scotian
bore that carries with it
fish, gulls, tourists, all squawking, mouth gaping
toward the sea serpent and stare
at my reflection in the world

of the living, then sink
back to the bottom again. Morphine makes faces
alike in their fastidious repose, austere
in their dedication to sleep. I was a servant
of sleep, luminous and white, the stretcher
emptied of everything. All I wanted

was to crawl onto a face, mouth
to mouth sucking its coma, and even
though the nurses pulled me back
from its bed, saying—but what
does it matter what they said?—once I saw
a picture of the first human face

reproduced in art, translucent alabaster
turned upward into the dirt: rubbish, millennia
of disasters burying the eyes,
which were wide open—you have to be born
with a face like mine to understand
how dangerous the world is,

to know from inside out—still, the tenderness,
the compassion hovering about
the mouth, as if flayed angelic
with its sense of escape
from the body. I see it as clearly
as I see the great stone

angel I climbed as a child
which towered outside
the church I did not belong to, the pitted
cheeks scraping skin from
my cheeks as I pushed my lips
against its freezing bliss.

PAUL MONETTE ❖

Brother of the Mount of Olives

> *Mine, O thou lord of life, send my roots rain.*
> —Gerard Manley Hopkins

combing the attic for anything extra
missed or missing evidence of us I sift
your oldest letters on onionskin soft-
cover Gallimard novels from graduate school
brown at the edges like pound cake and turn up
an undeveloped film race it to SUNSET
PLAZA ONE-HOUR wait out the hour wacko
as a spy smuggling a chip that might decode
World War III then sit on the curb poring over
prints of Christmas '83 till I hit paydirt
three shots of the hermit abbey on the moors
southeast of Siena our final crisscross
of the Tuscan hills before the sack of Rome
unplanned it was just that we couldn't bear
to leave the region quite the Green Guide barely
gave it a nod *minor Renaissance pile*
but the real thing monks in Benedictine white
pressing olives and gliding about in hooded
silence Benedict having commanded *shh*
along with his gaunt motto *ora et labora*
pray work but our particular brother John
couldn't stop chattering not from the moment
he met us grinning at the cloister door
seventy years olive-cheeked bald and guileless
no matter we spoke no Italian he led us
gesturing left and right at peeling frescoes
porcelain Marys a limpid row of arches
across the court like a trill on a harpsichord
little did he know how up to our eyeballs
we were on the glories of Florence the Bach
geometry of the hill towns their heart-
stopping squares with the well in the middle
and a rampant lion on the governor's roof

Most Recent Book: LOVE A LOVE (St. Martin's Press, 1988)

we'd already scrutinized every *thing* and now
before we left wished to see it peopled
going about their business out of time
keeping bees holy offices raisin bread
as if nothing had happened since Galileo
instead this voluble little monk pulling us
into the abbey church its lofty Gothic vault
overlaid in sugared Baroque plaster like a bad
cake then Brother John grips us by the biceps
and sweeps us down the cypress-paneled choir
to the reading desk where the Gutenberg
is propped on feast-days he crouches and points
to the inlay on the base and there is a cat
tail curled seeming to sit in a window
every tiger stripe of him laid in jigsaw
as we laughed our rapturous guide went *mew mew*
like a five-year-old *How long have you been here*
we ask a question requiring all our hands
fifty years he tosses off as if time had
nothing to do with it one hand lingering
on my shoulder is it books we like then come
and we patter round the cloister in his wake
duck through a door up a stone stairs and peer
through a grill wrought like a curtain of ivy
into the library its great vellum folios
solid as tombstones nobody copying out
or illuminating today unless perhaps
all of that has died and there's a Xerox
glowing green in the abbot's study John
pokes you to look at the door carvings it seems
he is not a bookish man but who has time
to read anymore we must descend and see
the frescoes fifty years without the world
pray work pray work and yet such drunken gaiety
gasping anew at the cloister's painted wall
clutching my hand before the bare-clad Jesus
bound at the pillar by the painter so-called
Sodoma the parted lips the love-glazed eyes
JUST WHAT KIND OF MEN ARE WE TALKING ABOUT
are we the heirs of them or they our secret
fathers and how many of our kind lie beneath
the cypress alley crowning the hill beyond
the bell tower how does one ask such things
with just one's hands then we took three pictures

me and John John and you you and me *click*
as the old monk takes my arm I'm certain now
that he likes touching us that we are a world
inside him whether he knows or not not that
I felt molested I can take care of myself
but a blind and ancient hunger not unspeakable
unsayable you think he knew about us Rog
how could he not pick up the intersect
the way we laughed the glint in our eyes as we
played our Italian for four hands but my sole
evidence is this sudden noon photograph
the two of us arm in arm in the cloister
delirious gold November light of Tuscany
washing our *cinquecento* faces splashing
the wall behind us a fresco of the monks
at dinner high above them in a pulpit
a reader trilling in Latin you can't even
eat without *ora et labora* and we look
squinting at John as if to wonder how
he will ever click the shutter right it's like
giving a watch to a savage but we look
quite wonderful you with the Green Guide me
clutching the pouch with the passports we look
unbelievably young our half smiles precisely
the same for that is the pierce of beauty
that first day of a rose barely started
and yet all there and Brother John so geeky
with the Canon A-1 did he even see what
he caught we look like choirboys or postulants
or a vagabond pair of scholars here to
pore over an undecoded text not religious
but brotherly enough it's a courtly age
where men are what they do and where they go
comrades all we look like no one else Rog
here's the proof in color now the tour is over
we are glided into a vestibule where cards
slides rosaries prayers that tick are gauntly
presided over by a monk senior to John
if not in years then officialdom the air
is strict in here we cut our laughter short
this one's got us pegged right off this keeper
of the canonical cash drawer withering John
with a look that can hardly wait to assign vast
and pointless rosaries of contrition we buy

the stark official guide to Monte Oliveto
leave a puddle of lire *per restauro*
for restorations and then we're free of His
Priestliness and John bundles us off still
merry and irrepressible too old perhaps
to fear the scorn and penitence of those
racked by sins of the flesh who never touch
a thing and ushers us out to the Fiat
bidding us safe journey who's never been
airborne or out to sea or where Shiva
dances or Pele the fire-god gargles
the bowels of the earth we wave him off
and leap in the car we're late for Rome flap
open the map but we're laughing too *Did that
just happen or what* and we drive away
winding up past the tower towards the grove
of graves where the tips of the cypress lean
in the breeze and a hooded monk is walking
head bent over his book of hours in passing
I see that it's John wave and grin *rividerci*
startled at his gauntness fixed on his text dark
his reverie no acknowledgment good-bye
that is the whole story you know about Rome
and flying tourist opening weeks of mail
putting a journey to bed and on and on
but I've thought of John ever since whenever
the smiling Pope makes another of his sub-
human attitudes the law he drives our people
from the temples and spits on the graves of his
brother priests who are coughing to death in cells
without unction and boots the Jesuit shrink
who calls all love holy he wants his fags
quiet *shh* and I try to think of John
and the picture he saved three years for me
till the lost roll of Tuscany came to light
and turned out to hold our wedding portrait
the innocent are so brief and the rigid world
doesn't marry its pagans anymore but John
didn't care what nothing we professed he joined
us to join him a ritual not in the book
but his secret heart it doesn't get easier Rog
even now the night jasmine is pouring
its white delirium in the dark and I
will not have it if you can't I shut all

windows still it seeps in with the gaudy
oath of spring oh help be somewhere near
so I can endure this drunk intrusion
of promise where is the walled place where we
can walk untouched or must I be content
with a wedding I almost didn't witness
the evidence all but lost no oath no ring
but the truth sealed to hold against the hate
of the first straight Pope since the Syllabus of
Errors this Polack joke who fears his women
and men too full of laughter far brother
if you should pass beneath our cypresses
you who are a praying man your god can
go to hell but since you are so inclined
pray that my friend and I be still together
just like this at the Mount of Olives blessed
by the last of an ancient race who loved
youth and laughter and beautiful things so much
they couldn't stop singing and we were the song

DAVID MURA ❖

The Colors of Desire

1 Photograph of a Lynching (circa 193_)

These men? In their dented felt hats,
in the way their fingers tug their suspenders or vests,
with faces a bit puffy or too lean, eyes narrow and close together,
they seem too like our image of the South,
the Thirties. Of course they are white;
who then could create this cardboard figure, face
flat and grey, eyes oversized, bulging like
an ancient totem this gang has dug up? At the far right,
in a small browed cap, a boy of twelve smiles,
as if responding to what's most familiar here:
the camera's click. And though directly above them,
a branch ropes the dead negro in the air,

Most Recent Book: AFTER WE LOST OUR WAY (E. P. Dutton, 1989)

the men too focus their blank beam
on the unseen eye. Which is, at this moment, us.

Or, more precisely, me. Who cannot but recall
how my father, as a teenager, clutched his weekend pass,
passed through the rifle towers and gates
of the Jerome, Arkansas camp, and, in 1942,
stepped on a bus to find white riders
motioning, "Sit here, son," and, in the rows beyond,
a half dozen black faces, waving him back,
"Us colored folks got to stick together."
How did he know where to sit? And how is it,

thirty-five years later, I found myself sitting
in a dark theatre, watching *Behind the Green Door*
with a dozen anonymous men? On the screen
a woman sprawls on a table, stripped, the same one
on the Ivory Snow soap box, a baby on her shoulder,
smiling her blond, practically pure white smile.
Now, after being prepared and serviced slowly
by a handful of women, as one of them
kneels, buries her face in her crotch,
she is ready: And now he walks in—

Lean, naked, black, streaks of white paint on his chest
and face, a necklace of teeth, it's almost comical,
this fake garb of the jungle, Africa and All-America,
black and blond, almost a joke but for the surge
of what these lynchers regarded as the ultimate crime
against nature: the black man kneeling to this kidnapped
body, slipping himself in, the screen showing it all, down
to her head shaking in a seizure, the final scream
before he lifts himself off her quivering body . . .

I left that theater, bolted from a dream into a dream.
I stared at the cars whizzing by, watched the light change,
red, yellow, green, and the haze in my head from the hash,
and the haze in my head from the image, melded together, reverberating.
I don't know what I did afterwards. Only, night after night,
I will see those bodies, black and white (and where am I,
the missing third?), like a talisman, a rageful, unrelenting release.

2 1957

Cut to Chicago, June. A boy of six.
Next year my hero will be Mickey Mantle,

but this noon, as father eases the Bel-Air past Wilson,
with cowboy hat black, cocked at an angle,
my skin dark from the sun, I'm Paladin,
and my six guns point at cars whizzing past,
blast after blast ricocheting the glass.
Like all boys in such moments, my face
attempts a look of what—toughness? bravado? ease?—
until, impatient, my father's arm wails
across the seat, and I sit back, silent at last.

Later, as we step from IGA with our sacks,
a man in a serge suit—stained with ink?—
steps forward, shouts, "Hey, you a Jap?
You from Tokyo? You a Jap? A Chink?"
I stop, look up, I don't know him,
my arm yanks forward, and suddenly,
the sidewalk's rolling, buckling, like lava melting,
and I know father will explode,
shouts, fists, I know his temper.
And then,
I'm in that dream where nothing happens—
The ignition grinds, the man's face presses
the windshield, and father stares ahead,
fingers rigid on the wheel . . .

That night in my bedroom, moths,
like fingertips, peck the screen;
from the living room, the muffled tv.
As I imagine Shane stepping into the dusty street,
in the next bed, my younger brother starts
to taunt—*you can't hurt me, you can't hurt me* . . .—
Who can explain where this chant began?
Or why, when father throws the door open,
shouts stalking chaos erupted in his house,
he swoops on his son with the same swift motion
that the son, like an animal, like a scared and angry little boy,
fell on his brother, beating him in the dark?

3 Miss June 1964

I'm twelve, home from school
with a slight fever. I slide back the door
of my parents' closet—my mother's out shopping—
rummage among pumps, flats, lined in a rack,
unzip the garment bags, one by one.

It slides like a sigh from the folded sweaters.
I flip through ads for cologne, L.P.'s, a man
in a trench coat, lugging a panda-sized Fleischman's fifth.
Somewhere past the photo of Schweitzer
in his pith helmet, and the cartoon nude man
perched as a gargoyle, I spill the photo
millions of men, white, black, yellow, have seen,
though the body before me is white, eighteen:
Her breasts are enormous, almost frightening
—the aureoles seem large as my fist.
As the three glossy pages sprawl before me,
I start to touch myself, and there is
some terror, my mother will come home,
some delight I've never felt before,
and I do not cry out, I make no sound . . .

How did I know that photo was there?
Or mother know I knew?
Two nights later, at her request,
father lectures me on burning out too early.
Beneath the cone of light at the kitchen table,
we're caught, like the shiest of lovers.
He points at the booklet from the AMA
—he writes their P.R.—"Read it," he says,
"and, if you have any questions . . ."

Thirty years later, these questions remain.
And his answers, too, are still the same:
Really, David, it was just a magazine.
And the camps, my father's lost nursery,
the way he chased me round the yard in L.A.,
even the two by four he swung—why connect them
with years you wandered those theatres?
Is nothing in your life your own volition?
The past isn't just a box full of horrors.
What of those mornings in the surf
near Venice, all of us casting line after line,
arcing over breakers all the way from Japan,
or plopping down beside my mother,
a plateful of mochi, *pulling it like taffy*
with our teeth, shoyu *dribbling*
down our chins. Think of it, David.
There were days like that. We were happy . . .

4

Who hears the rain churning the forest to mud,
or the unraveling rope snap, the negro
plummet to rest at last? And what flooded my father's eyes
in the Little Rock theatre, sitting beneath the balcony
in that third year of war? Where is 1944,
its snows sweeping down Heart Mountain,
to vanish on my mother's black bobbing head,
as she scrurries towards the cramped cracked barracks
where her mother's throat coughs through the night,
and her father sits beside her on the bed?
The dim bulb flickers as my mother enters.
Her face is flushed, her cheeks cold. She
bows, unwraps her scarf, pours the steaming
kettle in the tea pot; offers her mother a sip.
And none of them knows she will never
talk of this moment, that, years later,
I will have to imagine it, again and again,
just as I have tried to imagine the lives
of all those who have entered these lines . . .

Tonight snow drifts below my window,
and lamps puff ghostly aureoles
over walks and lawns. Father, Mother,
I married a woman not of my color.
Tell me: What is it I want to escape?
These nights in our bed, my head
on her belly, I can hear these thumps,
and later, when she falls asleep,
I stand in our daughter's room,
so bare yet but for a simple wooden crib
(on the bulletin board I've pinned the sonogram
with black-and-white swirls like a galaxy
spinning about the fetal body),
and something plummets inside me,
out of proportion to the time
I've been portioned on this earth.
And if what is granted erases nothing,
if history remains, untouched, implacable,
as darkness flows up our hemisphere,
her hollow still moves moonward,

small hill on the horizon, swelling,
floating with child, white, yellow,
who knows, who can tell her,
oh why must it matter?

JACK MYERS ❖

Visitation Rites

My gentle son is performing tricks for me on his bicycle.
He's fourteen and has just cracked open the storm door
to manhood with his gently lowered voice shredding
into shadows until he's surrounded by the calls of
tan young girls whose smooth brown skin calls out, "We're alone."

It will not be long before he masters standing still
on one wheel, elegant jumps over obstacles, riding
upside down and backwards until he will have made
of danger a pretty colored bird to delight him,
sending it away, calling it home, calling it home
as it sails and grows larger, darkens and adds weight.

I watch how well he has done without me all these years,
me with my iron sled of guilt, my cooked-out piles of
worry smouldering. I have been his only model, he says,
and shares with me what a typical day of winning is like.
I sit on a little hill watching my son show off his
light dominion over gravity, knowing in the next few minutes

I will leave again for another year, and again our lives
will pull apart and heal over like bubbles separating in two.
This is how he says good-bye—without speech or reasons or
the long looking after that I have honed through time—
just in a flash in the sun he's suddenly perfected, and I'm gone.

Most Recent Book: BLINDSIDED (David R. Godine, Publisher, forthcoming)

Jake Addresses the World from the Garden

Rocks without ch'i [spirit] are dead rocks.
—Mai-mai Sze, *The Way of Chinese Painting*

It's spring and Jake toddles to the garden
as the sun wobbles up clean and iridescent.

He points to the stones asleep and says, "M'mba,"
I guess for the sound they make, takes another step

and says, "M'mba," for the small red berries crying
in the holly. "M'mba" for the first sweet sadness

of the purplish-black berries in the drooping monkey grass,
and "M'mba," for the little witches' faces bursting into blossom.

That's what it's like being shorter than the primary colors,
being deafened by humming stones while the whole world billows

behind the curtain "M'mba," the one word. Meanwhile I go on
troweling, slavering the world with language as Jake squeals

like a held bird and begins lallating to me in tongues.
I follow him around as he tries to thread the shine of a stone

through the eye of a watchful bird. After a year of banging
his head, crying, the awful falling down, now he's trying

to explain the vast brightening in his brain by saying "M'mba"
to me again and again. And though I follow with the sadness

above which a stone cannot lift itself, I wink and say
"M'mba" back to him. But I don't mean it.

The Experts

When the man in the window seat
flying next to me
asks me who I am
and I tell him I'm a poet,
he turns embarrassed toward the sun.
The woman on the other side of me
pipes up she's 4′10″ and is going to sue
whoever made these seats.

And so it is I'm reminded how I wish I were
one of the aesthetes
floating down double-lit canals
of quiet listening, the ones
who come to know something as
mysterious and useless
as when a tree has decided to sleep.

You would think for them
pain lights up the edges of everything,
burns right through the center of every leaf,
but I've seen them strolling around,
their faces glistening with the sort of peace
only sleep can polish babies with.

And so when a waitress in San Antonio
asks me what I do, and I think
how the one small thing I've learned
seems more complex the more I think of it,
how the joys of it have overpowered me
long after I don't understand,

I tell her "Corned beef on rye, a side of salad,
hold the pickle, I'm a poet," and she stops to talk
about her little son who, she says, can hurt himself
even when he's sitting still. I tell her
there's a poem in that, and she repeats
"Hold the pickle, I'm a poet,"
then looks at me and says, "I know."

Not Thinking of Himself

"Today," he said to the mirror, "the person I am inside of
will not be allowed to think of himself. Not once!"

And immediately he smashed his toe on the corner of the sink
but thought only of his mother who used to pinch his cheeks
like this—"Ow!"—and crush his chest like that—"Ow!"

He wondered briefly if under his rules it would be allowable
to do something nice for someone who didn't know he existed.

And immediately he stood up and banged his head on the water tank
but thought only of his father who used to hit him on the head
like this—"Ow!"—and punch him in the stomach like that—"Ow!"

It was then that he thought of his life as an inside-out sock
and wondered if calling himself by another name completely
might give him a bigger head start.

Have a Nice Day

No, no I don't want my heart broken again today.
I don't want to hear the slosh and slide of another country-
western tune about bars and broken-down love and junky pickups,
though they're more than real enough. And I don't want to feel
the sentimental night sweats rising up from someone's childhood,
or tangle with the slashes of abstract art drying in the track-lit air
of grown-up feelings, watching the colors of memory and fact intersect
and crash like trucks, as if thought were feeling, and feelings, trucks.

I just want what we used to wish for back in the 1950s, to have
"a nice day," back when a woman would seriously ask without blinking,
"If I take off my clothes, will you take care of me the rest of my life?"
Back when most of the guys I knew would've given this serious thought
though it all seems sort of silly now, almost heartbreakingly incompetent
in its innocence, in its presumption of real loss, like the guys
elbowing each other on the corner, asking "How far did you get?" as if
the body, like the expression "nice," were a place you could retire to.

Everyone's suffered real losses, which means there is no "far enough."
And I don't want to harken back to yesteryear when being good or bad
was the simple difference between an open heart (now a surgical procedure)
and a closed door (signifying power), back when work was poetically
called "earning a living," as if merely living weren't work enough.
Everyone seems headed for his own compulsory heart attack, proving, yes,
the heart has gone far enough. And I'm not sure what's coming next

though yesterday I saw some kids with Day-Glo hair and deathheads
on their teeth. They were sloppily slam-dancing on ice which was just
their way of probably saying yes, we're broken-hearted, without taking
their clothes off. That seems more than hard enough. Today I just want
to relax, bring my blood pressure down to the level of rush hour traffic.
I suppose that makes me as outdated as this tree I'm sitting under,
on whose every leaf is a black-eyed, green-bellied cicada buzz-sawing
its wire-and-cellophane grade-school wings in the last-chance blood lust
of August. They seem willing and able to leave the burning husks
of their bodies behind in the trees, as I seem to be doing,
for the sake of a kind word.

What Brings Us Out

Something about pumpkins caused
the man who had not spoken in three years
to lean forward, cough, open his mouth.
How the room heaved into silence,
his words enormous in that air:
"I won't . . . be . . . afraid . . .
of my . . . father . . . anymore."
And what silence followed,
as if each heart had spoken
its most secret terror,
had combed the tangled clump
for the hardest line
and pulled it, intact,
from the mass.

I bless that man forever
for his courage, his voice
which started with one thing
and went to many, opening up and up
to the rim of the world.
So much silence had given him
a wisdom which held us all at bay,
amazed. Sometimes when I see
mountains of pumpkins by the roadside,
or watermelons, a hill of autumn gourds
piled lavishly on crates, I think
perhaps this one, or that, were it to
strike someone right,
this curl of hardened stalk,
this pleated skin . . .

or, on an old bureau drawer,
the vegetable-like roundness of a glass knob
that the baby turns and turns
emerging, later, from a complicated dream . . .

the huge navigational face of a radio
which never worked while I was alive

Most Recent Book: YELLOW GLOVE (Breitenbush Books, 1986)

but gave me more to go on than most sounds:
how what brings us out may be
small as that black arrow, swinging
the wide arc, the numbers where silent voices lived,
how fast you had to turn to make it move.

Rain

A teacher asked Paul
what he would remember
from third grade, and he sat
a long time before writing
"this year sumbody tutched me
on the sholder"
and turned his paper in.
Later she showed it to me
as an example of her wasted life.
The words he wrote were large
as houses in a landscape.
He wanted to go inside them
and live, he could fill in
the windows of "o" and "d"
and be safe while outside
birds building nests in drainpipes
knew nothing of the coming rain.

Streets

A man leaves the world
and the streets he lived on
grow a little shorter.

One more window dark
in this city, the figs on his branches
will soften for birds.

If we stand quietly enough evenings
there grows a whole company of us
standing quietly together.
Overhead loud grackles are claiming their trees
and the sky which sews and sews, tirelessly sewing,

drops her purple hem.
Each thing in its time, its place,
it would be nice to think the same about people.

Some people do. They sleep completely,
waking refreshed. Others live in two worlds,
the lost and remembered.
They sleep twice, once for the one who is gone,
once for themselves. They dream thickly,
dream double, they wake from a dream
into another one, they walk the short streets
calling out names, and then they answer.

The House Made of Rain

Our voices poured out through
a hole in the floor.
Some days the woman with a bucket
came swaggering up the block
singing our names, the song that goes
old old very old
and we rose toward her, echoing
the thrum of her lowest note.

At night the house would tilt
like small boats on the Mississippi
and we fell away from one another
into the laps of our own beds
deep deep very deep
where I dreamed I held a hand
after the person who owned it
was dead.

Already I felt the press of currents,
the taunt of a word like *blend*.
Our school herded us to see where rivers met
and we marched, expecting the pour
of purple into blue. Beyond us loomed
just a hint of subtle gray confluence,
gray into gray, we folded our arms.
They should see my house, I thought.
They should stand on the porch one afternoon
and listen.

In my house tears welled up from
underground pools, shadowy streams we rode
from room to room, paddling.
Sometimes my brother pulled me out
though he had been premature and took
twenty years to grow huge.
A girl in my class said she had never seen
her parents sad; I wanted to drown in her life.

The tornado that razored away whole blocks
might be coming back so I rode my horse
fast as I could to escape, and threw up.
Huddled in the hall, Mama stroked my back.
Next time, she said, listen.
And I swear everything was next.

A floor furnace we had to leap over
or scorch our feet, a barrel where we lit
what we wanted to lose, a red stove
that has followed me like a dog.
After so long it makes its own temperatures,
it does what it wants.
That house without arms or legs
still floats among houses where neighbors
used crutches, measured hems.
Living among them one could almost believe
the bucket might be used for watering,
thrum thrum from the bottom of the lung,
that trees might erupt, whole gardens,
that finally the weather might shift
to the glazed blue stare of summer,
or that anything could be enough.

Hello

Some nights
the rat with pointed teeth
makes his long way back
to the bowl of peaches.
He stands on the dining room table
sinking his tooth
drinking the pulp
of each fruity turned-up face

knowing you will read
this message and scream.
It is his only text,
to take and take in darkness,
to be gone before you awaken
and your giant feet
start creaking the floor.

Where is the mother of the rat?
The father, the shredded nest,
which breath were we taking
when the rat was born,
when he lifted his shivering snout
to rafter and rivet and stone?
I gave him the names of the devil,
seared and screeching names,
I would not enter those rooms
without a stick to guide me,
I leaned on the light, shuddering,
and the moist earth under the house,
the trailing tails of clouds,
said he was in the closet,
the drawer of candles,
his nose was a wick.

How would we live together
with our sad shoes and hideouts,
our lock on the door
and his delicate fingered paws
that could clutch and grip,
his blank slate of fur
and the pillow where we press our faces?
The bed that was a boat is sinking.
And the shores of morning loom up
lined with little shadows,
things we never wanted to be, or meet,
and all the rats are waving hello.

Sharon Olds ❖

The Quest

The day my girl is lost for an hour,
the day I think she is gone forever and then I find her,
I sit with her awhile and then I
go to the corner store for orange juice for her
lips, tongue, palate, throat,
stomach, blood, every gold cell of her body.
I joke around with the guy behind the counter, I
walk out into the winter air and
weep. I know he would never hurt her,
never take her body in his hands to
crack it or crush it, would keep her safe and
bring her home to me. Yet there are
those who would. I pass the huge
cockeyed buildings massive as prisons,
charged, loaded, cocked with people,
some who would love to take my girl, to un-
do her, fine strand by fine
strand. These are buildings full of rope,
ironing boards, sash, wire,
iron cords woven in black-and-blue spirals like
umbilici, apartments supplied with
razor blades and lye. This is my
quest, to know where it is, the evil in the
human heart. As I walk home I
look in face after face for it, I
see the dark beauty, the rage, the
grown-up children of the city she walks as a
child, a raw target. I cannot
see a soul who would do it, I clutch the
jar of juice like a cold heart,
remembering the time my parents tied me to a chair and
would not feed me and I looked up
into their beautiful faces, my stomach a
bright mace, my wrists like birds the
shrike has hung by the throat from barbed wire, I
gazed as deep as I could into their eyes

Most Recent Book: THE GOLD CELL (Alfred A. Knopf, 1987)

and all I saw was goodness, I could not get past it.
I rush home with the blood of oranges
pressed to my breast, I cannot get it to her fast enough.

Summer Solstice, New York City

By the end of the longest day of the year he could not stand it,
he went up the iron stairs through the roof of the building
and over the soft, tarry surface
to the edge, put one leg over the complex green tin cornice
and said if they came a step closer that was it.
Then the huge machinery of the earth began to work for his life,
the cops came in their suits blue-grey as the sky on a cloudy evening,
and one put on a bullet-proof vest, a
black shell around his own life,
life of his children's father, in case
the man was armed, and one, slung with a
rope like the sign of his bounden duty,
came up out of a hole in the top of the neighboring building
like the gold hole they say is in the top of the head,
and began to lurk toward the man who wanted to die.
The tallest cop approached him directly,
softly, slowly, talking to him, talking, talking,
while the man's leg hung over the lip of the next world
and the crowd gathered in the street, silent, and the
hairy net with its implacable grid was
unfolded near the curb and spread out and
stretched as the sheet is prepared to receive at a birth.
Then they all came a little closer
where he squatted next to his death, his shirt
glowing its milky glow like something
growing in a dish at night in the dark in a lab and then
everything stopped
as his body jerked and he
stepped down from the parapet and went toward them
and they closed on him, I thought they were going to
beat him up, as a mother whose child has been
lost will scream at the child when it's found, they
took him by the arms and held him up and
leaned him against the wall of the chimney and the
tall cop lit a cigarette
in his own mouth, and gave it to him, and

then they all lit cigarettes, and the
red, glowing ends burned like the
tiny campfires we lit at night
back at the beginning of the world.

May 1968

The Dean of the University said
the neighborhood people could not cross campus
until the students gave up the buildings
so we lay down in the street,
we said The cops will enter this gate
over our bodies. Spine-down on the cobbles—
hard bed, like a carton of eggs—
I saw the buildings of New York City
from dirt level, they soared up and stopped,
chopped off cleanly—beyond them the sky
black and neither sour nor sweet, the
night air over the island.
The mounted police moved near us
delicately. Flat out on our backs
we sang, and then I began to count,
12, 13, 14, 15, I
counted again, 15, 16, one
month since the day on that deserted beach when we
used nothing, 17, 18, my
mouth fell open, my hair in the soil,
if my period did not come tonight
I was pregnant. I looked up at the sole of the
cop's shoe, I looked up at the
horse's belly, its genitals—if they
took me to Women's Detention and did the
exam on me, jammed the unwashed
speculum high inside me, the guard's
three fingers—supine on Broadway, I looked
up into the horse's tail like a
dark filthed comet. All week, I had
wanted to get arrested, longed to
give myself away. I lay in the
tar, one brain in my head and another
tiny brain at the base of my tail and I
stared at the world, good-luck iron

arc of the gelding's shoe, the cop's
baton, the deep curve of the animal's
belly, the buildings streaming up
away from the earth. I knew I should get up and
leave, stand up to muzzle level, to the
height of the soft velvet nostrils and
walk away, turn my back on my
friends and danger, but I was a coward so I
lay there looking up at the sky,
black vault arched above us, I
lay there gazing up at God, at his
underbelly, till it turned deep blue and then
silvery, colorless, *Give me this one
night*, I said, *and I'll give this child
the rest of my life*, the horses' heads
drooping, dipping, until they slept in a
dark circle around my body and my daughter.

The Moment of My Father's Death

When he breathed his last breath it was he,
my father, although he was so transformed
no one who had not been with him
for the last hours would know him, the gold
skin luminous as cold animal fat,
the eyes cast all the way back into his head,
the whites gleaming like a white iris, the
nose that grew thinner and thinner every minute, the
open mouth racked open with that
tongue in it like all the heartbreak of the mortal,
a tongue so dried, scalloped, darkened and
material. You could see the mucus
risen like gorge into the back of his mouth
but it was he, the huge slack yellow arms,
the spots of blood under the skin
black and precise, we had come this far with him
step by step, it was he, his last
breath was his, not taken with desire but
his, light as the sphere of a dandelion seed
coming out of his mouth and floating across the room.
Then the nurse pulled up his gown and
listened for his heart, I saw his stomach

silvery and hairy, it was his stomach, she
moved to the foot of the bed and stood there, she
did not shake her head she stood and
nodded at me. And for a minute it was fully
he, my father, dead but completely
himself, a man with an open mouth and
no breath, gold skin and
black spots on his arms, I kissed him and
spoke to him. He looked like someone
killed in a violent bloodless struggle, all that
strain in his neck, that look of pulling back, that
stillness he seemed to be holding at first and
then it was holding him, the skin
tightened slightly around his whole body
as if the purely physical were claiming him,
and then it was not my father,
it was not a man, it was not an animal, I
stood and ran my hand through the silver hair,
plunged my fingers into it gently and
lifted them up slowly through the grey
waves of it, the unliving glistening
matter of this world.

William Olsen ❖

Tomorrow

A water sprinkler empties into parabolas
which, before they collapse into the past,
hang in air unencumbered by the ones before,
each as irreplaceable as the gauzy streetlights
blossoming above the electric leaves
of the tall clouds of elms staring across the street.
Though it's midnight and the black material of being
crumbles between the tendril tips of stars
that poke and rummage through the compost of the summer sky,
as late as it is the old cop is sweeping
our common driveway, the sound of his labor

Most Recent Book: THE HAND OF GOD AND A FEW BRIGHT FLOWERS (University of Illinois
Press, 1988)

wearing as thin as the sucking tide of cars.
And every tomorrow comes down to the next
moment like the first green sticky hand-grenade
bud of spring about to explode into leaf.
Soon the trees have crowns, and the blue rugs of their
shadows. Then the first leaf kisses the ground
and scuttles on its rusted tips across our driveway
until the sycamores are bleached antlers in the sunlight.
But this occurs gradually, this neat, bare ascent to absence.
As it happens, the old cop gets knocked off on duty
many tomorrows ago, and many tomorrows later
it occurs to me I haven't seen him raking,
his bicycle tangled in morning glory vines,
and still more tomorrows later I started this poem
one morning when I looked back at the bed
my sleep had messed, betraying me to the knowledge
that we vacate the past by looking on it.

Wasn't that you I saw slumming around there,
enjoying an hour by the pond, watching
the children fold up newspapers into boats and set them afloat?
The water took the tragic newsboats oh so lightly.
A big wind overturned them without looking back
and the geese pulling out from the marges
were leaving their Christmas-tree wakes intact
to ravel outward to possibility or was it
extinction? Yet in spite of everything
afternoons are everything while they are happening
and you are walking home by beef-red houses
drowning in blue sky till the extraordinary moments of dusk—
every night thins to the sucking tide of cars on the street,
a few mysterious sprinklers on manicured lawns,
the canners squeaking down the avenues their
shopping carts burdened like mules with bulging Glad Bags,
about to turn the corner toward whatever will
be the thing they have lost all track of.
Each tomorrow staggers by, like the steps
of the bum tottering giraffelike on two crutches,
a bottle of Thunderbird stuck in his crotch.
He swears at every hermetic car hissing by. But soon
he's a stick figure at the end of a tunnel of oaks,
too small and contemptible to worry over much,
even if part of what tomorrow slurs is true about us.

So the language of the past is too easy a sadness,
whereas we always generalize from within the cool,
spacious, eternal living room of the present.
And though our neighbors are deepened by autumn,
we don't even know what they do there in their windows.
And tomorrow seems entirely indifferent to charity,
so who can blame us if we watch an hour of TV
with the stars unnoticed overhead, raw papery buds
untouched by frost, and car lights swim through ink
and turn the trunks of sycamores into glowworms
and if it happens to be Christmas, archipelagoes of bulbs
celebrate a beautiful innocence, and by spring
the sprinklers turn out their parabolas
while the next century already mists in the trees.
But one day you fall backwards into a night that matters,
kamikaze into an armchair, and all the people
who ever sat there put their arms around you,
the lives that seek you out because you
can't betray them, and while pools of TV blue
make rings around your ankles, on comes
some thirty-second spot about some disaster
on the other side of the world, tonight it's an earthquake,
German shepherds running in and out of the rubble
of a downtown Mexico City hospital, and outside
in an electronic ear, a boy's faint heartbeat
taps like a blind man's cane for a way out.

For a moment you look up and it's raining so hard
you can't even see the myrtles giving up their blossoms.
Tomorrow is a stone on the other side of the world
you can't move. It is the fact that a little boy
will die, out of the long, bright, slamming, hammering sunlight,
that the volunteers know it, and still they work.
Tomorrow has the one face of our television sets,
which are dumb enough to want to spend their whole
portable existences staring out at whoever
lives behind the other faces, the ones safely concerned,
our dumb, troubling, troubled faces staring into tomorrow.

The Unicorn Tapestries

The things we leave behind must, for those
who find them flattened, scentless inside books
or in a gesture they make that isn't theirs,
be very much like the desk I found in the alley
one night, coming out of one way down another,

when I couldn't sleep or write letters, and walked.
The desk had lost a leg, and couldn't get away.
Some initials cut through oak had outlasted love.
Turning over the drawer to interpret
the contents, I thought of the farmer centuries ago
and the stack of "curtains" he found in a chest.
All the crazy things he couldn't understand—

the unicorn, Christ reborn; the seductive
damsel, Mary, who lured Him into the circular fence,
Her dress lifted ever so slightly, Her glance askew,
His smiling as if all the world centered on Him,
a field of lilies, violets, passionate roses
and periwinkles, "joy of the ground"—

he took them to the barn to cover the potatoes.
Little worked that winter. The potatoes darkened
the light that hid inside them. They grew eyes
until they were nothing but vision drained of life:
the unicorn bleeding and braying all winter
as the farmer lifted it and saw his work

ruined, for all his efforts.

The Oasis Motel

I touch you like the waves admire the weirs.
It is themselves they push out from, toward what
they are a part of, and it is transportation,
and this is why palms rustle, why the moon
drops shamelessly below the horizontal
off the Gulf of Mexico, and why you, too,

are something else, and utterly familiar.
And when I turn from comfort to a fight
picking up in the outdoor bar below,

one angel has asked another if he'd like
his face pushed in on this fantastic evening—
here at the edge of our nation the ravening void

fills with his sobbing, tearless plea for mercy,
convincing me I too have dearly suffered,
I too am equally amazed at terror's
lucidity and broachable distance.
The coward angel with a bloodied face
stumbles across new silences to his car

for everyone leaves exactly when he wants to,
and the way the coastal highway freight trucks rumble
beyond all sad reproach is just too awful,
for why else would the reading lamp enclose us,
why else would your arm be thrown across
the pillow in its unforgettable journey

all the way securely to your fingers
unless the night has nothing more nor less
to do with us than some small boatlight now
heading out from shore, and where it is
is not so far from where it was, and it
is lost to sight, and it is heading forth.

The Dead Monkey

A face framed in a pink lace baby's hood was youth and age
collapsed to a wizened black walnut. It had no idea
that we were there, New Orleans, 1981, or that we were
growing envious of its owner, an unshaven but rich looking Mexican
who hoisted it from the ground, not altogether modest
about the attention he and it were getting from all of us,
eating our beignets, watching this binary configuration,
man and monkey, kiss, kiss again, patching up
some make-believe quarrel between lovers.
Suddenly it leapt up a trellis of morning glory vines,
swung from a brass chandelier over the human circus of breakfasters
and scrambled across the street into a moving bus,
arms and legs toppling one over the other
as it tried to keep up with its death.
The man walked out to the ridiculous end to his happiness,
stealing the delight from us, like surreptitious newlyweds,

poor enough in spirit to be amazed by fact.
Taking it in his arms, crying to make himself alone,
this Mexican was living proof that suffering
is not all that crazy about company.
When the crowd dispersed, he seemed relieved,
as if too much had already been suffered
without us adding our thimbleful.
That night we saw the Mexican without his monkey in a bar,
buying everyone drinks and laughing hysterically
about the whole thing, saying *death is my life*.
If that sounds a bit dramatic, blame it
on sweet bourbon, this is just what he said,
being just lucid enough to mix up life and death
and stupid enough to want to share in their confusion.
We toasted with him to stupidity because
there's not always enough stupidity around to celebrate,
and when we were good and drunk we turned ourselves out
    into the night,
between more bars we saw more bars,
windows like photographs fleshed out with
bodies that destroyed their secrets,
we took the journey across the dangerous street,
entranced by the idea of getting somewhere,
sick for everything but home.

FRANKIE PAINO ❖

Horse Latitudes

In horse latitudes sailors once lashed
   the flanks of stallions, mares, until
      those wild-eyed, gentle beasts plunged overboard,

cleaved the still surface, water churning
   grey froth on their muzzles while trumpets
      of brash neighs turned to whinnies, turned

to what they'd say was nothing more
   than a sudden breeze which filled sails,
      pushed the ship, water lifting in an eerie

Most Recent Book: The Rapture of Matter (Cleveland State University Press, 1991)

swell like the cold silk of your marriage bed,
   unnatural white, and you weren't even innocent
      though you tried to be until he pressed his mouth

to yours and you snaked your tongue between
   his teeth so you both knew but didn't care.
      After twenty-five years, you say, even passion,

that universal desire, that voracious brat,
   grows lean, simple. You learned to go farther
      on less and less while your fingers grew slender,

then ugly, slack, and your rings slipped
   over bone meaning, *one* and *one* and *one makes one*
      and you tried to make it back to the beginning

of your past when he was a stranger, all arms
   and legs gone bronze with sun and you leaned
      in the window so he could see your breasts,

how they were shapped like his cupped palms
   and he gave you his ring which you let dangle
      at the center of that fleshy parabola. But

there was a past before that past, someone
   who had a name only he remembers and when you ask
      he shrugs and drifts off toward another night

pissing beer downtown on the backstreets
   in front of whores who stamp their feet
      against the cold, and anyway, to say that name

would be nothing more than the ruined music
   of this windchime, its crystals snapped
      to jagged teeth in last autumn's last storm

so it thunks its flat voice, a sound which is
   no longer a song. Or it is. The way this wind
      wraps around my bones, bites salty, cold, and I too

am thinking, *one*, though I want you to know,
   goddamnit, I've always loved you but couldn't
      say it because that music is impossible,

ruined, and we're like those horses, really,
   mad with fright, their deep lungs singed
      with brine. They must have taken comfort

in mutual loss, corded necks jutting
    from that flat field of North Atlantic
        as if they were merely chest deep in prairie

grass. And maybe it's useless to believe
    in forever; maybe I'm wrong to think any poem
        will let me get it right, how your hair,

just now, long and coarse as a wild mare's mane,
    is frayed by wind, utterly beautiful, restless,
        as it shifts north, northwest.

The Truth

My father died near evening, having spent
most of the day straining towards that release.
In the end, I watched the monitor count down
the beats of his heart's surrender, his eyes
fixed on nothing I could see, though I'd like to believe
he was looking at something, his own father, say,
coming to show him the way into a different world.

I never knew dying could take such effort, as if Death,
at the last, pulls back his outstretched hand
and we must chase and we must chase after the shroud of his dark wings.
All day I'd held my father's hand, leaned over
his thin form the way, I remember, he'd leaned over my bed
when I was a child. I ran my fingers through his fine, black
hair, matching my breath to the respirators hiss—

as if desire alone could save him. The truth is,
I wanted nothing more than a flat line on the screen,
the steady hum which means the heart has lost its music,
blood going cool and blue in the veins. I wanted
it to be the way that cliche goes, the one which says
we don't die, really, we just go to sleep. But his heart
refused romantic notions, hammering an unsteady beat

hours after I told the doctor to disengage
that machine which kept the pulse constant against his body's will.
I started to write how his muscles, deprived of oxygen,
rippled like the smooth flanks of a horse in the home stretch,
that graceful and sure, but it's a lie—the truth is,

the spasms were strong enough to make our own hearts
quicken, our arms strain as his head slipped over the pillow,

his legs quivering, pitiful. I wanted to tell you I saw
a boy, slight and beautiful, leaning against the waiting room
door, his right shoulder transparent, half in, half out of
the dark oak grain, as if he wanted me to see there is a life
beyond the one we know. But that, too, would be a lie.
The truth is, that room was empty except for the boys on tv,
the ones in Soweto who doused a man with gasoline, set him

alight, his head engulfed in flame like an infernal nimbus,
fire folding its terrible wings around him as he fell
to the ground, silent as snow. When my father died
the sun was just beginning to set. Friday. High summer.
Though I couldn't see them from the tight, dim room, I knew
cars crowded the streets, everyone anxious to get home where,
perhaps, someone else waited. Or maybe it was just solitude

they rushed toward. I didn't begrudge them such happiness,
but blessed their ignorance as they squinted against the light,
cursed the grass, too long to be ignored, and the mailbox
with its freight of bills, news, catalogues which promised
to satisfy any desire. Standing by my father's bed, I needed
him to live because my own heart was breaking. The truth is,
we never have all we need. I came to understand how my hand,

grasping his, must have made him hesitate between two
worlds, the way a child learning to swim glances from
a parent's hand to the pool's blue-green shimmer, then back
again, or maybe the way I hope those boys in Soweto paused
before they turned toward their neighbour, small fires
in their palms fingering air. My father moved his head
against his shoulder as if, already, he were looking back

at us from some vast distance. Perhaps Death is more timid than we
imagine, slipping off the soul the way love might begin
with the shy undoing of an evening gown. I held on to my
father's feet—how elegant they were, even then, like the feet
of a Bernini seraph, sleek, cool, too perfect to believe
they'd carried him through the world so long, and finally,
to that bed. I didn't want to hold him back but, if

such a thing is possible, to push his spirit out
through the crown of his head, give him the power to rise
from that body, its twisted spine, thighs thin, hollow, ready
for flight, and the cancer we'd measured in the deliberate

spreading of red, mottled skin like a map being drawn in front
of our eyes. What world, I wonder, did it describe?
We talked about the times my sister and I went with him

after bluegill, grayling, bass—the week in Canada
we didn't catch a thing, the evening's loons would cry
across still water while we sat around a fire,
our faces amber, otherworldy in that light. It must have
been those memories which gave him strength to move
towards that other shore which only the dead can know,
where perhaps he rose from dark waters deep as sleep

and remembered this life as a dream. In his room, the monitor
pushed an incandescent line across its screen as if to
underscore mortality. A nurse removed the needles, the tube
which ran like a tap root into the sweet cave of my father's
chest. His mouth, open, filled with the machine's emerald glow,
as if the tongue he now spoke were a language of light. Sometimes
we have nothing to grasp but such implausible fire. Just that.

MOLLY PEACOCK ❖

Say You Love Me

What happened earlier I'm not sure of.
Of course he was drunk, but often he was.
His face looked like a ham on a hook above

me—I was pinned to the chair because
he'd hunkered over me with arms like jaws
pried open by the chair arms. "Do you love

me?" he began to sob. "Say you love me!"
I held out. I was probably fifteen.
What had happened? Had my mother—had she

said or done something? Or had he just been
drinking too long after work? "He'll get *mean*,"
my sister hissed, "just *tell* him." I brought my knee

Most Recent Book: TAKE HEART (Random House, 1989)

up to kick him, but was too scared. Nothing
could have got the words out of me then. Rage
shut me up, yet "DO YOU?" was beginning

to peel, as of live layers of skin, age
from age from age from him until he gazed
through hysteria as a wet baby thing

repeating, "Do you love me? Say you do,"
in baby chokes, only loud, for they came
from a man. There wouldn't be a rescue

from my mother, still at work. The same
choking sobs said, "Love me, love me," and my game
was breaking down because I couldn't do

anything, not escape into my own
refusal, *I won't, I won't*, not fantasize
a kind, rich father, not fill the narrowed zone,

empty except for confusion until the size
of my fear ballooned as I saw his eyes,
blurred, taurean—my sister screamed—unknown,

unknown to me, a voice rose and leveled
off, "I love you," I said. *"Say 'I love you,
Dad!' "* "I love you, Dad," I whispered, leveled

by defeat into a cardboard image, untrue,
unbending. I was surprised I could move
as I did to get up, but he stayed, burled

onto the chair—my monstrous fear—she screamed,
my sister, "Dad, the phone! Go answer it!"
The phone wasn't ringing, yet he seemed

to move toward it, and I ran. He had a fit—
"It's not ringing!"—but I was at the edge of it
as he collapsed into the chair and blamed

both of us at a distance. No, the phone
was not ringing. There was no world out there,
so there we remained, completely alone.

How I Had to Act

One day I went and bought a fake fur coat
from two old ladies in a discount shop
no young woman should have walked into: taupe

fluff with leopard spots for four hundred bucks
which I charged—no cash till my paycheck—
admired by the two old saleslady crooks.

Five minutes later I was at my shrink's
casually shoving the bag by a chair,
one arm flopping out synthetically. Trinkets,

all belonging to my crooked grandmother,
floated across the wall already filled with the shrink's
trinkets. Afterwards, among the minks

on the street, I caught sight of my grandmother
in a shopwindow. The wind was howling.
I wore the fake coat with a babushka. Another

possibility was: that was *me*. I didn't
have four hundred dollars and felt humiliated
by what I had acted out and berated

myself for buying a blazer in the size
of my sister the week before! You MESS!
I called myself a lot of names. Eyes

on the bus looked up when I barreled on
in the coat I couldn't return to the store.
I refused to go shopping alone anymore.

My rich friend said, "A fun fur . . . how daring."
How daring to become my clever, lying
grandmother and before that my sister, whose loved,

dirty stuffed leopard Gram craftily destroyed.
I had promised myself a real fur coat
which I wanted as I did a real self, employed

with real feelings. Instead I bought a fake
which I couldn't afford. "What a mistake!"
I chortled to my shrink, who agreed,

though I did not want her to. How terrible,
I wanted her to say, How terrible
you have to act this way.

Don't Think Governments End the World

Don't think governments end the world. The blast,
the burnings, and the final famine will
be brought on *by mistake.* "I'm sorry," the last
anxious man at the control panel will
try to say, his face streaked with panic, red
hives rising on his neck. He'll have been a jerk
all his life, who couldn't get through his head
that his mother couldn't love him. Work
at the panel would give him the control
that she had denied him again and again.

Thus the world will burn through the central hole
of his being. He won't really be sure—again,
having never been assured of her—of what
he is supposed to do. That is, he'll be sure
at every exercise until the shut
blank door of the final moment injures
his gerrybuilt control and BANG, BANG, BANG.

It won't be his fault, his childish mother's fault,
or the fault of what produced her or what
produced what produced her back through the vault
of savage centuries. If he'd just known what,
he'd have done it to please. He might have known himself
through what he'd felt, and thus might be clear.
She might have said, "That's nice, dear,"
and we wouldn't be dead.

The Surge

Maybe it is the shyness of the pride
he has when he puts my hand down to feel
the hardness of his cock I hadn't tried

by any conscious gesture to raise,
yet it rose for my soft presence in the bed:
there was nothing I did to earn its praise

but be alive next to it. Maybe it is
the softness of want beneath his delight
at his body going on without his . . .

his will, really, his instructions . . . that
surges inside me as a sort of surrender
to the fact that I am, that I was made, that

there is nothing I need do to please but be.
To do nothing but be, and thus be wanted:
so, this is love. *Look what happened*, he says as he

watches my hand draw out what it did not raise,
purpled in sleep. The surge inside me must
come from inside me, where the world lies,

just as the prick stiffened to amaze us
came from a rising inside him. The blessing
we feel is knowing that *out there* is nothing.
The world inside us has come to praise us.

MICHAEL PETTIT ❖

Sparrow of Espanola

Here's to that bedraggled sparrow
at the Sonic Drive-In
in Espanola, New Mexico, famous
Low Rider Capital of the World.
Sunday there is a holy day of cars;
the summer afternoon we passed through
all the discount auto parts stores
were open, their lots full,
and out on the drag a parade
of huge Dodges and souped-up Chevys
crept along, engines throbbing,
drivers in mirrored shades just visible
above the steering wheels made from chain,
the carpeted dashboards, soft dice
bouncing as car after car reared up
and dropped down, reared and dropped
like perfect black stallions
in movies at El Pasatiempo down the road.
Sunlight ricocheted off tinted windshields,

Most Recent Book: CARDINAL POINTS (University of Iowa Press, 1988)

metallic-flake paint and chrome trim
as the drivers idled bumper to bumper
up and down U.S. 285, route
of the Pueblos, route of Escalante and Cortez,
of Spanish priests, American trappers, traders
and tourists on their way somewhere else,
stopping for coffee, a bite to eat,
a tank of gas to get them out.
In Espanola the low riders drove all afternoon,
all evening, all their lives
for all we knew. For half an hour
we ate in our car and watched them go by
and go by. They were home there,
with the hard-luck sparrow
that accosted us at the Sonic:
small, brown, skinny, half its feathers
gone, others poking out
at odd angles, it looked ravaged
and incapable of flight,
sparrow of present misery forever.
Yet it flew, popping from beam to beam
holding up the corrugated steel roof
above us, flying about
or bouncing around on the ground, peeping
its one note over and over.
There, out of the hot sun
that bore down, crowning the cars out on the strip,
softening the asphalt everywhere
except in the shadow of the Sonic,
was home, was the known world:
cheap speakers squawking,
waitresses hustling trays, overheated
aroma of fries and tacos, crumbs
all the sparrows fought over.
Ours and the others of the flock—
those bigger, less tattered, maybe
not so hopelessly stuck in Espanola—
went begging shamelessly from car to car,
ours and the hot machines of low riders
in for a rest, a break in their ceaseless
revolutions up and down 285.
Give them tenacity. Here's to that
lost sparrow, that least bird
cheeping on the hood of our car, ornament

of desire that creates and defeats
failure. Here's to the insistent
call of its belly and heart
that won our hearts and tongues:
when we rolled out of the Sonic
into the parade and away
from Espanola forever, we were singing
its song over and over and over.

Pavlov's Dog

Last night, late, a light rain
beading the windshield,
I held you and we listened
to the static and old songs on the radio.
Filled with the past, the failure
of love to last, beyond our breath
on the glass I saw coming
down the wet street a great dog,
his chestnut coat long and curling,
soaked as though he'd walked all night
to stand there before us.
I held you close and watched him
shut his yellow eyes
and shake slowly his massive head,
water slinging from his muzzle
in threads of light.
I watched him drive the muscles
of his neck and shoulders,
his back, flanks, hips a blur
of motion and water flowering.

And so I believed
love and sorrow must be foreign
to each other, the heart so large
they never meet, never speak.
Why is it not so? Why the old song,
desire and heartbreak we can sing
word for word after all these years?
Why as I held you did that dog
appear and seem to shake clean,
only to roll his eyes open

and stand unmoving, staring our way
through the rain? Cold and steady
and long into the night it fell,
into his thick coat, into my heart
where you walk, filled with love
and unafraid. I am afraid. Of Pavlov,
of his bell and saliva at work
in my life. Tell me how I am
to join you, to shake free for good
of that cold man's rain,
his dog standing wet, obedient,
and brutal as a bell ringing,
always ringing, for sorrow.

Driving Lesson

    for Suzanne

Beside him in the old Ford pickup
that smelled of rope and grease and cattle feed,
sat my sister and I, ten and eight, big
now our grandfather would teach us
that powerful secret, how to drive.
Horizon of high mountain peaks visible
above the blue hood, steering wheel huge
in our hands, pedals at our toe-tips,
we heard his sure voice urge us
Give it gas, give it gas. Over the roar
of the engine our hearts banged
like never before and banged on
furiously in the silence after
we bucked and stalled the truck.
How infinitely empty it then seemed—
windy flat rangeland of silver-green
gramma grass dotted with blooming cactus
and jagged outcrops of red rock, beginnings
of the Sangre de Cristos fifty miles off.
All Guadelupe County, New Mexico,
nothing to hit, and we could not
get the damn thing going. Nothing to hit
was no help. It was not the mechanics
of accelerator and clutch, muscle and bone,

but our sheer unruly spirits
that kept us small with the great desire
to move the world by us, earth and sky
and all the earth and sky contained.
And how hard it was when,
after our grandfather who was a god
said *Let it out slow, slow* time and again
until we did and were at long last rolling
over the earth, his happy little angels,
how hard it was to listen
not to our own thrilled inner voices
saying *Go, go*, but to his saying
the *Good, good* we loved but also
the *Keep it in the ruts* we hated to hear.
How hard to hold to it—
single red vein of a ranch road
running out straight across the mesa,
blood we were bound to follow—
when what we wanted with all our hearts
was to scatter everywhere, everywhere.

Legless Boy Climbing In and Out of Chair

Plate 90, *The Human Figure in Motion*

It seems a trick of lighting, his legs lost
only in shadow, not in fact. A stunt,
like a solar eclipse or Jesus missing
from the tomb. Astonishing, but you know
they'll be back. In fact, they won't. Imagine
the nights he can't sleep, the sheet that lies flat
just beyond his fingertips: fields of snow
stretching trackless before him, the fair girls
he will never have. On the street he spies
their hips swinging and remembers running
toward the freight car, the leap that falls short
by inches. He catches hold with his hands,
swings gracefully under the great iron wheels
that barely leave the track. He's left staring
across the rail at his legs. His blood flows
before him. His brother begins to scream
like a steam whistle. Now his mother says

The good Lord moves in mysterious ways.
Mr. Muybridge wants to take your picture.
See what a lucky, lucky boy you are!
On his face you see nothing but bitter
determination. There's no trick to this.

ROBERT PINSKY ❖

The Questions

What about the people who came to my father's office
For hearing aids and glasses—chatting with him sometimes

A few extra minutes while I swept up in the back,
Addressed packages, cleaned the machines; if he was busy

I might sell them batteries, or tend to their questions:
The tall overloud old man with a tilted, ironic smirk

To cover the gaps in his hearing; a woman who hummed one
Prolonged note constantly, we called her "the hummer"—how

Could her white fat husband (he looked like Rev. Peale)
Bear hearing it day and night? And others: a coquettish old lady

In a bandeau, a European. She worked for refugees who ran
Gift shops or booths on the boardwalk in the summer;

She must have lived in winter on Social Security. One man
Always greeted my father in Masonic gestures and codes.

Why do I want them to be treated tenderly by the world, now
Long after they must have slipped from it one way or another,

While I was dawdling through school at that moment—or driving,
Reading, talking to Ellen. Why this new superfluous caring?

I want for them not to have died in awful pain, friendless.
Though many of the living are starving, I still pray for these,

Dead, mostly anonymous (but Mr. Monk, Mrs. Rose Vogel)
And barely remembered: that they had a little extra, something

---

Most Recent Book: THE WANT BONE (The Ecco Press, 1990)

For pleasure, a good meal, a book or a decent television set.
Of whom do I pray this rubbery, low-class charity? I saw

An expert today, a nun—wearing a regular skirt and blouse,
But the hood or headdress navy and white around her plain

Probably Irish face, older than me by five or ten years.
The Post Office clerk told her he couldn't break a twenty

So she got change next door and came back to send her package.
As I came out she was driving off—with an air, it seemed to me,

Of annoying, demure good cheer, as if the reasonableness
Of change, mail, cars, clothes was a pleasure in itself; veiled

And dumb like the girls I thought enjoyed the rules too much
In grade school. She might have been a grade school teacher;

But she reminded me of being there, aside from that—as a name
And person there, a Mary or John who learns that the janitor

Is Mr. Woodhouse; the principal is Mr. Ringleven; the secretary
In the office is Mrs. Apostolacus; the bus driver is Ray.

Shirt

The back, the yoke, the yardage. Lapped seams,
The nearly invisible stitches along the collar
Turned in a sweatshop by Koreans or Malaysians

Gossiping over tea and noodles on their break
Or talking money or politics while one fitted
This armpiece with its overseam to the band

Of cuff I button at my wrist. The presser, the cutter,
The wringer, the mangle. The needle, the union,
The treadle, the bobbin. The code. The infamous blaze

At the Triangle Factory in nineteen-eleven.
One hundred and forty-six died in the flames
On the ninth floor, no hydrants, no fire escapes—

The witness in a building across the street
Who watched how a young man helped a girl to step
Up to the window sill, then held her out

Away from the masonry wall and let her drop.
And then another. As if he were helping them up
To enter a streetcar, and not eternity.

A third before he dropped her put her arms
Around his neck and kissed him. Then he held
Her into space, and dropped her. Almost at once

He stepped to the sill himself, his jacket flared
And fluttered up from his shirt as he came down,
Air filling up the legs of his gray trousers—

Like Hart Crane's Bedlamite, "shrill shirt ballooning."
Wonderful how the pattern matches perfectly
Across the placket and over the twin bar-tacked

Corners of both pockets, like a strict rhyme
Or a major chord. Prints, plaids, checks,
Houndstooth, Tattersall, Madras. The clan tartans

Invented by mill-owners inspired by the hoax of Ossian,
To control their savage Scottish workers, tamed
By a fabricated heraldry: MacGregor,

Bailey, MacMartin. The kilt, devised for workers
To wear among the dusty clattering looms.
Weavers, carders, spinners. The loader,

The docker, the navvy. The planter, the picker, the sorter
Sweating at her machine in a litter of cotton
As slaves in calico headrags sweated in fields:

George Herbert, your descendant is a Black
Lady in South Carolina, her name is Irma
And she inspected my shirt. Its color and fit

And feel and its clean smell have satisfied
Both her and me. We have culled its cost and quality
Down to the buttons of simulated bone,

The buttonholes, the sizing, the facing, the characters
Printed in black on neckband and tail. The shape,
The label, the labor, the color, the shade. The shirt.

The New Saddhus

Barefoot, in unaccustomed clouts or skirts of raw muslin,
With new tin cup, rattle or scroll held in diffident hands
Stripped of the familiar cuffs, rings, watches, the new holy-men

Avoid looking at their farewelling families, an elaborate
Feigned concentration stretched over their self-consciousness and terror,
Like small boys nervous on the first day of baseball tryouts.

Fearful exalted Coptic tradesman; Swedish trucker; Palestinian doctor;
The Irish works foreman and the Lutheran Optometrist from St. Paul:
They line up smirking or scowling, feeling silly, determined,

All putting aside the finite piercing recklessness of men
Who in this world have provided for their generation: O they have
Swallowed their wives' girlhoods and their children's dentistry,

Dowries and tuitions. And grown fat with swallowing they line up
Endless as the Ganges or the piles of old newspapers at the dumps,
Which may be blankets for them now; intense and bathetic

As the founders of lodges, they will overcome fatigue, self-pity, desire,
O Lords of mystery, to stare endlessly at the sun till the last
Red retinal ghost of actual sight is burned utterly away,

And still turn eyes that see no more than the forehead can see
Daily and all day toward the first faint heat of the morning.
Ready O Lords to carry one kilo of sand more each month,

More weight and more, so the fabulous thick mortified muscles
Lurch and bulge under an impossible tonnage of stupid,
Particulate inertia, and still O Lords ready, men and not women

And not young men, but the respectable Kurd, Celt, Marxist
And Rotarian, chanting and shuffling in place a little now
Like their own pimply, reformed-addict children, as they put aside

The garb, gear, manners and bottomless desires of their completed
Responsibilities; they are a shambles of a comic drill-team
But holy, holy—holy, becoming their own animate worshipful

Soon all but genderless flesh, a cooked sanctified recklessness—
O the old marks of elastic, leather, metal razors, callousing tools,
Pack straps and belts, fading from their embarrassed bodies!

STANLEY PLUMLY ❖

Infidelity

The two-toned Olds swinging sideways out of
the drive, the bone-white gravel kicked up in
a shot, my mother in the deathseat half
out the door, the door half shut—she's being
pushed or wants to jump, I don't remember.
The Olds is two kinds of green, hand painted,
and blows black smoke like a coal-oil fire. I'm
stunned and feel a wind, like a machine, pass
through me, through my heart and mouth; I'm standing
in a field not fifty feet away, the
wheel of the wind closing the distance.
Then suddenly the car stops and my mother
falls with nothing, nothing to break the fall . . .

One of those moments we give too much to,
like the moment of acknowledgment of
betrayal, when the one who's faithless has
nothing more to say and the silence is
terrifying since you must choose between
one or the other emptiness. I know
my mother's face was covered black with blood
and that when she rose she too said nothing.
Language is a darkness pulled out of us.
But I screamed that day she was almost killed,
whether I wept or ran or threw a stone,
or stood stone-still, choosing at last between
parents, one of whom was driving away.

Hedgerows

How many names. Some trouble
or other would take me outside
up the town's soft hill, into the country,
on the road between them.
The haw, the interlocking bramble, the thorn,

Most Recent Book: BOY ON A STEP (The Ecco Press, 1989)

head-high, higher, a corridor, black windows.
  And everywhere the smell of sanicle
    and tansy, the taste
  of the judas elder, and somewhere
the weaver thrush that here they call *mistle*,
  as in evergreen, because of the berries.
    I'd walk in the evening,
  into the sun, the blue air almost cold,
wind like traffic, the paper flowering of the ox-eye
    and the campion still white,
      still lit, like spring.
    I'd walk until my mind cleared,
with the clarity of morning, the dew transparent
    to the green, even here, in another
      country, in the dark,
    the hedgework building and weaving
and building under both great wings of the night.
    I'd have walked to the top of the next
      hill, and the next, the stars,
    like town lights, coming on,
the next town either Ash Mill or Rose Ash.
    Then sometimes a car, sometimes a bird, a magpie,
      gliding. This is voicelessness,
    the still breath easing.
I think, for a moment, I wanted to die,
    and that somehow the tangle
      and bramble, the branch and flowering of the hedge
    would take me in, torn, rendered down
to the apple or the red wound or the balm,
    the green man, leaf and shred.
      I think I wanted the richness, the thickness,
    the whole dumb life gone to seed,
and the work to follow, the hedger with his tools,
    ethering and cutting, wood and mind.
      And later, in this life,
    to come back as a pail made of elm
or broom straw of broom or the heartwood of the yew
    for the bow, oak for the plow—
      the bowl on the wild cherry of the table for the boy
    who sits there, having come from the field
with his family, half hungry, half cold,
    one more day of the harvest accounted,
      yellowing, winnowing,

the boy lost in the thought
of the turning of the year and the dead father.

Birthday

An old mortality, these evening doorways into rooms,
this door from the kitchen and there's the yard,
the grass not cut and filled with sweetness,
and in the thorn the summer wounding of the sun.

And locked in the shade the dove calling down.

The glare's a little blinding still but only
for the moment of surprise, like suddenly
coming into a hall with a window at the end,

the light stacked up like scaffolding. I am
that boy again my father told not to look
at the ground so much looking at the ground.

I am the animal touched on the forehead, charmed.

In the sky the silver maple like rain in a cloud
we've tied: and I see myself walking from what looks like
a classroom, the floor waxed white, into my father's
arms, who lifts me, like a discovery, out of this life.

Cedar Waxwing on Scarlet Firethorn

for John Jones

To start again with something beautiful,
and natural, the waxwing first on one
foot, then the other, holding the berry
against the moment like a drop of blood—
red-wing-tipped, yellow at the tip of the
tail, the head sleek, crested, fin or arrow,
turning now, swallowing. Or any bird
that turns, as by instruction, its small, dark
head, disinterested, toward the future; flies
into the massive tangle of the trees, slick.
The visual glide of the detail blurs.

The good gun flowering in the mouth is done,
like swallowing the sword or eating fire,
the carnival trick we could take back if
we wanted. When I was told suicide
meant the soul stayed with the body locked in
the ground I knew it was wrong, that each bird
could be anyone in the afterlife,
alive, on wing. Like this one, which lets its
thin lisp of a song go out into
the future, then follows, into the wood-
land understory, into its voice, gone.

But to look down the long shaft of the air,
the whole healing silence of the air, fire
and thorn, where we want to be, on the edge
of the advantage, the abrupt green edge
between the flowering pyracantha and
the winded, open field, before the trees—
to be alive in secret, this is what
we wanted, and here, as when we die what
lives is fluted on the air—a whistle,
then the wing—even our desire to die,
to swallow fire, disappear, be nothing.

The body fills with light, and in the mind
the white oak of the table, the ladder
stiffness of the chair, the dried-out paper
on the wall fly back into the vein and
branching of the leaf—flare like the waxwings,
whose moment seems to fill the scarlet hedge.
From the window, at a distance, just more
trees against the sky, and in the distance
after that everything is possible.
We are in a room with all the loved ones,
who, when they answer, have the power of song.

Toward Umbria

                    It isn't the poppies,
their red and accidental numbers,
nor the birdfoot-violets, their blue lines
wasted, nor the sheer, uninterrupted
wayside pastures—nor along the river

the centuries-faded terra-cotta farmhouses,
outbuildings, floatings of iron, iron windmills,
                              pastoral or neutral,
like the ancient towns walled-up in sunlight
and the failed machinery left abandoned.
From a summer I can still see the sidewalk
broken by a root and follow, in a thought,
the bull-blue thistle wild along the fence-wire
into the country. Here the thistle blooms

too tall, the color of clover, Great Marsh and Musk,
and spiked like roses. Something about its
conference and size, its spine indifference—.
                              We are drift and flotsam,
though sometimes when we stop to look out over
the landscape, outcrops of limestone and a few
stone sheep, the ground itself seems torn,
and when we drive along the white glide of the river,
the high wheat grass like water in the wind,
someone in joy running from the house,
the story is already breaking down.
The season is ending, fire on the wing,
or the season is starting endlessly again,
sedge and woodrush and yellow chamomile,

anywhere a field is like a wall, lapsed, fallow
or filled, a stain of wildflowers or a wave
of light washing over stone, everything in time,
                              and all the same—
if I pick this poppy, as I used to
pull up weeds, wild strawberries, anything,
a city will be built, we'll have to live there,
we'll have to leave. Once, and in one direction only.
And the figure on the landscape coming toward us
will be someone we knew and almost loved, or loved,
for whom this moment is equally awkward,
as for those ahead of us it is equally condemned,
ploughmen and gleaners, shepherds-of-the-keep,
                      those on the road, those lost.

Thomas Rabbitt ❖

Bernadette Murphy, 1943–1955

Fat girls have more fun in the woods
Is what boys said. What did I know?

An Indian fell from the cliff
To name Sally's Rock. This was truth.

What did I know? The Army Camp
Was built to keep the Russians out.

This was truth. Ike was President.
Bernadette did it if you asked.

To keep Russians out of our woods.
	All day we slunk from tree to rock.

If you ask now what I saw then
I have to say what I said then.

Nothing. Bernadette was climbing
Sally's Rock. It's what we all did.

From tree to rock to cliff. For fun.
She'd found a cave where she could watch

While I looked everywhere for her
And no matter how mad I got

She would watch. She would not call out.
I saw then that she must hate me,

So I got mad. It did no good.
I found the ledge. It did no good.

I hated her. And ran away.
And told them at the Army Camp

That a stupid fat girl was naked
In a cave high on Sally's Rock.

The Army Camp turned out to look
For Bernadette, and found her

Most Recent Book: The Abandoned Country (Carnegie Mellon University Press, 1988)

Dead on the stones beneath the cliff,
And asked me again what I knew.

Fat girls have more fun in the woods.
The Army keeps the Russians out.

Bernadette does it if you ask.
An Indian fell from the cliff.

Beneath the cliff the soldiers found
Nothing. What did I know? Nothing.

Ike was President. This was truth.
Bernadette loved you if you asked.

Blue Lights

A madman has threatened my life. I mean
An insane human being, adult, male,
Has expressed his need to terminate me.
I carry a pistol. Like an itch. Strange
How desire turns itself over. It's all
I can do to keep from tracking him down.

Some winter nights I drive to the airport
And park off the road that circles the field.
Winter is best. The clear air. I drink beer
And watch the runway lights, strung like blue pearls,
Send themselves off into air, into space.
A signal. To call us in. Send us home.

I carry the gun in my coat pocket.
I never forget it is there. I'd like
To get it over with soon, to kill him
And leave. To leave the gun behind, to be
Free of this weight so alien I begin
To believe he is right: I deserve to die.

When I was a child the Cibottis wrapped
Their house in blue lights. It was Christmas
And they were Italians. Blue was still strange.
Their bungalow pulsed. Each night while I watched it
I·was sure I could see the house rise.
Others watched. I pointed. No one else believed.

The sheriff's throbbing blue cherry is lovely,
More like an echo than sound itself, sometimes
Too green, but always more than we can tear
Away from—is what I tell him the night
He asks what the fuck I think I'm doing parked
At the end of the runway. Drunk. And armed.

The world makes of itself a target is what
Any sane lover of blue lights would say
To any fool who would question the gift
The lights offer: this color is unearthly.
There's no gentian, no sea, no burning gas
Accounts for what you see, for your desire.

These blue lights at the airport suck you in
Is what, instead of shooting him, I tell
The sheriff. He needs to understand. It must
Be sexual. Italian. It must be
Otherworldly madness makes us believe
These lights are taking back our alien souls.

The Power of Faith

The man on the phone says he is blind.
What reassurance is that meant to give?
That if I am naked or peeing or dead,
He cannot tell? But the blind have a gift,
We're told, a consolation: the blind can see
Over miles and miles of telephone lines
What the sighted can only guess from what is said.
Perhaps the FCC requires the blind to give
Some warning: Hello, I'm blind, I can't
Actually see that you're naked, peeing and dead,
But I know that you are, which, for us blind
Telephone salesmen is an unfair advantage.
So, consider yourself seen.
The point is, he says, I'm selling light bulbs.
This is rich, I think, this is poetry,
This is Ronnie Reagan hosting *Death Valley Days*
All over again. Homer's back in Attica
And the old fool is selling light bulbs.
So how does he convince me? His is the quick way
Around the steel trap of my bitter wit.

No fooling you, he says. A blind man
Selling light bulbs over the phone, he says,
Is irony. Yes, I says, no shit.
But that was not my point, he says. Boraxo,
I think, like Ronald Reagan, he's really selling
Boraxo, so we all can have clean hands.
How is it, the salesman asks, that nowadays
You who see that dignity is all that I should
Save from my life have never been fools,
At one time or another, for money or love,
Have never lost these, have failed to try?
Now you pretend to have everything. How can
The stupid and the very hard still believe
That the intellect, bee in a jar, rules
At all the world it sees? One sting.
Passion and risk. One sting is all you get.
It's not, he says, like I am selling
Preparation H or God. It's not as though
I've promised that you'll never die.
I just want to do for you what I
Cannot do for me. I want to sell you this thing
You cannot see, this bee in a jar, this
Buzz under glass, this miracle. I kiss
Your eyelids. I turn it on. See there now.
You can see. Never mind the cost.

For Thomas Stearns Eliot on the Occasion of His One Hundredth Birthday

There he is, Mars rising, a purulent red dot,
Mere pimple, closest he can get for three trillion years,
Live, on screen, 9/26/88, one day past
The full moon. I've checked the calendar.

Today Old Possum turns a hundred and is dead.
Last night, in the kitchen, in the full moon,
I checked the calendar, took up the breadknife,
Hooted, hollered, danced in the full moon's light,

Sober, self-conscious, while the airwaves sent
Beyond air, beyond Alpha Centuri, the last debate:

Out there—what must they think? Surely
They must think, have some opinion

Of the disturbance we create, the particles,
The waves, the data flow, the flood of knowledge
Since Heinrich Rudolph Herz, a hundred years ago,
First generated microwaves and got us cooking.

There was, of course, a lapse between
The picture and the sound. Hanna-Barbera,
Dukakis-Bush. The wonder was that these
Would travel while the pop your planet made

Was lost in space and time, was never seen
Or heard three trillion years ago
Except, perhaps, as recorded on this screen—
Faint echo, tiny flash—a disturbance

On the "Howdy Doody Show" or, just as likely,
A flip-flop on the news, film at eleven
Showing Mars rising in the sky at seven
Over the shoulder of that woman in Beirut:

I am the Sybil of Cumae, she said, I
Am the poetess of witness. Oh, look. Listen. I
Am the reason the dead die. On and on. I. I.
I am witless. I am disjunction. *Und so weiter.*

I am the naked man with the breadknife
In the dark kitchen at the foot of the stairs
You can just now hear beginning to creak.
Like craps, the news at eleven. At seven.

I am the child blown to chopped liver, darling.
I am the mother whipped into borscht
Says the scared white lady with the long brown hair.
Voice-over hurries to overtake the video it describes.

Happy birthday to you, happy birthday to you . . .
Over her right shoulder, Mars, a bright carbuncle
With a life of its own. Over her left, the moon,
Playing possum in the middle of the road.

Madre Sofia

My mother took me because she couldn't
wait the second ten years to know.
This was the lady rumored to have been
responsible for the box-wrapped baby
among the presents at that wedding,
but we went in, anyway, through the curtains.
Loose jar-top half turned
and not caught properly in the threads
her head sat mimicking its original intention
like the smile of a child hitting himself.
Central in that head grew unfamiliar poppies
from a face mahogany, eyes half yellow
half gray at the same time, goat and fog,
slit eyes of the devil, his tweed suit, red
lips, and she smelled of smoke, cigarettes,
but a diamond smoke, somehow; I inhaled
sparkles, I could feel them, throat, stomach.
She did not speak, and as a child
I could only answer, so that together
we were silent, cold and wet, dry and hard:
from behind my mother pushed me forward.
The lady put her hand on the face
of a thin animal wrap, tossing that head
behind her to be pressured incredibly
as she sat back in the huge chair and leaned.
Then I saw the breasts as large as her
head, folded together, coming out of her dress
as if it didn't fit, not like my mother's.
I could see them, how she kept them
penned up, leisurely, in maroon feed bags,
horse nuzzles of her wide body,
but exquisitely penned up
circled by pearl reins and red scarves.
She lifted her arm, but only with the tips
of her fingers motioned me to sit opposite.
She looked at me but spoke to my mother

Most Recent Book: TEODORA LUNA'S TWO KISSES (W. W. Norton & Co., 1990)

words dark, smoky like the small room,
words coming like red ants stepping occasionally
from a hold on a summer day in the valley,
red ants from her mouth, her nose, her ears,
tears from the corners of her cinched eyes.
And suddenly she put her hand full on my head
pinching tight again with those fingertips
like a television healer, young Oral Roberts
half standing, quickly, half leaning
those breasts swinging toward me
so that I reach with both hands to my lap
protecting instinctively whatever it is
that needs protection when a baseball is thrown
and you're not looking but someone yells,
the hand, then those breasts coming toward me
like the quarter-arms of the amputee Joaquin
who came back from the war to sit
in the park, reaching always for children
until one day he had to be held back.
I sat there, no breath, and could see only
hair around her left nipple, like a man.
Her clothes were old.
Accented, in a language whose spine had been
snapped, she whispered the words of a city
witch, and made me happy, alive like a man:
The future will make you tall.

The Inquietude of a Particular Matter

Ventura had hair of the jungle
Long like the gatling words
Of the monkeys and the parrots
Like the vines and roots without end
All pulled back and knotted tight
With the help, the insistence
Of her mother who had cheeks
Like persimmons, her face
Always tasting their peel,
Her mother using the energy
Of that taste to pull
So that the face part
Of Ventura's young girl head

Became skull, white bone
And sockets, big clack teeth
Like in the cartoon, unconnected,
Almost, clack clacking so
She could not help
Sounding like the fat ducks
That every day she fed
After she stopped her work
In the peeling secretariat
Of a third but ambitious
Supervisor to the federal railroads,
Fed the ducks every day popcorn,
Palomitas, and the one day
She could not because of the snow,
Snow for the first time
She could remember this early,
This far to the south,
The ducks opened their mouths anyway
And ate the snow, the white bits
They thought had come from her.
She laughed and opened
Her mouth, also, making a sound
In that late afternoon
So sacred in its one freedom
That the crickets stopped to listen
But no less than he.

Clemente had watched her
From behind the bougainvilleas,
Had smoked his colored cigarette
Watching her in this moment
Then letting her go, simply,
Like smoke to its most secret place,
To the place smoke always goes,
This Ventura leaving a memory
Sweet like cane in his eyes
So that the rest of his body
Caught fire with jealousy.
The world had always erupted
Through him, always bad,
But not this time: this time
He wished to whisper the Spanish
Love words he had dreamed,
How long they were, he wished

To let these words kick
Their fine heels through the fat
Wall of freedoms
Breaking through to the side
Of what might be
But he dared not.
In this town, he knew well,
In this life, one must wait.
Nothing could be more simple.
He blew circles of new smoke
The size of himself standing,
The large himself
Where the pain most certainly was,
Wishing he could so easily
Erase the pain with his hands,
Put his hands fisted
Into the face of a bad man
But he could not.
The inquietude of this matter
Of love, of loving how she saw
The ducks, how she laughed out
Her true self in that moment,
How he wanted her
He could not endure.
But he would. This was his test,
To say nothing.

True Story of the Pins

Pins are always plentiful
but one day they were not
and your Uncle Humberto
who collected all the butterflies
you see here on the walls,
was crazy looking for some
and he went to your cousin
Graciela the hard seamstress
who has pins it is rumored
even in hard times
but when she found out
why he wanted them
because the wind from the south

who was her friend
since the days of her
childhood on the sea
told her, she firmly refused
your poor Uncle Humberto
whose picture is here
on the wall behind you,
did you feel his eyes,
and he went into the most terrible
of rages, too terrible
for a butterfly collector
we all said afterward
and he burst the vein
that grew like a great snake
on his small forehead
and he died on the dirt
floor of Graciela's house
who of course felt sick
and immediately went
and put pins, this is what has
made her hard, through
the bright wings of the butterflies
Humberto had prepared
since he was after all
her father and she
could afford no better
light of perpetuity.

DAVID RIVARD ❖

Summons

Suppose I can convince myself this world
is my home only by claiming it could
never be & then assuming we all
share that feeling, a bond which anchors us
each to the planet, even those hired
to populate this photo, spread across
pages twenty-five & twenty-six, of a beach

Most Recent Book: TORQUE (University of Pittsburg Press, 1988)

party, the magazine scented, because
what else should summon us to delusion
but perfume, drifting up from the tanned
and fiercely healthy faces, a massaged
glow, in precise attunement to the means
implied by the Queen Anne porch & gables,
women in summer evening dresses, barefoot,
heels tossed in clumps of eel grass, lightly
wavering stalks, & two men in tuxes
about to heap driftwood atop a bonfire
while a third lugs the straw hamper of food
and wines, the models' laughter unheard but
booming, out over dunes & waves, joyful
efflorescent laughing, easy to envy,
and hidden inside their shouts another shot
of them, later, clothes stripped off, drunken,
running down the beach into a warm
plankton-lit surf, as if these were the seas
from which we had once evolved crawling
and skittering over one another's backs.

Naive Invocation

We weave up a switchback gully & out to sloping pasture,
canary grass checkered with olive saplings.
                                        Not like
the goddess, braided, unfolding wreck & trials,
and Odysseus, who gives ear to her omens while he axes
pine for hull puncheons & rigs halyards
to sail from this island.
                        No, I
wouldn't say like those two.
                                    So why shouldn't I lag
back a little, watching you hike up the path,
your thighs, & the other places my skin loves,
last meandering pulse of the last moments
of sleep,
hair tucked under a duckbill baseball cap, sun-streaked,
coarsened by weeks of swimming.
                                        Up ahead, smoke
downdrafts across the field from a low ridge.
                                        And walking through

we're just two more shallow-breathing members of the creation,
like the cicadas
on these dry gold hills, who sound as if pleading,
pleading for the return of their souls.
                                    And what necessary thing
have I learned yet about begging, to stop love abandoning
the shell skin is?
                        Nothing more than that calf & those
dozen belled goats just off the path, as they whirl & shit
themselves in a corner of their pen.
                                    The smoke like a drover,
caressing, rubbing shut their eyelids, preparing
them.
        It waits for us to go.
                        Soon enough, I think, to catch up
with ourselves, as if already we're stretched out
naked in the cove a kilometer ahead, ocean drawling, undulant,
belly & nipples breathing into warm sand.

Earth to Tell of the Beasts

Because it's summer a trellis of Gulf air curves over the day,
buckling, resiny.
                        Six-thirty one morning,
you killed yourself.
                        And in one of the minutes since then
I'm drawn out to the porch by a ripsaw's
E-flat run through plywood, blade shrieking its crude lullaby
about shelter & endurance. Between cuts, from the shade
of a hawthorn, a jay whistles
the sassy hymns & palpitations
fate will never be able to outlaw.
                                    So, ears filled by all
this singing, fate cowers, & trembles,
and agrees to the erasure of every word placing your Toyota
on Maui, parked off a cliff road. Words like *the syringe*,
your deft fingers tying-
off, & shooting, while flames eat the wick of rags
you stuffed in the gas tank. *Junkies*, you'd laugh,
just cheaters. As for mercy, when the gas ignites
no words will be allowed to flare outward with the explosion,
each syllable elided that would scorch

clumps of fuchsia, fleshy leaves of wild ginger.

It's a good bet.
It's easy. It's a sure thing. That the warmth & abiding
plenitude of this morning would permit me
to call your pain a fugue, an intricately feathered
spiral, because it sounds lovely. And lovely implies consolation
and accuracy. But all the while, buried inside, hurt
is still hurt, shame still shame.

And though you turned, once,
at the edge of a pool in Tucson, green eyes intensified
by the water, snub nose pierced by a tiny silver stud, gossiping,
you would never have claimed
your laughter was a music, as I could now,
the run of notes
a stampede, & after the stampede just tracks in the earth
to tell of the beasts & their escape.

Later History

for Michael McGuire

No, it isn't so bad being
the tail end of a life form, & even when it is
over for good, when the rivers slow to a stop
and we are eradicated from this planet
with its hierarchies of golden wasp, conqueror, & clerk,
it still won't be over. Our extermination
will allow us to survive ourselves, but changed
in our ways, humble, less sullen, quickened,
like dust driven along by a risen wind.
Each of us like a skater
who sidles down a corridor of wind & snowflakes, without
loneliness or fear. I think we will communicate
with one another the way,
in a bright kitchen on Sundays, a worn & disheveled pajama bottom
can deliver a message simply by clinging
to a thigh, quietly
but with a sly impunity. Doubt will defeat itself,
perfectly aware of its own
weaknesses, & all the treaties & accords of history
will be honored. All the subtle fragrances & intensities
of axel grease, of sails on the Nile & tangerines,

will be recalled & sung,
while our faces in the mirrors of innumerable
bathrooms will no longer loom up to obsess us.
But sorrow, sorrow will be unchanged.
So that we may recognize each other.

PATTIANN ROGERS ❖

The Hummingbird: A Seduction

If I were a female hummingbird perched still
And quiet on an upper myrtle branch
In the spring afternoon and if you were a male
Alone in the whole heavens before me, having parted
Yourself, for me, from cedar top and honeysuckle stem
And earth-down, your body hovering in mid-air
Far away from jewelweed, thistle and beebalm;

And if I watched how you fell, plummeting before me,
And how you rose again and fell, with such mastery
That I believed for a moment *you* were the sky
And the red-marked bird diving inside your circumference
Was just the physical revelation of the light's
Most perfect desire;

And if I saw your sweeping and sucking
Performance of swirling egg and semen in the air,
The weaving, twisting vision of red petal
And nectar and soaring rump, the rush of your wing
In its grand confusion of arcing and splitting
Created completely out of nothing just for me,

Then when you came down to me, I would call you
My own spinning bloom of ruby sage, my funneling
Storm of sunlit sperm and pollen, my only breathless
Piece of scarlet sky, and I would bless the base
Of each of your feathers and touch the tine
Of string muscles binding your wings and taste
The odor of your glistening oils and hunt
The honey in your crimson flare

Most Recent Book: SPLITTING AND BINDING (Wesleyan University Press, 1989)

And I would take you and take you and take you
Deep into any kind of nest you ever wanted.

The Next Story

All morning long
they kept coming back, the jays
five of them, blue-grey, purple-banded,
strident, disruptive. They screamed
with their whole bodies from the branches
of the pine, tipped forward, heads
toward earth, and swept across the lawn
into the oleanders, dipping low
as they flew over the half-skull
and beak, the blood-end of the one wing
lying intact, over the fluff
of feathers scattered and drifting
occasionally, easily as dandelion—
all that the cat had left.

Back and forth, past one another,
pausing as if listening, then sharply
cutting the morning again into shard
upon shard of frantic and crested descent,
jagged slivers of raucous outrage,
they kept at it, crying singly, together,
alternately, as if on cue, discordant
anthem. The pattern of their inconsolable
fear could be seen against the flat
spring sky as identical to the pattern
made by that unmendable shatter
of disjointed rubbish on the lawn,
all morning long.

Mothers, fathers, our kind, tell me again
that death doesn't matter. Tell me
it's just a limitation of vision, a fold
of landscape, a deep flax-and-poppy-filled
gully hidden on the hill, a pleat
in our perception, a somersault of existence,
natural, even beneficent, even a gift,
the only key to the red-lacquered door

at the end of the hall, "water
within water," those old stories.

But this time, whatever is said,
when it's said, will have to be more
reverent and more rude, more absolute,
more convincing than these five jays
who have become the five wheeling spokes
and stays of perfect lament, who, without knowing
anything, have accurately matched the black
beaks and spread shoulders of their bodies
to all the shrill, bird-shaped histories
of grief; will have to be demanding enough,
subtle enough, shocking enough, sovereign
enough, right enough to rouse me, to move me
from this window where I have pressed
my forehead hard against the unyielding pane,
unyielding all morning long.

The Power of Toads

The oak toad and the red-spotted toad love their love
In a spring rain, calling and calling, breeding
Through a stormy evening clasped atop their mates.
Who wouldn't sing—anticipating the belly pressed hard
Against a female's spine in the steady rain
Below writhing skies, the safe moist jelly effluence
Of a final exaltation?

There might be some toads who actually believe
That the loin-shaking thunder of the banks, the evening
Filled with damp, the warm softening mud and rising
Riverlets are the facts of their own persistent
Performance. Maybe they think that when they sing
They sing more than songs, creating rain and mist
By their voices, initiating the union of water and dusk,
Females materializing on the banks shaped perfectly
By their calls.

And some toads may be convinced they have forced
The heavens to twist and moan by the continual expansion
Of their lung-sacs pushing against the dusk.
And some might believe the splitting light,

The soaring grey they see above them are nothing
But a vision of the longing in their groins,
A fertile spring heaven caught in its entirety
At the pit of the gut.

And they might be right.
Who knows whether these broken heavens
Could exist tonight separate from trills and toad ringings?
Maybe the particles of this rain descending on the pond
Are nothing but the visual manifestation of whistles
And cascading love clicks in the shore grasses.
Raindrops-finding-earth and coitus could very well
Be known here as one.

We could investigate the causal relationship
Between rainstorm and love-by-pondside if we wished.
We could lie down in the grasses by the water's edge
And watch to see exactly how the heavens were moved,
Thinking hard of thunder, imagining all the courses
That slow, clean waters might take across our bodies,
Believing completely in the rolling and pressing power
Of heavens and thighs. And in the end we might be glad,
Even if all we discovered for certain was the slick, sweet
Promise of good love beneath dark skies inside warm rains.

Geocentric

Indecent, self-soiled, bilious
reek of turnip and toadstool
decay, dribbling the black oil
of wilted succulents, the brown
fester of rotting orchids,
in plain view, that stain
of stinkhorn down your front,
that leaking roil of bracket
fungi down your back, you
purple-haired, grainy-fuzzed
smolder of refuse, fathering
fumes and boils and powdery
mildews, enduring the constant
interruption of sink-mire
flatulence, contagious
with ear wax, corn smut,

blister rust, backwash
and graveyard debris, rich
with manure bog and dry-rot,
harboring not only egg-addled
garbage and wrinkled lip
of orange-peel mold but also
the clotted breath of over-ripe
radish and burnt leek, bearing
every dank, malodorous rut
and scarp, all sulphur fissures
and fetid hillside seepages, old,
old dependable, engendering
forever the stench and stretch
and warm seeth of inevitable
putrefaction, nobody
loves you as I do.

MICHAEL RYAN ❖

Not the End of the World

What flew down the chimney
into the cold wood stove
in my study? Wings
alive inside cast iron
gave the cold stove a soul
wilder than fire, in trouble.
I knocked the window-screen out
with a hand-heel's thunk,
and dropped the shade over
the top half of the window,
and shut the study door,
and wadded the keyhole,
hoping whatever it was
would fly for the light,
the full, clean stream of light
like the sliding board from heaven
our guardian angels slid to earth on
in *The Little Catholic Messenger*

Most Recent Book: GOD HUNGER (Viking Penguin, 1989)

weekly magazine. I genuflected once,
but only to flick the stove-latch
and spring behind a bookcase
through a memory-flash
of church-darkness, incense-smoke
mushrooming as the censer
clanks and swings back
toward the Living Host
in His golden cabinet.
A dull brown bird no bigger
than my fist hopped modestly
out, twisting its neck like a boxer
trying to shake off a flush punch.
And there on my rug, dazed,
heedless of the spotlight, it stayed,
and stayed, then settled down
as if to hatch an egg it was hallucinating.
So I scooped it into my two hands,
crazed heart in a feathered ounce,
and sat it outside on the dirt.

And there I left it.
It didn't even try its wings,
not one perfunctory flap,
but staggered a few rickety steps
before collapsing, puffing its tiny bulk.
I watched behind a window
other identical little dull birds
land within inches and chart
circles around it. Five of them,
cheeping, chased an inquiring cat.
Then all of them one by one—
by this time, a dozen—mounted its back
and fluttered jerkily like helicopters
trying to unbog a truck,
and, when that didn't work,
pecked it and pecked it,
a gust of flicks, to kill it
or rouse it I couldn't tell
until they all stepped back to wait.
It flapped once and fell forward
and rested its forehead on the ground.

I've never seen such weakness.
I thought to bring it back in

or call someone, but heard my voice
saying, "Birds die, we all die,"
the shock of being picked up again
would probably finish it,
so with this pronouncement
I tried to clear it from my mind
and return to the work I had waiting
that is most of what I can do
even if it changes nothing.

Do I need to say I was away
for all of a minute
before I went back to it?
But the bird was gone.
All the birds were gone,
and the circle they had made
now made a space so desolate
that for one moment I saw
the dead planet.

TV Room at the Children's Hospice

Red-and-green leather-helmeted
maniacally grinning motorcyclists
crash at all angles
on Lev Smith's pajama top

and when his chocolate ice cream
dumps like a mud slide down its front
he smiles, not maniacally, still nauseous
from chemotherapy and bald already.

Lev is six but sat still four hours
all afternoon with IVs in his arms,
his grandma tells everyone. Marcie
is nine and was born with no face.

One profile has been built in increments
with surgical plastic and skin grafts
and the other looks like fudge.
Tomorrow she's having an eye moved.

She finds a hand-mirror in the toy box
and maybe for the minute I watch

she sees nothing she doesn't expect.
Ruth Borthnott's son, Richard,

cracked his second vertebra
at diving practice eight weeks ago,
and as Ruth describes getting the news
by telephone (shampoo suds plopped

all over the notepad she tried
to write on) she smiles like Lev Smith
at his ice cream, smiles also saying
Richard's on a breathing machine,

if he makes it he'll be quadriplegic,
she's there in intensive care every day
at dawn. The gameshow-shrill details
of a Hawaiian vacation for two

and surf teasing the ankles
of the couple on a moonlit beachwalk
keep drawing her attention
away from our conversation.

I say it's amazing how life can change
from one second to the next,
and with no apparent disdain
for this dismal platitude,

she nods yes, and yes again
at the gameshow's svelte assistant
petting a dinette set, and yes
to Lev Smith's grandma

who has appeared beside her
with microwaved popcorn
blooming like a huge
cauliflower from its tin.

Switchblade

Most of the past is lost,
and I'm glad mine has vanished
into blackness or space or whatever nowhere
what we feel and do goes,
but there were a few cool Sunday afternoons

when my father wasn't sick with hangover
and the air in the house wasn't foul with anger
and the best china had been cleared after the week's best meal
so he could place on the table his violins
to polish with their special cloth and oil.
Three violins he'd arrange
side by side in their velvet-lined cases
with enough room between for the lids to lie open.
They looked like children in coffins,
three infant sisters whose hearts had stopped for no reason,
but after he rubbed up their scrolls and waists
along the lines of the grain to the highest sheen,
they took on the knowing posture of women in silk gowns
in magazine ads for new cars and ocean voyages,
and, as if a violin were a car in storage
that needed a spin around the block every so often,
for fifteen minutes he would play each one—
though not until each horsehair bow was precisely tightened
and coated with rosin, and we had undergone an eon of tuning.
When he played no one was allowed to speak to him.
He seemed to see something drastic across the room
or feel it through his handkerchief padding the chinboard.
So we'd hop in front of him waving or making pig-noses
the way kids do to guards at Buckingham Palace,
and after he had finished playing and had returned to himself,
he'd softly curse the idiocy of his children
beneath my mother's voice yelling to him from the kitchen
That was beautiful, Paul, play it again.

He never did, and I always hoped he wouldn't,
because the whole time I was waiting for his switchblade
to appear, and the new stories he'd tell me
for the scar thin as a seam
up the white underside of his forearm,
for the chunks of proud flesh on his back and belly,
scarlet souvenirs of East St. Louis dance halls in the twenties,
cornered in men's rooms, ganged in blind alleys,
always slashing out alone with this knife.
First the violins had to be snug again
inside their black cases
for who knew how many more months or years or lifetimes;
then he had to pretend to have forgotten
why I was sitting there wide-eyed across from him
long after my sister and brother had gone off with friends.

Every time, as if only an afterthought,
he'd sneak into his pocket and ease the switchblade
onto the bare table between us,
its thumb-button jutting from the pearl-and-silver plating
like the eye of some sleek prehistoric fish.
I must have known it wouldn't come to life
and slither toward me by itself,
but when he'd finally nod to me to take it
its touch was still warm with his body heat
and I could feel the blade inside aching
to flash open with the terrible click
that sounds now like just a *tsk* of disappointment,
it has become so sweet and quiet.

IRA SADOFF ❖

Nazis

Thank God they're all gone
except for one or two in Clinton Maine
who come home from work
at Scott Paper or Diamond Match
to make a few crank calls
to the only Jew in New England
they can find

These make-shift students of history
whose catalogue of facts include
every Jew who gave a dollar
to elect the current governor
every Jew who'd sell this country out
to the insatiable Israeli state

I know exactly how they feel
when they say they want to smash my face

Someone's cheated them
they want to know who it is
they want to know who makes them beg
It's true Let's Be Fair

Most Recent Book: EMOTIONAL TRAFFIC (David R. Godine, Publisher, 1990)

it's tough for almost everyone
I exaggerate the facts
to make a point

Just when I thought I could walk to the market
just when Jean the check-out girl
asks me how many cords of wood I chopped
and wishes me a Happy Easter
as if I've lived here all my life

Just when I can walk into the bank
and nod at the tellers who know my name
where I work who lived in my house in 1832
who know to the penny the amount
of my tiny Jewish bank account

Just when I'm sure we can all live together
and I can dine in their saltbox dining rooms
with the melancholy painting of Christ
on the wall their only consolation
just when I can borrow my neighbor's ladder
to repair one of the holes in my roof

I pick up the phone
and listen to my instructions

I see the town now from the right perspective
the gunner in the glass bubble
of his fighter plane shadowing the tiny man
with the shopping bag and pointy nose
his overcoat two sizes too large for him
skulking from one doorway to the next
trying to make his own way home

I can see he's not one of us

At the Half Note Café

for Gene Ammons

Once I heard him play
"Willow Weep for Me"
in a tone so full
and sentimental, I felt
a gap between my ribs

and lungs, a dearth of air
sorrow soon enough would fill.
I found the blues unfair
to boys like me who came to bars
unprepared for grief
that wasn't strictly personal.

I told my girl
I knew all you had to know
about suffering and love, but when
I heard a woman drunk, cry out,
in front of everyone, "Don't go, Jug—
I'll give you all of what you want,"
my face went blank
and limp as an infant
when a stranger shakes
a rattle in his face. Later,
when he hit bottom,
the last broken chorus
of "Body and Soul," I collapsed in
my girl's arms, my composure crushed
by one note on the saxophone.
I couldn't think of what to tell her.
What the hell did she know anyhow?
We both came from the same suburban town.

It was a brittle winter night.
We had nowhere to go
except her parents' house,
so we drifted down Greenwich Ave.
hand in hand. I'd never seen
streets so crowded after dark—
with drunks, half-dead, and kids
who should have been in bed.
I'm shocked we made it out alive.
I know if I'd seen my stupid grin,
my wide-eyed stare, my gaping face,
I would have smashed it
just for the experience. We were lucky
though we didn't know it then. We ended up
parking in my mother's car. We kissed,
then I stripped off her blouse,
grabbed her breast,
put her stiffened nipple in my mouth.

The Bath

1

Mother might have drowned me,
had she caught me watching her.
I watched her scrub her skin so hard
it seemed to blush. I saw desire there,
before a mother wants to be a mother.
The keyhole—ring of light that skims the flesh—
drew me to the pleasure. I understood
the glistening surface of the belly, the bumpy
shadows of the ribcoast range. I understood
that water scalds, dripping from the wrist.
Everything else, like a lamp
turned on and off, was thought: pure, impure, pure.

2

Years later, I can't repair the shock of hair
crackling to the static of her brush,
or grant her mermaid's wishes. I can't
re-trace her hands: the first amphibians
waiting to emerge. In the beginning
we know too much of everyone
until we fail them, until we see them
as they can't be seen. When Actæon
came upon Diana's naked body
and the dogs made cloth of his flesh,
he knew he'd truly burn. His voice
was not his own, his face not his face.
How could one touch heal all of us?

3

Since I can't go back
to what I wanted, since the flesh
refuses its own flesh, I can't suggest
what might have pleased them,
those long-haired creatures whose touch
soothed and satisfied. What pleases them,
these mothers, sisters, lovers,
whose oars row out to the island
I keep lonely? What pleased her
she never said. That night I saw her dream
so sheer, so self-contained, that mist surrounded it.

I never knew its subject matter.
The flesh has its cannibals, its boiling pots.
We prepare the body badly for its future.
Every household is full of crimes.
A moon shines in every window, wanting.
Each night I hold a different woman in my arms.

DAVID ST. JOHN ❖

Terraces of Rain

And the mole crept along the garden,
And moonlight stroked the young buds of
The lemon trees, and they walked the five lands . . .
Sheer terraces, rocks rising
Straight up from the sea; the strung vines
Of the grapes, the upraised hands of the olives,
Presided and blessed. Between Vernazza
And Monterosso, along a path
Cut into the sea cliff, a place for lovers
To look down and consider their love,
They climbed up to the double-backed lane
Where a few old women gathered herbs
By the roadside. Voices—
Scattered in the hills above—
Fell like rushes in a wind, their rasp and echo
Traveling down and forever in the clear sea air . . .
Then clouds, then mist, then a universal gray . . .
Where Signore and Signora Bianchini are having lunch,
She stops to talk with them, weather being
The unavoidable topic. Slips of rain, a child's
Scrawl, sudden layers and pages—then, at last,
The fan of sunlight scraping clean
The sky. Here, the world's
Very old, very stubborn, and proud. In the twilight:
Shadow and other, watching the painted foam of
Waves running from the sunset
To the coves, the overturned skiffs, the white nets
Drying in the reddening air. She stood

Most Recent Book: No HEAVEN (Houghton Mifflin Co., 1985)

Behind him, resting her hand on his shoulder. Night
Spread above them like a circling breeze,
The way a simple memory had once
Returned to Montale, calming his childhood
And a troubled winter sea. The air still cleansing,
She said, the heart that was uncleansable. The unforgiving
One, that heart . . . A boy in an emerald sweater
Passed, out walking a mongrel in good spirits. Across
The scallop of bay, the boats began
Returning to the harbor. Silent. Harsh. Such country
Breaks the selfish heart. There is no original sin:
To be in love is to be granted the only grace
Of all women and all men.

(The Cinque Terre)

I Know

I know the moon is troubling;

Its pale eloquence is always such a meddling,
Intrusive lie. I know the pearl sheen of the sheets
Remains the screen I'll draw against the night;

I know all of those silences invented for me approximate
Those real silences I cannot lose to daylight . . .
I know the orchid smell of your skin

The way I know the blackened path to the marina,
When gathering clouds obscure the summer moon—
Just as I know the chambered heart where I begin.

I know too the lacquered jewel box, its obsidian patina;
The sexual trumpeting of the diving, sweeping loons . . .
I know the slow combinations of the night, & the glow

Of fireflies, deepening the shadows of all I do not know.

Leap of Faith

No less fabulous than the carved marble inner
Ear of a lost Michelangelo & more

Blinding than the multiple courts & interior facets
Of a black diamond held up in broken moonlight

This final geography acknowledges its trunks of
Ebony & its boughs of summer rain

Though there at the gate where Dante burned his
Initials into the face of the oak shield
I hesitated before following the switchback trail up
To the precipice overlooking the canyon the abyss
So relished by philosophy & when I saw you
On the opposite cliff in your long cape & gold
Shoes with frayed thin ribbons snaking up your ankles

Like anyone approaching from the foot of a bridge
I simply stepped toward you & below the bones
Of the fallen shone in the lightning & the prayers

& certainly it was there in that country
Braced between twin brackets of stone I saw only one
Belief remains for a man whose life is spared by

A faith more insupportable than air

Wavelength

They were sitting on the thin mattress
He'd once rolled & carried up the four floors
To his room only to find it covered nearly all
Of the bare wood
Leaving just a small path alongside the wall

& between them was the sack
Of oranges & pears she'd brought its neck
Turned back to expose the colors of the fruit
& as she opened a bottle of wine
He reached over to a tall stack of books
& pulled out *The Tao* & with a silly flourish
Handed it across the bed to her she looked up
& simply poured the two squat water glasses
Half-full with wine & then she
Took the book reading silently not aloud
As he'd assumed & suddenly he felt clearly
She knew the way
Two people must come upon such an understanding

Together of course but separately
As the moon & the wave remain individually one

Meridian

The day seemed suddenly to give to black-&-white
The falcon tearing at the glove
Clare yanking down the hood over its banked eyes
& handing the bird
Its body still rippling & shuddering & flecked
Here or there with blood
                              to her son Louis
& as we walked back up the overgrown stone trail
To the castle now in the public trust
For tax reasons she admitted
Supposing one more turn in the grave couldn't harm
Her father the Count much at this point anyway
Though she flew his favorite red flag
From one of the towers every year
To mark each anniversary of his death
& though her beauty had acquired the sunken
Sheen of a ship's figurehead lifted
From the clear Mediterranean
As she walked ahead of me in her high chocolate boots
I could think only of her body still muscled like a
Snake's & how she lay sprawled last night
Naked on the blue tiles of the bathroom floor
& as I stepped into the doorway
I could see the bathtub speckled with vomit
The syringe still hanging limply from a vein in her
Thigh & she was swearing
As she grasped for the glass vial
That had rolled out of reach behind the toilet
Then she had it
Drawing herself up slowly as she
Turned her body slightly to look up at me
& she said nothing
Simply waiting until I turned & walked away
The door closing with its soft collapse
Behind me
                    now over lunch on the terrace
I pin a small sprig of parsley to her jacket lapel

A kind of truce a soldier's decoration
& above us the sun drags the day toward its meridian
Of heat & red wine & circumstance from which
We can neither look back nor step ever
Visibly beyond yet as we
Look at each other in the brash eclipsing glare
We know what bridging silence to respect
Now that neither of us has the heart to care

SHEROD SANTOS ❖

Inspiration

Say what we will, at times it seems the rarest
Moments, the most splenetic trills, the most
Ecstatic gestures, are conceived in sloth
And degradation and executed by a great unstaggered
Surge of feeling which bursts forth suddenly
Like a yard given over to day lilies, surprise lilies,
Naked ladies, to the spiked, thumbed, overlooked
Phallus of the yucca plant, to the carmined
Secret of the flowering dogwood's uninfected petals
Falling around you sunbathing naked in the grass
Like Susanna among the Elders, to the goat-horned
Furl of the climbing fern, to the certain posture
The May apple chooses to display itself, to the heart-
Raking itch of wood lice in the oak, to the coming
Darkness, to the secret balance, to the extreme
And desolate flowering of the night-blooming cereus,
And to all those things, all that loosestrife,
Spiderwort, tickweed and flax, all those hidden
Gothic amplitudes which leave us finally,
Tattooed and senseless, trembling on the stair.

Most Recent Book: THE SOUTHERN REACHES (Wesleyan University Press, 1989)

Nineteen Fifty-five

After all the late suppers of that faraway
Summer at his grandparents' house,
He would wait outside on the screened
Back porch with the screams of the blue jays
Plundering in the trees, and the sun-drunk
Yellow jackets droning, and he would count
The minutes backwards until the world
Grew distant, like the ocean inside
A shell. But that day dull, gray and
Heavy-headed clouds had risen unexpectedly

Into the evening sky, and he hadn't seen
The dark begin to spread across
The lawns and bushes, and he was afraid
At first and so went indoors
To sit in the kitchen while the coffee
Was poured, and the dishes were put back
In the cupboards. Then almost just as
Suddenly, he was quiet again, and happy,
And he wondered at the way the light
From the kitchen formed a glimmering square

That lay out on the side yard, a square
In which he could see played back, as on
A movie screen, small things he'd felt himself
Feel that day: the smoke from the coal
Train winding through the hills,
The cat's milk soured and yellowing
In its bowl, his new shoes crackling
Down the gravel drive while the eyes
Of a stranger who'd paused at the gate
Watched him without speaking in the morning.

It was the hour when a hush settles over
A town, when porches darken and voices
Bloom in drowsy clouds above the rooftops,
And much as he might have wanted to then,
He could not stop that flood
Of things, and he thought of the earth
As a sphere that spun in a crazy arc
That looped and hung, while the planets
Coursed, and the moon and sun
Moved through the star lanes unchanging.

For the earth was somehow different from them,
With all its facts and histories,
Its scalloped oceans and desert sands,
Its flowers and rains and long seasons
Of trouble, with its wars he'd heard called
Beautiful names—"Korean" and "Roses"
And "Holy." And he thought of the shuffle
Of soldiers' feet, thousands of soldiers
With dumbstruck eyes, and of the spiraling
Planes and overturned carts he'd seen

In magazines and movies; and he thought
Of the cities all over the globe, cities
Bombed into streets and burning, and as
He whispered their names he could feel
On his tongue the terrible impermanence
Of nations: *Bangkok* and *London, Guernica*
And *Rome, Dresden* and *Moscow* and *Hiroshima.*
But they were names he was still unable
To see except in small and momentary glimpses
Of things, of a woman kneeling in the rubble

Beside a horse whose belly had been ruptured,
Of a man hunched over a wood-spoked
Wheel in a frozen ditch in the tundra,
Of a naked girl whose head had been shaved
And who was tied to a chair in the middle
Of a crowd that milled about her like
Shoppers. . . . All this time the boy had sat
Tilting forward in his straight-backed chair,
His elbows on the table for balance,
And he felt in his throat there were unknown

Words that would never in his lifetime
Get spoken, never be given a name,
And he was afraid to think he might
Take them away, take them away forever
Into that black and dividing night even now
Unraveling the edges of the light
That fell in a golden square
From the window. So he turned his head
Away from the glass, and let his chair
Tip back to the floor, and just beyond

His outspread hands there were dark coffee
Circles that had deepened to stain, and flies

Had settled in quiet rings, which were all
I'd remember thirty years from then
When rising from dinner with my wife
And son, news of warships gathering
In the Gulf was broadcast on the radio
In the kitchen—and the kitchen,
Whose windows had blurred from within,
Would grow ludicrous before it grew dim.

The Air Base at Châteauroux, France

In the American schoolyard
where we lunged headfirst
onto the rocky ground scrab-
bling for a ball
                    as if
for love, the crossed chalk-
line still electrified our
tough boyish hearts, and no
one much cared
                    for such
exotic gods as loomed up
out of the Palatine Hills
in the required guidebooks
dumped in heaps
                    behind our
makeshift goal. We knew
what we knew. Sweatstains
darkened our blue school
shirts while
                    our fathers'
fighters strafed the mock-
ups in the practice fields,
never far enough from town
it didn't thunder
                    all day
through the blackened
cottages' stony stares locked
up tight behind their shot

bolts; nor through
                    the evening,
either, when drifting home,
stripped to the waist, we'd
dance feet-chalked across
the marketplace
                    like young,
uneasy gods, a little drunk
on our shame, our power.

PHILIP SCHULTZ ❖

The Quality

There is in each body something splendid, I think,
        a kind of sheltering, say, the suit of
hours we wear like weather, or instinct striking
        the spine's cold accordion, that ripening
of reflex that is the mind's appetite for testimony,
        yes, in darkness there is strength hoarded

against damage, say, the flowering of desire imprinted
        in the infant's smile as it awakens out of
its dream of creation, I mean pain is not sentiment only,
        but a fierce healing, like light rebuilding,
out of darkness, our original boundaries, yet something
        is lost in the growing, yes, the greater

the gift the more troubling the sleep, like lovers lost
        in the body's cold spin, we are naked
within the shell of our temperament, beings greater in
        mystery after violation, yes, like strips
of horizon, the spirit unwinds its gift of a single life,
        moment by moment, say, that quality of love

that is not physical, but sensed, like vision burning
        in the eye's garden, yes, once again spring
arrives after winter's long ash & I accept despair's
        selfish fruit as the fermenting of wonder

Most Recent Book: DEEP WITHIN THE RAVINE (Viking Penguin, 1984)

that springs out of everything lost & dying, say,
    that furthering of instinct, which, like

the spider's ambition to infinitely extend its life
    another inch of light, glistens like rain
over the attic window where I sat as a boy entranced
    with the radiance of first longing, yes,
a quality so distinctly human we glow like light burning
    over all the fire-struck windows of our lives.

For My Mother

The hand of peace you sent from Israel
hangs on my wall like an ironic testament
to the one quality we have never shared.
I imagine you peering into that ancient vista
as if discovering God in the brilliant sunlight,
worrying no doubt about your bunions & weak ankles.
These words have been a long time in coming.
Once I wrote only to the dead but grief has an end.
The living are more demanding. I have seen the scar
big as a zipper on your belly where they cut you open
& ripped out six pounds of hunger demanding to be adored.
You named me Big Mouth, Big Pain, Big Wanting. Sons,
you said, suck a woman dry & leave for someone
with stronger ankles & a back better suited
to their talent for self-eulogy. Yes, men
are more selfish. Nothing demands of us
so absolute a generosity. But I have given up
the umbilicus of rage which for so long has fed me.
Now I understand why you paste every scrap of my existence
in a black book like a certificate of blood, but achievement
is not redemption & even now I cannot hold a woman
without fearing she might take too much of me. Perhaps
this is why I love a woman most during her time
when the earth is lush within her & her embrace
gives forth such privilege my passion for distance
becomes a cry for forgiveness, a desire to return
always to the beginning. No, I have not forgotten
the Saturday afternoons in movie houses when you
cried so softly I imagined I was to blame.
I remember those long walks home,

our hands a binding of such unbreakable vengeance
I can still taste the cool blue wafers of your eyes.
Believe me, there was nothing I would not have given,
nothing I would not have done for you. Remember our game
when I held your leg so tightly you had to drag me
like a ball & chain around our unhappy house? Neither of us
understood that the grip of consanguinity is nothing less
than an embrace with time. Mother, though I cannot unhinge
all this lasting sorrow or make your flesh sing, cannot
return the gift of such remarkable expansion, I am always
thinking: This is for you, this word, this breath, this tiny light,
this, my hand of peace, this wound which does not heal.

Pumpernickel

Monday mornings Grandma rose an hour early to make rye,
onion & challah, but it was pumpernickel she broke her hands for,
pumpernickel that demanded cornmeal, ripe caraway, mashed potatoes
& several Old Testament stories about patience & fortitude & for
which she cursed in five languages if it didn't pop out fat
as an apple-cheeked peasant bride. But bread, after all,
is only bread & who has time to fuss all day & end up
with a dead heart if it flops? Why bother? I'll tell you why.
For the moment when the steam curls off the black crust like a strip
of pure sunlight & the hard oily flesh breaks open like a poem
pulling out of its own stubborn complexity a single glistening truth
& who can help but wonder at the mystery of the human heart when you
hold a slice up to the light in all its absurd splendor & I tell you
we must risk everything for the raw recipe of our passion.

Ode

Grandma stuffed her fur coat into the icebox.
God Himself couldn't convince her it wasn't a closet.
"God take me away this minute!" was her favorite Friday night prayer.
Nothing made sense, she said. Expect heartburn & bad teeth, not sense.
Leave a meat fork in a dairy dish & she'd break the dish & bury the fork.
"I spit on this house, on this earth & on God for putting me
in this life that spits on me night & day," she cried, forgetting the barley
in barley soup. It wasn't age. She believed she was put here to make

one unforgivable mistake after another. Thou shalt be disappointed
was God's first law. Her last words were: "Turn off the stove
before the house blows up." Listen, I'm thirty-four already
& nothing I do is done well enough. But what if disappointment
is faith & not fate? What if we never wanted anything enough to hurt
    over?
All I can say is spring came this year with such a wallop
the trees are still shaking. Grandma, what do we want from them?
What do we want?

The Answering Machine

My friends & I speak mostly to one another's machine.
We badger, cajole & manipulate without compunction
& often don't even remember who it is we're calling.

These machines don't counterfeit enthusiasm by raising
their volume or use a disdainful static to imply indignation.
They don't hold grudges & aren't judgmental. They're never

too busy or bored or self-absorbed. They have no conscience
& possess a tolerance for sadness which, admittedly, we lack.
Even cowardice is permitted, if enunciated clearly. I broke off

with Betsey by telling her machine I couldn't go rafting
with her in Colorado. I meant *anywhere* & it understood perfectly.
They appreciate, I think, how much intimacy we can bear

on a daily basis. When one becomes overburdened it buries
all pertinent information by overlapping; whatever happened,
say, to Jane's sweet birthday song, hidden now under so many

solicitations about my appendix operation, or Bill's news
of his father's death which was so rudely preempted by Helen's
wedding invitation? Yes, the conflict which evolves through

direct contact is softened & our privacy protected, but
perhaps the price we pay is greater isolation. Under all
these supplanted voices is a constant reminder of everything

we once promised & then forgot, or betrayed. The guilt
can be overwhelming, especially late at night when I replay
my messages to hear the plaintive vowels & combative consonants

rub like verbals sticks into a piercing vibrato of prayerlike
insistence. What is essential, after all, cannot be understood
too quickly & unessential facts get equal time. I mean

even in our silence there is evidence of what we feared
to say or mean—that ongoing testimony of remorse & affection
which, however crippling, we replay nightly & then, sadly, erase.

Tim Seibles ❖

Wind

José, the wind is just the restless walking of air
in and out of itself—just as anyone walks
into and out of himself for no reason
other than the constant itching of the soul.
What is looking but leaving through the eyes?
And look at that East Indian lady over there
with that dark nation of hair, those robes,
her brown skin, smooth as a smooth wind after rain.
Just reaching her with my eyes, I am light as a child's wish—
I am a gnat holding the hard kiss of a hurricane,
I am blown halfway to Sri Lanka with this glance.

But you will never fly, José. You will roll
on your huge balls—you will probably break yourself
with those bolos. I would tell you to sing,
but your heart is all full of sperm—you and your
sticky music. For you the wind
is the collective sigh for all those loves
that might have been, but really it blows
because each molecule of air itches
for the next and cannot sleep—

like you with your Samsonite luggage of balls
always going somewhere to worship the black women
with their immaculate cha-cha of hips, to hear
the señoritas spilling that silky Spanish into the wind—
like Yadira with the Aztec night roiling in her eyes.
Seeing her, I'm gone again like a harmless germ

Most Recent Book: Body Moves (Corona Press, 1988)

from a sneeze. I am flying like shimmer
from the sweat of a star—without feathers,
without a ladder, with my hands tied at the wrists,
I am climbing the wind above trees and tall offices,
but you will roll, José. You will look at her and roll
because of your balls.

Trying for Fire

Right now, even if a muscualar woman wanted
to teach me the power of her skin
I'd probably just stand here with my hands
jammed in my pockets. Tonight
I'm feeling weak as water, watching the wind
bandage the moon. That's how it is tonight:
sky like tar, thin gauzy clouds,
a couple lame stars. A car rips by—
the driver's cigarette pinwheels past
the dog I saw hit this afternoon.
One second he was trotting along
with his wet nose tasting the air,
next thing I know he's off the curb,
a car swerves and, bam, it's over. For an instant,
he didn't seem to understand he was dying—
he lifted his head as if he might still reach
the dark-green trash bags half-open
on the other side of the street.

I wish someone could tell me
how to live in the city. My friends
just shake their heads and shrug. I
can't go to church—I'm embarrassed by the things
preachers say we should believe.
I would talk to my wife, but she's worried
about the house. Whenever she listens
she hears the shingles giving in
to the rain. If I read the paper
I start believing some stranger
has got my name in his pocket—
on a matchbook next to his knife.
When I was twelve I'd take out the trash—
the garage would open like some ogre's cave

while just above my head the Monday Night Movie
stepped out of the television, and my parents
leaned back in their chairs. I can still hear
my father's voice coming through the floor,
"Boy, make sure you don't make a mess down there."
I remember the red-brick caterpillar of row houses
on Belfield Avenue and, not much higher than the rooftops,
the moon, soft and pale as a nun's thigh.

I had a plan back then—my feet were made
for football: each toe had the heart
of a different animal, so I ran
ten ways at once. I knew I'd play pro
and live with my best friend, and
when Vanessa let us pull up her sweater
those deep-brown balloony mounds made me believe
in a world where eventually you could touch
whatever you didn't understand.

If I was afraid of anything it was
my bedroom when my parents made me
turn out the light: that knocking noise
that kept coming from the walls,
the shadow shapes by the bookshelf,
the feeling that something was always there
just waiting for me to close my eyes.
But only sleep would get me, and I'd
wake up running for my bike, my life
jingling like a little bell on the breeze.
I understood so little that I
understood it all, and I still know
what it meant to be one of the boys
who had never kissed a girl.

I never did play pro football.
I never got to do my mad-horse,
mountain goat, happy-wolf dance
for the blaring fans in the Astro Dome.
I never snagged a one-hander over the middle
against Green Bay and stole my snaky way
down the sideline for the game-breaking six.

And now, the city is crouched like a mugger
behind me—right outside, in the alley behind my door,
a man stabbed this guy for his wallet, and
up the block a four-year-old disappeared. When I

turn on the radio the music is just like the news.
So, what should I do—close my eyes and hope
whatever's out there will just let me sleep?
I won't sleep tonight. I'll stay near my TV
and watch the police get everybody.

Across the street a woman is letting
her phone ring. I see her in the kitchen
stirring something on the stove. Farther off
a small dog chips the quiet with his bark.
Above me the moon looks like a nickel
in a murky-little creek. This
is the same moon that saw me twelve,
without a single bill to pay, zinging
soup can tops into the dark—I called them
flying saucers. This is the same
white light that touched dinosaurs, that
found the first people trying for fire.

It must have been very good, that moment
when wood smoke turned to flickering, when
they believed night was broken
once and for all—I wonder what almost-words
were spoken. I wonder how long
before that first flame went out.

For Brothers Everywhere

There is a schoolyard that runs
from here to the dark's fence
where brothers keep goin to the hoop, keep
risin up with baske'balls ripe as pumpkins
toward rims hung like piñatas, pinned
like thunderclouds to the sky's wide chest
an' everybody is spinnin an' bankin
off the glass, finger-rollin off the boards
with the same soft touch
you'd give the head of a child, a child
witta big-ass pumpkin head, who stands
in the schoolyard lit by brothers givin and
goin, flashin off the pivit, dealin
behind their backs, between their legs,
cockin the rock an' glidin like mad hawks—

swoopin black, with arms for wings—
palmin the sun an' throwin it down,
an' even with the day gone, without even
a crumb of light from the city, brothers
keep runnin-gunnin, fallin away takin
fall-away jumpers from the corner,
their bodies like muscular saxophones
body-boppin better than jazz, beyond
summer, beyond weather, beyond
everything that moves, an' with one shake
they're pullin-up from the perimeter,
shakin-bakin brothers be sweet
pullin-up from the edge of the world,
hangin like air itself hangs in the air,
an' gravidy gotta giv'em up:
the ball burning like a fruit with a soul
in the velvet hands while the wrists whisper
"*back-spin*" an' the fingers comb the rock
once—lettin go, lettin it go like good news—
'cuz the hoop is a well, *Shwip!* a well
with no bottom, *Shwick!*
an' they're fillin that sucker up.

DAVE SMITH ❖

Championship Fight

The big Plymouth shuddered with all the speed
it could give us, jammed by my father's
planted right foot. We wallowed through days
and nights, struck at the feints of curves,
bobbing and weaving, shooting in and out
of neighborhoods long dark as old sweats.
We liked the smoky rooms, the night's smells
that heaved us right and left, then back,
so we seemed always to be rolling on shocks
belly-soft. That wheezy hulk wouldn't quit.

Most Recent Book: CUBA NIGHT (William Morrow, 1990)

My sister and I learned how to laugh, bounced
over the fabric that still prickles my face.
We were quick and capable of anything then,
little faces darting in that tub of darkness,
howling until once again we were stopped
inside the float of dust that rose up to say
like a bodiless voice Ladies and Gentleman,
arrived all the way from . . . Wherever. Now

I don't know, I can't remember who it was
my father had come to fight, why it mattered,
only that he leaps from the car onto rocks,
instantly slinks into the shape of Marciano,
whom he loved, no one man enough anywhere
to take down the Brockton Bomber and live.
Yet I saw that black fighter make the spit
lick from that broken mouth before the bar
emptied its first row of booths. It was fast.

Wherever we went after that, my mother's gaze
glared back at the moon cool on the windshield.
His knockout, he called her. Driving at all
the things we never saw ahead, he'd reach
back for us, grabbing arm or leg, and squeeze
until the fat car rocked, and left us grinning.
I never thought this would be what I'd remember
when I had curled into the black corner, not
sleeping, afraid. I thought it would be him
crying, drooling blood into a stranger's ditch,
who said Jesus, oh Jesus, it's over so quick.

A Quilt in the Bennington College Library

What should we see in this artifact? Incredible
colors, yet not so stunning as the peasant girl
seen once, perhaps, by her maker, cheek-red
and eye-blue pure, as if frozen in hope's dream.
We're always driven to demand from the useless
beauty that stares us down: what do you serve?
This white was a pet goat's inner thigh. Love's
lesson tells us to covet well whatever stinks.
Isn't it lessons we've come for? Pretty is

as pretty does, this tidy architecture says,
its squares like houses stitched in firm.
A village of cloth American as a Currier & Ives.

But this too-perfect Puritan fantasy rankles,
moves us back, forward to focus, find the room
with that girl ended in some posture of abandon
near the piss-pot toppled to a reeking stain.
From the shadows of books comes the dying cough
of a dreamer. A chair scrapes like a scream.
Who bursts past into the light? We look back,
see a patch left off-angle like a troubled
face whose question has one answer replicated
endlessly: faith. Our eye follows little fences
of thread binding all a house gets. If fear
makes us hang up pretty pictures, art invites

pain to show us what we know we'll lie under—
the first soft gargle of blood at a goat's slit
throat, the pus sealing a baby blind, a girl
who measures her years by the stones shoveled
aside for the bodies she's put into the dirt.
Where is she, the one who fled under ribbons
of punk-wood smoke, choosing the black rain
with only this homemade skin to surround her,
until God's voice in a spruce sent her home?
Hung here, the quilt's a shapeless play-pretty,
American abstract, survivor of no one's evil.
They've nailed it up in the air, out of reach
of the sun that remembers the bed, the woman
groaning and bleeding until she was colorless,
a dark space no one looked at or questioned.

Pulling a Pig's Tail

The feel of it was hairy and coarse
like new rope in A.W. Johnson's
hardware store but I never touched it
or any part of a pig
until that day my father took me
where the farm was, woods
a kind of green stillness, the hanging
leaves from so much rain

I guess—it felt as if I was upside
down underwater trying to swim
for my life. The farmer, Uncle Bern,
said I could have one
if I could catch it. A little one
looked easy, about my size,
not so wary because he wasn't unsure
of anything yet—I must have
thought, but quick and hungry
as small lives always are
so I chased him until the foul mud
hardened on me like a skin,
the big men crying with laughter.
My father said it was just
that funny like some kind of soul's
testing to see I wanted
badly enough to catch myself, black
eyes not seeming to watch,
fixed on the horizon past the weird
way I talked to it. Finally
it listened to something and I took
a grip, held, grunting, dug
my sneakers into the shit. Why he ran
and didn't try to bite me
I don't know. By then I almost had
everything straight but felt
at last what wasn't right, the uncoiled
helplessness of anything
dragged small and screaming while
the big ones watch and grin.
I let go. I didn't say I was thinking
about school that was over
that summer, the teacher that yanked
my hair, who said she'd see
I got myself straightened out. I hid
my hands in shame. How could I
tell my father a pig's tail burns
your hands like lost beauty?
I only knew I loved school
until that raw day when she let me loose.

Cuba Night

The small of the back has its answers
for all our wrong turns, even the slightest,
those aches there's no name for, or source,
and the mole in the mirror, a black moon
of sudden importance, can turn your hours
into love's rapt attention. As you shave
an innocent glance into the yard pulls
your gaze to the glass—is anything there
more than a choice, a will to live? When

the fly on its back, feet up in dead air
between the storm-doubled panes, stiffens
it seems to remind you of the big words
you can't speak, history or love, but feel
as once you felt the shuffle and slap
of your father's feet on heartwood floors.
He would be bathed then, as you are now,
unshirted, coffee starting, his lathered
clownish cheeks white, the dawn oozing red.

Quizzical, you hear the razor pull closer,
strokes deliberate, hard, then stopped
as you see the black place in your head.
Is it death? Only a cafe memory, you two
standing outside, soft night, a radio,
Kennedy declaring over the dirt his one
line only a war could cross. Your mother
wasn't yet meat that a drunk's Ford would
leave in a sunny ditch. Then your father
stopped to visit, shy, held your man's hand,

while along the block many leaned, listening.
Dusk steadily bled all the light from each
face, a voice—maybe Bob Dylan's—said this
is history, and you said what? Same word
when your wife cried I can't stand any more,
whose crying had started under your yes, yes.
You can't smell her stale sheets and no
memory's kiss mushrooms. No late show's
rerun of Bikini atoll keeps flaring at you.

What then? Only azaleas beginning to explode
that must have been planted in that year,

the smudged hand now earth's, with questions
he couldn't answer. His eyes brimmed wetly.
Nobody you know's been to Cuba or cries out
what history means. There's blood on your lip.
The mole has grown. You're starting over,
remembering the floor that seemed to shake
with love, then with the unslipping of her
nakedness, its soap-white. Then the shaving.

MARCIA SOUTHWICK ❖

Brothers

In a story called
"The Poor Boy in the Grave,"
the master says, "I'll be back
in five hours. If the straw
isn't cut in half by then,
I'll beat you senseless."
Your older brother is like that.
He locks you out of the house
and throws your French book
out the window. Later, mother
finds you studying beneath
a street lamp. The next day,
after you've failed the test,
he twists your arm behind your back.
Mother won't be home till four.
You can feel his hot breath on your neck
as he pins you down
on the slick cement,
your face pressed against the cool
basement floor.
The boy in the story
cuts the straw, but by mistake
also rips his coat.
Afraid of what his master will do,
he swallows a jar of poison.
But you kick and scratch,

Most Recent Book: WHY THE RIVER DISAPPEARS (Carnegie Mellon University Press, 1990)

scurrying away. You run upstairs,
through the kitchen, overturning chairs
behind you as you go,
worried about what mother will say
when she opens the door and sees
the mess: ripped curtains, plates
tossed, and chairs that look
like kindling—her face
frozen in shock. You think of the poor boy
half-drunk on poison,
stumbling over roots and stones in the cemetery,
looking for an empty grave
to leap into.

The Rain's Marriage

In an African folk tale, the rain
falls in love with a blacksmith.
At the wedding, the downpour dies out
to a single stream, a column of water.
As the first drop touches soil,
feet appear, then legs, a torso, arms. . . .
The woman, waves of transparent hair
falling over her shoulders, is called
the *Water Bride* and doesn't fully lose
her identity as rain. Once,
I was certain of the boundaries between my body
and whatever it touched, as if
touch itself were a way of defining exactly where *I* stopped
and the rest of the world began.
Then I lost the sense that I was hemmed in
by skin. My body felt like something loaned to me—
it might break, or dissolve to ashes,
leaving me stranded,
a pure thought without a skull to inhabit—
like rain falling into any shape that accepts it,
every hollow place made equal by its touch.
The mind of rain
contemplates even the smallest crack in the parched dirt
where nothing will grow.
Why can't I fall effortlessly in love?
If I knew the exact place where my body stops

and everything else begins, I'd marry.
Like the *Water Bride*, I'd be unafraid,
though surely trouble would exist, as between rain
and a blacksmith's fire.

Horse on the Wall

She deserted you,
the aunt who sang you to sleep.
On your birthday years ago,
she gave you a figurine,
a blue china horse
that broke as you dragged it
across the floor. At five,
you felt the twinge you'd later recognize
as guilt. So here you are,
thirty-three years later,
standing on a street corner,
looking for answers:
It's evening and the first stars
will soon spot you
waving and calling to your friend
who wants to quit writing poetry
but can't. He should have stopped
his car for you.
You hear yourself
call his name again,
and the shock of it is like
the screech of tires rounding a corner.
Maybe you've just called
a name into history,
your voice flying past the great poets,
who lean out of doorways
into the gray rain. Unheard,
a call like that cannot turn back
and loses itself among the vacant
parking lots and side streets.
It's the way your aunt
must have disappeared, leaving you
awake at night, your mind
patching together bits of shadow
into a figure that looked like

a flattened version of the china horse
galloping on the wall.
Maybe your friend,
without a poem in his head,
adjusts the rearview mirror
and sees his own face
staring back at him like a stranger's.

Child, Invisible Fire

One day, the bread knife wasn't a bread knife anymore,
and she held it to my throat.
She wasn't a child anymore, and I hadn't aborted her.
She passed, unseen,
through the wall of the house and stood
at the end of the bed.
The muscles in my throat twitched
and I turned over.
I don't know where she is now, I know that.
But I would like to remove the small splinters,
bandage the small cuts, stop
her confused blood
from flowing every which way.
I hate these days playing themselves out
like piano scales,
and the redbuds exercising their right to bloom.
Someone sensible should put a stop to this.
A long winter should be called for.
The word love is abstract, less real
than the slippery oil on the roads.
I walk down the road
to our old house and think we could have lived there,
we could have blessed the moths
that invaded the house each year,
we could have sat in the cool shade of the oak
and talked. But talk is abstract, unsafe,
a shore that deserts us.
What was it you said as we crossed the lake one day
in the rickety boat?
You wanted a fire to burn the trees on the other side.
You wanted approval.
You wanted vocabulary to be simple, like a child's.

But a child has a head and shoulders.
Now, as I enter the house, the feeling begins:
I am observed by the chairs
and the white walls.
The continuous dreaming,
done by the narrow windows,
has nothing to do with the view.
And outside, the empty street slides into place,
its only oblivion.

ELIZABETH SPIRES ❖

Sunday Afternoon at Fulham Palace

Putney Bridge, London

A Sunday afternoon in late September, one of the last
good weekends before the long dark, old couples
taking the air along the Thames, sunning themselves,
their arms and legs so pale, *exposed*,
eyes closed against the slanting autumn light,
while the young press forward, carry us
along in the crowd to the fair at Fulham Palace
where a few people have already spread blankets and tablecloths
for the picnics they've brought, laughing and talking
as they wait for the music to begin at three o'clock.
Inside the palace gates, a man inflates
a room-size, brightly painted rubber castle,
the children impatiently waiting for the walls and turrets to go up,
the spongy floor they like to jump on.
The palace is empty. The Bishop gone.
Now overfed goldfish swim slowly round and round
in the crumbling courtyard fountain, and farther on,
a white peacock stands still as a statue,
still as a stone, whether in pride or sorrow
at being the last of its kind here I don't know.
A low door opens into the Bishop's walled garden, but once
inside nothing miraculous or forbidden tempts us,
just a few flowers and herbs among weeds

Most Recent Book: ANNONCIADE (Viking Penguin, 1989)

(unlike those illuminated scenes in books of hours),
the past passing away too quickly to catch or recognize.

Out on the other side, we pick our way
among booths put up for the day,
one woman, predictably, passing out pamphlets
on nuclear winter and cruise missiles, as if she could stop it alone.
The Fulham Band takes its place on the platform,
the conductor announcing as the overture,
"Those Magnificent Men in Their Flying Machines,"
the crossed shadow of coincidence, of airplanes from Gatwick
passing over at two-minute intervals, touching us
for a moment before they fly into the day's
unplanned pattern of connections, the music
attracting more of a crowd, men, women, and children
making their entrances like extras in a movie,
in pairs, in families, no one alone that I can see
except one girl, no more than ten,
lagging behind the others, lost completely
in a vivid, invisible daydream until her mother finds her,
brings her back with a touch on the arm,
and the daughter says, unbelievably,
"I was thinking about what kind of anesthesia
they'll give me when I have my first baby."

The future expands, then contracts, like an eye's iris opening
        and closing,
walling me into a room where light and sound come and go,
first near, then far, as if I had vertigo.
It is easy, too easy, to imagine the world ending
on a day like today, the sun shining and the band playing,
the players dreamily moving now into Ellington's "Mood Indigo."
Easy to see the great grey plane hovering briefly overhead,
the grey metal belly opening and the bomb dropping,
a flash, a light "like a thousand suns,"
and then the long winter.
The white peacock. Erased. The goldfish in the fountain
swimming crazily as the water boils up around them, evaporates.
The children's castle. Gone. The children. The mothers
        and the fathers.
As if a hand had suddenly erased a huge blackboard.
Thank God you don't know what I'm thinking.
You press my hand as if to ask, "Am I here with you?
Do you want to go?" pulling me back to this moment,
to this music we are just coming to know, the crowd around us

growing denser, just wanting to live their lives,
each person a *nerve*, thinking and feeling
too much as sensation pours over them
in a ceaseless flow, the music, as we move to go,
jumping far back in time, the conductor oddly choosing
something devotional, a coronet solo
composed, and probably played here, by Purcell three centuries ago.
All is as it was as we make our way back along the Thames
to Putney Bridge, the old souls still sleeping unaware,
hands lightly touching, as the river bends in a gentle arc
around them. Mood indigo. The white peacock.
The walled garden and the low door.
As if, if it did happen, we could bow our heads
and ask, once more, to enter that innocent first world.

The Beds

London

Each day, I take the lift from the sublet down
    to the ground floor.
Out on the street, I pass the shop that sells the beds,
the sumptuous beds, made up each morning anew, afresh,
by smiling clerks who please their own moods,
doing the beds up one day in flaming sunrise and sunset tones,
and the next, in shades of white on white, with satin piping,
pillowcases threaded with ribbons and bows,
like a bride's too-delicate underclothes.
And yet, nobody sleeps in the beds, makes love in the beds.
They wait, like a young girl with too much imagination,
to be taken away for a weekend in the country,
to a great house where stylish lovers flirt and scheme
in preliminary maneuvering, but know, in the end,
what beds are for. Know, no matter what they do,
all will be plumped and tucked and smoothed,
all made as it was, by knowing maids the morning after.

The anxious clerks stare out at the soiled street,
the racing cars and taxis, the passers-by, waiting for money
to stop, walk in the door, and ask to buy a bed.
There are circles under their eyes,
as if they've been sleeping badly.
Beds must make way for other beds,

pillows for other pillows, new sheets, new lives!
The seconds tick on the big clock
a block from the bed shop, the minute hand
moves with a jerk, and suddenly whole hours have flown,
    the day vanishes,
pulled by an unseen hand through a small hole in the sky
somewhere in the darkening East End.
Night falls so quickly on this street of Dream Merchandise!
Now all of us reverse ourselves and change direction
to come home to well-intentioned stews
    with husbands and wives,
yesterday's leftovers made to stretch so economically,
my heels on the sidewalk clicking in silver tones,
like the small change in my pocket falling end
    over end over end,
all that remains of a day's hard buying.
Already the new moon is backlighting the city's
    towers and spires,
illuminating shadowy shop windows up and down
    Fulham Road.
It drapes itself casually across the beds,
like the misplaced towel or bathrobe
of a woman who has just stepped out for the evening,
wearing new evening clothes, made up so carefully
she can't be recognized, who secretly knows
she will not be coming back until morning
to sleep, if she sleeps then,
in the perfect bed of her own making.

Mutoscope

Swirl and smash of waves against the legs
and crossgirders of the pier, I have come to Brighton,
come as the fathers of our fathers came,
to see the past's Peep Show.
On two good legs, on one, they came,
veterans and stay-at-homes of the Great War,
all casualties, to stroll the West Pier's promenade,
past bands, flags, and minstrel shows,
past Gladys Pawsey in a high-necked bathing costume
riding her bicycle off the high board,
past Hokey-Pokey and Electric Shocker,

the old Penny Palace, pennies burning hotly
in their hands, the worn watery profile
of Queen Victoria looking away from it all.
I bend to the mutoscope's lit window
to see "What the Butler Saw": a woman artlessly
taking off her clothes in a jerky striptease
I can slow down or speed up
by turning the handle of the mutoscope.
Easily I raise her from darkness—
the eye eternally aroused by what it can't touch—
to watch her brief repeating performance
that counts for so little. Or so much.
I can't be sure which.
Abruptly, THE END shuts down the image, but her story
continues as she reverses time's tawdry sequence
to dress and quickly disappear
down a maze of narrow streets and alleys
filled with the ghostly bodies and bodiless ghosts
of causality, the unredeemed and never-to-be-born
bearing her along to a flight
of shabby stairs, a rented room where she is free
as anyone to dream her dreams and smoke a cigarette,
smoke from the lit tip spiraling
in patternless patterns toward the room's bare light bulb,
the light I see her by harsh, violently
unforgiving as she makes tomorrow into a question
of either/or: to leave this room, this vacancy
forever, or go on exactly as she has before.
Old ghost, your history is nameless and sexual,
you are your own enigma, victim
or heroine of an act of repetition that, once chosen,
will choose you for a lifetime.
I peer into the tunneled past,
so small, so faraway and fragmentary,
and yet, not unconnected to what I am now.
Dilapidation upon dilapidation, Brighton
is crumbling, fading to sepia tones,
as your unfunny burlesque continues past
your life, perhaps past mine,
the past preserved and persevering,
the sentimental past.

Maura Stanton ❖

The Grocery Store

At first I used to read headlines
At checkout stands with a laugh:
WOMAN CAPTURES SHRIEKING GHOST,
or else, SHIP RETURNS FROM LIMBO.
I only wanted what I saw,
Apples, ginger root, and beans,
Or gleaming flasks of vinegar.
I didn't need a mystery world
Where spirits knocked, or aliens
Landed in a humming saucer.
I drove to shop past fields of corn,
Saw the corn turned to stubble,
And never thought of death in fall
But only of the Christmas hams.
Then one day the produce man,
A neighbor I had known for years,
Wept to say his wife had died
By her own perverse desire,
Locked inside their big garage.
I stood near him at the funeral.
He told me she was not in heaven
But only somewhere in the air
Just beyond our narrow vision.
Later he spoke about a séance.
Friends had held his sweating hands.
He called his wife until she rapped
A message on the table top.
The medium whispered in the dark:
Yes, she loves you tenderly
But she trembles with the cold.
Light a candle and she'll come.
So every night he lights a candle
And he feels the faint rustle
As she steps in from the dark
To scorch her invisible hands.

Most Recent Book: TALES OF THE SUPERNATURAL (David R. Godine, Publisher, 1988)

Every week the garish headlines
Insist there is another world
That ordinary people see—
Spaceships land in backyards;
A baby cures a multitude;
An angry ghost destroys the china
To the amazement of a waitress;
A dentist shouts from his coffin—
For even when we die there's still
Hope for revenge, or true love.
Deep inside my chest I feel
Blood moving through the arteries.
Sometimes I'm dizzy when I stand.
I know my body's nothing more
Than a side of beef in the freezer,
Mapped, ready for cutting.
But when I wait at the register
At busy times, I seem to feel
Some buzz or hum or energy
Coming from the hands in motion,
Talking mothers, businessmen,
Old women buying bran flakes,
Teenagers in line with pizzas—
Everyone reads the shocking news,
Silently, or to a friend,
Eyebrows moving in irony
Or lips in private wonder,
And on every stranger's face
I see a flash of agony:
Why not? Why not a miracle?

Living Apart

I leave our house, our town, familiar fields
Below me at take off when I fly to you
Deep in these shadowed mountains. Now at dawn
I wake to the horse-clop of passing carriages
As if I'd passed through time as well as space.
Yesterday we saw an Amish farmer
Bearded and calm, stroking his horse's mane

Under a flaming maple as he watched
Hang-gliders drifting down from Hyner View.
We stopped to watch them, too. I was amazed
To see men falling toward the scarlet treetops
On out-spread wings. That's when I grabbed your hand
To tell myself we were alive and human
Not lost in hell which must resemble this—
A place where souls from many centuries
Stand side by side, united but unhappy,
To watch the angels fall from fiery mountains.

A Portrait by Bronzino

Once older than me, now certainly younger,
This unnamed woman stares into my room
On this bleak, final day in February
When my head aches from reading, and my eyes
Seem dulled by words that glide without impression.
I close my book, then rise to study her,
Noting the folds of her violet undersleeves
And the wedding ring, prominent on her finger.
I take a breath, and as I feel my body,
I feel hers, too, solid under drapery,
Cold pearls clasping her bare neck.
She must have had trouble keeping her mouth
Closed so tightly, as she held her pose
For all those hours in the carved armchair.
My reproduction is too small for details—
I can't make out the words on her gold chain.
She holds an open book in one hand
But I can't read the illuminated letters.
Yet Bronzino has painted the book so finely,
Even the decorated border and gilt edges,
That surely he meant the viewer to know
Something about her mind, not just her face.

But who was she? Of course she was real.
She almost seems to sigh as our eyes meet
As if at last I've understood her meaning,
Though I'm still puzzled. What does she want?
I put on my blue parka and wool cap,
And walk to the Library, my face hardening

nd turning red against the northeast wind.
On a shelf I find a volume on Bronzino,
And turn the glossy pages with stiff hands
Until I find her: Lucrezia Panciatichi.
This larger print reveals the delicate pleats
Of her white guimpe, and at last I know
That her chain says *Amour Dure San Fin*—
And here's her husband on another page,
Ethereal against his palace walls,
Bartolomeo, both scholar and poet . . .
I see them reading books side by side
In their tall, bare salon, a brazier
Sending waves of heat through the cold air.
A black dog sleeps and dreams near his feet
While hers are propped on a small velvet stool
As she turns the illuminated pages,
Then smiles at him to read some bright passage
From Ariosto . . .
           But ten years later,
Dressed in black, the first grey in her hair,
Her ankle bleeding where the chain galled it,
She heard the iron door of the dungeon clank
As the hooded priests led her husband out
To crawl the streets of Florence on his knees.
Gagged, almost choking, his head bare,
Holding a drizzling torch in his bruised hand,
He struggled forward, hiding the pain,
While all along the way crowds jeered and spat
And laughed to see his genius brought so low.
In her cell, listening to the rats,
Lucrezia imagined the whole stony route,
Saw him drag his bloody knees up
The steps of the Cathedral, where all his poems,
His witty epigrammi, his meditations,
Were heaped in a pile. He had to burn
The words he'd labored over. Greasy smoke
Rose from the orange flames as he abjured
His heretical writings in a hollow tone,
Watching his books and unbound manuscripts
Brown at the edges, curl, then disappear.

Two days later, Lucrezia herself crawled
To San Simone, weighed down by her skirt,
A gag around her mouth. She felt the globs

Of spittal gather in her unloosed hair,
And rotten vegetables splatter her back.
She had to burn her sonnets, and cross herself,
While the Inquisition's hooded officers
Looked on through slits . . .
                              Some lines remained
Inside her head, and she repeated them
As vellum pages shriveled into ash,
Remembering how she had posed for Bronzino
So long ago, holding in her left hand
Her immortal book to show posterity.
She watched a spurred boot stamp out the fire,
Scatter and smear the grey film. She rose
On trembling legs, and all through the Mass
She now had to attend, she told herself

That she was free inside her silent mind
Although she stood between two hooded devils.
But later, reunited with Bartolomeo,
She gasped to see how he had aged in prison,
His thin hair almost white, his skin loose,
A permanant catch in his beloved voice.

I look around the room, surprised and dazed
To find myself still sitting in the Library
Staring at crushed milk cartons, old tissues,
A student hunched over a Chemistry book,
Highlighting facts in yellow. I close my eyes,
Remembering the rolled print I carried
Away from the Loggia when I was twenty-two—
I'd thumbed through the stalls for an hour
Looking for the woman in the Uffizi
I'd admired. I wanted to be like her.
A book always in my hand, my brow calm.
I fended off all the vendors waving Venus
Gleaming in her shell, or pressing Madonnas
Into my unwilling hand. At last I found her.
Later, smoothing the print across my lap
I looked at her bright face and saw my future—
But not the monsterous one that sprouted and grew
Within the womblike vault behind her chair.

GERALD STERN ❖

The Founder

There was a kind of drooping bronze head
I stole in the Catskills and put in my living room
in Philadelphia. I put a sledge hammer
beside it so my friends and I could smash him
and change his shape from thoughtful oppressor
to tortured victim. This was just to show
the close connection between the two, the liquid
life of Capitalism; we got to kick him,
we got to gouge his eyes out, we were elated
breaking his nose and flattening his ear; it was
a kind of funeral rite, sometimes the hammer
      hummed in our hands, there was a jolt, his pain
was in our wrists; sometimes we were exhausted
from so much pounding; after a while his face
was old and twisted, it was a little shameful.
I finally sold him—by the pound, I think;
he was too ugly for us, too demented;
we were starting to turn to pity—we pitied
that bronze bastard, he who must have presided
over the burning of mountains, he who managed
the killing of souls, the death of every dream.

I reached inside once to get the brain
but it was only rough casting in there,
nothing to suck on, even though the cavity
was widened at the base of the skull. He was
a brainless founder, his eyes stared at the wall,
or if we turned him around his eyes stared
with a kind of wonder at the dining-room table
catching the pools of beer. I remember
it wasn't all raw Socialism and hatred
of the rich; there was a little terror in it.
I think sometimes I got out of bed early
and put a towel or a T-shirt over his face
to cover his eyes and his ugly deformities.
He was for a while a mutilated ancestor,
someone we had buried twice, a monster,

Most Recent Book: LEAVING ANOTHER KINGDOM: SELECTED POEMS (HarperCollins, 1990)

something that could ruin us. It took an effort
to put him on the back of a station wagon
and free ourselves from fright. I had to struggle.
Although I'm sorry I sold him, he deserved
to be buried somewhere. I should have driven
to one of the dumps and thrown him into a valley
between a sofa and a refrigerator,
or just gone into the woods and made a grave
between two birches and shoved him in. I'm glad
there wasn't a river; I would have dropped him down
in the muck somewhere with the black Budweiser,
and one cold spring the current would have carried him
through a park or into a muddy backyard
on top of the poison and the wild strawberries,
or carried him into the open, his crushed head
going faster and faster, turning around in the garbage,
his face forever swollen, his eyes squinting,
the sorrow coming from his metal lips,
the sun shining down, the melodies never ending.

What It Is Like

I will have to tell you what it is like
since I was the one lying on my back
with my arms in the air and a blanket up to my
chin, since I was the one on a mattress
and the one trying to make up my mind
whether it was an early heaven just being there
or whether it was another bitter vertigo.

There were great parties where I went out
on a back porch and stared through the sycamores,
and there were parties, mostly lawless gatherings,
where we stood on the beach apart from each other
studying the sky. For me it's always
the earth; I'm one of the addicts; I can hardly
stand the dreaminess; I get burnt, I blister

at night as others do in the day. Last summer
I lay there crying. It was California
and the sheep vision. I was on a mattress
looking up. I started to talk. Aside
from the stars, aside from the beating heart, I only

member two things: both hands were in the air
and I was, for the first time in twenty years,

lying down without fear. My friend Robin
was there beside me; she was sobbing; I have
such gratitude towards her. It was her house,
it was her stars. She took me down to see
the sheep first, then she showed me the ocean.
It was an outside room; one wall was a maple,
one wall was made of planter boxes. There were

tomatoes and eggplants in one, there was lavendar
and basil in another. I remember
the trees on every side; I know there was oak
and redwood; there was a twisted madrone with leaves
in leathery piles, almost like rhododendron.
Robin knew the shadows, she knew the edges,
she knew the clouds, she knew the sky. It was

the summer of 1989. The charts
have already registered my odd affliction
and the stars absorbed my happiness. Standing—
or lying—you could see a horse to the right,
if you were facing north, and a white dragon,
if you were facing south. I think I never
slept that night. I only dozed. And ranted.

The Bull-roarer

I

I only saw my father's face in butchery
once—it was a horror—there were ten men
surrounding a calf, their faces were red, my father's
eyes were shining; there might have been fewer than ten,
some were farmers, some were my father's friends
down from the city. I was nine, maybe eight;
I remember we slept a few hours and left
at four in the morning, there were two cars, or three,
I think it was West Virginia. I remember
the pasture, the calf was screaming, his two eyes
were white with terror, there was blood and slaver
mixed, he was spread-eagled, there was a rope
still hanging from his neck, they all had knives

or ice picks—is that possible?—they were beery,
drunk, the blood was pouring from the throat
but they were stabbing him, one of them bellowed
as if he were a bull, he was the god
of the hunters, dressed in overalls and boots,
the king of animals; they seemed to know—
some of them seemed to know—the tendons and bones,
they were already cutting and slicing, pulling
the skin off, or maybe that was later, I stood there
staring at them, my father with a knife;
we didn't even have a dog—my mother froze
whenever she saw one—we were living in Beechview,
we had the newest car on the street, it was
an ugly suburb, everything was decent,
there was a little woods, but it was locust,
it would be covered with houses, we didn't even have
a parrot, my father left at eight in the morning
and drove his car downtown, he always wore
a suit and tie, his shoes were polished, he spent
the day with customers, he ate his lunch
at a little booth, I often sat with him,
with him and his friends, I had to show off, I drew
their likenesses, I drew the tables and chairs,
it was the Depression, none of them had brass rings
hanging from their ears, they all wore socks,
and long-sleeved shirts, they ate and drank with passion.

2

My mother is eighty-seven, she remembers
the visit to the farm, there was her brother,
my uncle Simon, and there was his friend, MacBride,
Lou MacBride, he was the connection, he was
a friend of the farmer's, maybe a cousin. I asked her
about the killing—"that is the way those farmers
got their meat, they lived like that, they butchered
whatever they needed." I asked if she could remember
anything strange, was she nervous or frightened?
"There was the tail, they cut the tail off
and chased each other; it was like pinning the tail
to the donkey." Both of us laughed. I didn't have the heart
to mention my father's face, or mention the knife—
and, most of all, my pain. What did I want?
That he should stay forever locked inside

his gold-flecked suits? That he should get up in the dark
and put his shoes on with a silver knife?
That he should unbutton his shirts and stuff the cardboard
into a chute? That he should always tie
his tie with three full loops, his own true version
of the Windsor knot? And what did I want for myself?
Some childish thing, that no-one would ever leave me?
That there would always be logic—and loyalty?
—I think that tail goes back to the Paleolithic.
I think our game has gory roots—some cave,
or field, they chased each other—or they were grimmer,
pinning that tail, some power was amassed,
as well as something ludicrous, always that,
the tail was different from the horns, or paws,
it was the seat of shame—and there was envy,
not just contempt, but envy—horns a man has,
and he has furry hands and he has a mane,
but never a tail. I remember dimly
a toy we had, a kind of flattened stone,
curved at the sides, with a long rope at the end
we whirled around to make a thundering noise.
This was a "bull-roarer"; we made thunder
and felt the power in our shoulders and legs.
I saw this toy in southern Italy;
I saw children throwing it over their heads
as if they were in central Australia
or ancient Europe somewhere, in a meadow,
forcing the gods to roar. They call it Uranic,
a heavenly force, sometimes almost a voice,
locked up in that whirling stone, dear father.

SUSAN STEWART ❖

The Gypsy

A late afternoon in July, too early to begin
making supper, too hot
to work in the garden.
A Saturday, then, and after

Most Recent Book: THE HIVE (University of Georgia Press, 1987)

the war, for the three of them
are there: mother, father, daughter.
But what should be clear,
should be said, from the start
is that the father
always doubts, can't be sure
this is his
daughter and so has pulled
back gradually to the edges
of the house, re-entering
only in fury and shame.

But now he is sleeping.
Her mother and she look in the doorway
at this man, on his back,
completely clothed, against
the candlewick spread.
He is snoring, his mouth
precisely locked into a wide,
slightly vibrating O.
From the doorway they can see
his arms wide, his palms up,
his shoes in opposing directions.

Whose idea was it?
They say they can't remember,
but one of them goes
to the sliding velvet trays
of the jewel box and untangles
a green crystal earring,
then attaches it
with delicate turns of the vise
to his left, slightly tufted,
lobe. The green globe
dangles from its chain
to the pillow, casting a bright
leafy shadow.

Next a vermilion disk for
the right ear, a white plastic bow
for his hair:
the room seems hotter, more still, by now
and the locusts start to wind
into a wilder cadenza.
When he stops snoring

they try to hold their breath,
but his mouth lies slack
in deeper sleep, his breathing
pale and regular.
By this point they have taken
out the cigar-box cache
of brushes, tubes, and puffs.
They powder his coarse cheeks
layer by layer and draw the faintly
bruising blusher down
his jaw: they stencil
the eyebrows to match
the latest style—1946,
a year of constant,
mild surprises.

Brazenly, they flourish
the mascara's viscous wand:
and then the fiery lipstick; what red
lips and coal-black lashes!
They discover, for the first time,
they can't look at each other.

————

As dusk falls, they sit on the porch
and wait—snapping beans,
shelling peas, for supper. When he finally wakes
he is hungry, sour, and dazed a little from sleep;
he cuts everything with his fork, scrapes
his plate, without a word
goes out for the night.
When he's gone the house
seems to fill with a hundred random sounds—
the dishes jarring, the tick
and hum of someone's mower,
an idling car, the darning needles
hovering, some dogs, and then
a bright disk clack-clacking
on the spokes of a distant bicycle.
The mother says, "He's looking
like a gypsy." They wonder
how long this spell can last—
this invention as new
as a homemade fairy tale

where the father,
who is always the real father,
never bothers to look in the mirror.
And those who have lived in
the giant's shadow
for years, find one day
they can speak, they can speak.

Mouth of the Wolf

In my photograph of the Sphinx,
wearing black robes extended heavily
like open bat wings, two men

as big as this pen point
steady themselves
on the bright side of His neck.

Each stretches a left arm
to the collarlike ridge that forms a pediment
for the god's enormous head.

And though a shadow
obscures him, it seems from
this distance that the closer of the two

has held his right arm forward
with considerable eloquence toward what must
have been the mysteriously

elevated position
of the photographer.
Yet this picture-taker has everything

in focus: the faces of the men,
the Pharaoh's delicate ear, the serrated mane,
and even the far grains of sand

in the visible, though cut-off,
triangle of the pyramids, making up
what could be called the background.

The shadowed, more bulbous
side of the head-dress casts a mark to His left
in a patch of overexposed sand.

This mark is confusing,
    shallow or deep, a point
    of absorption or an after-thought—

    like a cavernous, yet
silent, and displaced mouth.
    In other words,

what rain there is
    can be found in this shadow's
    shadow. The rain which falls

    alike upon every country,
and the other rain, too, which disappears
    from the picture.

The Memory Cabinet of Mrs. K.   1960

Top Right Drawer
    Aspirin and pumice stone; emory board and
peach stone; hourglass, lost its sand; a postcard from
Watkins Glen; piece of quartz; sequinned belt; red barrette;
vermilion disc; a diary, *January 8 saw R skating, in the dark,
a branch in an icy glove . . . that line before, something
breaking*; a white shoe buckle; half-knit mitten.

Top Left Drawer
    Packet of pins with gold foil backing; six grosgrain
ribbons—red, yellow, blue, pink, chartreuse, and candy-striped;
a reel of hem tape; a very straight nail; envelope with a
negative (girl on a tire swing); plug on a brass-beaded chain
for a sink; five keys shaped like spades, diamonds, clubs.

Middle Drawer
    Hammer and picture wire; flowered pajamas; cross-stitched
dresser scarf; kimono, missing belt; velveteen sandals from
Panama, huts and palm trees carved into the heel; a squirt
gun; detachable collar with lip print; postcard from the
Poconos; pack of cards; a trivet made of popsicle sticks.

Bottom Drawer
    Souvenir pillow from Watkins Glen; presser foot; zipper
foot; flywheel belt; an ink bottle, rubber stopper askew;
inside *a bevy of charred wings rising, over a black, but*

moonlit pond; extension cord, box of bobbins, belt for
a blue kimono; diploma; certificate of perfect attendance.

RUTH STONE ❖

Where I Came From

My father put me in my mother
but he didn't pick me out.
I am my own quick woman.
What drew him to my mother?
Beating his drumsticks
he thought—why not?
And he gave her an umbrella.
Their marriage was like that.
She hid ironically in her apron.
Sometimes she cried into the biscuit dough.
When she wanted to make a point
she would sing a hymn or an old song.
He was loose-footed. He couldn't be counted on
until his pockets were empty.
When he was home the kettle drums,
the snare drum, the celeste,
the triangle throbbed.
While he changed their heads,
the drum skins soaked in the bathtub.
Collapsed and wrinkled, they floated
like huge used condoms.

Curtains

Putting up new curtains,
other windows intrude.
As though it is that first winter in Cambridge
when you and I had just moved in.
Now cold borscht alone in a bare kitchen.

Most Recent Book: SECOND-HAND COAT (David R. Godine, Publisher, 1987)

What does it mean if I say this years later?

Listen, last night
I am on a crying jag
with my landlord, Mr. Tempesta.
I sneaked in two cats.
He screams NO PETS! NO PETS!
I become my Aunt Virginia,
proud but weak in the head.
I remember Anna Magnani.
I throw a few books. I shout.
He wipes his eyes and opens his hands.
OK OK keep the dirty animals
but no nails in the walls.
We cry together.
I am so nervous, he says.

I want to dig you up and say, look,
it's like the time, remember,
when I ran into our living room naked
to get rid of that fire inspector.

See what you miss by being dead?

Happiness

We were married near the base,
with three days' leave;
a wife's allotment, a widow's pension.
The first night in our rented basement room,
as we came together . . .
Port Chicago exploded!
Several thousand pounds of human flesh
shot like hamburger through the air;
making military funerals, even with wax,
even with closed caskets, bizarre.
As well as certain facts:
there were no white males
loading ammunition on that ship.
From twenty miles away
shock waves rattled the roof,
the walls, the windows.

Our bed danced on the floor
as if we had created a miracle.

Then you went with your unit
in a leaky Liberty Ship to Kiska.
There in the shadow of a Russian church,
you began to notice birds.
One day you followed a snowbird over the tundra.
You followed it beyond sight of the camp, of the others,
as if for a moment there was a choice.
You felt a kind of happiness.
Your letters which told me this, with certain lines
removed, stamped out, sealed by the censor,
have been lost for years.
As the bird, filaments burning in a web of moss,
its tiny skeleton, its skull
that searched ahead of you like radar.

Turn Your Eyes Away

The gendarme came
to tell me you had hung yourself
on the door of a rented room
like an overcoat
like a bathrobe
hung from a hook;
when they forced the door open
your feet pushed against the floor.
Inside your skull
there was no room for us,
your circuits forgot me.
Even in Paris where we never were
I wait for you
knowing you will not come.
I remember your eyes as if I were
someone you had never seen,
a slight frown between your brows
considering me.
How could I have guessed
the plain-spoken stranger in your face,
your body, tagged in a drawer,
attached to nothing, incurious.

My sister, my spouse, you said,
in a place on the other side of the earth
where we lay in a single bed
unable to pull apart
breathing into each other,
the Gideon Bible open to the Song of Songs,
the rush of the El-train
jarring the window.
As if needles were stuck
in the pleasure zones of our brains,
we repeated everything
over and over and over.

CHASE TWICHELL ❖

The Shades of Grand Central

You could tell that the flowers
splayed in the vendor's buckets

had come from the hothouse factories

lit all night to force more blooms.
Among the blue and scarlet flames
the eyes of the homeless flicked

from no one to no one,
and the name for them came to me
sharp in the winter dark

as if it had always been a word.

I climbed the heavy stairs
up out of the pit that steams
and quakes with machine life,

past flowers for the lover
and the lonely self,

flowers for the longtime dead and for
the fresh-cut holes in the frozen hill,

Most Recent Book: PERDIDO (Farrar, Straus & Giroux, 1991)

and for all the children
locked out of the world,

including my own
about whom I know nothing,

not even how many, not even their names

which are like thin ice and do not bear
the weight of my wondering about them.

I came up into the purifying cold,

the small, stinging arrows of snow,
and when I turned my head against it

I saw the hulk of a dumpster
out back of a rib-house, in an alley.
A man in a hooded burlap robe

had led his flock of vagrant dogs to food.

What is an individual grief
but a flake in the storm?

He threw to the dogs the gnawed-on ribs
the restaurant had thrown away.

Snow diffused the harsh
halo of the streetlamp and lit
the folds of his strange apparel.

The dog bodies took each rib with a seizure,
white-backed and ravenous.

Six Belons

The ruckled lips gaped slightly, but when
I slipped the knife in next to the hinge,
they closed to a stone.
The violence it took to unlock them!
Each wounded thing lay in opalescent milk
like an albino heart,
muscle sliced from the roof-shell.
I took each one pale and harmless
into my mouth and held it there,
tasting the difference between

the ligament and the pure, faintly
coffee-colored flesh that was unflinching
even in the acid of lemon juice,
so that I felt I was eating
not the body but the life in the body.
Afterward my mouth stayed greedy
though it carried the sea-rankness
away with it, a taste usually transient,
held for a moment beyond its time
on mustache or fingertip.`
The shells looked abruptly old,
crudely fluted, gray-green, flecked
with the undersea equivalent of lichens,
and pearly, slick, bereft of all their meat.
The creatures themselves were gone,
the succulent indecent briny ghosts
that caused this arousal, this feeding
and now a sudden loneliness.

The Condom Tree

Pleasure must slip
right through memory's barbed wire,
because sex makes lost things reappear.
This afternoon when I shut my eyes
beneath his body's heavy braille,
I fell through the rosy darkness
all the way back to my tenth year,
the year of the secret
place by the river,
where the old dam spilled
long ropes of water and the froth
chafed the small stones smooth.
I looked up and there it was,
a young maple
still raw in early spring,
and drooping pale
from every reachable branch,
dozens of latex blooms.
I knew what they were,
that the older kids
had hung them there,

but the tree—was it beautiful
caught in that dirty floral light,
or was it an ugly thing?
Beautiful first, and ugly afterward,
when I saw up close
the shrivelled human skins?
That must be right,
though in the remembering
its value has been changed again,
and now that flowering
dapples the two of us
with its tendered shadows,
dapples the rumpled bed as it slips
out of the damp present
into our separate pasts.

Chanel No. 5

Life had become a sort of gorgeous elegy,
intimate with things about to be lost.

The waiter's hand on the wineglass
seemed an intermediary flame,

the atoms rampant inside it,

though it moved slowly
and hesitated slightly
before it was withdrawn

as if it meant to ask
whether anything more was wanted.

Abstracted by the static of the surf,

I dined alone, the beach hotel
half-empty in the off-season,

the honeymooning couple
at the table next to mine

caressing with their voices
the still-folded map of their future,

their two armies still in reserve,

the flowers massed between them
a flimsy barricade
against their wakening grief.

The long pin of her corsage
pierced the thin silk on her breast:
white flower, green leaf, black dress.

In her perfume I smelled
the residue of all their recent happiness,
a sweetness corrupted by the sea, and yet

she wore it innocently, that target.

It was a fledgling bitterness I caught
off a shred of air that had touched her dress
as she rose to follow her husband-mystery.

The little emblem inside the flame,
the male and female become one,

was blackening back in their room

overlooking the sea, but before they
hurried back to it, she looked at me,
and, as if to innoculate herself against me,

inclined her head to smell her own gardenia.

LESLIE ULLMAN ❖

Dawn Feeding

Darkness has feathered all night
downward into drifts. Vague bits of
dream. Discarded socks and shirt.
My feet sink in and track it
outside, where what's near
still recedes—woodpile, corral, the bay
mare's heavy head nodding
between the rails—I'm not
ready to open my other eyes.

Most Recent Book: DREAMS BY NO ONE'S DAUGHTER (University of Pittsburgh Press, 1987)

The hungry horses loom like ships,
restless and dark against the sky.
One pokes a blunt nose out of the night,
into my hand, and a dream I had before waking
takes shape again—a familiar child,
my brother's new daughter left to my care
like the life-sized doll I was given
one birthday, a time I was really part horse.
She was too expensive to be taken from her box.
"When you're older," they promised. Nearly
forty now, I kept forgetting to carry crackers
and milk to the hidden room where this child
drifted in her crib. Little by little she stopped
inventing words. Her warm cheeks
cooled to wax. I never even thought
to pick her up, my arms weren't real
as they weren't in the days when I
flourished my silk scarf of a tail.
When I munched what I was fed. When I tossed
my head and slept hard. Daylight
abruptly has flooded this yard.
My neglect, my night track, does not
burn off, but the horses turn to me
anyway, the bringer of buckets and hay.
All night they held some shape
of me in their heads like a dream—
a snip of red, perhaps, a weightless thing
drifting in and out of their view.
Now they dip their heads in the circle
of my arms. Their jaws closing over
the charged and magical grains are engines
churning up steam that would startle
their vast bodies away, even now,
if I raised a hand to them suddenly.

Desire

While the pulse in my neck
taps "trouble, trouble," I think about
deep sea fish—their calm gills,
eyes like iced flowers, cold hearts
pumping. I think, *tons of water*

could be holding me down, the vast
blue pressure shot with light that doesn't
break the darkness, but turns
whole fields of minnows to stars.
How slowly they move in the immense

privacy, while grasses wave in slow motion
as they have forever, fanning time,
not this fever, not tongues of flame
springing from this face. . . .

I imagine I breathe water,
suddenly skilled at drawing
what little air I need and sending
the rest back to its heavy world—
that's the miracle of fish, what I
envy—then I remember the striped bass
I once lifted from fresh water to my
natural element, this giddy vanishing
of all substance, that drowning.

Mauve

I

At night, late, the men I loved began
my instruction. One spoke a tongue
foreign to me at first
as it must have been to him, a river
of syllables pumped from sleep's
sure heart. By day he spoke
through locked teeth, an old anger,
his words hard as buckshot.
I got out of range by
leaving my body, leaving
in my place a cold blue light
he came to know well; whenever he
flared, my own words sharpened
into metal and good sense.

But at night I opened myself
to his other tongue—I glimpsed
his father taken early by illness

and hidden in the heart's
walled city, while his mother refused
to hold a man's hand again, or laugh
from the center of her body—
I glimpsed the boy cutting a path through
trees and tall grass, then dozing
in a hayloft while horses munched below—
I followed his sounds until they
ran through my head like a song.
He led me to a garden taken over
by thistles, by briars, fragile
and lovely in their frost.

I found myself kneeling,
a child just big enough to seek
refuge from those who would protect her,
studying my own hand
as though it had just sprung from the ground.

*

The other gathered me
and arranged me across the table
as though I were green and full
of sun. He coaxed me with talk,
with hands, to love my own hands
as different from others, to love
my breasts. My skin grew supple
over the way I was made.
Another me sprang up
like one of my own ribs turning
to blossom, to red fruit.
She made my voice sound like bells.
In her company I began to talk to myself.

Then in his sleep he turned wholly
away. If wakened he curled
around his hands, his back
a shield. I found myself
pinned beneath the ghosts
of women—the longings
and quarrels gathered in his heart
like silt, all that was left
of the light their hands might have
given him at first. I could hear
his breath fill with sand, clay,

with bedrock grown thick—
that's when I knew what had
grown in me had not
grown there.

For a while then, every nightfall
passed something like a hand
over my cheek and made me
grateful to be lowered
gently into the lamplight
of myself until daybreak.
Until thin light sneaked back,
casting the shadow of mountain
over my door and over the fields
behind this house, where all the green
had bled into sand.
Every morning I'd put on something red
or the clear blue the sky might
or might not offer, and step out of my house
as though into a stranger's body.

2

Now I've grown lighter, my skin
sometimes sponge instead of flesh,
sometimes air. Now the nights
bring silence, then sleep.
Sometimes rain. Then dawn
and its simple changes.
I follow them, passing in and out
of my house while the fields' flowering
passes in and out of me.
Sometimes what I'm writing keeps me
dreamily indoors, as pages
turn to dune and river beneath my pen.
Or the telephone lifts me from work
and passes me into other, possible lives:

Esther is dazed from the pull of others'
secrets, from opening and closing
doors of herself to let them pass.
She only half-knows others' dreams
are her first language.
She only half-knows she is
brave. She listens hard

to their stories until she finds
herself at their source—
the sister, the mirror,
the dark saint—then gathers
herself from her jeweled hive of rooms
to greet husband or son or lover
who cracks a secret door in himself
while thinking her his own, his single
blue- or white- or rose-colored stone.

Susan, who stopped painting for years, now
sleeps at night between the Pacific Ocean
and the first man she's ever known who doesn't
need to talk. Who doesn't need
to shelter in the tropics of her heart,
its thick roots and tribal mothers.
She picked him for his hands, fluent
with chisel and nails. She picked him for
glancing calmly out the window now and then,
not knowing himself observed.
At first he didn't notice her bottomless eyes.
Now she begins to paint again,
beach glass or shells. Bits of wood
washed a long way, worn smooth, not broken.
Her dreams, she says, have lost their furious colors.

MICHAEL VAN WALLEGHEN ❖

Meat

It was early Saturday, dawn
the day for buying meat . . .

My father had this friend
way over in Hamtramck

who knew all about meat
and so we'd drive uxorious

drunk mornings after payday
halfway across Detroit

Most Recent Book: BLUE TANGO (University of Illinois Press, 1989)

to meet this expert
at the slaughter house

where they sold everything:
brains, testicles, tripe

all that precious offal
grocery stores disdained—

whole hog heads for headcheese
fresh duck blood, fresh feet

kidneys, giblets, pancreas . . .
The freshest meat in the world

my father's friend would shout
above the squealing, bleating

foaming panic of the animals
and my father would repeat it

all day long. *The freshest
goddamn meat in the world*

he'd croon to the barmaids
along our long route home

forgetting, even as he said it
that all that lovely meat

was spoiling in the car.
But I remembered. I knew

the trouble we were in.
I could already see us

opening the bloody packages—
our poor brains, our testicles

smelling up the whole kitchen
again, and in the sorry face

of all my father's promises
to come home early, sober

a fine example for his son
a good husband for a change

one of those smart guys
who knew all about meat.

The Age of Reason

Once, my father got invited
by an almost perfect stranger

a four-hundred-pound alcoholic
who bought the drinks all day

to go really flying sometime
sightseeing in his Piper Cub

and my father said *perfect!*
Tomorrow was my birthday

I'd be seven years old, a chip
off the old daredevil himself

and we'd love to go flying.
We'd even bring a case of beer.

My father weighed two-fifty
two-seventy-five in those days

the beer weighed something
the ice, the cooler. I weighed

practically nothing: forty-five
maybe fifty pounds at the most—

just enough to make me nervous.
Where were the parachutes? Who

was this guy? Then suddenly
there we were, lumbering

down a bumpy, too short runway
and headed for a fence . . .

Holy Shit! my father shouts
and that's it, all we need

by way of the miraculous
to lift us in a twinkling

over everything—fence, trees
and powerline. What a birthday!

We were really flying now . . .
We were probably high enough

to have another beer in fact,
high enough to see Belle Isle

the Waterworks, Packard's
and the Chrysler plant.

We could even see our own
bug-sized house down there

our own backyard, smaller
than a chewed down thumbnail.

We wondered if my mother
was taking down the laundry

and if she'd wave . . . Lightning
trembled in the thunderheads

above Belle Isle. Altitude:
2500, air speed: one-twenty

but the fuel gauge I noticed
quivered right on empty . . .

I'd reached the age of reason.
Our pilot lit a big cigar.

Blue Tango

After stumbling around for months
like arthritic wooden puppets

unaccountbly brain-damaged
and unable to count—failing

to fox-trot, failing to waltz
failing in the church basement

even to two-step correctly
it was decided we had danced

beyond all mere appearance
to some mystical new plateau

where henceforth we should learn
to tango. Our Dominican nuns

were adamant. The seventh grade
at the Assumption of Our Blessed

Virgin Mary School would tango!
The Saint Elizabeth's Sodality

with whom we shared the basement
on Wednesday afternoons agreed.

They loved that music; it helped
them sew. That year, I remember

they were busy sewing things
the nuns called "cancer pads."

And when the long, elliptical orbit
of our tango brought us twirling

close to the glimmering windows
the flimsy tables where they sewed

I'd hear the whispered variations
of a single, incessant conversation:

By the time they opened him up
repeated someone, *it was everywhere.*

Then off I'd go again, mincing
with my awkward too-tall partner

toward the gloomy furnace room.
Listening to those ladies talk

you'd think that suppurating cancers
had hit our parish like the plague.

Nor was there anything to do for it
but sewing cancer pads, communion

and learning, of course, to tango—
as if preparing for a long cruise

among the romantic blue islands
of the southern ocean. Some heaven

where even cabin boys could tango
and no one had to get up for work

at Packard's, Dodge Main, Cadillac . . .
where no one got pregnant, got cancer

lost their fingers in a punch press
or had even heard of Detroit, at all.

MARILYN NELSON WANIEK ❖

Balance

He watch her like a coonhound watch a tree.
What might explain the metamorphosis
he underwent when she paraded by
with tea-cakes, in her fresh and shabby dress?
(As one would carry water from a well—
straight-backed, high-headed, like a diadem,
with careful grace so that no drop will spill—
she balanced, almost brimming, her one name.)

She think she something, stuck-up island bitch.
Chopping wood, hanging laundry on the line,
and tantalizingly within his reach,
she honed his body's yearning to a keen,
sharp point. And on that point she balanced life.
That hoe Diverne think she Marse Tyler's wife.

Chosen

Diverne wanted to die, that August night
his face hung over hers, a sweating moon.
She wished so hard, she killed part of her heart.
If she had died, her one begotten son,
her life's one light, would never have been born.
Pomp Atwood might have been another man:
born with a single race, another name.
Diverne might not have known the starburst joy
her son would give her. And the man who came
out of a twelve-room house and ran to her
close shack across three yards that night, to leap
onto her cornshuck pallet. Pomp was their
share of the future. And it wasn't rape.
In spite of her raw terror. And his whip.

Most Recent Book: THE HOME PLACE (Louisiana State University Press, 1990)

Star-fix

for Melvin M. Nelson (1917–1966)
Capt. USAF (ret.)

At his cramped desk
under the astrodome,
the navigator looks
thousands of light-years
everywhere but down.
He gets a celestial fix,
measuring head-winds;
checking the log;
plotting wind-speed,
altitude, drift
in a circle of protractors,
slide-rules and pencils.

He charts in his Howgozit
the points of no alternate
and of no return.
He keeps his eyes on the compass,
the two altimeters, the map.
He thinks, *Do we have enough fuel?*
What if my radio fails?

He's the only Negro in the crew.
The only black flyer on the whole base,
for that matter. Not that it does:
this crew is a team.
Bob and Al, Les, Smitty, Nelson.

Smitty, who said once
after a poker game,
I love you, Nelson.
I never thought I could love
a colored man.
When we get out of this man's Air Force,
if you ever come down to Tuskaloosa,
look me up and come to dinner.
You can come in the front door, too;
hell, you can stay overnight!
Of course, as soon as you leave,
I'll have to burn down my house.

Because if I don't
my neighbors will.

The navigator knows where he is
because he knows where he's been
and where he's going.

At night, since he can't fly
by dead-reckoning,
he calculates his position
by shooting a star.

The octant tells him
the angle of a fixed star
over the artificial horizon.
His position in that angle
is absolute and true:
Where the hell are we, Nelson?
Alioth, in the Big Dipper.
Regulus. Antares, in Scorpio.

He plots their lines
of position on the chart,
gets his radio bearing,
corrects for lost time.

Bob, Al, Les and Smitty
are counting on their navigator.
If he sleeps,
they all sleep.
If he fails
they fall.

The navigator keeps watch
over the night and the instruments,
going hungry for five or six hours
to give his flight-lunch
to his two little girls.

Lonely Eagles

for Daniel "Chappie" James, General, USAF
and for the 332nd Fighter Group

Being black in America
was the Original Catch,
so no one was surprised
by 22:
The segregated airstrips,
separate camps.
They did the jobs
they'd been trained to do.

Black ground-crews kept them in the air;
black flight-surgeons kept them alive;
the whole Group removed their headgear
when another pilot died.

They were known by their names:
"Ace" and "Lucky,"
"Sky-hawk Johnny," "Mr. Death."
And by their positions and planes.
Red Leader to Yellow Wing-man,
do you copy?

If you could find a fresh egg
you bought it and hid it
in your dopp-kit or your boot
until you could eat it alone.
On the night before a mission
you gave a buddy
your hiding-places
as solemnly
as a man dictating
his will.
There's a chocolate bar
in my Bible;
my whiskey bottle
is inside my bed-roll.

In beat-up Flying Tigers
that had seen action in Burma,
they shot down three German jets.
They were the only outfit

in the American Air Corps
to sink a destroyer
with fighter planes.
Fighter planes with names
like "By Request."
Sometimes the radios
didn't even work.
They called themselves
"Hell from Heaven."
This Spookwaffe.
My father's old friends.

It was always
maximum effort:
A whole squadron
of brother-men
raced across the tarmack
and mounted their planes.

      My tent-mate was a guy named Starks.
      The funny thing about me and Starks
      was that my airmattress leaked,
      and Starks' didn't.
      Every time we went up,
      I gave my mattress to Starks
      and put his on my cot.

      One day we were strafing a train.
      Strafing's bad news:
      you have to fly so low and slow
      you're a pretty clear target.
      My other wing-man and I
      exhausted our ammunition and got out.
      I recognized Starks
      by his red tail
      and his rudder's trim-tabs.
      He couldn't pull up his nose.
      He dived into the train
      and bought the farm.

      I found his chocolate,
      three eggs, and a full fifth
      of his hoarded-up whiskey.
      I used his mattress
      for the rest of my tour.

It still bothers me, sometimes:
I was sleeping
on his breath.

BELLE WARING ❖

When a Beautiful Woman Gets on the Jutiapa Bus

babies twist in their mothers' arms. The men
yearn so the breath snags, Ai! in their chests.
The women flick their eyes over her,
discreet, and turn back to each other.
                    When
a beautiful woman steps on the bus, she scowls
with the arrogance of the gorgeous. That face,
engrave it on commemorative stamps. A philatelist's
dream. That profile should be stamped on centennial
coins. Somebody quick take a picture of her,
la señora in the azure frock. Sculpt her image
to honor Our Lady.
                Just how did she land here,
Miss Fine Mix? As a matter of course, her forefather,
El Conquistador, raped a Mayan priestess,
Anno Domini 1510. At the moment of her own conception,
her parents met each other's eyes. Don't stare.

What's she doing squeezed in here with campesinos
carrying chickens? Squawk. Save that face.

When a beautiful woman gets off the bus, everyone
sighs, Ai! and imagines her fate: she's off
to Sunday dinner with mama who's groomed her
to marry an honest farmer happy to knock her up
every spring. Her looks (no doubt) will leach out,
washing the dead, schlepping headloads of scavenged
firewood, grinding, grinding, grinding corn,
hanging the wash in the sun and wind, all
by hand, all by her graceful brown hand.

Most Recent Book: REFUGE (University of Pittsburgh Press, 1990)

Baby Random

tries a nosedive, kamikaze,
when the intern flings open the isolette.

The kid almost hits the floor. I can see the headline:
DOC DUMPS AIDS TOT. Nice save, nurse,

Why thanks. Young physician: "We have to change
his tube." His voice trembles, six weeks

out of school. I tell him: "Keep it to a handshake,
you'll be OK." Our team resuscitated

this Baby Random, birth weight
one pound, eyelids still fused. Mother's

a junkie with HIV. Never named him.
Where I work we bring back terminal preemies,

No Fetus Can Beat Us. That's our motto. I have
a friend who was thrown into prison. Where do birds

go when they die? Neruda wanted to know. Crows
eat them. Bird heaven? Imagine the racket.

When Random cries, petit fish on shore, nothing
squeaks past the tube down his pipe. His ventilator's

a high-tech bellows that kicks in & out. Not
up to the nurses. Quiet: a pigeon's outside,

color of graham crackers, throat oil on a wet street,
wings spattered white, perched out of the rain.

I have friends who were thrown into prison, Latin
American. Tortured. Exiled. Some people have

courage. Some people have heart. *Corazon.*
After a shift like tonight, I have the usual

bad dreams. Some days I avoid my reflection in store
windows. I just don't want anyone to look at me.

Back to Catfish

The cafe with the hotwire
boys is where you are and me

I'm back to cooking catfish
with banana, disguised
as a Guadeloupan delicacy,
but it's still its old ugly-snout
self. Now, when you bon temps roulez,
you booze in a fancy French joint
where the ladies get menus
with no price list. My little sun-
king, who knows when you'll blow
in. A woman like me
with a fine arts degree
could have been a master
engraver. Counterfeiter.
Not the counterfeiter's moll.

Sure. I'm back to cooking
catfish, a creature with purpose
in life, to sweep the creek bottom
clean as the moon.
I'm waiting for thee,
wearing this swamp-green
shirt you left. I could never
just throw it away,
the color of a hangover, a bruise.

But I could start without you.
Scarf up bananafish by myself.
Clean this kitchen with your keepsake
shirt, scrub every bad business
I can reach. Go out for some middlebrow
cappuccino. Swing by the Tastee Diner
for some brawlproof pie. I'll smile
when I'm ready and feel
complete. Who knows who I might meet?

I could swim the night in my cherry Nova
and sweep down the state road
crossing the river
on its long goddamn way home.

Breeze in Translation

Me I like to putz in the kitchen and regard
fat garlic and hum about nothing. Make it up. Word
for *blues*. Like dragging down the street
in a hundred-and-four heat—you know
when air temp tops body temp, how buzzed and weird

you get? Word for *trance*. So this character
taps me: remember me, *mon amie?* Name's
Breeze. Then she dictates most fabulous. I'm
blessed. She's benign. Word for *pixilated*.

She's a scholarship girl at the School of Beaux-Arts
so she drags me down the line to an out-of-town
show. Rattle express. Word for

kismet. This lady with the face of an old walnut
sits by us making lace with an eye-fine
hook and when the train dives into the tunnels
she keeps on working in the dark. Word's

exquisite. Breeze sings
scat all the way to the opening:
sculpture of heating ducts, stovepipes and stones.
Breeze is prole to the bone. The tablecloth's

spattered with blood of the lamb,
wine on the lace. The critic pronounces optimism
vulgar, and asks: Why have there been so few
great women artists?
                    We ask ourselves. The word is

jerkoff. Breeze, who is terrifyingly fluent,

challenges him to sew a bride's dress. From
scratch. *Femmes aux barricades!* The critic can't weave
a cat's cradle. Breeze spits: By hand. French lace.

BRUCE WEIGL ❖

The Black Hose

A boy who knew enough to save for something
like the whim that took me downtown on the bus
one lost Saturday, morning of my mother's birthday,
I sat in the back where the gasoline smell
made me dizzy and I closed my eyes but didn't
think of her, only of myself basking in the light
and love that would fall down on me when I
handed her the box and she untied the bow to save
and lifted something shining out and held it up before us
like a promise taking shape for once in her hands
though I didn't know what to buy, the bus door
hissing behind me because I'm in some kind of
state now, a trance that comes when you pull at the
cords of light that connect the mother to the boy,
the 1959 department store opening up before me
like a jeweled city.

In lingerie I found myself
surrounded by those torsos sheened in silk,
dreaming my mother, feeling that silk against me,
the two of us moving through a cloudy room
in a dance I can't remember until shame comes.
From out of nowhere the matron frowned,
asked me what I wanted, hovered over me.
Confused and afraid I whispered, without thinking,
The black hose with rhinestones down the seams please
and pointed to the pair across the room
stretched over the legs standing on the glass counter
as if about to step off
and I saw her in my mind put them on,
her skirts hiked up above the garters, the sun
catching in her tangled hair
until the matron made a sound in her throat
and looked at me with eyes that said
What's wrong with you dirty boy.

Most Recent Book: SONG OF NAPALM (The Atlantic Monthly Press, 1988)

All the way home a sweet ache rocked me,
the silver package riding my lap
like a heavy wrong thing
I couldn't give up no matter how it
dragged me down to a place
where I could barely breathe or see or feel.
I was holding on for a last few moments
to the woman I could never have again in the old way.
I was breaking loose at the same time,
the boy trying to die inside me.
Whatever happened that spinning afternoon—
she ran her fingers over the rhinestone seams or
she didn't; she wore them out into any evening
or kept them forever in her drawer of impossible things
doesn't matter or is lost in the storm of years
but I would find my way to the light
of another woman into whose arms I fall
nights my fingers can't tear through the dark
that eats me, the silk stretched across her breasts,
the need for something womanly to raise me up
pounding in my head until I curl in sleep away
from those longings ancient and blue.

What Saves Us

We are wrapped around each other in
the back of my father's car parked
in the empty lot of the highschool
of our failures, the sweat on her neck
like oil. The next morning I would leave
for the war and I thought I had something
coming for that, I thought to myself
that I would not die never having
been inside her long body. I pulled
her skirt above her waist like an umbrella
blown inside out by the storm. I pulled
her cotton panties up as high as
she could stand. I was on fire. Heaven
was in sight. We were drowning on our
tongues and I tried to tear my pants off
when she stopped so suddenly
we were surrounded only by my shuddering

and by the school bells grinding in the
empty halls. She reached to find something,
a silver crucifix on a silver
chain, the tiny savior's head hanging
and stakes through his hands and his feet.
She put it around my neck and held
me so long the black wings of my heart
were calmed. We are not always right
about what we think will save us. I
thought that dragging the angel down would
save me, but instead I carried the crucifix
in my pocket and rubbed it on my
face and lips nights the rockets roared in.

People die sometimes so near you
you feel them struggling to cross over,
the deep untangling, of one body from another.

Anna's Grace

And with damp rags she bathes him, brings him
his whiskey in the evenings, says the rosary
before the crucifix and dried palm leaves on the wall.
He can't stand by himself or walk
or lift his arms. He doesn't know the children
or grandchildren who come to this bed to hold
his swollen hands and kiss his face.
On the plain of stroke he sleeps in the day bed
where the sun may find him and the toilet isn't far
when she must carry him in to piss.
He can't hold his cock so she holds it
for him, as when in love they tumbled
into the same bed. He lies
in the consuming shock of the brain assaulting
itself and calls in the language he would not
abandon, to the old country dying out
in his heart. And the old woman who shaves him
with such grace he doesn't bleed,
sleeps on the hard couch to be near him, the flashlight
on the table beside her, so she can shine and move
the light under her blankets, before sleep,

when he demands each night to see
no other man sleeps with her.

The Confusion of Planes We Must Wander in Sleep

I stood naked in the corner as my mother
changed the wet sheets and clucked her tongue though spoke
as kindly as she could, my father stirring angrily
in the bed across the hall. Lost, my legs sheened in piss
I stumbled, drugged with the kind of grieving
children practice to survive. I was apart from
the cold and the heavy smell. I was not attached
to the world though I followed my young and weary
mother into the timeless dark,
                              and tonight I
pull my own son's blankets back and speak to him:
how nice a dry bed will be, how good to get up
without a fuss and go. I lift him to stand, his
penis a wand waving its way magically
before us, and something makes sense for once in my head,
the way that what we pass on is not always a gift,
not always grace or strength or music, but sometimes
a burden and that we have no choice but to live as
hard as we can inside the storm of our years and
that even the weaknesses are a kind of beauty
for the way they bind us into what love, finally, must be.

Meditation at Pearl Street

The steelyards, the long lines of workers
changing shifts, hunched in the predawn cold,
caught in light from mill towers like
searchlights. Or the beauty of gas flaming up
blue and white from the open-hearth that blasted
ingots of iron and carbon into
steel. Or the beauty of the slag heaps, our
black desert by the lake where we met
in secret as boys to smoke and to touch
ourselves, our legs stiffening, the gull's cry

an accusation. Or the beauty of
our small company houses painted in
pastels against the fly ash that came down
on us like dogwood dust. . . . Into what grief,
into what family of grief were we born
and did we grow that these things are grace.
Or the beauty of the quiet hours when the
chronic angers were still and the father's curses
did not slam down on the table and a
rough love bound us all in a knot. Or the
beauty of the feast, when all our hearts were opened.

They Name Heaven

I saw the moon over Plaza Espana
but it's not my moon
because of what this pale one has seen
pass in dark cells at the hands
of crazy rich men,
murder on their lips like salt.
Not the moon my little boy will see tonight
safe in the place of the great Republic,
near enough his mother
so he may find her even in his sleep.
Not the clean and round moon he calls to,

this one rises over Cuesta del Plomo
where the bones have already grown
back into the earth until
there is nothing to mark
the graves of the disappeared. The moon
who will no longer let us understand each other,

how in darkness they'd come for you,
how in moonlight you'd pass through the city,
your hands bound,
your shirt ripped over your face.
How you must have known you would die
only you wondered how long it would take,
what parts of the body they would relish
with their sticks and their long knives,
those who made pacts under the moon,
who washed away the blood with rum,

who returned to their sleeping families
and lifted the acquiescent
nightgowns of their wives,
their drunken lips
fumbling upwards, always
upwards to the moons of flesh they name heaven.

ROGER WEINGARTEN ❖

Father Hunger and Son

A pedestal ashtray next to the son who hadn't seen
or spoken to his father for years of blame, and another
man wrapped in a coat, both hands pressed
into a fist between his thighs, the cleanshaven
pendulum of his chin muttering under a petrified
tear that magnified the bloodshot corner. Jealous
of his thirty years side-by-side with my father
working the phones for sales, I assumed his grief
was for the tenuous life at the far end
of the corridor suspended between
a bag of blood and a monitor's
vigilance. I touched his shoulder like a stranger
interrupting another on an empty bus. He'll be okay.
Who? he answered, as he grabbed
the ashtray and pulled it to him, whispering
through something stuck in his throat
that he'd found an unmailed
letter from his wife to another man
sticking out from under
the car seat as he'd reached to turn the key
that morning in the garage. I want him to masturbate
to death, he said. You can see
your father now, the nurse told me.
After I passed my stepsister and Aunt Delilah, her eyebrows
raised into dollar signs beneath a pale
beehive, my stepmother pulled me aside and said,
Why are you here? You're not welcome. You'll kill him
if you step foot in that room. I pushed

Most Recent Book: INFANT BONDS OF JOY (David R. Godine, Publisher, 1990)

my sad cuckold into a cab that dropped us
in the industrial flats under cranes looming
by the revolving bridge of my childhood
over the river that burned once. While we tried
to light it again with matchbooks and wads
of old receipts from his pockets, scraps
of smoke drifting nowhere, he wanted to know
what I thought he should say to his wife. I asked him
if my father loved me. He hunkered down
and stared at his wingtips. When your mother
left him for that other guy, something
died inside of him. I'm not saying he didn't laugh
or give a shit about anyone. But if
your name came up—which was almost
never—you could see something
sidestep in his face, like he was dodging
a sucker punch. What do I know after thirty years
of lunches and hustle? I worked for the bastard.
He signed the checks like clockwork every week.
As I started to cry, he said, C'mere, child,
crying too and pulling me
to his sandpaper cheek. I don't know my wife
any better than your old man. Or anyone else
for that matter. I don't know.

From the Temple of Longing

The moment the children climb
into my ex-wife's car they buckle
themselves into a faraway look.
The little one
never cries, the eldest
counts white hairs that sneak
like the future up the side of his arm.
Camel, tent, oasis, storm—their ancestors
longed to pause and longed even more
to press on. But on a cobalt dark
night like this, following
an invisible need at the other
end of a leash, I want to hear
from my wild nomads dreaming
on the other side of the state. I want

to hear them say papa, it's alright,
don't cry—always thirsty at three a.m.
for something more than water. Maybe
you think this is all about a dime-
a-dozen emotional flotsam who left a furious
marriage only to miss his children from one
school holiday to the next, who exaggerates
the tangled heartworms that pressed
his ribcage when his
parents divorced. Maybe you just
want to tell me that children
are not that fragile. But I wonder
what I would hear, a dozen
years from now, waiting for the last
solar eclipse of the century, my arms relaxed
around my teenage boys, hovering
over a jerryrigged
cardboard theater, watching
the little moon erase the little sun—
I wonder what they would say
in that strange light, if I asked them
to remember.

Four Seasons of His Discontent

I've been digging a hole in sunlight.
I've been running uphill
on a sheet of ice. I've taken
my innermost being by the collar
and hurled it at the first
hawk of spring gliding
above its furry breakfast. You can bet
that I wanted to make
the right impression on a cluster fly
thrashing in the window, that I yearned
even more to have the Bureau of Motivation
inspect every cobwebbed corner
of my self-respect. One moonlit morning,
as I slept in a mudhole in front of my shack,
a yellow butterfly landed on peach fuzz
above my lip, whispering into the two-way
tunnel of my slumbering nose, Hey Weingarten

of The Lake, I'm the reincarnation
of your Uncle Hyman and I'll fricassee
your *tuchas* with a Bunsen burner
if you don't cut the crap. I wanted to wake
from that beauty sleep and pull
the sword out of the stone of my
sickness unto death; I wanted to climb the bald
mountain of my anxiety, turn my shoulder
blades of resentment into wings flying
out of the quicksand of my self-contempt, but instead
I've been tunneling away at daylight, trying to defy
gravity up an icy hill. Stopped a man of the cloth
in his car, who took one look, crossed himself
and ran the light. Reader, though I haven't
resolved a damn thing, I promise not
to let you down: My dentist said nowadays
it's hard to find a good hygienist, but you
can find me almost anytime with a half-eaten
pickled egg in one hand and a warped
cue over my shoulder, pacing
around the table at the Miss Montpelier
Tap and Grill. Remember the schoolboy
who overheard a cockroach telling God
on the ceiling of the Sistine Chapel
that becoming was superior to being, and who
can argue that? So slide your quarter
into the slot and rack 'em tight,
so the black ball you've been waiting for
lingers, while the rest explode. House rules.
Winner breaks, but I'll aim
to leave you a shot.

Jungle Gliders

I was kneeling with my daughter into a chaos
of frog-shaped jigsaw cutouts guaranteed
to coalesce into animal acrobats that range
the upper levels of South Asian jungles, when,
looking up at the Dragon Lizard's ribs spread
into wings pictured on the box my son,
making bomber sounds, held
over my head, I remembered the roach that fell

out of the fist-sized hole in the ceiling
of my first furnished room, almost
eighteen and kneeling
between your pale
knees in the air, mine dug into the heap
of coats and blankets that covered the concrete
carpet of my basement palace, where
we were struggling for warmth
and pleasure, when the gold-bellied
angel of retribution, like a miniature
landlord, dropped through the punch-drunk
hole in my character, through the onion-scented
fumes from the heater jammed in the window
and landed on your freckle we'd christened
The Third Eye. Watching the impossibly
thin legs, upside-down and flailing,
spinning the hard shell, my jungle-
gliding Paradise Tree Snake slid
out of you into the bedclothes. Your cupped hand
pulled me toward your tongue hovering
between your teeth, like the barely
visible eye of a Red-tailed
Flying Squirrel, as if to will
our privacy and concentration
no matter what. Just as your other
hand splayed across the small
of my lower back nudged
me into you, the insect,
whose family tree had inhabited
every Eden, oasis, every four-star
constellation of food and drink,
righted itself and ran
like three little bodies portaging
an upturned canoe toward the secret
passageway of memory, where
I loved you when I wasn't running
on anger, an adolescent
ground predator, dogfaced
and tracking the family
blood into the trap
of my first poem. Is this
the Flying Lemur of Colugo, my daughter
wondered, reaching
for the upside-down creature, its claws

around a branch, sheltering a smaller
version of itself on its belly, the passenger
staring at the gecko
gliding toward tropical bark, where yellow-flowered
Spider Orchids trail out of ferns, like your hair
between my fingers, while our bodies collided
and turned toward separate futures, and the moonlit
shadow of the jet bearing Kennedy's body
swept a million dreams into the ocean.

DARA WIER ❖

Holidays

How many times our hands will enter
water to brighten our faces,
wash our glasses, clean our plates,
to rush through the turkey's carcass,
clean it of fat and blood,
whatever offends. We have gathered
to tell about the worlds we've left
to gather and tell of ourselves.

Your grandmother has recently lost
her husband. This is the first
time you remember her quiet,
letting herself be helped.
This is her daughter's house.
The last time she visited ten years
ago for your wedding. It is odd to see
your grandmother's hands out of water.

Your sister spells out the duties
of her latest part-time job, a gopher
for circuit court judges.
It is better than hamburgers,
better than the graveyard shift.
It's easy to fill an urn
with water for coffee, take down
brief messages from callers.

Most Recent Book: THE BOOK OF KNOWLEDGE (Carnegie Mellon University Press, 1989)

Your brother tells of gallons
of water he drank in Arizona,
fossil water, once secret
and hidden in the earth for centuries,
tapped for a growing population
in need of a clean source
of water for table flowers and
bright green squares of soft lawn.

Your other brother puts on the table
a rock the size of your dead grandfather's
fist, covered with lumps, having
the look of a brain.
He has brought it with him
from Australia, down under.
He has chiseled it from its place,
checked it through customs and flown

with it eleven thousand miles.
It is 2.8 billion years old.
When you heft it, you think
what you are holding should send you
through the seat of your chair, through
your mother's terrazo floor, through
Louisiana's hard, wet dirt, through
the earth's center and out into space.

But you go on sitting at the table.
There is the smell of boiled potatoes.
Your father is filling your glass
with water; your mother's head
is waiting for Grace. We mention
friends who will marry
during the holiday season.
We avoid the names of the recently dead.
We ask that no one give us details
of painful and critical operations.
No one wants to move
the 2.8 billion-year-old rock.
It is something to look at
when we won't look at one another.

Old-fashioned

Next to my best friend I woke up,
    small and deep
in the unfamiliar middle

of her parents' late night quarrel
    over faithlessness,
terrible to find her in such danger.

I wanted her whom I pictured the picture
    of happy-go-lucky to sleep.
I didn't want to turn my face to see

what hers showed or if now she knew
    or had known all along or never.
Her mother was so young, beautiful,

dark-eyed and quick; their walls, thick-
    textured and creamy like cake frosting,
were fancy and rich with filigreed frames,

watercolors of Italian bridges
    and pastels of Parisian streets.
Her father's dog was a dangerous German shepherd,

her mother's car an exotic Buick Electra
    she could take for granted.
This was the modern world I'd been denied.

Her mother wanted to know who the other woman was;
    her father didn't care.
While I listened to their familiar voices

I pictured them a foot apart, no closer
    than my friend, fat, faceless, sleeping
next to me in her bed. I pictured the dark

house shrink around us like a muscle.
    Her parents' voices rose over the pale moon
globe we'd left lit in the room for our own

late night talk of travel beyond our planet
    and the men we knew would soon walk
on the moon above us. Her parents' voices

traveled through a new atmosphere,
    one from which no words escaped.
We were on our way to somewhere unknown together

when over something I don't remember
    we parted company.
Soon her father would be gone and later

she'd grow slim and pretty as her mother,
    her mother the same
as if she were a picture.

When I went back to visit we sat together
    on the side of the same bed,
working hard to say what we'd become.

Her mother called us through the house
    for supper. Glowing in the golden light
of too many candles, Italian bridges

and Parisian streets glowed in their beautiful faces.
    When to emphasize her thought
my friend touched me on my knee

I flinched. It made me think she'd forgiven
    everything I'd understood and not forgotten.

The Flood

The obese man with a goiter,
it looked so tender,
sloshed a bucket of dirty water
over my windshield's streaks of dust
and dead insects. He had tires
to sell me and oil and air
and for half a dollar
he'd unlock his cellar
where he kept his spectacular
two-headed calf.

By his way of asking he wanted to know
why I was passing through Rush,
and where, if I could remember, was there.
He motioned me over, took my money,
pointed where the river turned nearer,
added I shouldn't worry,
odds were good against another disaster.
How was I to explain to a stranger
how deep in love I was, and stunned.

Up the road the flood had set dead deer
to rot up high in trees. Cedars, elms
and sycamores, all the scraggly bushes
and tall grasses leaned hard in one direction.
Every broken post and twisted guardrail
descended down its gully.
Over the clean new sand of a roadside park

I stopped and watched two lovers
open the green wings of their car doors
to let their sweet music drift down
to the fish in the river and up
to the quarter moon.

Two nights before they'd have been underwater.
They'd have lost one another.
There'd have been no time to wave good-bye.
Maybe she'd have seen his eyes
through the instant flash
as they fell apart, almost bowing
to one another in the last, liquid notes
of a slow, sexy dance.
Maybe he gave her his last breath
of air when he kissed her. Maybe
he held a loose swatch of her billowing sleeve.

So she seemed to struggle, but didn't,
but couldn't be still any longer.
Maybe she knew this would happen.
Maybe he wanted it to.
Today they're safe from danger.
Their kisses come and go
and when they breathe they take time
to breathe one another's air.
They hold one another as though their bodies
fold the seam of a spectacular current,
and lean hard into one another
like headwaters joining a flood.

DAVID WOJAHN ❖

The Assassination of John Lennon as Depicted by the Madame Tussaud Wax Museum, Niagara Falls, Ontario, 1987

Smuggled human hair from Mexico
Falls radiant around the waxy O

Of her scream. Shades on, leather coat and pants, Yoko
On her knees—like the famous Kent State photo

Where the girl can't shriek her boyfriend alive, her arms
Windmilling Ohio sky.
                    A pump in John's chest heaves

To mimic death-throes. The blood is made of latex.
His glasses: broken on the plastic sidewalk.

A scowling David Chapman, his arms outstretched,
His pistol barrel spiraling fake smoke

In a siren's red wash, completes the composition,
And somewhere background music plays *Imagine*

Before the tableau darkens. We push a button
To renew the scream.
                    The chest starts up again.

Matins: James Brown and His Fabulous Flames Tour the South, 1958

Please, Please, Please, on the charts permits
Four canary yellow sequined suits
And a hulking Coupe de Ville—bought on credit—
For the Alabama-Georgia roadhouse circuit.
Half last night they drove from Athens, taking turns
At the wheel. The radio hissed National Guards
in Little Rock, static filling Jackie Wilson's
Lonely Teardrops. Parked near Macon in a soybean field,

Most Recent Book: MYSTERY TRAIN (University of Pittsburgh Press, 1990)

They sleep with heads in towels to protect
Their kingly pompadours, and as the predawn
Mist burns off, they wake to knocks against
The windshield. A cruiser with its siren on
Dyes the fog bright red. *Don't you niggers know your place?*
A billy club, a face, the windshield breaks.

White Lanterns

i.
Visiting Accounting, 1960
(The numbers hypnotize.)

Beside her desk, three squat adding machines
Confetti the floor with paper strips in ever
Widening spirals, and her gaze dances to ledgers
Exhaling their breath of dust, a Dickens scene
Transplanted to the '60s, to General Tire
Or Northwest Bank.
                    (The columns hypnotize.)
                    Released from Doctor Thorson,
My molar wrapped in tissue in my hand,
I peer into her office door. Lost in her lacemaker's
Trance,
        (The figures hypnotize.)
        she sees numbers constellate into rows,

But not her son. Sixes and zeros comet down
Relentlessly as sleet, the addition
And subtraction of these moments that compose
A life: this one to debit, this one to credit,
(She looks up.)
This one to crimson lipstick, vapor lights.

ii.
Study, 1989

Her lipstick's crimson in the vapor light.
The funeral home basement, and the undertaker's bent
To pry the casket hinges up for us. No lambent
Painterly shadowplay, only stark fluorescent

Clarity. She's no one anymore,
Only the Christmas-and-New Year's dress
Tentlike on the wasted body, only a face
Half hers, half a cosmetician's caricature

Jerrybuilt from photos in a borrowed
Family album. Why must my mind so brokenly
Conjure this stranger's distracted study

Of wig and cheekbones, dental plates, of each bad
Polaroid of birthday dinners, summer cookouts,
His tools fixing the exact shape of her mouth?

iii.
Harlequins, 1962

I remember the exact shape of her mouth,
The dimestore novels on her lap, the lips
Working silent incantations, the threadbare couch.
She's in Rio tonight, or Pernambuco, and I'm up

Past midnight, creeping to the living room
To tell her I can't sleep. My father's on the road again,
The Fargo-Minot-Whitefish run, and I'm alone
With her all week, The Man Of The House. Her gin

Glass sweating on the table, I watch her doze,
The book dropped to the floor. All night she's tangoed
With suave pencil-mustached generalisimos,

A rose in her teeth, absinthe and milky pernod.
But now she's mine again, waking with a start:
David, fill the glass for me, I've got such a thirst.

iv.
Morphine, 1989

Johnny, fill the syringe for me. All the pain's come back.
Perhaps then she can sleep or watch TV,
Or stare at Midwest winter, snow falling vertically
From here to Hudson's Bay. The flakes strike

The new picture window, and he fumbles with the syringe,
Waits through the game shows that she hates, until
She's gentled into sleep. And when she's still
He dozes too, fetal on the couch, the sponge

He dabbed her forehead with falling damp
From his hand to the floor. Refrigerator hum,
The clock spitting seconds, the seething storm,

The dog chasing rabbits in dream. Let them sleep,
Sleep as the spectral evening shadows come
To blur the window, the snowflakes' numb white lanterns.

v.
Walking to School, 1964

Blurring the window, the snowflakes' numb white lanterns.
She's brewed her coffee, in the bathroom sprays cologne
And sets the lipstick upright on the sink.
The door ajar, I glimpse the yellow slip,

The rose-colored birthmark on her shoulder.
Then she's dressed—the pillbox hat and ersatz fur,
And I'm dressed too, mummified in stocking cap
And scarves, and I walk her to the bus stop

Where she'll leave me for my own walk to school,
Where she'll board the bus that zigzags to St. Paul
As I watch her in the window, the paperback

Romance already open on her lap,
The bus laboring off into snow, her good-bye kiss
Still startling my cheek with lipstick trace.

vi.
Picture Window, 1988

Spattering the room with a snowy trace
Of plaster dust, the carpenters have worked all week,
And the pane they're fitting will be huge, posed to frame
The brown November lawn. Thanksgiving break,

And we arrive to stacked lumber, saw horses,
The living room a stage or excavation.
Wig askew, she slowly rises: the pain is worse
Since last month's visit. But she only complains

About the carpenters. "Two of them are *negroes*,
And you know how they are. Your father has
To watch them all the time." The chemo's

Bleached her eyebrows to down, her voice a rasp
From radiation, red burn etching her throat and face.
Pineboards, hammers, sacks of nails. And now the stiff embrace.

vii.
Writing Desk, 1990

Frost starred window, rented house, the stiff embrace
We hold in photographs above my desk.
Mother and father, mother and son, faces
Sharing noses, cheekbones, our immeasurable strangeness

To each other. Perspective is a lie,
A blurred collage, and where does it carry us,
This trio waving from a thirty-year-old Chevy
Christmas morning, window spattered with frost,

Colorless now, outside of history?
How would she tally fragments such as these?
I must be watching from the half-lit hallway

As she bends to the numbers. Neither of us speaks.
I move to the door, the churn of the adding machines
Fixing us here. The columns hypnotize.

C. D. WRIGHT ❖

Our Dust

I am your ancestor. You know next-to-nothing
about me.
There is no reason for you to imagine
the rooms I occupied or my heavy hair.
Not the faint vinegar smell of me. Or
the rubbered damp
of Forrest and I coupling on the landing
en route to our detached day.

You didn't know my weariness, error, incapacity.
I was the poet

Most Recent Book: FURTHER ADVENTURES WITH YOU
(Carnegie Mellon University Press, 1986)

of shadow work and towns with quarter-inch
phone books, of failed
roadside zoos. The poet of yard eggs and
sharpening shops,
jobs at the weapons plant and the Mabelline
factory on the penitentiary road.

A poet of spiderwort and jacks-in-the-pulpit,
hollyhocks against the tool shed.
An unsmiling dark blond.
The one with the trowel in her handbag.
I dug up protected and private things.
That sort, I was.
My graves went undecorated and my churches
abandoned. This wasn't planned, but practice.

I was the poet of short-tailed cats and yellow
line paint.
Of satellite dishes and Peterbilt trucks. Red Man
Chewing Tobacco, Black Cat Fireworks, Triple Hit
Creme Soda. Also of dirt dobbers, nightcrawlers,
martin houses, honey, and whetstones
from the Novaculite Uplift. What remained
of The Uplift.
I had registered dogs 4 sale; rocks, shit,
and straw.
I was a poet of hummingbird hives along with
redheaded stepbrothers.

The poet of good walking shoes—a necessity
in vernacular parts—and push mowers.
The rumor that I was once seen sleeping
in a refrigerator box is false (he was a brother
who hated me).
Nor was I the one lunching at the Governor's
mansion.

I didn't work off a grid. Or prime the surface
if I could get off without it. I made
simple music
out of sticks and string. On side B of me,
experimental guitar, night repairs and suppers
such as this.
You could count on me to make a bad situation
worse like putting liquid make-up over
a passion mark.

I never raised your rent. Or anyone else's by God.
Never said I loved you. The future gave me chills.
I used the medium to say: Arise arise and
come together.
Free your children. Come on everybody. Let's start
with Baltimore.

Believe me I am not being modest when I
admit my life doesn't bear repeating. I
agreed to be the poet of one life,
one death alone. I have seen myself
in the black car. I have seen the retreat
of the black car.

Kings' Daughters, Home for Unwed Mothers, 1948

Somewhere there figures a man. In uniform. He's not white. He
could be AWOL. Sitting on a mattress riddled with cigarette burns.
Night of a big game in the capitol. Big snow.
Beyond Pearl river past Petal and Leaf River and Macedonia;
it is a three-storied house. The only hill around. White.
The house and hill are white. Lighted upstairs, down.
She is up on her elbows, bangs wet and in her eyes. The head
of the unborn is visible at the opening. The head
crowns. Many helping hands are on her. She is told not to push.
But breathe. A firm voice.
With helping hands. They open the howl of her love. Out of her issues:

volumes of letters, morning glories on a string trellis, the job
at the Mabelline Factory, the job at the weapons plant, the hummingbird
hive, her hollyhocks, her grandmother's rigid back next to her
grandfather's bow, the briefest reflection of her mother's braid
falling below her wing blades, her atomizers and silverbacked
brush and comb, the steel balls under her father's knuckles, the
moon's punched-out face, his two-dollar neckties, the peacock
coming down the drive; there was the boy shuffling her way with
the melon on his shoulder, car dust all over his light clothes, the
Black Cat fireworks sign on the barn, her father's death from
moving the barn by himself, the family sitting in the darkened
room drinking ice tea after the funeral, tires blown out on the
macadam, the women beaten like eggs, the store with foundation
garments, and boys pelting the girls with peony buds, the meatgrinder
cringing in the corner of the store, the old icebox she couldn't

fix and couldn't sell so buried to keep out the kids, her grandmother's
pride, the prettiest lavalier, the pole houses; there was the boy
with the melon shifted to the other shoulder, coming her way,
grown taller and darker, wiping his sweat with his hand, his beautiful
Nubian head, older and set upon by the longingly necked girls
from the bottoms, his fishing hole, learning the equations of equality:
six for the white man and none for the rest; the sloping shadows
and blue hollows behind his shack, what the sunflowers saw, the
wide skirts she wore, the lizards they caught, the eagerness with
which they went through each other's folds of hair and skin, the
boy's outnumbered pride.

This couldn't go on, the difficulty of concealment, putting make-up
over a passion mark. 1947, summer of whiskey and victory and
fear. It was long, then over. The letters burned. She heaves. Bleeds.
In the words of the grandmother: Do not eat oranges under the moon,
eat fruit that is green and cold. What was meant by that, really.
The infant's head is huge. She tears. He's white. He'll make it
just fine. The firm voice. The hands that helped.
What would become of this boychild. The uniformed man and she
will never know. That they will outlive him. They will never know.
That he will do things they never dreamed.

Scratch Music

How many threads have I broken with my teeth. How many
times have I looked at the stars and felt ill. Time here is
divided into before and since your shuttering in 1978. I remember
hanging onto the hood of the big-fendered Olds with a mess
of money in my purse. Call that romance. Some memory
precedes you: when I wanted lederhosen because I'd read
Heidi. And how I wanted my folks to build a fall-out shelter
so I could arrange the cans. And coveting mother's muskrat.
I remember college. And being in Vista: I asked the librarian
in Banks, the state's tomato capitol, if she had any black
literature and she said they used to have *Lil Black Sambo*
but the white children tore out pages and wrote ugly words
inside. Someone said if I didn't like Banks I should go to
Moscow. I said, Come on, let's go outside and shoot the hoop.
I've got a jones to beat your butt. I haven't changed. Now
if I think of the earth's origins, I get vertigo. When I think
of its death, I fall. I've picked up a few things. I know if

you want songbirds, plant berry trees. If you don't want
birds, buy a rubber snake. I remember that town with the
Alcoa plant I toured. The manager kept referring to the
workers as Alcoans. I thought of hundreds of flexible metal
beings bent over assemblages. They sparked. What would
I do in Moscow. I have these dreams—relatives loom over
my bed. We should put her to sleep Lonnie says. Go home
old girl, go home, my aunt says. Why should I go home before
her I want to say. But I am bereft. So how is Life in the
Other World. Do you get the news. Are you allowed a pet.
But I wanted to show you how I've grown, what I know:
I keep my bees far from the stable, they can't stand how
horses smell. And I know sooner or later an old house will
need a new roof. And more than six years have whistled
by since you blew your heart out like the porch light. Reason
and meaning don't step into another lit spot like a well-meaning
stranger with a hat. And mother's mother who has lived
in the same house ten times six years, told me, We didn't
know we had termites until they swarmed. Then we had
to pull up the whole floor. 'Too late, no more . . . ,' you know
the poem. But you, you bastard. You picked up a gun in winter
as if it were a hat and you were leaving a restaurant: full,
weary, and thankful to be spending the evening with no one.

More Blues and the Abstract Truth

In the mornings we're in the dark;
even at the end of June
the zucchini keep on the sill.
Call Grandmother for advice
and she says O you know
I used to grow so many things.

Hair appears on my chest in dreams;
I back the car over a soft, large object.
The paperboy comes to collect
with a pitbull. Ring Grandmother
and she says Well you know
death is death and none other.

Then there's the frequent bleeding,
the tender nipples and the rot
under the floormat. If I'm not seeing

a cold-eyed doctor it is
another gouging mechanic.
Grandmother says Thanks to the blue rugs
and Eileen Briscoe's elms
the house keeps cool.

Well. Then. You say. Grandmother
let me just ask you this:
How does a body rise again and rinse
her mouth from the tap. And how
does a body put in a plum tree
or lie again on top of another body
or string a trellis. Or go on drying
the flatware. Fix rainbow trout. Grout the tile.
Buy a bag of onions. Beat an egg stiff. Yes,

how does the cat continue
to lick itself from toenail to tail hole.
And how does a body break
bread with the word when the word
has broken. Again. And. Again.
With the wine. And the loaf.
And the excellent glass
of the body. And she says,

Even. If. The. Sky. Is. Falling.
My. Peace. Rose. Is. In. Bloom.

FRANZ WRIGHT ❖

Certain Tall Buildings

J.A.

I know a little
about it: I know
if you contemplate suicide
long enough, it
begins to contemplate you—
oh, it has plans for you.
It calls to your attention

Most Recent Book: Entry in an Unknown Hand: (Carnegie Mellon University Press, 1989)

the windows of certain tall
buildings, wooded snow fields
in your memory where you might cunningly vanish
to remotely, undiscoverably
sleep. Remember your mother
hanging the cat
in front of you when you were four?

Why not that? That
should fix her. Or deep drugs
glibly prescribed by psychiatrists weary
as you of your failure to change
into someone else—
you'll show them
change.

These thoughts, occurring once too often,
are no longer your own. No,
they think you.
The thing is not to entertain them
in the first place, dear
life, friend.
Don't leave me here without you.

The Needle: For a Friend Who Disappeared

Just one more time. Only one—
the small rose of blood blooming in the syringe—
one to compel haunted speech to the lips,
sure. Some immense seconds pass. Dusk's
prow slowly glides right up Avenue B;
the young Schumann's two personalities
continue discussing each other
in the diary. Your eyes
move to the warning
on a pack of cigarettes—
good thing you're not pregnant!
Still no speech, but no pain either,
no New York,
nothing,
sweet.
You happen to know that you're home.
And how simple it was, and how smart

to come back: in the moon
on its oak branch
the owl slowly opens
its eyes like a just severed head
that hears its name called out,
and spreads its wings
and disappears;
and the moth leaves the print
of its lips on the glass, lights
on the lamp's still-warm bulb,
the napper's forehead,
his hand, where it rests
down the chair arm,
fingers
slowly opening.

Entry in an Unknown Hand

And still nothing happens. I am not arrested.
By some inexplicable oversight

nobody jeers when I walk down the street.

I have been allowed to go on living in this
room. I am not asked to explain my presence
anywhere.

What posthypnotic suggestions were made; and
are any left unexecuted?

Why am I so distressed at the thought of taking
certain jobs?

They are absolutely shameless at the bank—
you'd think my name meant nothing to them. Non-
chalantly they hand me the sum I've requested,

but I know them. It's like this everywhere—

they think they are going to surprise me: I,
who do nothing but wait.

Once I answered the phone, and the caller hung up—
very clever.

They think that they can scare me.

I am always scared.

And how much courage it requires to get up in the morning and dress yourself. Nobody congratulates you!

At no point in the day may I fall to my knees and refuse to go on, it's not done.

I go on

dodging cars that jump the curb to crush my hip,

accompanied by abrupt bursts of black-and-white laughter and applause,

past a million unlighted windows, peered out at by the retired and their aged attack-dogs—

toward my place,

the one at the end of the counter,

the scalpel on the napkin.

Elegy: Breece D'J Pancake

We can always be found
seated at a bar
the glass before us
empty, with our halos
of drunk flies—
or standing
in the dark across the street
from the Sacramento
Coroner's. (And my friend
we're all in there
floating along
the ceiling, tethered
to our laughing gas canisters). We are
old people shopping,
next winter's ghosts,
the prostitute
in her mortician's make-up
strolling York Avenue at 3 a.m.,
the fellow in Atlantic City

furtively pawning a doll.
Quick suture,
lightning,
hush-finger—
cheap eeriness of windchimes—
summer thunder
from a cloudless sky . . .
The abandoned abandon.
There are no adults.
You're dead,
but look who's talking.

DEAN YOUNG ❖

Storms

I've been sweating again, a symptom
so far only of itself just as those stray
explosions belong to no holiday,
no larger sequence of battle. Years ago
in another house, I'd wake like this
and stalk the other rooms, naked and
monstrously alive as if a thousand ears
had sprung from my skin. Sometimes
back in bed, a woman would be sobbing hard,
hiccupping, so I'd get a glass of water
that would harp the walls, get the pills
from her purse, stroke her until they worked.
Other nights she'd be waiting,
wetting herself with her hand and rapidly
we'd fuck, panting like harnessed dogs
who didn't know miles ago their master
had frozen in the sled. Stop? No one
can stop. It starts out Wednesday then
it's Tuesday and you're sitting with A
in a cafe under some ornamental masks.
She's disturbed. You're disturbed.
A whole cloudburst of disturbance.
Inside the purple mask, there's more feathers,

Most Recent Book: DESIGN WITH X (Wesleyan University Press, 1988)

each with a quill directed inward, against
the face. Awful to be in it as well as
outside of it, hooting with fear. Will A
stay with B and is B's cancer-riddled mother
choosing this exact moment to die, can anyone
actually choose a moment to die, choose
to die at all and what is a moment anyway
but a thing made entirely of its own vanishing?
It all gets complex fast. You're just
sitting there, nodding, then BOOM, the temple's
in ruins and the emperor has you up at dawn
beating the ocean with chains. I wonder
if C will ever forgive me and will D ever
pick up his phone? Then the dream of the sun.
Then the dream of the black dogs and
saying yes in the desert. There were those
masks on the terrified wall. Maybe she *should* go.
Maybe I should explain. When the fire next door
is out, the firemen loiter and smoke in the rain.
Who hasn't wanted to be a fireman
in a rubber raincoat, everything ash and hissing?
In the rain she decided to leave him
and in the rain she decided to go back.
Such friendships and fires. Such lies
and masks and love. I've only myself to blame.
In the rain we were singing. In the rain
I am empty. I am struck. In the rain
I am pilfering and wanton and struck.

Threshold

After the sagittal and lateral cuts
with the .07 saw into the parietal
and frontal bones, I peel back
the fibrous dura mater. The brain
is glossy, tied in and upon itself
like worms mating. 231
says my friend's brass earring
but, laying my hand across his frontal lobe,
I should know him better. Imagine
touching someone like this,
someone I wouldn't know on the street

even if I held a match to his cigarette,
even if the match didn't seem to light
until a long time after striking.
Under my palm is what the texts call
the region of higher intellect,
which means I could be handling
his life's work on chemical thresholds,
the microscopy of water about
to boil. Next week, I'll cut down
to the hypothalamic nuclei, no bigger
than a thumb, where some neurologists say
there's a spot that could keep us
happy forever.

I'm lucky my lab's this close
to the school of music, the carillon,
and I wish I could make that music
of ice and ice's melting. Yes, I know all about
how it's just a keyboard connected to a computer
and there's no ropes, no harsh November air
unless a window's open. And I know there's no
pulling hard then being lifted
by the low notes that thicken like clouds.
Still, at any moment we can be carried skyward,
there's so little to us.

Other Obit

Night, what more do you want? Why this second per second
scream? My friend Nick used to sit all night in the same
booth all night with a pile of quarters for pinball and
jukebox. He loved the one where the balls disappeared
up the bonus-lit chute. He loved the song where the wife
smelled shirts, all tilt and jilt and sometimes he'd
bring back a waitress who'd play the records we never
played. You know the ones, everyone has those records. It
was the age of Aquarius and once we wanted to remember
the comedy, movies, the primitive flutes. I'd come down
and there they'd be, nearly glamorous with smoke and wine,
all the shades pulled. Night, even then you couldn't give
up, there was your lariat in the corner, your ashes
everywhere. It might have been the drugs we kept zip-

locked in the cranial cavity of, a pig, a skull Nick
found where a pig had died or at least a pig's head had
died. Aren't I cute? Don't you like my legs? Night, what
pleases you? From the beginning, the body's full of
holes. Night, these are the facts and the philosophy of
facts. See how they grin back fast faces like the 23
windows he fell past. Jumped past. When does a jump
become a fall? There were a few more floors but 23 was
enough, enough climbing he must have thought then opened
the window by the stairs. I thought at least there'd be
a note. Help or a simple declarative sentence. They
seemed to take forever with the organ, the hothouse
arrangements and how his parents hated me that open-hole
day. Adios, au revoir, good night. You want me on my
knees? I'm on my knees. When I was a child I'd listen to
the owls rouse their fiefdoms. Say the little prayer.
When I was a child. When I was a cantaloupe. When I was
an enemy spacecraft hovering over the Pentagon. Tick
tock and such a puddle. Tick tock my soul to keep. Tick
tock and such deep wagons on so many panged wheels.

Lace

While crickets tighten their solitary bolts
and morning's still dark-tousled,
the steady fan, steady turbine of summer mist,
each engine, planet, floating spark,
each person roams a room in my heart,
mother snaps beans into a bowl, father
blows smoke out through the screen door
and my wife lifts her arm to look at her arm,
the amethyst-and-platinum bracelet, in slats
of amber light, caught like a bee in sap.

After the afternoon hammock, beer bottles
loosening their labels with sweat, after
fireflies ignite like far city lights
that tease, devouring and devoured like stars
that fall, hampered with lust and weight,
I wait for her to come to bed, the water
in the pipes a kind of signal like locking
doors, turning the sheets and sleep

like a shell smoothed in the waves' lathe
and the kiss cool with fatigue and mint.

Before the delicate downward yearning of snow,
the winter wools and wafts of cedar, naphtha
and dry winter heat, the opaque wrapping
done and undone, burning in the grate,
before the gray vaulted shape of each burned thing,
the bitter medicinal dust, old lace and its cobweb
dream breaking in my hand, each thread frays, knots
give and knot again like roots into stem,
the stem unraveling into flower, into flame,
into seed and wind, into dirt, into into into.

Acknowledgments

Barbara Anderson: "Deuce: 12:23 a.m." is used by permission of the author. Copyright © 1991 Barbara Anderson.

Ralph Angel: "The River Has No Hair to Hold Onto" first appeared in *Cimarron Review* and is used by permission of the author. Copyright © 1990 Ralph Angel. "Shadow Play" first appeared in *Poetry* and is used by permission of *Poetry* and the author. Copyright © 1987 Modern Poetry Association. "Man in a Window" is reprinted from *Anxious Latitudes* by permission of Wesleyan University Press, University Press of New England and the author. Copyright © 1986 Ralph Angel. "Breaking and Entering" is used by permission of the author. Copyright © 1991 Ralph Angel.

Jimmy Santiago Baca: "I Am Here," "Green Chile," and "Main Character" are reprinted from *Black Mesa Poems* by permission of New Directions and the author. Copyright © 1989 Jimmy Santiago Baca.

Stephen Berg: "The Coat" and "Self-Portrait at Six" are used by permission of the author. Copyright © 1991 Stephen Berg. "And the Scream" is reprinted from *In It* by permission of University of Illinois Press and the author. Copyright © 1986 Stephen Berg.

Linda Bierds: "Off the Aleutian Chain" and "The Stillness, The Dancing" are reprinted from *The Stillness, The Dancing* by permission of Henry Holt and Company and the author. Copyright © 1988 Linda Bierds. "For the Sake of Retrieval" first appeared in *Atlantic Monthly* and is reprinted by permission of the author. Copyright © 1990 Linda Bierds.

Lorna Dee Cervantes: "Raisins" and "From the Bus to E.L. at Atascadero State Hospital" are used by permission of the author. Copyright © 1991 Lorna Dee Cervantes. "Colorado Blvd." is reprinted from *From the Cables of Genocide: Poems on Love and Hunger* by permission of Arte Publico Press and the author. Copyright © 1990 Lorna Dee Cervantes.

David Clewell: "We Never Close" and "This Book Belongs to Susan Someone" are reprinted from *Blessings in Disguise* by permission of Viking Penguin, a division of Penguin Books USA, Inc. and the author. Copyright © 1989 David Clewell.

Peter Cooley: "The Soul," "Holy Family: Audubon Zoo, New Orleans," and "The History of Poetry" are reprinted from *The Astonished Hours* by permission of Carnegie Mellon University Press and the author. Copyright © 1991 Peter Cooley. "The Zouave" and "Self-Portrait as Van Gogh" are reprinted from *The Van Gogh Notebook* by permission of Carnegie Mellon University Press and the author. Copyright © 1987 Peter Cooley.

Mark Cox: "Archaic Torso of My Uncle Phil," "Geese," "Poem for the Name Mary," "In This His Suit," and "The Word" are reprinted from *Smoulder* by permission of David R. Godine, Publisher, and the author. Copyright © 1989 Mark Cox.

Kate Daniels: "Christmas Party" and "For Miklos Radnoti: 1909-1944" are reprinted from *The White Wave* by permission of University of Pittsburgh Press and the author. Copyright © 1984 Kate Daniels. "Bathing" is reprinted from *The Niobe Poems* by permission of University of Pittsburgh Press and the author. Copyright © 1988 Kate Daniels.

Toi Derricotte: "Blackbottom," "Christmas Eve: My Mother Dressing," "The Minks," and "On the Turning Up of Unidentified Black Female Corpses" are reprinted from *Captivity* by permission of University of Pittsburgh Press and the author. Copyright © 1989 Toi Derricotte.

Deborah Digges: "Rock, Scissors, Paper" is used by permission of the author. Copyright © 1991 Deborah Digges.

Stephen Dobyns: "Tomatoes" is reprinted from *Cemetery Nights* by permission of Viking Penguin, a division of Penguin Books, USA, Inc. and the author. Copyright © 1987 Stephen Dobyns. "Desire" and "Shaving" are reprinted from *Body Traffic* by permission of Viking Penguin and the author. Copyright © 1990 Stephen Dobyns.

Mark Doty: "Adonis Theater," "Heaven," and "Night Ferry" are reprinted from *Bethlehem in Broad Daylight* by permission of David R. Godine, Publisher, and the author. Copyright © 1991 Mark Doty.

Rita Dove: "Elevator Man, 1949" first appeared in *The Black Scholar* and is used by permission of the author. Copyright © 1988 Rita Dove. "Used" first appeared in *Atlantic Monthly* and is used by permission of the author. Copyright © 1989 Rita Dove. "Sonnet in Primary Colors" first appeared in *Sojourner* and is used by permission of the author. Copyright © 1989 Rita Dove. "Persephone, Falling" and "Persephone Underground" first appeared in *Sequoia* and are used by permission of the author. Copyright © 1988 Rita Dove. "Cameos" first appeared in *Agni* and is used by permission of the author. Copyright © 1982 Rita Dove.

Norman Dubie: "Radio Sky" first appeared in *Kenyon Review* and is used by permission of the author. Copyright © 1989 Norman Dubie. "The Diatribe of the Kite" first appeared in *American Poetry Review* and is used by permission of the author. Copyright © 1990 Norman Dubie. "The Apocrypha of Jacques Derrida" and "Trakl" are reprinted from *Groom Falconer* by permission of W.W. Norton & Company, Inc. and the author. Copyright © 1990 Norman Dubie. "The Elegy for Integral Domains" is reprinted from *The Springhouse* by permission of W.W. Norton & Company, Inc. and the author. Copyright © 1986 Norman Dubie.

Stephen Dunn: "The Routine Things Around the House" is reprinted from *Not Dancing* by permission of Carnegie Mellon University Press and the author. Copyright © 1984 Stephen Dunn. "At the Smithville Methodist Church" and "He/She" are reprinted from *Local Time* by permission of William Morrow and Co., Inc. and the author. Copyright © 1986 Stephen Dunn.

Lynn Emanuel: "Frying Trout while Drunk," "When Father Decided He Did Not Love Her Anymore," and "Of Your Father's Indiscretions and the Train to California" are reprinted from *Hotel Fiesta* by permission of University of Georgia Press and the author. Copyright © 1984 Lynn Emanuel. "Inspiration" and "Blond Bombshell" are reprinted from *The Technology of Love* by permission of Abattoir Editions and the author. Copyright © 1988 Lynn Emanuel and Abattoir Editions. "On Waking after Dreaming of Raoul" is used by permission of the author. Copyright © 1991 Lynn Emanuel.

John Engman: "Mushroom Clouds," "Atlantis," and "One Minute of Night Sky" are reprinted from *Keeping Still, Mountain* by permission of Galileo Press and the author. Copyright © 1983 John Engman. "Staff" first appeared in *Virginia Quarterly* and is used by permission of the author. Copyright © 1988 John Engman. "Another Word for Blue" is reprinted from *Minnesota Writes: Poetry* by permission of Milkweed Editions/Nodin Press. Copyright © 1987 John Engman.

Alice Fulton: "Cherry Bombs," "Powers Of Congress," and "Self-Storage" are reprinted from *Powers Of Congress* by permission of David R. Godine, Publisher, and the author. Copyright © 1990 Alice Fulton.

Tess Gallagher: "Each Bird Walking" is reprinted from *Amplitude: New and Selected Poems* by permission of Graywolf Press and the author. Copyright © 1987 Tess Gallagher. "Strange Thanksgiving," "Red Poppy," and "Now That I Am Never Alone" first appeared in *The New Yorker* and is reprinted from *Moon Bridge Crossing* by permission of Graywolf Press and the author. Copyright © 1989 Tess Gallagher. "After the Chinese" is reprinted from *Moon*

Bridge Crossing by permission of Graywolf Press and the author. Copyright © 1991 Tess Gallagher.

Louise Glück: "Brown Circle," "Paradise," "Widows," "Lullaby," and "Amazons" are reprinted from *Ararat* by permission of The Ecco Press and the author. Copyright © 1990 Louise Glück.

Albert Goldbarth: "How the World Works: an essay" and "The Nile" are reprinted from *Heaven and Earth: A Cosmology* by permission of University of Georgia Press and the author. Copyright © 1991 Albert Goldbarth.

Beckian Fritz Goldberg: "The Possibilities," "In the Middle of Things, Begin," and "To a Girl Writing Her Father's Death," first appeared in *Crazyhorse* and are used by permission of the author. Copyright © 1991 Beckian Fritz Goldberg. "Monsoon" first appeared in *American Poetry Review* and is used by permission of the author. Copyright © 1990 Beckian Fritz Goldberg. "In the Badlands of Desire" is reprinted by permission of the author. Copyright © 1991 Beckian Fritz Goldberg.

Barry Goldensohn: "The Marrano," "American Innocents, Oberlin, Ohio, 1954," "Honeymoon," and "Post Mortem as Angels" are reprinted from *The Marrano* by permission of the National Poetry Foundation and the author. Copyright © 1988 Barry Goldensohn.

Jorie Graham: "Salmon" is reprinted from *Erosion* by permission of Princeton University Press and the author. Copyright © 1983 Princeton University Press. "What the End Is For" is reprinted from *The End of Beauty* by permission of The Ecco Press and the author. Copyright © 1987 Jorie Graham.

Mark Halliday: "Reality U.S.A." and "Seventh Avenue" first appeared in *Crazyhorse* and is used by permission of the author. Copyright © 1989 Mark Halliday. "Population" first appeared in *New England Review/Bread Loaf Quarterly* and is used by permission of the author. Copyright © 1986 Mark Halliday.

Joy Harjo: "Petroglyph" is reprinted from *The Jaune Quick-To-See Smith Catalogue* by permission of the University Art Museum of the University of California at Long Beach and the author. Copyright © 1990 Joy Harjo. "Grace" first appeared in *Rhetoric Review* and is used by permission of the author. Copyright © 1989 Joy Harjo. "Santa Fe" is reprinted from *In Mad Love and War* by permission of Wesleyan University Press, University Press of New England and the author. Copyright © 1989 Joy Harjo. "Blue Elliptic" first appeared in *Continental Drifter* and is used by permission of the author. Copyright © 1986 Joy Harjo.

Robert Hass: "Human Wishes," "Vintage," "A Story about the Body," and "The Privilege of Being" are reprinted from *Human Wishes* by permission of The Ecco Press and the author. Copyright © 1989 Robert Hass.

William Hathaway: "A Poem in Response to Doom" first appeared in *Crazyhorse* and is used by permission of the author. Copyright © 1989 William Hathaway. "Wan Hope" is reprinted from *Looking into the Heart of Light* by permission of University of Central Florida Press and the author. Copyright © 1988 William Hathaway.

Edward Hirsch: "After the Last Practice" first appeared in *The Kenyon Review* and is used by permission of the author. Copyright © 1990 Edward Hirsch. "Art Pepper" is used by permission of the author. Copyright © 1991.

Tony Hoagland: "One Season" and "Sweet Ruin" are reprinted from *History of Desire* by permission of Moon Pony Press and the author. Copyright © 1990 Tony Hoagland. "Poem for Men Only" is used by permission of the author. Copyright © 1991 Tony Hoagland.

Jonathan Holden: "Wisdom Tooth" and "Against Paradise" are reprinted from *Against Paradise* by permission of University of Utah Press and the author. Copyright © 1990 Jonathan Holden. "Tumbleweed" first appeared in *Cimarron Review* and is used by permission of the author. Copyright © 1989 Jonathan Holden.

Garrett Hongo: "Four Chinatown Figures," "The Underworld," and "The Legend" are reprinted from *The River of Heaven* by permission of Alfred A. Knopf and the author. Copyright © 1988 Garrett Hongo.

Marie Howe: "The Split," "Without Devotion," "Part of Eve's Discussion," and "Death, the Last Visit" are reprinted from *The Good Thief* by permission of Persea Books, Inc. and the author. Copyright © 1988 Marie Howe.

Lynda Hull: "Love Song During Riot with Many Voices: Newark, 1967," "Frugal Repasts," and "Shore Leave" are reprinted from *Star Ledger* by permission of University of Iowa Press and the author. Copyright © 1991 Lynda Hull.

Terry Hummer: "Austerity in Vermont," "Mississippi 1955 Confessional," "A Heart Attack in the Country," and "Spring Comes to Mid-Ohio in a Holy Shower of Stars" are reprinted from *The 18,000-Ton Olympic Dream* by permission of William Morrow and Co., Inc. and the author. Copyright © 1990 Terry Hummer.

Cynthia Huntington: "Breaking" first appeared in *The Kenyon Review* and is used by permission of the author. Copyright © 1989 Cynthia Huntington. "The Hackeysack Players," "Party," and "Rhapsody" by permission of the author. Copyright © 1991 Cynthia Huntington.

Richard Jackson: "Homeric" first appeared in *Passages North* and is used by permission of the author. Copyright © 1991 Richard Jackson. "A Violation" first appeared in *Crazyhorse* and is used by permission of the author. Copyright © 1991 Richard Jackson. "The Angels of 1912 and 1972" first appeared in *The Indiana Review* and is used by permission of the author. Copyright © 1989 Richard Jackson.

Mark Jarman: "Ground Swell" first appeared in *The Indiana Review* and is used by permission of the author. Copyright © 1988 Mark Jarman. "The Black Riviera" and "The Shrine and the Burning Wheel" are reprinted from *The Black Riviera* by permission of University Press of New England. Copyright © 1990 Mark Jarman. "The Black Riviera" first appeared in *The New Yorker* magazine.

Richard Jones: "The Bell," "The Mechanic," "The Hearing Aid," "The Birds," and "Leaving Town after the Funeral" are reprinted from *Country of Air* by permission of Copper Canyon Press and the author. Copyright © 1986 Richard Jones. "Wan Chu's Wife in Bed" first appeared in *The Quarterly* and is used by permission of the author. Copyright © 1990. "Certain People" is used by permission of the author. Copyright © 1990 Richard Jones.

Rodney Jones: "Mule," "Caught," and "The Weepers" are reprinted from *Transparent Gestures* by permission of Houghton Mifflin and the author. Copyright © 1989 Rodney Jones.

Richard Katrovas: "The Beating" and "A Dog and a Boy" are reprinted from *Snug Harbour* by permission of Wesleyan University Press, University Press of New England and the author. Copyright © 1986 Richard Katrovas. "The Public Mirror" and "My Friends the Pigeons" are reprinted from *The Public Mirror* by permission of Wesleyan University Press, University Press of New England and the author. Copyright © 1990 Richard Katrovas.

Brigit Pegeen Kelly: "Young Wife's Lament" and "Those Who Wrestle with the Angel for Us" are reprinted from *To the Place of Trumpets* by permission of Yale University Press. Copyright © 1988 Yale University Press. "Wild Turkeys: The Dignity of the Damned" and "Silver Lake" are used by permission of the author.

Yusef Komunyakaa: "Temples of Smoke" and "Blackberries" first appeared in *Ploughshares* and are used by permission of the author. Copyright © 1989 Yusef Komunyakaa. "Venus's-flytraps" first appeared in *Ploughshares* and is used by permission of the author. Copyright © 1988 Yusef Komunyakaa. "Sunday Afternoons" first appeared in *Literary Supplement* and is used by permission of the author. Copyright © 1989 Yusef Komunyakaa.

Sydney Lea: "Prayer for the Little City" and "Museum" are reprinted from *Prayer for the Little City* by permission of Scribners and the author. Copyright © 1990 Sydney Lea.

Li-Young Lee: "The Cleaving" is reprinted from *The City in Which I Love You* by permission of Boa Editions and the author. Copyright © 1990 Li-Young Lee.

David Lehman: "Enigma Variations" is reprinted from *An Alternative to Speech* by permission of Princeton University Press and the author. Copyright © 1986 David Lehman. "Spontaneous Combustion," "Operation Memory," "Perfidia," and "Fear" are reprinted from *Operation Memory* by permission of Princeton University Press and the author. Copyright © 1990 Princeton University Press.

Larry Levis: "The Widening Spell of the Leaves" is reprinted from *The Widening Spell of the Leaves* by permission of University of Pittsburgh Press and the author. Copyright © 1990 Larry Levis.

Robert Long: "Have a Nice Day," "What Happens," "Saying One Thing," and "Found and Lost" are reprinted from *What Happens* by permission of Galileo Press and the author. Copyright © 1988 Robert Long. "Fumetti" first appeared in *Cimarron Review* and is used by permission of the author. Copyright © 1990 Robert Long.

Adrian C. Louis: "Wakinyan," "Rhetoric Leads to Cliché," "Indian College Blues," "Couch Fantasy," and "The First of the Month" are reprinted from *Fire Water World* by permission of West End Press and the author. Copyright © 1989 Adrian C. Louis.

Heather McHugh: "Earthmoving Malediction," "Inflation," "Place Where Things Got," and "Third Person Neuter" are reprinted from *Shades* by permission of Wesleyan University Press, University Press of New England and the author. Copyright © 1988 Heather McHugh.

Lynne McMahon: "Convalescence," "Barbie's Ferrari," and "Ann Lee" first appeared in *American Poetry Review* and are used by permission of the author. Copyright © 1988 Lynne McMahon. "Devolution of the Nude" first appeared in *Pacific Poetry and Fiction Review* and is used by permission of the author. Copyright © 1988 Lynne McMahon. "Little Elegy for the Age" first appeared in *Crazyhorse* and is used by permission of the author. Copyright © 1989 Lynne McMahon.

Gail Mazur: "Spring Planting" is reprinted from *The Pose of Happiness* by permission of David R. Godine, Publisher, and the author. Copyright © 1986 Gail Mazur. "Phonic" and "Family Plot, October" first appeared in *Agni* and are used by permission of the author. Copyright © 1990 Gail Mazur. "May, Home after a Year Away" is used by permission of the author. Copyright © 1991 Gail Mazur.

Susan Mitchell: "Havana Birth" first appeared in *Ploughshares* and is reprinted by permission of the author. Copyright © 1989 Susan Mitchell. "Feeding the Ducks at the Howard Johnson Motel" first appeared in *The Quarterly* and is reprinted by permission of the author. Copyright © 1989 Susan Mitchell. "The Face" first appeared in *Ironwood* and is used by permission of the author. Copyright © 1988 Susan Mitchell.

Paul Monette: "Brother of the Mount of Olives" is reprinted from *Love Alone* by permission of St. Martin's Press and the author. Copyright © 1988 Paul Monette.

David Rivard: "Summons" first appeared in *North American Review* and is used by permission of the author. Copyright © 1991 David Rivard. "Naive Invocation" first appeared in *Ironwood* and is used by permission of the author. Copyright © 1989 David Rivard. "Earth to Tell of the Beasts" first appeared in *Crazyhorse* and is used by permission of the author. Copyright © 1989 David Rivard. "Later History" first appeared in *Antioch Review* and is used by permission of the author. Copyright © 1991 David Rivard.

Pattiann Rogers: "The Hummingbird: A Seduction" and "The Power of Toads" are reprinted from *The Tattooed Lady in the Garden* by permission of Wesleyan University Press, University Press of New England and the author. Copyright © 1986 Pattiann Rogers. "Geocentric" first appeared in *Poetry East* and is used by permission of the author. Copyright © 1986 Pattiann Rogers. "The Next Story" is reprinted from *Splitting and Binding* by permission of Wesleyan University Press, University Press of New England and the author. Copyright © 1989 Pattiann Rogers.

Michael Ryan: "Not the End of the World," "TV Room at the Children's Hospice," and "Switchblade" are reprinted from *God Hunger* by permission of Viking Penguin, a division of Penguin Books, USA, Inc. and the author. Copyright © 1989 Michael Ryan.

Ira Sadoff: "Nazis," "At the Half Note Café," and "The Bath" are reprinted from *Emotional Traffic* by permission of David R. Godine, Publisher, and the author. Copyright © 1990 Ira Sadoff.

David St. John: "Terraces of Rain" and "I Know" originally appeared in *Anteaus*. Copyright © 1990 David St. John. "Leap of Faith," "Wavelength," and "Meridian" are reprinted from *No Heaven* by permission of Houghton Mifflin Co. and the author. Copyright © 1985 David St. John.

Sherod Santos: "Inspiration," "Nineteen Fifty-five," and "The Air Base at Châteauroux, France" are reprinted from *The Southern Reaches* by permission of Wesleyan University Press, University Press of New England and the author. Copyright © 1989 Sherod Santos.

Philip Schultz: "The Quality," "For My Mother," "Pumpernickel," and "Ode" are reprinted from *Deep Within the Ravine* by permission of Viking Penguin, a division of Penguin Books, USA, Inc. and the author. Copyright © 1984 Philip Schultz. "The Answering Machine" first appeared in *Poetry* and is used by permission of the author. Copyright © 1988 Philip Schultz.

Tim Seibles: "Trying for Fire" first appeared in *Cimarron Review* and is used by permission of the author. Copyright © 1990 Tim Seibles. "Wind" and "For Brothers Everywhere" are used by permission of the author. Copyright © 1991 Tim Seibles.

Dave Smith: "Championship Fight," "A Quilt in the Bennington College Library," "Pulling a Pig's Tail," and "Cuba Night" are reprinted from *Cuba Night* by permission of William Morrow and Co., Inc. and the author. Copyright © 1990 Dave Smith.

Marcia Southwick: "Brothers," "The Rain's Marriage," "Horse on the Wall," and "Child, Invisible Fire" are reprinted from *Why the River Disappears* by permission of Carnegie Mellon University Press and the author. Copyright © 1990 Marcia Southwick.

Elizabeth Spires: "Sunday Afternoon at Fulham Palace," "The Beds," and "Mutoscope" are reprinted from *Annonciade* by permission of Viking Penguin, a division of Penguin Books, USA, Inc. and the author. Copyright © 1989 Elizabeth Spires.

Maura Stanton: "The Grocery Store" and "Living Apart" are reprinted from *Tales of the Supernatural* by permission of David R. Godine, Publisher, and the author. Copyright © 1988 Maura Stanton. "A Portrait by Bronzino" is reprinted by permission of the author. Copyright © 1991 Maura Stanton.

Gerald Stern: "The Founder" first appeared in *Antaeus* and is used permission of the author. Copyright © 1989 Gerald Stern. "What It Is Like" first appeared in *The New Yorker* and is used by permission of *The New Yorker* and the author. Copyright © 1991 Gerald Stern. "The Bull-Roarer" first appeared in *Poetry* and is used by permission of *Poetry* and the author. Copyright © 1988 Modern Poetry Association.

Susan Stewart: "Mouth of the Wolf" is reprinted from *The Hive* by permission of University of Georgia Press and the author. Copyright © 1987 Susan Stewart. "The Gypsy" is reprinted by permission of the author. Copyright © 1991 Susan Stewart. "The Memory Cabinet of Mrs. K. 1960" first appeared in *Virginia Quarterly Review* and is used by permission of the author. Copyright © 1988 Susan Stewart.

Ruth Stone: "Where I Came From," "Curtains," "Happiness," and "Turn Your Eyes Away" are reprinted from *Second-Hand Coat* by permission of David R. Godine, Publisher, and the author. Copyright © 1987 Ruth Stone.

Chase Twichell: "The Shades of Grand Central," "Six Belons," "The Condom Tree," and "Chanel No. 5" are reprinted from *Perdido* by permission of Farrar, Straus & Giroux and the author. Copyright © 1991 Chase Twichell.

Leslie Ullman: "Dawn Feeding" is reprinted from *Dreams by No One's Daughter* by permission of University of Pittsburgh Press. Copyright © 1987 Leslie Ullman. "Desire" first appeared in *Denver Quarterly* and is used by permission of the author. Copyright © 1987 Leslie Ullman. "Mauve" first appeared in *Poetry* and is used by permission of *Poetry* and the author. Copyright © 1989 Modern Poetry Association.

Michael Van Walleghen: "The Age of Reason," "Meat," and "Blue Tango" are reprinted from *Blue Tango* by permission of University of Illinois Press and the author. Copyright © 1989 Michael Van Walleghen.

Marilyn Nelson Waniek: "Balance," "Chosen," "Star-Fix," and "Lonely Eagles" are reprinted from *The Homeplace* by permission of Louisiana State University Press and the author. Copyright © 1990 Marilyn Nelson Waniek.

Belle Waring: "When a Beautiful Woman Gets on the Jutiapa Bus," "Baby Random," "Back to Catfish," and "Breeze in Translation" are reprinted from *Refuge* by permission of University of Pittsburgh Press and the author. Copyright © 1990 Belle Waring.

Bruce Weigl: "The Black Hose" first appeared in *The Missouri Review* and is used by permission of the author. Copyright © 1990 Bruce Weigl. "Anna's Grace" first appeared in *American Poetry Review* and is used by permission of the author. Copyright © 1990 Bruce Weigl. "The Confusion of Planes We Must Wander in Sleep" first appeared in *The Kenyon Review* and is used by permission of the author. Copyright © 1990 Bruce Weigl. "Meditation at Pearl Street" first appeared in *The Ohio Review* and is used by permission of the author. Copyright © 1990 Bruce Weigl. "They Name Heaven" first appeared in *American Poetry Review* and is used by permission of the author. Copyright © 1990 Bruce Weigl.

Roger Weingarten: "Father Hunger and Son," "From the Temple of Longing," and "Four Seasons of His Discontent" are reprinted from *Infant Bonds of Joy* by permission of David R. Godine, Publisher, and the author. Copyright © 1990 by Roger Weingarten. "Jungle Gliders" first appeared in *Missouri Review* and is used by permission of the author. Copyright © 1991 Roger Weingarten.

Dara Wier: "Old-Fashioned," "The Flood," and "Holidays" are reprinted from *The Book of Knowledge* by permission of Carnegie Mellon University Press and the author. Copyright © 1989 Dara Wier.

David Wojahn: "The Assassination of John Lennon as Depicted by the Madame Tussaud Wax Museum, Niagara Falls, Ontario, 1987" and "Matins: James Brown and his Fabulous Flames Tour the South, 1958" are reprinted from *Mystery Train* by permission of University of Pittsburgh Press and the author. Copyright © 1990 David Wojahn. "White Lanterns" is reprinted by permission of the author. Copyright © 1991 David Wojahn.

C. D. Wright: "Our Dust" first appeared in *The Paris Review* and is used by permission of the author. Copyright © 1989 C. D. Wright. "Kings' Daughters, Home for Unwed Mothers, 1948" first appeared in *Raccoon* and is used by permission of the author. Copyright © 1987 C. D. Wright. "Scratch Music" is reprinted from *Further Adventures with You* by permission of Carnegie Mellon University Press and the author. Copyright © 1986 C. D. Wright. "More Blues and the Abstract Truth" first appeared in *The Paris Review* and is used by permission of the author. Copyright © 1989 C. D. Wright.

Franz Wright: "The Needle: For a Friend Who Disappeared" first appeared in *The New Yorker* and is used by permission of the author. Copyright © 1989 Franz Wright. "Entry in an Unknown Hand" is reprinted from *Entry in an Unknown Hand* by permission of Carnegie Mellon University Press and the author. Copyright © 1989 Franz Wright. "Elegy: Breece D'J Pancake" and "Certain Tall Buildings" first appeared in *Field* and are used by permission of the author. Copyright © 1991 Franz Wright.

Dean Young: "Storms" is reprinted by permission of the author. Copyright © 1991 Dean Young. "Other Obit" first appeared in *Indiana Review* and is used by permission of the author. Copyright © 1990 Dean Young. "Threshold" and "Lace" are reprinted from *Design with X* by permission of Wesleyan University Press and the author. Copyright © 1988 Dean Young.

Jack Myers

is the author of six poetry books, including *As Long As You're Happy*, winner of the 1986 National Poetry Series (Graywolf Press) and *Blindsided*, forthcoming from Godine, and is the co-editor of critical works on poetry and the anthology *New American Poets of the '80s*, with Roger Weingarten. He is currently a professor of English at Southern Methodist University in Dallas, Texas, and a faculty member in the MFA in Writing Program at Vermont College of Norwich University.

Roger Weingarten

is the author of seven books of poetry, including *Shadow Shadow* and *Infant Bonds of Joy*, both published by Godine, and is the co-editor of two other anthologies. He currently teaches in and directs the MFA in Writing Program at Vermont College of Norwich University.

New American Poets of the '90s

was set in Galliard, a typeface designed by Matthew Carter and introduced in 1978 by the Mergenthaler Linotype Company. Based on the types created by Robert Granjon in the sixteenth century, Galliard is the first of its genre to be designed exclusively for phototypesetting. A type of solid weight, it possesses an authentic sparkle that is lacking in most current Garamonds. The italic is particularly felicitous and reaches back to the feeling of the chancery style, from which Claude Garamond's italic departed. The display type is Bembo.

Designed by Robert G. Lowe. Composition by PennSet, Inc., Bloomsburg, Pennsylvania. Printed and bound by Maple-Vail Book Manufacturing Group, Binghamton, New York.